J. MUIR.

— ALEX T. MUIR —

MINISTRY OF TECHNOLOGY

The Law relating to Safety and Health in Mines and Quarries

PART 2

MINES OF COAL, STRATIFIED IRONSTONE, SHALE AND FIRECLAY

1970

Regulations and Orders under the Mines and Quarries Acts 1954 and 1969, Approved Specifications and Procedures, and Mining Qualifications Board Rules.

LONDON

HER MAJESTY'S STATIONERY OFFICE

1970

SBN 11 410074 8

CONTENTS

INTRODUCTION

This Part is one of a new series on "The Law relating to Safety and Health in Mines and Quarries". The full series is

Part 1— The Mines and Quarries Act 1954, as amended by Part I of the Mines and Quarries (Tips) Act 1969;
The Mines and Quarries (Tips) Act 1969.

Part 2— Mines of Coal, Stratified Ironstone, Shale and Fireclay—Regulations and Orders made under the Mines and Quarries Acts 1954 and 1969, Approved Specifications and Procedures, and Mining Qualifications Board Rules.

Part 3— Miscellaneous Mines—Regulations and Orders made under the Mines and Quarries Acts 1954 and 1969 and related matters.

Part 4— Quarries—Regulations and Orders made under the Mines and Quarries Act, 1954 and 1969, Approved Specifications and Procedures.

Parts **2**, **3** and **4** should be read in association with Part **1**, the footnotes in which refer the reader to the appropriate Regulations, Approved Specifications, Procedures, etc. in the other Parts.

2. The Ministry of Technology prepares annual lists of amendments to the respective Parts which may be obtained from the address below.

3. The Minister of Technology Order 1969, made by Order in Council on 22nd October, 1969, came into operation on 23rd October, 1969. This provided for the dissolution of the Ministry of Power and the assumption of the functions of the Minister of Power by the Minister of Technology. The Order provides for anything done by the Minister of Power before 23rd October, 1969, to remain valid and for anything in the process of being done by the Minister of Power on that date to be continued by the Minister of Technology. Approvals, Certificates, Regulations and other instruments made by the Minister of Power before that date and still in force will have effect as though made by the Minister of Technology.

4. Legislation requires the Minister's approval for use of certain types of apparatus in mines. Lists of such apparatus may be obtained from the address below.

5. The Mines and Quarries Act 1954, provides for any certificate, exemption, approval, authority, etc. granted under earlier legislation and in force at the commencement of that Act (1st January, 1957), in so far as it could have been granted thereunder, to remain effective. A Schedule of the earlier legislation which has been re-enacted is given in pages 333 to 336.

6. Where a statutory provision requires that a report or other information shall be recorded in a form directed or specified by the Minister, a reference is made in a footnote to the appropriate M. & Q. Form; a full list appears on pages 337 to 339.

MINISTRY OF TECHNOLOGY,
THAMES HOUSE SOUTH,
MILLBANK,
LONDON, S.W.1.

ACCIDENTS

THE MINES

(NOTIFICATION OF DANGEROUS OCCURRENCES) ORDER 1959

S.I. 1959 No. 2117

(As amended by the Mines (Notification of Dangerous Occurrences) (Amendment) Order 1969, S.I. 1969 No. 963)

1. This order shall come into operation on the first day of January, nineteen hundred and sixty, and may be cited as the Mines (Notification of Dangerous Occurrences) Order 1959.

2. (1) In this order the following expressions have the meanings hereby respectively assigned to them, that is to say—

"the Act" means the Mines and Quarries Act 1954;

"auxiliary fan" means a fan used or intended to be used below ground wholly or mainly for ventilating a heading, drift or blind end.

(2) The Interpretation Act 1889, shall apply to the interpretation of this order as it applies to the interpretation of an Act of Parliament, and as if this order and the orders hereby revoked were Acts of Parliament.

3. The provisions of the said section one hundred and sixteen of the Act are hereby extended to occurrences at a mine of each of the following special classes (whether death or serious bodily injury is thereby caused or not), that is to say occurrences in which—

(*a*) any gas, other than gas in a safety-lamp, or dust is ignited below ground;

(*b*) any gas in a part of a firedamp drainage system on the surface or in an exhauster house is ignited accidentally;

(*c*) any fire breaks out below ground;

(*d*) any person, in consequence of any smoke or any other indication that a fire may have broken out below ground, has been caused to leave any place pursuant to paragraph (1) of regulation eleven of the Coal and Other Mines (Fire and Rescue) Regulations 1956*, or section seventy-nine of the Act;

(*e*) any fire breaks out on the surface endangering the operation of any winding or haulage apparatus installed at a shaft or unwalkable outlet, or any mechanically operated apparatus for producing ventilation below ground in the mine;

(*f*) there is any violent outburst of gas together with coal or other solid matter into the mine workings except when such an outburst is caused intentionally;

*See page 115.

(*g*) there is any inrush of noxious or inflammable gas from old workings;

(*h*) there is any inrush of water, or material which flows when wet, from any source;

(*i*) any rope, chain, coupling or other gear of a similar kind, by which persons are carried through any shaft, staple-pit or unwalkable outlet, breaks;

(*j*) any rope, chain, coupling or other gear of a similar kind, used for the transport of persons below ground, breaks;

(*k*) any cage being used for the carriage of persons is overwound; or any cage not being so used is overwound and becomes detached from its winding rope; or any cage operated by means of the friction of a rope on a winding sheave is brought to rest by the apparatus provided in the headframe of the shaft or in the part of the shaft below the lowest landing for the time being in use, being apparatus provided for bringing the cage to rest in the event of its being overwound;

(*l*) there is any explosion from, or collapse or burst of, any apparatus which is used for generating a pressure of air, gas or steam greater than atmospheric, or for storing air, gas or steam at such a pressure:

Provided that the provisions of this paragraph shall not apply to an explosion from any boiler to which the Boiler Explosions Act 1882, applies;

(*m*) any ventilating apparatus other than an auxiliary fan breaks down causing a substantial reduction in the ventilation of the mine lasting for a period exceeding thirty minutes;

(*n*) any headframe, winding engine house, screen or tippler house, or vehicle gantry collapses;

(*o*) any mechanically powered crane, crab or other lifting machine overturns, or any part thereof (other than the hoisting rope of a stock pile gantry crane) fails and causes the load of the machine to fall or, in the case of such a machine with a jib, the jib to fall;

(*p*) breathing apparatus or a smoke helmet or other apparatus serving the same purpose, while being used, fails to function safely or develops a defect likely to affect its safe working;

(*q*) forthwith after using and arising out of the use of breathing apparatus or a smoke helmet or other apparatus serving the same purpose, any person receives at the mine first aid or medical treatment by reason of his unfitness or suspected unfitness;

(*r*) any person suffers such an electric shock or burn, by coming into contact with any conductor in a circuit in which the voltage for the time being exceeds twenty-five, that he receives therefor at the mine first aid or medical treatment;

(*s*) any person suffers such bodily injury, resulting from an explosion or discharge of any blasting material or device as defined in subsection (4) of section sixty-nine of the Act, that he receives therefor at the mine first aid or medical treatment;

(*t*) any movement of material or any fire or any other event indicates that a tip to which Part I of the Mines and Quarries (Tips) Act 1969 applies is, or is likely to become, insecure.

4. (1) Article three shall not apply to any occurrence (other than such an occurrence as is mentioned in paragraph (*e*) or (*t*) thereof) at any place on the surface of a mine where building operations undertaken by way of trade or business, or for the purpose of any industrial or commercial undertaking, are being carried on, being an occurrence arising out of those operations.

(2) In the preceding paragraph the expression "building operation" has the meaning assigned thereto in section one hundred and fifty-two of the Factories Act 1937.

(3) Paragraphs (*p*) and (*q*) of article three shall not apply to any occurrence at a mine other than a mine of coal, stratified ironstone, shale or fireclay.

5. The Mines and Quarries (Notification of Dangerous Occurrences) Order 1957, and the Order dated December 22, 1906, made by the Secretary of State under the Notice of Accidents Act 1906, requiring the reporting of certain classes of dangerous occurrences in mines and quarries whether personal injury is caused or not, and having effect by virtue of section one hundred and ninety-one of the Act, are hereby revoked.

DUST

THE COAL MINES
(PRECAUTIONS AGAINST INFLAMMABLE DUST) REGULATIONS 1956

S.I. 1956 No. 1769

(As varied by the Coal Mines (Precautions against Inflammable Dust) (Variation) Regulations 1960, S.I. 1960 No. 1738)

Arrangement of Regulations

PART I

Precautions as regards screens

1. This Part of these regulations shall apply at every mine in which coal is worked other than a mine in which the floor, roof and sides of the roads are naturally wet throughout.

2. It shall be the duty of the manager of every mine to make and ensure the efficient carrying out of arrangements to secure that the entry of coal dust from screens into any downcast shaft is minimised.

3. At any such mine newly opened after the sixteenth day of December, nineteen hundred and eleven, no plant shall be used for screening or sorting coal within a distance of two hundred and forty feet from any downcast shaft:

Provided that an inspector may by notice served on the manager exempt a mine from the provisions of this regulation.

PART II

Maintenance of incombustible matter in dust in roads

4. This Part of these regulations shall apply, at every mine in which coal is worked, to every length of road therein other than—

(*a*) a length of road used only in connection with the working of anthracite; or

(*b*) a length of road which is within thirty feet of a coal face or which is a shoot from the coal face down which coal is thrown.

5. (1) It shall be the duty of the manager of every mine to make and ensure the efficient carrying out of arrangements to secure that, as respects every length of road to which this Part of these regulations applies and which is required to be ventilated, any dust on the floor, roof or sides thereof which can be raised into the air shall contain not less than the minimum percentage of incombustible matter determined in accordance with the schedule to these regulations in relation to coal in connection with the working of which that length of road is used.

(2) For the purposes of these regulations the incombustible matter in any dust includes moisture contained therein.

6. No incombustible dust shall be used for the purposes of these regulations unless in tests carried out at intervals not exceeding ninety days it is found to comply with the following requirements, that is to say—

(*a*) it is of such fineness that of the dry dust which passes through a 60-mesh sieve of a specification approved* by the Minister not less than fifty per cent by weight and not more than seventy-five per cent by weight, or such larger percentage as may be authorised by an inspector by notice served on the manager, shall pass through a 240-mesh sieve of a specification so approved,* and

(*b*) it is of such character that it is readily dispersable into the air and, if in use in places where it is not directly wetted by water from the strata, it does not cake but is dispersed into the air when blown upon by the mouth or by a suitable appliance.

7. (1) For the purpose of establishing the efficacy of his arrangements made in pursuance of regulation five it shall be the duty of the manager of the mine to ensure that at intervals not exceeding thirty days a sufficient number of samples of the dust on every length of road to which that regulation applies are systematically collected and analysed.

(2) In the case of any such length of road which is used for the transport of coal or which is within six hundred feet of a working face and is used as a return airway in respect of that face, the number of samples so collected and analysed shall not be less than in the proportion of ten per mile:

Provided that an inspector may by notice served on the manager permit the taking and analysis of a lesser number of samples in any such length of road.

(3) If in the case of any length of road every analysis of a sample taken within the preceding six months indicates that the natural conditions of the road are such that the requisite percentage of incombustible matter is maintained without the application of incombustible dust or if, in the case of a length of road to which the last preceding paragraph does not apply, every such analysis indicates that the application of incombustible dust is not necessary at intervals of less than six months, it shall be sufficient for samples to be collected and analysed at intervals not exceeding ninety days or at such longer intervals as may be authorised by an inspector by notice served on the manager:

*The sieves approved for this purpose are the 60-mesh and 240-mesh sieves made to the specification in British Standard Specification for Test Sieves, No. 410, dated April, 1931.

Provided that if there is any change in the natural conditions or in the method of working which affects or may affect substantially the percentage of incombustible matter in any such length of road, samples shall be taken and analysed as soon as any effect of the change would be apparent.

(4) The manager shall ensure the result of every analysis required to be made by this regulation is within twenty-one days of the collection of the sample entered in a book* provided by the owner of the mine for the purpose. Except at a mine at which less than one hundred persons are employed below ground, entries in that book relating to each length of road shall be distinguished by colour, number, letter or mark which shall be identified with that length of road by means of a suitable plan preserved with that book.

(5) The manager shall ensure that a notice specifying the result of every analysis required to be made by this regulation is kept in the covered accommodation provided in pursuance of section one hundred and thirty-five of the Act for a period of thirty days commencing when that result is entered in the book in pursuance of the last preceding paragraph.

8. (1) When any sample is collected to ascertain the percentage of incombustible matter in any dust in any road for the purposes of these regulations it shall (subject to the following provisions of this regulation) be collected—

(*a*) over a length of road not less than one hundred and fifty feet in length;

(*b*) in the case of dust on the roof or sides, to a depth not exceeding a quarter of an inch or, in the case of dust on the floor, to a depth not exceeding one inch; and

(*c*) in the manner specified in paragraph (5) of this regulation.

(2) If since samples were last collected from any length of road in pursuance of regulation seven some part of it has been treated with incombustible dust more frequently or more recently than other parts, separate samples shall for the purposes of that regulation be collected from those parts respectively irrespective of their lengths.

(3) Samples of the dust on the roof and sides of any length of road shall be taken together in the case of a length of road supported by steel arches and in the case of any other length of road unless there is in force a direction given by an inspector by notice served on the manager that samples of the dust on the roof and sides of that length of road are to be taken separately.

(4) If in the case of any length of road the dust on the floor is systematically treated in a manner approved† by the Minister so as to consolidate it and render it indispersable, samples of the dust on that floor shall be taken to a depth of a quarter of an inch, as nearly as may be, and be taken together with dust from the roof and sides of that length of road unless there is in force a direction to the contrary given by an inspector by notice served on the manager.

(5) Every sample shall be so taken as to be representative of the whole surface of the floor, roof or sides, roof and sides or all of them, as the case may be, of the length of road in question and shall be collected—

*M. & Q. Form No. 207.

†See page 11.

(*a*) by a method of strip sampling by which the dust is collected from a succession of transverse strips as nearly as may be of equal width and equally spaced, not more than fifteen feet apart and of an aggregate area not less than one per cent of the total area sampled; or

(*b*) by a method of spot sampling by which it is collected from one point for each three feet of that length of road.

9. When any sample of dust is to be analysed for the purposes of these regulations it shall be well mixed and a representative portion which is passed through a 60-mesh sieve of a specification approved* by the Minister shall be analysed by a method so approved.†

Part III

General

Precautions as regards vehicles containing coal dust

10. It shall be the duty of the manager of every mine to ensure that no vehicle is used therein for the transport of material consisting wholly or mainly of coal dust (not being anthracite dust) along any length of road in which there is any electric cable or apparatus unless such steps are taken to enclose the material as would prevent the dust being thrown into the air if the vehicle were upset.

Stone dust barriers

10A. (1) In every area of a mine of coal—

(*a*) in which there are one or more lengths of road on which any coal (other than anthracite) is carried by means of a conveyor, and

(*b*) which is an area throughout which the flame that may be caused by an ignition of inflammable gas or dust occurring at a working coal face or at such other place as the manager may determine is likely to extend,

the manager shall ensure that stone dust barriers of a type approved‡ by the Minister are provided and maintained in or near to one or more such lengths of road.

(2) The manager shall prepare a scheme in respect of each such area specifying the position and type of each such barrier and such scheme or a copy thereof shall be kept at the office at the mine or at such other place as an inspector may approve.

(3) If an inspector is of the opinion that for reasons of safety it is advisable that the scheme should be amended, he may serve on the manager a notice stating that he is of that opinion and requiring him to make such amendment to the scheme as may be specified in the notice.

(4) The provisions of Part XV of the Act§ with respect to references upon notices served by inspectors shall apply to a notice served under the last preceding paragraph, and the relevant grounds of objection shall be that compliance

---

*The sieve approved for this purpose is the 60-mesh sieve made to the specification in British Standard Specification for Test Sieves, No. 410, dated April, 1931.

†See page 13.

‡See page 15.

§See Section 170 the of 1954 Act.

with any requirement sought to be imposed by, or by virtue of, the notice is wholly, or to a particular extent, unnecessary, inadvisable for reasons of safety or impracticable.

(5) In this regulation "conveyor" means a single conveyor not less than one hundred and fifty feet long, or two or more conveyors operating as one unit which together are not less than one hundred and fifty feet long.

11. The Interpretation Act 1889, shall apply to the interpretation of these regulations as it applies to the interpretation of an Act of Parliament.

SCHEDULE

Minimum percentage of incombustible matter

1. For the purposes of regulation five the minimum percentage of incombustible matter in relation to any coal shall be determined by reference to the volatile matter content of that coal calculated on an ash-free dry basis in accordance with the following table:

Volatile matter content of coal (Per cent)	Minimum percentage of incombustible matter required
Not exceeding	
20	50
22	55
25	60
27	65
30	68
32	70
35	72
Exceeding 35	75

2. For the purposes of this schedule the volatile matter content of any coal shall be deemed to be that determined by analysis of a representative section of the seam or of a representative sample of run-of-mine coal from the seam taken within the preceding twelve months or where no such determination has been made shall be deemed to exceed thirty-five per cent.

3. Where any road is used in connection with the working of coal from more than one seam the volatile matter content of the coal shall be deemed to exceed thirty-five per cent unless such a determination has been made in respect of each seam and in the excepted case shall be deemed to be the highest percentage so determined.

4. No account shall be taken for the purposes of this schedule of any analysis of a representative sample of coal unless forthwith after the making thereof notice containing particulars thereof was served on the inspector for the district.

5. Where in the seam or seams of coal in connection with the working of which any road is used inflammable gas is unknown and no explosive, which is not permitted explosive and sheathed explosive within the meaning assigned to those terms by the Coal Mines (Explosives) Regulations 1956,* is used in that road, the minimum percentage of incombustible matter required shall not exceed sixty per cent in a case in which the road is treated with incombustible dust or fifty per cent in a case in which it is not so treated.

*Now replaced by the Coal Mines (Explosives) Regulations 1961, see page 35.

APPROVED MANNER OF CONSOLIDATING DUST ON THE FLOOR OF A ROAD AND RENDERING IT INDISPERSABLE

The method of treatment with calcium chloride described below is approved, for the purpose of Regulation 8 (4) of the Coal Mines (Precautions against Inflammable Dust) Regulations 1956, as a manner of consolidating the dust on the floor of a road and rendering it indispersable:

1. *Preparation*

Preparation shall consist of the following processes undertaken in the order in which they are set out:

(*a*) the road shall be cleaned and all loose material except dust removed from the floor;

(*b*) stone dust shall be applied freely to the floor, roof and sides;

(*c*) the floor dust shall be smoothed down;

(*d*) if the layer of dust on the floor is in any place less than one inch deep, additional stone dust shall be applied in that place to make the dust on the floor one inch deep;

(*e*) the floor dust shall be thoroughly and uniformly wetted to a depth of at least one inch by spraying over it a solution of a wetting agent, and afterwards water; so however that, if the dust in that sector of the road can be wetted as required by this sub-paragraph by spraying water only, no wetting agent need be used.

2. *Application*

Not less than one hour after preparation of a sector of the road has been completed, flaked calcium chloride shall be spread evenly over the floor of the sector with a shovel.

3. *Required condition after initial treatment*

The floor is required to have after treatment a uniform surface sufficiently plastic to take and retain, if trodden upon, sharp impressions of heel marks. If this condition is not achieved at the first application, additional calcium chloride shall be applied on the next and (if necessary) following days.

Subsequent treatment

4. *Preparation*

Any deterioration in the required condition of the floor (as specified in paragraph 3) shall be remedied by preparing the sector of the road concerned, and applying calcium chloride, as provided in this and the following paragraph. Preparation shall consist of the following processes undertaken in the order in which they are set out:

(*a*) all coal and other loose material shall be removed;

(*b*) all fine coal and coal dust shall be swept out of the sector;

(*c*) stone dust shall be applied freely to the roof and sides;

(*d*) water shall be lightly sprayed over the floor.

5. *Application*

Approximately one hour after preparation has been completed, flaked calcium chloride shall be spread evenly over the floor with a shovel.

APPROVED METHODS OF ANALYSIS OF MINE DUST

The methods of analysis of mine dust described below are approved for the purposes of Regulation 9 of the Coal Mines (Precautions against Inflammable Dust) Regulations 1956:

1. (*a*) *The High Temperature Incineration Method*

(i) The residue of a weighed quantity of dust after that quantity of dust has been dried at a temperature not exceeding 140°C. and the weight loss attributable to moisture ascertained or (in any case where the percentage of incombustible matter, excluding moisture, is likely to exceed the minimum required by the said regulations) a weighed quantity of dust, shall be heated in an open vessel to a temperature of not less than 950°C. until it no longer loses weight. The incinerated residue shall be weighed.

(ii) The sum of the weights of moisture and incinerated residue or, as the case may be, the weight of incinerated residue shall be reckoned as incombustible matter and be expressed as a percentage of the total weight of the dust.

If in any case where the dust contains carbonates a weighed quantity of that dust has been treated with dilute acid to ascertain the weight of carbon dioxide present, the weight of that carbon dioxide shall be reckoned as incombustible matter and shall be taken into account in expressing, in pursuance of sub-paragraph (*a*) (ii), the percentage of incombustible matter.

(*b*) *The Low Temperature Incineration Method*

(i) The residue of a weighed quantity of dust after that quantity of dust has been dried at a temperature not exceeding 140°C. and the weight loss attributable to moisture ascertained or (in any case where the percentage of incombustible matter, excluding moisture, is likely to exceed the minimum required by the said regulations) a weighed quantity of dust, shall be heated in an open vessel to a temperature of not less than 480°C. until the coal is completely burnt away. The incinerated residue shall be weighed.

(ii) The sum of the weights of moisture and incinerated residue or, as the case may be, the weight of incinerated residue shall be reckoned as incombustible matter and be expressed as a percentage of the total weight of the dust.

2. Except where gypsum dust is used for stone dusting, the following method of analysis is approved for the purposes of regulation nine aforesaid in addition to any other approved method:—

The Volumeter Method

The volume of solid matter in a weighed quantity of dust shall be ascertained by immersion in a fluid and the incombustible matter in the dust estimated by a comparison of the volume so ascertained with volumes of other similar dust containing known proportions of incombustible matter.

3. Where limestone dust or a dust of a similar colour is used for stone dusting, the following method of analysis is approved for the purposes of regulation nine aforesaid, in addition to any other approved method:—

The Colorimeter Method

The colour of a sample of dust shall be compared with that of a representative sample of similar dust known to contain eighty per cent or a higher percentage of incombustible matter and if, on such a comparison, the colour of the sample is found to be lighter than that of the representative sample, the incombustible matter in the dust shall be taken to exceed eighty per cent or, as the case may be, the higher percentage of the total weight of the dust.

4. *Moisture Correction*

If it is necessary for a dust sample to be air dried before being sieved through a 60-mesh sieve in accordance with regulation nine aforesaid, a correction may be made to the incombustible matter content of the dust determined by method 1(*a*), 1(*b*) or 2.

The corrected total incombustible content of the dust is equal to $M + \frac{I(100 - M)}{100}$

where M is the percentage loss of weight during the air drying, and I is the percentage of total incombustible matter in the dust as determined by method 1(*a*), 1(*b*) or 2.

STONE DUST BARRIERS

The following types of stone dust barriers are approved for the purposes of Regulation 10A(1).

(i) Stone Dust Barrier Approvals Nos. 1 and 2 expired on 31st December, 1962.

(ii) Stone Dust Barrier Approval No. 3 (Revised)
Primary Stone Dust Barrier

Type of Barrier

Each stone dust barrier shall consist of a number of light and heavy shelves placed parallel, or as near as may be, to each other along the road, and in any such barrier the number of light shelves shall not be less than half the number of heavy shelves, and the light shelves shall be placed at each end of the barrier so that there are an equal number at each end. Each shelf, whether light or heavy, shall consist of a number of dust boards, running parallel to the direction of the road, and a frame, on which the dust boards shall rest and which shall run at right angles to that direction.

For the purposes of this approval a 'heavy shelf' means a shelf in which the dust boards are at least fourteen inches, but do not exceed twenty inches, in length, and a 'light shelf' means a shelf in which the dust boards do not exceed fourteen inches in length.

The distance between the nearest parts of adjacent shelves shall, in any case where the adjacent shelves are heavy shelves or a heavy shelf and a light shelf, be at least four feet six inches and shall not exceed six feet, and in any case where the adjacent shelves are light shelves, be at least three feet and shall not exceed four feet six inches.

The two main members of each frame shall be at least six inches in depth, shall be set parallel, or as near as may be, to each other with their outside edges not more than eight inches apart, and shall rest on edge on a horizontal bar comprised in a bracket at each side of the road. Each bracket shall be rigidly attached to the road supports or side of the road. Each frame shall be free to slide in the direction of the road. No frame or dust board shall be fastened to each other or to any bracket, and each shall, so far as is practicable, be so constructed and installed that, in the event of an explosion, it may fly without obstruction along the road.

Conditions of Approval

(*a*) The manager of every mine of coal in which stone dust barriers are required to be provided by the said paragraph* shall ensure that each barrier in the mine of the type to which this approval relates holds not less than eighty pounds of stone dust per square foot of the average cross-section of the length of road in which it is placed, that no heavy shelf forming part of any such barrier is loaded with more than forty pounds or less than twenty pounds of stone dust for each foot of its length, that no light shelf forming part of any such barrier is loaded with more than twenty pounds of stone dust for each foot of its length, and that, so far as is practicable, no stone dust, other than a type which will not cake under the normal atmospheric conditions of the length of road in which it is to be used, is used in connection with any such barrier.

(*b*) The manager of every mine shall further ensure that no part of any such shelf and no stone dust thereon is less than four inches from the roof or sides of any road or any prop or other support therein.

---

*i.e., Paragraph (1) of Regulation 10(A).

(*c*) No barrier of the type to which this approval relates shall on or after the first day of January, nineteen hundred and sixty-two be provided or on or after that date be erected after removal either in the same place or elsewhere.

(iii) Stone Dust Barrier Approval No. 4 (Revised)
Secondary Stone Dust Barrier

Type of Barrier

Each stone dust barrier shall consist of a number of shelves placed parallel, or as near as may be, to each other along the road, and each shelf shall consist of a number of dust boards, not exceeding fourteen inches in length and running parallel to the direction of the road, and a frame, on which the dust boards shall rest and which shall run at right angles to that direction. The distance between the nearest parts of adjacent shelves shall be at least three feet and shall not exceed four feet six inches.

The two main members of each frame shall be at least six inches in depth, shall be set parallel, or as near as may be, to each other with their outside edges not more than eight inches apart, and shall rest on edge on a horizontal bar comprised in a bracket at each side of the road. Each frame shall be free to slide in the direction of the road. No frame or dust board shall be fastened to each other or to any bracket, and each shall, so far as is practicable, be so constructed and installed that, in the event of an explosion, it may fly without obstruction along the road.

Conditions of Approval

(*a*) The manager of every mine of coal in which stone dust barriers are required to be provided by the said paragraph* shall ensure that each barrier in the mine of the type to which this approval relates holds not less than twenty pounds of stone dust per square foot of the average cross-section of the length of road in which it is placed, that no shelf forming part of any such barrier is loaded with more than twenty pounds of stone dust for each foot of its length, and that, so far as is practicable, no stone dust, other than a type which will not cake under the normal atmospheric conditions of the length of road in which it is to be used, is used in connection with any such barrier.

(*b*) The manager of every such mine shall further ensure that no part of any such shelf and no stone dust thereon is less than four inches from the roof or sides of any road or any prop or other support therein.

(*c*) No barrier of the type to which this approval relates shall on or after the first day of January, nineteen hundred and sixty-two be provided or on or after that date be erected after removal either in the same place or elsewhere.

(iv) Stone Dust Barrier Approval No. 5
Light Stone Dust Barrier

Type of Barrier

Each stone dust barrier shall consist of a number of shelves placed parallel, or as near as may be, to each other along the road. The distance between the nearest parts of adjacent shelves shall be not less than three feet and not more than seven feet. Each shelf shall rest on brackets rigidly attached to the road supports or sides of the road. No shelf shall be loaded with more than twenty pounds of stone dust per foot of shelf length. Each shelf shall consist of a number of dust boards, in length not exceeding fourteen inches resting on a frame consisting of two main members at least six inches in depth set parallel to each other with their outside edges not more than eight inches apart and fastened together by connecting pieces. The frames shall be

*i.e., Paragraph (1) of Regulation 10(A).

placed at right angles to the direction of the road and the dust boards parallel to it. No dust board or frame shall be fastened to each other or to any bracket and each shall so far as is practicable be so constructed and installed that, in the event of any explosion, it may fly without obstruction along the roadway. Each frame shall rest on horizontal bars comprised in or resting on the brackets so that the frame is free to slide in the direction of the road.

Conditions of Approval

(*a*) The manager of every mine of coal in which stone dust barriers are required to be provided by the said paragraph* shall ensure that each barrier in the mine of the type to which this approval relates holds not less than twenty-two pounds of stone dust per square foot of the average cross-section of the length of road in which it is placed.

(*b*) The manager of every such mine shall further ensure that no part of any shelf and no stone dust on any shelf is less than four inches from the roof or sides of the road or of any prop or other support.

(*c*) The manager of every such mine shall further ensure that so far as is practicable no stone dust, other than of a type which will not cake under the normal atmospheric conditions of the length of road in which it is to be used, is used in connection with any such barrier.

(v) Stone Dust Barrier Approval No. 6
Intermediate Stone Dust Barrier

Type of Barrier

Each stone dust barrier shall consist of a number of lightly loaded shelves and heavily loaded shelves placed parallel, or as near as may be, to each other along the road. The distance between the nearest parts of adjacent shelves shall be, in a case where both adjacent shelves are lightly loaded shelves, not less than three feet and not more than seven feet, and in any other case not less than four feet and not more than eight feet six inches. Each shelf shall rest on brackets rigidly attached to the road supports or sides of the road. Each shelf shall consist of a number of dust boards resting on a frame consisting of two main members at least six inches in depth set parallel to each other with their outside edges not more than eight inches apart and fastened to each other by connecting pieces. Such dust boards shall be in length in the case of a lightly loaded shelf not more than fourteen inches and in the case of a heavily loaded shelf more than fourteen inches and not more than twenty inches. The frames shall be placed at right angles to the direction of the road and the dust boards parallel to it. No dust board or frame shall be fastened to each other or to any bracket and each shall so far as is practicable be so constructed and installed that, in the event of any explosion, it may fly without obstruction along the roadway. Each frame shall rest on horizontal bars comprised in or resting on the brackets so that the frame is free to slide in the direction of the road. Not more than one-third of the shelves in the barrier shall be heavily loaded shelves arranged together at one end of the barrier and the remainder of the shelves shall be lightly loaded shelves ('lightly loaded shelf' means a shelf loaded with not more than twenty pounds of stone dust per foot of shelf length and 'heavily loaded shelf' means a shelf loaded with more than twenty pounds, but not more than forty pounds of stone dust per foot of shelf length).

Conditions of Approval

(*a*) The manager of every mine of coal in which stone dust barriers are required to be provided by the said paragraph* shall ensure that each barrier in the

*i.e., Paragraph (1) of Regulation 10(A).

mine of the type to which this approval relates holds not less than forty pounds of stone dust per square foot of the average cross-section of the length of road in which it is placed.

(*b*) The manager of every such mine shall further ensure that no part of any shelf and no stone dust on any shelf is less than four inches from the roof or sides of the road or of any prop or other support.

(*c*) The manager of every such mine shall further ensure that so far as is practicable no stone dust, other than of a type which will not cake under the normal atmospheric conditions of the length of road in which it is to be used, is used in connection with any such barrier.

(vi) Stone Dust Barrier Approval No. 7
Heavy Stone Dust Barrier

Type of Barrier

Each stone dust barrier shall consist of a number of lightly loaded shelves and heavily loaded shelves placed parallel, or as near as may be, to each other along the road. The distance between the nearest parts of adjacent shelves shall be, in a case where both adjacent shelves are lightly loaded shelves, not less than three feet and not more than seven feet, and in any other case not less than four feet and not more than eight feet six inches. Each shelf shall rest on brackets rigidly attached to the road supports or sides of the road. Each shelf shall consist of a number of dust boards resting on a frame consisting of two main members at least six inches in depth set parallel to each other with their outside edges not more than eight inches apart and fastened to each other by connecting pieces. Such dust boards shall be in length in the case of a lightly loaded shelf not more than fourteen inches and in the case of a heavily loaded shelf more than fourteen inches and not more than twenty inches. The frames shall be placed at right angles to the direction of the road and the dust boards parallel to it. No dust board or frame shall be fastened to each other or to any bracket and each shall so far as is practicable be so constructed and installed that, in the event of any explosion, it may fly without obstruction along the roadway. Each frame shall rest on horizontal bars comprised in or resting on the brackets so that the frame is free to slide in the direction of the road. Not less than one-third of the shelves in the barrier shall be lightly loaded shelves arranged together at one end of the barrier and the remainder of the shelves shall be heavily loaded shelves ('lightly loaded shelf' means a shelf loaded with not more than twenty pounds of stone dust per foot of shelf length and 'heavily loaded shelf' means a shelf loaded with more than twenty pounds, but not more than forty pounds of stone dust per foot of shelf length).

Conditions of Approval

(*a*) The manager of every mine of coal in which stone dust barriers are required to be provided by the said paragraph* shall ensure that each barrier in the mine of the type to which this approval relates holds not less than eighty pounds of stone dust per square foot of the average cross-section of the length of road in which it is placed.

(*b*) The manager of every such mine shall further ensure that no part of any shelf and no stone dust on any shelf is less than four inches from the roof or sides of the road or of any prop or other support.

(*c*) The manager of every such mine shall further ensure that so far as is practicable no stone dust, other than of a type which will not cake under the normal atmospheric conditions of the length of road in which it is to be used, is used in connection with any such barrier.

---

*i.e., Paragraph (1) of Regulation 10(A).

ELECTRICITY

THE COAL AND OTHER MINES

(ELECTRICITY) REGULATIONS 1956

S.I. 1956 No. 1766

(As amended by the Coal and Other Mines (Electricity) (Amendment) Regulations 1967, S.I. 1967 No. 1083)

Application

1. These regulations shall apply to every mine of coal, stratified ironstone, shale or fireclay and in these regulations 'mine' means such a mine.

Notice of introduction of electricity

2. (1) Electrical apparatus shall not be installed below ground in any part of a mine, being a part in which electrical apparatus is not already installed, unless the manager of the mine has served on the inspector for the district notice of the intention so to do in such form* and accompanied by such particulars as may be specified by the Minister, and an inspector has not within thirty days of the service of that notice served a notice on the manager in relation to such installation in pursuance of subsection (2) of section sixty-eight of the Act.

(2) Nothing in this regulation shall apply—

(*a*) to the installation of electrical apparatus in any part of a mine, being a part in which the installation of such apparatus was lawful immediately before the commencement of the Act;

(*b*) to the installation of telephone or signalling apparatus, and for the purposes of this regulation no account shall be taken of such apparatus already installed.

Plan of electrical apparatus

3. It shall be the duty of the manager of every mine in which there is installed below ground electrical apparatus, other than telephone or signalling apparatus, to keep at the office at the mine or at such other place as may be approved by an inspector, plans, on the same scale as the plans of the workings in the mine so kept, showing the position of all such electrical apparatus other than portable apparatus and cables.

Main switchgear for cutting off electricity

4. (1) There shall be provided at the surface at every mine in which there is installed below ground electrical apparatus, other than telephone or signalling apparatus, suitable switchgear for cutting off the supply of electricity therefrom.

(2) The manager of every such mine shall make and secure the efficient carrying out of arrangements whereby a competent person appointed by him for the purpose of operating such switchgear is in attendance at the surface at the mine whenever any cable below ground in the mine is live.

---

*M. & Q. Form No. 263.

(3) There shall be provided effective means of telephonic communication or other equivalent means of transmitting speech between the place at which such switchgear is situate and a place at or near every such entrance below ground to every shaft or outlet as is regularly used for affording means of ingress and egress by persons employed in a part of the mine in which electrical apparatus is installed or a place at or near the main distributing centre (if any) for the part of the mine to which that entrance gives access. There shall be kept posted in a suitable position near such means of communication a notice in such characters as to be easily seen and read specifying how communication with the person in attendance at that switchgear is to be obtained.

Other means for cutting off electricity

5. (1) There shall be provided in relation to every electrical circuit at every mine (whether at the surface or below ground) effective means suitably placed for cutting off the supply of electricity from that circuit as may be necessary to prevent danger, and without prejudice to the generality of the aforesaid such means shall be provided for cutting off the supply from any flexible cable at the apparatus by which it is connected to fixed cable.

(2) There shall be provided in relation to every such electrical circuit such effective means for cutting off the supply of electricity automatically from that circuit in the event of any fault occurring in any part of that circuit as may be necessary to prevent danger.

(3) There shall be provided in relation to every motor at a mine such switchgear that the supply of electricity can be entirely cut off from the motor and any starter therefor, being switchgear so placed as to be easily operated by the person operating the motor.

Cutting off electricity where inflammable gas is found

6. (1) Where any person finds that at any place below ground in a mine an amount of inflammable gas is present in the general body of the air at that place exceeding one-and-a-quarter per cent by volume or sees an indication of gas at that place on the lowered flame of a safety-lamp, then, without prejudice to the generality of the application of sections seventy-nine and eighty of the Act, that person shall—

(*a*) forthwith cause the supply of electricity to be cut off from all electrical apparatus at that place, other than any telephone or signalling apparatus or any apparatus for detecting or measuring inflammable gas including ancillary apparatus operated by such apparatus or any electric safety-lamp, if the taking of those measures falls within the scope of his normal duties; or

(*b*) if not, forthwith report the matter to an official of the mine or a person whose normal duties include the taking of those measures.

(2) Any person to whom the presence of inflammable gas at that place is reported in pursuance of sub-paragraph (*b*) of the last preceding paragraph shall forthwith cause the supply of electricity to be cut off from all electrical apparatus at that place, other than any telephone or signalling apparatus or any apparatus for detecting or measuring inflammable gas including ancillary apparatus operated by such apparatus or any electric safety-lamp.

(3) After the supply of electricity has been cut off from electrical apparatus at that place in pursuance of sub-paragraph (*a*) of paragraph (1) or paragraph (2) of this regulation, no such supply shall be restored to that apparatus at that place until the senior official on duty at the mine, being satisfied that the amount of inflammable gas present in the general body of the air at that place does not exceed one-and-a-quarter per cent by volume, so directs.

Restriction on use of high voltages

7. Electricity at a voltage exceeding six hundred and fifty shall not be applied to—

(*a*) any portable apparatus; or
(*b*) any motor at a mine rated at less than twenty horse-power; or
(*c*) the rotating parts of any apparatus.

Housing of apparatus

8. (1) Wherever necessary to prevent danger therefrom or damage thereto electrical apparatus at the surface of any mine shall be installed in a room, compartment or box so constructed or treated as to be fire resisting.

(2) Wherever necessary to prevent danger therefrom or damage thereto any transformer or switchgear below ground in any mine shall be installed in a room, compartment or box which shall be of substantial construction and kept dry. Unless the apparatus so installed is so constructed, protected and worked as to obviate risk of fire, no inflammable material shall be used in the construction of any such room, compartment or box or of any of the fittings therein.

(3) No inflammable or explosive material shall be stored at any mine in any room, compartment or box containing any electrical apparatus or below ground in the vicinity of any electrical apparatus.

9. (1) All parts of electrical apparatus that require attention and all handles for the operation of electrical apparatus shall be so placed that there is safe means of access thereto and adequate working space thereat.

(2) All such handles shall be kept free of obstruction and conveniently placed for operation.

Protection of apparatus

10. Every person doing any work which may result in such damage to any electrical apparatus at a mine that that apparatus might be a source of danger to persons employed thereat shall take such steps to protect it from such damage as may be appropriate.

Suitability of apparatus

11. (1) No electrical apparatus shall be used at any mine unless it is of sufficient power or capacity to avoid dangerous overloading, and is protected against any danger arising out of such use.

(2) Wherever necessary to prevent danger, electrical apparatus at any mine shall be kept clean, dry and clear of obstruction.

Insulation

12. (1) Any material used in any mine for the purpose of insulating any conductor shall be suitable having regard to the degree of insulation and mechanical strength required and the conditions of temperature and moisture to which it is likely to be subjected and to any means provided for its protection.

(2) Every conductor forming part of an electrical system, except the outer conductor of a concentric cable, shall be kept efficiently insulated from earth:

Provided that—

(*a*) in the case of a system with polyphase supply, the neutral point thereof may be connected at one place but no more to earth at the surface of the mine; and

(*b*) in the case of a system with single-phase or direct current supply, the mid-voltage point may be connected at one place but no more to earth at the surface of the mine.

(3) In relation to every electrical system efficient means shall be provided whereby an indication is given of any defect in the insulation thereof.

Earthing

13. (1) There shall be connected to earth at the surface of the mine in such manner as will ensure immediate electrical discharge without danger—

(*a*) every metallic covering of any cable;

(*b*) the outer conductor of every concentric cable;

(*c*) every metallic part of any covering or container of, or mounting for, any other electrical apparatus; and

(*d*) any handle for the operation of any electrical apparatus:

Provided that the provisions of this paragraph shall not apply to a lamp-holder efficiently protected by a covering made of fire resisting material which is either insulated or earthed.

(2) Without prejudice to the generality of the last preceding paragraph, every earthing conductor installed for the purposes thereof shall have a conductivity throughout (including any joint) not less than half that of the conductor having the greatest current carrying capacity in relation to which it is provided and shall have a cross-sectional area not less than 0·022 square inches:

Provided that—

(*a*) in relation to a flexible cable by which electricity is supplied at a voltage not exceeding one hundred and twenty-five to portable apparatus, nothing in the preceding provisions of this paragraph shall require the earthing conductor to have a cross-sectional area greater than 0·01 square inches; and

(*b*) in relation to a flexible cable by which electricity is supplied to portable apparatus of capacity not exceeding three kilowatts at the surface of a mine, being a cable comprising an earthing conductor, nothing in the preceding provisions of this paragraph shall require the earthing conductor to have a cross-sectional area greater than that of any one of the other conductors in that cable.

(3) Subject to the preceding provisions of this regulation and to the provisions of regulation fifteen, the metallic covering of any cable may be used as an earthing conductor.

(4) No switch or circuit breaker* shall be placed in any earthing conductor.

(5) Nothing in this regulation shall apply to any apparatus in any circuit in which the voltage does not exceed two hundred and fifty direct current or one hundred and twenty-five alternating current, other than portable apparatus.

Cables

14. (1) The provisions of this regulation shall apply to all electric cables at a mine other than—

(*a*) flexible cables for portable apparatus;

(*b*) telephone and signalling apparatus; and

(*c*) at the surface, other cables so placed or otherwise safeguarded as to prevent danger.

(2) Every conductor in every cable to which this regulation applies, except an earthed outer conductor of a concentric cable and a metallic covering of a cable used as an earthing conductor in accordance with the provisions of paragraph (3) of regulation thirteen, shall be covered with insulating material.

(3) Every cable to which this regulation applies shall be efficiently protected from mechanical damage and supported at such intervals and in such manner as to prevent damage thereto or danger.

(4) Every such cable used—

(*a*) for transmitting electricity at a voltage exceeding two hundred and fifty; or

(*b*) in any length of road below ground in which vehicles moved otherwise than by hand or by animal traction or conveyors are used; or

(*c*) at a place at which there may be a danger of igniting any inflammable material (including gas or coal dust);

shall be a cable protected by a metallic covering containing all the conductors forming part of that electrical system at that place:

Provided that in the case of a system in which direct current at a voltage not exceeding six hundred and fifty is used there may be separate cables each protected by a metallic covering, so however that such coverings below ground shall be bonded together at points not more than one hundred feet apart.

(5) In the case of every cable to which this regulation applies and which is protected by a metallic covering that covering shall be electrically continuous throughout and where necessary having regard to its position protected against corrosion. At any place at which there may be a danger of igniting inflammable

*Includes 'fuse'—see definition in Regulation 26 (1).

material (including gas or coal dust) such metallic covering shall be so constructed as to minimise the risk of ignition of that material in the event of any fault in or leakage of current from a live conductor in the cable.

Flexible cables

15. (1) No single-core flexible cable shall be used for supplying portable apparatus at any mine. Each conductor in a flexible cable shall be covered with insulating material and the conductor and insulating material shall be efficiently protected from damage.

(2) A metallic covering provided to protect a flexible cable from damage shall not be used as the sole earthing conductor in respect of that cable or any apparatus connected thereto, unless that cable is of a specification approved* by the Minister.

(3) No flexible cable shall be connected to any other electrical apparatus except by means of a properly constructed connector.

Switchgear and electrical joints and connections

16. (1) All parts of switchgear and of electrical connections at every mine shall be of sufficient mechanical strength and current carrying capacity to prevent danger, in particular from rough usage.

(2) All live parts of such switchgear and connections shall be so enclosed or otherwise protected as to prevent a danger of persons accidentally coming into contact therewith, or from the deposit thereon of dust or other matter, or from water.

(3) Wherever any such switchgear or connection is at any place at which there may be a risk of igniting gas, coal dust or other material, all live parts thereof shall be so protected as to prevent external ignition thereof.

(4) Any material insulating any conductor in any cable shall be efficiently sealed at any point at which that conductor is connected to other apparatus where its insulating property might be diminished by moisture or otherwise.

(5) Wherever any cable protected by a metallic covering is connected to other apparatus that metallic covering shall be securely attached to that apparatus.

Transformers

17. In any transformer at a mine suitable provision shall be made to guard against danger arising from the charging of lower voltage components by contact with or leakage from higher voltage components.

Telephone and signalling apparatus

18. Adequate precautions shall be taken to prevent any telephone wire or signalling conductor wire coming into contact with any cable or other electrical apparatus.

19. The voltage in any circuit used for signalling (otherwise than by telephone) below ground in a mine shall not exceed twenty-five.

---

*See page 29.

20. (1) No electrical apparatus, other than apparatus of a type approved by the Minister for the purposes of this regulation, shall be connected into any circuit used for signalling (whether by telephone or otherwise) wholly or partly in a mine or part of a mine in which the use of lamps or lights, other than permitted lights, is unlawful:

Provided that this paragraph shall not apply to apparatus used solely to regulate the movements of cages or carriages in a shaft or unwalkable outlet:

Provided also that telephones not of a type so approved may be connected into a part of such a circuit which is on the surface of the mine or in a part of the mine in which the use of lamps or lights, other than permitted lights, is not unlawful by means of a coupling unit of a type approved by the Minister for the purpose.

(2) No source of current shall be used for operating electrical apparatus in any such circuit wholly or partly in a mine or part of a mine in which the use of lamps or lights, other than permitted lights, is unlawful except—

(*a*) for direct current signalling, a battery of three pint porous-pot Leclanché cells connected in simple series or a source of current approved by the Minister for the purpose;

(*b*) for alternating current signalling, a transformer of a type approved by the Minister for the purpose;

(*c*) for a magneto-call telephone of a type approved by the Minister, a generator of a type specified in that approval.

(3) No part of any such circuit shall be connected to earth or to more than one source of current, except—

(*a*) that the same line wires may be used for the calling and speaking circuits of telephones;

(*b*) as provided in paragraph (5) of this regulation.

(4) Any magneto-call telephones connected into any such circuit shall be connected in parallel, and, if such telephones of different types are so connected, each instrument shall include a condenser of a type approved by the Minister for the purpose connected in shunt with the calling bell.

(5) Any direct current bells or relays used in connection with any such circuit shall when connected in parallel be supplied from a single source of current or when connected in series be so supplied or supplied from two identical sources of current connected in opposition.

21. Contact makers used in telephone or signalling apparatus shall be so constructed as to prevent the accidental closing of the circuit.

Apparatus for detecting or measuring inflammable gas

21A. No electrical apparatus for detecting or measuring inflammable gas including ancillary apparatus operated by such apparatus, other than apparatus of a type approved by the Minister for the purpose of this regulation, shall be installed or used below ground in any part of a mine.

Apparatus for use where inflammable gas may occur

22. (1) In any part of a mine below ground in which inflammable gas although not normally present is likely to occur in a quantity sufficient to indicate danger, no electrical apparatus shall be used if there is in the normal working thereof a risk of incendive sparking* therefrom.

(2) In any such part of a mine all rubbing contacts in any motor shall be so arranged or enclosed as to prevent incendive sparking.

Notices

23. It shall be the duty of the manager of every mine to secure that notices are kept posted in such positions and such characters as to be easily seen and read, that is to say—

(*a*) a notice prohibiting unauthorised persons from tampering with electrical apparatus, wherever such persons have access to any place in which such apparatus other than cables is installed;

(*b*) a notice containing directions upon the procedure in case of fire, at every place at which electrical apparatus, other than cables or telephone or signalling apparatus, is installed; and

(*c*) a notice containing directions upon the treatment of persons suffering from electric shock, wherever apparatus is installed from which a dangerous shock might be received.

Saving

24. Nothing in these regulations shall apply to any electrical apparatus which is not used and is not intended to be used as, and does not form and is not intended to form, part of the equipment of a mine.

Exemptions

25. The Chief Inspector of Mines, if he is satisfied that the application of any provision of these regulations is inappropriate in relation to any mine or part of a mine or is not requisite for safety in relation to any electrical apparatus therein, may by notice served on the manager of that mine grant exemption from that provision in respect of that mine or part thereof or in respect of that apparatus, as the case may be.

Interpretation

26. (1) In these regulations, unless the context otherwise requires, the following expressions have the meanings hereby respectively assigned to them, that is to say—

'the Act' means the Mines and Quarries Act 1954;

'circuit breaker' includes a fuse;

'concentric cable' means a cable in which an outer conductor is disposed around an inner conductor;

---

*As defined in Regulation 26 (1). Apparatus complying with this requirement is certified by the Ministry.

'electrical apparatus' includes electric cables and any part of any machinery, apparatus or appliance being a part designed for the generation, conversion, storage, transmission or utilisation of electricity;

'flexible cable' means a cable which is designed to be movable while in use;

'incendive sparking' means, in relation to any electrical apparatus, sparking in such circumstances that inflammable gas present in the air outside the apparatus might be ignited directly or indirectly;

'metallic covering' in relation to any cable means an iron or steel wire covering and any lead or other metallic sheath provided in addition thereto or an iron or steel pipe;

'mine' has the meaning assigned thereto in regulation one;

'portable apparatus' includes any electrical apparatus that is designed to be moved while working.

(2) Expressions to which meanings are assigned by the Act or by these regulations shall (unless the contrary intention appears) have the same meanings in any document issued under the provisions of these regulations.

(3) The Interpretation Act 1889, shall apply to the interpretation of these regulations as it applies to the interpretation of an Act of Parliament.

APPROVED SPECIFICATION OF FLEXIBLE CABLE

(Regulation 15 (2) of the Coal and Other Mines (Electricity) Regulations 1956)

By an approval dated 31st December, 1956, the Minister, in pursuance of Regulation 15 (2) of the Coal and Other Mines (Electricity) Regulations 1956, approved the specification of Type No. 21 cable of British Standard Specification for Trailing Cables for Mining Purposes numbered 708, either as revised in February, 1940, and amended in August, 1940, or as revised in January, 1950, and amended in May, 1950.

The approval only has effect when the cables are used with portable apparatus in accordance with the following conditions:

(*a*) the cables must supply power to the portable apparatus on a three-phase circuit at a voltage between phases not exceeding 650 volts with the neutral point earthed;

(*b*) the portable apparatus must be interlocked electrically with an automatic switch, on an interlock circuit including the pilot core and the armouring of the cable; and

(*c*) the interlock circuit must be supplied with electricity at a voltage not exceeding 30 volts, and must be so arranged that, in the event of any interruption of the circuit, the supply of electricity to the flexible cable is cut off by the automatic opening of the switch.

EMPLOYMENT OF YOUNG PERSONS

THE COAL MINES

(MALE YOUNG PERSONS) ORDER 1960

S.I. 1960 No. 349

1. This order shall come into operation on the fourteenth day of March, nineteen hundred and sixty, and may be cited as the Coal Mines (Male Young Persons) Order 1960.

2. The thirty-first day of March, nineteen hundred and sixty, is hereby appointed as the day until which the provisions of paragraphs (*a*) and (*b*) of subsection (1) of section one hundred and twenty-nine of the Mines and Quarries Act 1954 shall have effect in relation to the county of Warwick, and the thirty-first day of December, nineteen hundred and sixty-one is hereby appointed as the day until which those provisions shall have effect in relation to the counties of Durham and Northumberland.

THE MINES (EMPLOYMENT OF YOUNG PERSONS) (APPOINTED DAY) ORDER 1957

S.I. 1957 No. 1093

1. This order shall come into operation on the first day of July, nineteen hundred and fifty-seven, and may be cited as the Mines (Employment of Young Persons) (Appointed Day) Order 1957.

2. The first day of July, nineteen hundred and fifty-seven, is hereby appointed in relation to mines of every class as the day after which no male young person who has not attained the age of sixteen shall be employed below ground in a mine of any class except for the purpose of receiving instruction of such description as may be prescribed.

EXPLOSIVES

THE COAL MINES

(EXPLOSIVES) REGULATIONS, 1961*

S.I. 1961 No. 854

Arrangement of Regulations

PART I

GENERAL

Commencement and citation

1. These regulations shall come into operation on the first day of June, nineteen hundred and sixty-one, and may be cited as the Coal Mines (Explosives) Regulations 1961.

---

*Certain words, which are used in these Regulations in a special sense which is defined in Regulation 2, appear too frequently to be footnoted separately. It is advisable, therefore, to read the definitions before studying any provision, and particularly one in which any of the following words occur: 'cross measure drift', 'detonator', 'explosive', 'round', 'safety fuse' or 'sheathed explosive'.

Interpretation

2. (1) In these regulations, unless the context otherwise requires, the following expressions have the meanings hereby respectively assigned to them, that is to say—

'the Act' means the Mines and Quarries Act 1954;

'cross measure drift' includes any drift driven otherwise than in coal or otherwise than for the purpose of getting coal therefrom;

'deputy' and 'deputy's district' have the meanings respectively assigned thereto in the Coal and Other Mines (Managers and Officials) Regulations 1956;

'detonator' includes safety fuse capped with a detonator;

'explosive' does not include a detonator;

'explosives store' has the meaning assigned thereto in paragraph (1) of regulation thirteen;

'firedamp content' means the percentage of inflammable gas present in the general body of the air;

'infusion method' has the meaning assigned thereto in paragraph (2) of regulation eight;

'mine' has the meaning assigned thereto in regulation six;

'the Minister' means the Minister of Power;

'miss-fire in a round by broken continuity' and 'miss-fire in a round after firing' have the meanings respectively assigned thereto in paragraph (1) of regulation sixty-five;

'permitted detonator' and 'permitted explosive' have the meanings respectively assigned thereto in regulation seven;

'round', in relation to shots, means (subject to the provisions of paragraph (1) of regulation sixty-one) a number of shots fired—

(*a*) electrically in one operation, by means of instantaneous or delay detonators; or

(*b*) by means approved by the Minister for firing more than four shots at one time by fuse; or

(*c*) by fuses lighted at one time;

'safety fuse' means fuse consisting of gun powder protected either by not less than three coverings of thread or by not less than two coverings of thread and one of tape or gutta-percha, being of such a quality that the rate of burning does not vary more than ten seconds above or below the rate of ninety seconds for each three feet of fuse;

'scheme of transit' has the meaning assigned thereto in paragraph (1) of regulation twenty;

'sheathed explosive' means explosive covered by an external sheath of incombustible material spread evenly over the sides of the cartridge, and includes explosive, in any type of cartridge, certified by the Minister to be equivalent in safety to sheathed explosive;

'shot firer' has the meaning assigned thereto in paragraph (1) of regulation eight;

'single-shot miss-fire' has the meaning assigned thereto in paragraph (2) of regulation sixty-one;

'trainee shot firer' has the meaning assigned thereto in paragraph (1) of regulation eight.

(2) In these regulations any reference to the use of explosive includes the charging of a shot hole therewith.

(3) Expressions to which meanings are assigned by the Act or by these regulations shall (unless the contrary intention appears) have the same meanings in any document issued under the provisions of these regulations.

(4) The Interpretation Act 1889, shall apply to the interpretation of these regulations as it applies to the interpretation of an Act of Parliament, and as if these regulations and the regulations hereby revoked were Acts of Parliament; and any reference in any other regulations made under the Act to any provision of the regulations hereby revoked shall be construed as a reference to the corresponding provision of these regulations.

Exemptions

3. An inspector may by notice served on the manager of any mine exempt that mine or any part thereof, or any person or thing or class of persons or things thereat, from the application of any provision of these regulations if he is satisfied that the safety of persons employed at the mine will not be prejudiced in consequence of the granting of the exemption.

Revocation

4. The Coal Mines (Explosives) Regulations 1956 are hereby revoked.

Savings

5. Nothwithstanding the revocation of the Coal Mines (Explosives) Regulations 1956 any certificate, exemption, consent, approval, authority, determination, permission or scheme granted or made, or having effect as if it had been granted or made, for the purposes of any provision of those regulations, or any other thing done for the purposes of any such provision, shall, if in force on the coming into operation of these regulations and so far as it could have been granted, made or done for the purposes of the corresponding provision of these regulations, have effect as if it had been so granted, made or done.

Part II

Application

6. These regulations shall apply to every mine of coal, and in these regulations 'mine' means such a mine.

Part III

Mines and Parts of Mines in which only Permitted Explosives and Permitted Detonators may be used

7. (1) At any mine in which the use of lamps or lights, other than permitted lights, is unlawful, no person shall take or use below ground any explosive or detonator other than an explosive or detonator of a type approved by the Minister for use in places hazardous by reason of the presence or possibility of the presence of inflammable gas or combustible dust. An explosive or detonator of a type so approved is hereinafter referred to as a 'permitted explosive' or a 'permitted detonator', as the case may be.

(2) No person shall take into or use in any part of a mine, being a part in which safety-lamps are for the time being in use by way of temporary precaution, any explosive other than a permitted explosive or any detonator other than a permitted detonator.

(3) No person shall use any explosive other than a permitted explosive or any detonator other than a permitted detonator—

(*a*) in a length of road which as regards any working face is an intake airway and which begins at a shaft or outlet or the current of air in which is subsequently split; or

(*b*) in a length of road through which coal is, or during the last preceding six months has been, transported by means of a conveyor or in vehicles moved otherwise than by hand or by animal traction; or

(*c*) in any place within thirty feet of such a road (not being a roadhead).

(4) If an inspector is of opinion that any part of a mine is dry and dusty he may serve on the manager a notice stating that he is of that opinion and requiring him to ensure that no explosive other than a permitted explosive and no detonator other than a permitted detonator is taken into or used in that part of the mine and any such notice shall, if it is so specified therein, become operative forthwith.

(5) The provisions of Part XV of the Act* with respect to references upon notices served by inspectors shall apply to a notice served under the last preceding paragraph and the relevant ground of objection to such a notice shall be that that part of the mine is not so dry and dusty as to make the use therein of explosives other than permitted explosives, or detonators other than permitted detonators, dangerous.

PART IV

APPOINTMENT AND QUALIFICATION OF SHOT FIRERS

8. (1) No person shall fire a shot in any mine other than—

(*a*) a competent person appointed to fire shots in that mine by the manager thereof (any person so appointed being, in these regulations, referred to as a 'shot firer'); or

(*b*) a person who is the holder of a shot firer's certificate granted by the Minister on the recommendation of the Mining Qualifications Board, and who, in firing the shot, is practising shot firing by means of electric shot firing apparatus under the close personal supervision of a shot firer in pursuance of an authority in that behalf given in writing by the

*See Section 170 of the 1954 Act.

manager (such a person being in these regulations referred to as a 'trainee shot firer').

(2) No person shall fire a shot in any mine—

(*a*) by means of a delay detonator;

(*b*) by the method known as infusion shot firing (in these regulations referred to as 'the infusion method'); or

(*c*) in a round of more than six shots;

unless he is a shot firer appointed so to do by the manager of that mine or, in the case of a shot fired by means of a delay detonator or in a round of more than six shots, he is a shot firer practising the firing of such shots in accordance with the provisions of regulation eleven. The manager shall include a record of any such appointment in the record of the appointment of that shot firer kept in pursuance of section one hundred and thirty-four of the Act.

(3) No person firing shots in the regular course of his employment in any mine or part of a mine in which no explosives other than permitted explosives may be used shall be paid by wages depending upon the amount of mineral gotten:

Provided that this paragraph shall not apply—

(*a*) by virtue of the firing of shots in a part of the mine in which no explosives other than permitted explosives may be used by reason only that safety-lamps are for the time being in use therein by way of temporary precaution; or

(*b*) to a shot firer who is a master sinker or who is a deputy whose district consists of a shaft in the course of being sunk.

Qualification of shot firers

9. (1) No person shall be qualified to be appointed or to be a shot firer unless—

(*a*) he has attained the age of twenty-two years, or such less age not being less than twenty-one years as may be approved* by the Minister having regard to any special qualification held by him, and has had the practical experience specified in paragraph (2) of this regulation; or

(*b*) he is the holder of a service certificate made under paragraph (6) of article twelve of the Coal Mines (Explosives) Order 1951.

(2) The practical experience referred to in the preceding paragraph is three years' practical experience below ground in a mine including employment for not less than eighteen months in one or more of the following, namely—

(*a*) getting or cutting coal;

(*b*) ripping in a roadhead;

(*c*) setting or withdrawing supports at or building packs at a face at which coal is being worked;

(*d*) drilling shot holes at a face at which coal is being worked;

*An age of 21 has been approved in respect of persons who hold the General Certificate in Mining or any higher qualification.

(*e*) for not more than six months, repairing or enlarging roads or driving cross measure drifts;

(*f*) in the case of a master sinker or a deputy whose district consists of a shaft in the course of being sunk, sinking operations.

10. (1) No person shall be qualified to be appointed or to be a shot firer at a mine in which no explosives other than permitted explosives may be used and no shot firer shall fire a shot or supervise the firing of a shot in a part of a mine in which no explosives other than permitted explosives may be used, not being such a mine or part of a mine by reason only that safety-lamps are for the time being in use therein by way of temporary precaution, unless (in addition to the qualification required under the last preceding regulation)—

(*a*) he is the holder of—

(i) a first or second class certificate of competency valid with respect to that mine; or

(ii) a shot firer's certificate granted by the Minister on the recommendation of the Mining Qualifications Board and he has spent not less than five shifts in practising shot firing in a mine under the close personal supervision of a shot firer; or

(iii) a service certificate made under paragraph (6) of article twelve of the Coal Mines (Explosives) Order 1951, being a certificate which states that he regularly fired shots in a mine to which Part II of the Explosives in Coal Mines Order 1934 applied; and

(*b*) he has within the last preceding five years obtained a certificate* that he was then able to make proper tests for inflammable gas and, in so far as concerned his hearing, to carry out his duties efficiently, being a certificate granted by a university or university college or by a school, college or institution maintained or assisted by a local education authority, or by another body† approved by the Minister for that purpose:

Provided that the certificate referred to in sub-paragraph (*b*) of this paragraph shall not be required in the case of any person who has within the last preceding five years obtained for the purposes of regulation five of the Coal Mines (Explosive) Regulations 1956, or for the purposes of paragraph (2) of regulation twenty-six of the Coal and Other Mines (Managers and Officials) Regulations 1956, a certificate that he was then able to recognise the various gas caps formed in a safety-lamp as required by the regulation in question.

(2) No person shall be authorised to practise shot firing, and no person shall practice shot firing, in any such mine or part of a mine unless that person, in addition to holding the certificate referred to in sub-paragraph (*b*) of paragraph (1) of regulation eight, has the qualification described in sub-paragraph (*b*) of the preceding paragraph subject to the proviso to that paragraph.

---

*M. & Q. Form No. 306.

†No other bodies have been approved for this purpose.

11. No shot firer shall be appointed to fire shots in any mine by means of a delay detonator or in a round of more than six shots unless he has spent not less than five shifts practising the firing of shots by such means or in such a round, as the case may be, under the close personal supervision of a shot firer authorised to fire the shots in question who was not then supervising any other person for the purposes of this regulation.

12. Any certificate required by the preceding provisions of this Part of these regulations to be held as a qualification by any person for the time being employed as a shot firer or trainee shot firer at any mine shall be kept at the office at that mine or at such other place as may be approved by an inspector.

PART V

STORAGE, ISSUE AND CONVEYANCE OF EXPLOSIVES AND DETONATORS

13. (1) The manager of a mine shall not permit any explosive, detonator or safety fuse to be stored thereat except in a place on the surface appointed by him for the purpose (in these regulations referred to as 'an explosives store').*

(2) The manager of every mine in which explosives are used shall appoint at least one place, which shall be situate conveniently near the top of each shaft or outlet normally used by workmen, as a place for the deposit of explosives and detonators brought out of the mine, and may appoint a place (other than an explosives store) for the issue thereof.

(3) The manager of every mine in which explosives are used shall appoint such number of competent persons and make such arrangements as to secure that a competent person is in charge of each explosives store or place appointed for the purposes of the last preceding paragraph whenever explosives or detonators are taken into the store or place, as the case may be, or are to be issued thereat.

14. No person shall cap safety fuse with a detonator at any place at a mine except at a workshop used in connection with an explosives store in pursuance of section forty-seven of the Explosives Act 1875.

Control of issue of detonators

15. (1) All detonators at an explosives store or at a place appointed in pursuance of paragraph (2) of regulation thirteen shall, except during a shift for which the manager of the mine has appointed a competent person to have charge of that store or place, be in the sole charge of the manager.

(2) No person shall be in possession of any detonator at any place at a mine other than an explosives store or a place appointed in pursuance of paragraph (2) of regulation thirteen except a shot firer or trainee shot firer to whom the detonator has been issued for use, or a person authorised in writing by the manager of the mine so to be, and save as aforesaid no person shall issue or take any detonator from such a store or place.

---

*See Memorandum on the Storage of Explosives at Mines, page 107.

Conveyance and care of detonators

16. (1) Except in pursuance of regulation fifty-seven, no person shall take any detonator below ground in a mine except in a securely locked detonator case provided by the owner of the mine.

(2) No person shall put a detonator into a detonator case if it would then contain a delay detonator as well as a detonator which is not a delay detonator.

(3) No person shall put a delay detonator into a detonator case unless the detonator is clearly marked with a number which indicates the period of delay and that period does not exceed five seconds.

(4) The manager of every mine in which detonators are used shall ensure that no detonator case is issued to any person unless it is so constructed and maintained that when the case is closed it is impossible for any detonator or the leads of any detonator contained in the case to touch any metal part thereof which is exposed outside the case or is in contact with any other metal part so exposed.

17. (1) Each shot firer or trainee shot firer to whom a detonator case has been issued shall—

(*a*) retain the key of the case in his own possession throughout the period during which he is on duty;

(*b*) ensure that, apart from any check sheet for recording shots fired by him, nothing except detonators is in it;

(*c*) keep it separate from any receptacle containing explosive;

(*d*) ensure that at any time at which it is not on his person it is in a safe place and, unless he remains in the immediate vicinity, in a securely locked box which does not contain any explosive; and

(*e*) if at the end of his period of duty it contains any detonator, return it to the explosives store or appropriate place on the surface appointed for the deposit of explosives.

(2) Subject to the provisions of regulation forty-four, no shot firer or trainee shot firer shall remove a detonator from a detonator case unless it is required immediately for charging a shot hole.

Conveyance and care of explosives

18. No person shall take any explosive below ground in any mine unless it is in the form of a cartridge.

19. (1) Except in pursuance of regulation twenty or regulation fifty-seven, no person shall take any explosive below ground in any mine unless it is in a closed canister stoutly constructed and containing not more than five pounds of explosive.

(2) Every person having any canister of explosives in his possession or control shall ensure that it is not deposited at any time elsewhere than in a place of safety, and in particular if at the end of his period of duty the canister contains any explosive shall return it to the explosives store or appropriate place on the

surface appointed for the deposit of explosives or, if he received it from a reserve station established for the purposes of a scheme of transit, to that reserve station or to a person and at a place appointed by the manager for the purpose of tha scheme.

(3) Subject to the provisions of regulation forty-four, no person below ground shall unlock or open any canister of explosives or take any explosive from any canister unless the shot firer or trainee shot firer concerned requires to check the quantity of the explosives or the explosive is required immediately for charging a shot hole or the act in question has been authorised by a deputy or other official of the mine.

Conveyance of explosives in bulk

20. (1) Subject to the following provisions of this regulation the manager of any mine may as respects that mine or any part thereof make a scheme for the conveyance of explosives in bulk (herein referred to as a 'scheme of transit') whereby explosives packed at an explosives store in securely locked canisters of any size may be conveyed in a special carriage to one or more reserve stations in that mine or part of the mine or to the working face.

(2) Every scheme of transit shall contain provisions for securing safety with respect to each of the following matters—

(*a*) the location, construction and marking of each reserve station and the custody of the keys thereof;

(*b*) the design and construction of the special carriage;

(*c*) supervision of and precautions to be taken during the transit of the carriage;

(*d*) supervision of any explosives at a reserve station;

(*e*) if explosives are to be taken in bulk to any working face, the manner of so doing;

(*f*) the maximum quantity of explosives to be at any reserve station at any time;

(*g*) the control of the issue of explosives from any reserve station;

(*h*) the return of explosives to a reserve station or other place appointed by the manager.

(3) Every scheme of transit shall contain provisions to ensure that—

(*a*) the quantity of explosives conveyed into the mine in pursuance thereof at any time together with any quantity so conveyed already in the mine does not exceed the quantity estimated to be required for use during the next full working day;

(*b*) except in pursuance of a provision of the scheme, no explosive shall while being conveyed in bulk be taken nearer to a working face (not being only a place in a road at which ripping or work of repair is in progress) than the reserve station nearest to that face.

(4) A scheme of transit may impose duties and prohibitions on persons employed at the mine and those persons shall comply therewith. It shall

be the duty of the manager of the mine to secure that the provisions of any scheme of transit for that mine are executed and enforced.

(5) If an inspector is of opinion with respect to a scheme of transit that the provisions contained therein in pursuance of paragraph (2) of this regulation are not adequate to secure safety, he may serve on the manager of the mine a notice stating that he is of that opinion, specifying the nature of the provision which in his opinion ought to be made and requiring the manager to amend the the scheme accordingly, and any such notice shall, if it is so specified therein, become operative forthwith.

(6) The provisions of Part XV of the Act* with respect to references upon notices served by inspectors shall apply to a notice served under the last preceding paragraph, and the relevant ground of objection shall be that the provisions contained in the scheme of transit in pursuance of paragraph (2) of this regulation are adequate to secure safety.

(7) The person in charge of the explosives at any reserve station shall ensure that—

(*a*) any explosives remaining thereat at the end of his period of duty are—

(i) if the mine will not be worked during the period of one hundred and twenty hours next following, returned to the explosives stores;

(ii) in any other case,

(A) delivered by him to a person appointed to have charge of them during the immediately following shift; or

(B) returned to the explosives store; or

(C) securely locked in the reserve station; and

(*b*) if any such explosives are locked in the reserve station as aforesaid, the key thereof is—

(i) delivered by him to a person appointed to have charge of those explosives during the immediately following shift; or

(ii) deposited in the explosives store.

(8) The manager of every mine at which a scheme of transit is in operation shall ensure that a copy thereof is provided in the covered accommodation provided in pursuance of section one hundred and thirty-five of the Act and that a copy thereof is supplied to each shot firer and trainee shot firer employed at the mine.

PART VI

EQUIPMENT OF A SHOT FIRER

21. (1) For each shot firer on duty there shall be provided by the owner of the mine—

(*a*) a tool made entirely of wood suitable for charging and stemming shot holes;

(*b*) a scraper suitable for cleaning out shot holes; and

*See Section 170 of the 1954 Act.

(*c*) in the case of a shot firer in a mine in which the use of lamps or lights, other than permitted lights, is unlawful or in the case of a shot firer on duty in a part of a mine in which safety-lamps are for the time being in use by way of temporary precaution, a break detector of a design approved* by the Minister (which detector may incorporate the scraper required by the last preceding sub-paragraph).

(2) Where a shot firer is to fire, or supervise the firing of, shots by means of electric shot firing apparatus he shall be provided by the owner of the mine with the necessary shot firing cable of a specification approved* by the Minister—

(*a*) if shots are to be fired in a round, for multi-shot firing; or

(*b*) in any other case, for single-shot firing.

22. No person shall fire a shot in any mine by means of electric shot firing apparatus or cable not provided by the owner of the mine.

23. (1) In any mine or part of a mine in which no explosives other than permitted explosives may be used, no person shall fire a shot except by means of electric shot firing apparatus of a type approved by the Minister—

(*a*) if shots are being fired in a round, for multi-shot firing with all explosives; or

(*b*) in any other case, for single-shot firing with all explosives:

Provided that if an inspector is of opinion in any case that it is expedient to allow the firing of a number of shots in a round, and no such multi-shot firing apparatus may be used to fire those shots by reason of the terms of the approvals of the apparatus, he may by notice served on the manager of the mine permit the use therefor of such electric shot firing apparatus as is specified in the notice, whether approved apparatus or otherwise.

(2) In a mine or part of a mine to which the preceding paragraph does not apply, no person shall fire a shot by means of electric shot firing apparatus other than apparatus of a type approved by the Minister—

(*a*) if shots are being fired in a round, for multi-shot firing with all explosives or with explosives which are not permitted explosives; or

(*b*) in any other case, for single-shot firing with all explosives or with explosives which are not permitted explosives.

(3) Nothing in this regulation shall prevent the use of shot firing apparatus in accordance with the following provisions of these regulations in connection with miss-fired shots and, in a case in which a shot or shots in a shaft are to be fired by means of shot firing apparatus on the surface, nothing in paragraph (1) shall prevent the use of apparatus of a type approved by the Minister for firing with explosives which are not permitted explosives.

24. (1) A shot firer or trainee shot firer to whom any electric shot firing apparatus has been issued shall retain the removable handle or key in his own possession throughout his period of duty:

---

*See page 65.

Provided that nothing in this paragraph shall make it unlawful for a shot firer to whom any such apparatus has been issued and who is supervising the firing of shots by a trainee shot firer to allow the trainee shot firer to have possession of the removable handle or key for so long as may be necessary to enable the trainee shot firer to fire those shots.

(2) Any person who is using any electric shot firing apparatus—

(*a*) shall not place the removable handle or key in position in the apparatus until he is about to fire a shot; and

(*b*) shall remove it from the apparatus immediately after firing each shot.

25. (1) If any electric shot firing apparatus appears to be defective, the person in charge of it shall not use it further but shall cause it to be returned to the surface forthwith and shall report the circumstances to the manager in writing.

(2) If any electric shot firing apparatus approved for multi-shot firing fails to fire all the shots in any properly connected round at one operation, it shall be deemed to be defective for the purposes of the preceding paragraph but notwithstanding the provisions of that paragraph it may be used to fire the shots in that round in accordance with the provisions of regulation sixty-seven.

26. It shall be the duty of the manager of every mine in which electric shot firing apparatus is used to make and secure the efficient carrying out of arrangements to ensure that—

(*a*) all such apparatus is thoroughly cleaned and overhauled at intervals not exceeding three months by the manufacturer thereof or by a competent person appointed for that purpose by the manager;

(*b*) all multi-shot firing apparatus is tested at the surface at intervals not exceeding seven days in a manner approved* by the Minister in respect of apparatus of that type;

(*c*) if in connection with the firing of a round of shots by means of any such apparatus any miss-fire in a round after firing occurs, that apparatus is tested at the surface in such a manner before it is again taken below ground;

(*d*) no such apparatus is taken or used below ground unless on the last previous test thereof it was found to be in satisfactory order; and

(*e*) the date of each cleaning and overhaul and the result of each test carried out in pursuance of this regulation are entered in a book† provided for the purpose by the owner of the mine.

Misuse of equipment

27. (1) No person shall open or tamper with any electric shot firing apparatus below ground.

(2) No person shall use shot firing cable for any purpose other than shot firing.

---

*See page 66.

†M. & Q. Form No. 240.

PART VII

SHOT FIRING—ALL MINES

Drilling and cleaning shot holes

28. (1) No person shall drill a shot hole or any part thereof with a drill of which the diameter does not exceed by at least one-eighth of an inch the diameter of any cartridge to be inserted in that shot hole.

(2) No person shall for the purpose of testing, cleaning out or charging any shot hole use any tool other than the appropriate tool provided for the purpose by the owner of the mine.

29. (1) No person shall begin to charge any shot hole unless it has been thoroughly cleaned out.

(2) No person shall use compressed air to clean out any shot hole unless he ensures that the giving off of any dust is minimised.

Charging shot holes

30. (1) No person shall charge a shot hole unless he is a shot firer or is doing so under the supervision of a shot firer, and no shot firer shall charge a shot hole, or permit a shot hole to be charged, before it is necessary to do so for the purpose of firing a shot.

(2) No person shall begin to charge any shot hole unless he has satisfied himself by taking all reasonable precautions that it is so placed and drilled as to be safe for the firing of a shot.

(3) Except in the case of shots to be fired in one round or of a relieving shot for the purposes of a miss-fire, no person shall charge a shot hole if there is a charged shot hole within ninety feet thereof measured in any plane.

(4) No person shall charge a shot hole to be fired as one of a round in a cross measure drift, heading or ripping or in a shaft or staple-pit until all shot holes for that round have been completely drilled.

31. (1) No shot firer shall permit more than one canister of explosives to be open at any one time for the charging of shot holes by him or under his supervision.

(2) No person shall charge a shot hole—

(*a*) otherwise than with a complete cartridge or complete cartridges; or

(*b*) subject to the provisions of paragraph (3) of regulation sixty-three with cartridges of different diameters or of explosives of different descriptions.

(3) No person shall remove any of the external sheath from a sheathed explosive.

(4) No person shall violently or forcibly press any cartridge into a shot hole.

(5) Any person charging a shot hole shall to the best of his judgment ensure that it is not overcharged having regard to the task to be performed.

32. (1) Except in accordance with the provisions of Part XI of these regulations in relation to a miss-fire, no person shall insert more than one detonator into a shot hole.

(2) No person shall fire a shot by means of a detonator other than an electric detonator or safety fuse capped with a detonator.

(3) No person shall use any detonator in firing a round of shots electrically in any mine unless—

(*a*) it is a low tension detonator or a delay detonator; and
(*b*) it has copper leading wires.

(4) No shot firer shall use a delay detonator unless it is clearly marked with a number which indicates the period of delay and that period does not exceed five seconds.

(5) Where a delay detonator is to be used and the charge is to consist of more than one cartridge, the person charging the shot hole shall insert the primer cartridge first with the detonator at the back of the hole.

33. (1) Except where the shot is to be fired by the infusion method, any person charging a shot hole shall ensure that it is stemmed with sufficient suitable and non-inflammable stemming to prevent a blown out shot.

(2) Except where—

(*a*) a device for pneumatic stemming approved by the Minister* is being used; or

(*b*) infusion apparatus is being inserted into the shot hole for the purpose of firing a shot by the infusion method; or

(*c*) a device approved by the Minister for removing a cartridge from a shot hole in the event of a miss-fire is being used in accordance with the proviso to paragraph (1) of regulation sixty-three or the proviso to paragraph (1) of regulation sixty-six;

no person shall insert any tool not made entirely of wood into a shot hole containing explosive.

34. (1) No person shall remove any stemming from any charged shot hole otherwise than by means of water.

(2) No person shall pull out any detonator lead from any charged shot hole.

(3) No person shall remove any explosive from any charged shot hole except—

(*a*) a cartridge or part of a cartridge which is left protruding out of the mouth of the hole as a result of the firing of a shot or round of shots; or

(*b*) in accordance with the proviso to paragraph (1) of regulation sixty-three or the proviso to paragraph (1) of regulation sixty-six.

Firing shots

35. (1) No person shall fire any shot unless he has satisfied himself by taking all reasonable precautions that it is in a shot hole so placed and drilled as to be

*There are no current approvals.

safe for the firing of a shot and is charged and stemmed in accordance with the provisions of these regulations.

(2) Subject to the provisions of the preceding paragraph, each shot firer shall, unless prevented by circumstances beyond his control, fire every shot which has been charged by him or by some person under his supervision and which has not been fired by a trainee shot firer.

36. Each shot firer and trainee shot firer shall keep a record of all shots fired by him on each shift of his in a book* provided by the owner of the mine for that purpose.

Firing shots electrically

37. (1) No shot firer shall, in any mine or part of a mine, fire a round of more than six shots in—

(*a*) a coal face; or

(*b*) any other place if an inspector has by notice served on the manager directed that no round of more than six shots shall be fired in that place.

The provisions of Part XV of the Act† with respect to references upon notices served by inspectors shall apply to a notice served under this paragraph, and the relevant ground of objection to such a notice shall be that compliance therewith is wholly, or to a particular extent, unnecessary for securing the safety of persons employed at the mine.

(2) Where a round of shots is to be fired by means of electric shot firing apparatus, the person who is to fire the round shall ensure that—

(*a*) the detonators are connected in series;

(*b*) no additional wire is used for connecting any detonator leads to each other.

(3) No person shall use any cable for firing shots if its length is less than any one of the following lengths which are applicable to the cable—

(*a*) sixty feet when a single shot is being fired otherwise than in a shaft in the course of being sunk;

(*b*) one hundred and fifty feet when a round of shots is being fired in coal;

(*c*) two hundred and ten feet when a round of six shots or less is being fired in stone;

(*d*) three hundred feet when a round of more than six shots is being fired in a ripping;

(*e*) six hundred feet when a round of more than six shots in a cross measure drift, or any shot in a shaft in the course of being sunk, is being fired.

(4) Any person who is about to use shot firing cable shall ensure that it is not in, and cannot make, contact with any other cable or electric apparatus.

---

*M. & Q. Form No. 241.

†See Section 170 of the 1954 Act.

(5) No person other than a shot firer or trainee shot firer shall couple any shot firing cable to any detonator or to shot firing apparatus.

(6) No person shall couple a shot firing cable to shot firing apparatus for the purpose of firing a shot unless the cable has already been coupled by him to the detonator or detonator circuit.

(7) No person shall fire any round of shots by means of electric shot firing apparatus unless he has tested the circuit for continuity by means of a testing device approved by the Minister and has found it to be satisfactory. No person shall make any such test unless all persons in the vicinity have withdrawn to a place of safety, and he himself has taken proper shelter.

Firing shots by fuse

38. (1) No shot firer shall fire a single shot by fuse less than three feet in length or any shot in a round by fuse less than four feet in length.

(2) Not more than one shot firer shall charge shot holes with shots to be fired by fuse or permit shot holes to be so charged or fire shots by fuse at any one time in any working place or at any working face which does not exceed one hundred and fifty feet in length.

(3) At any working face exceeding one hundred and fifty feet in length no shot firer shall fire any shot by fuse within one hundred and fifty feet of another charged shot hole unless he has satisfied himself that no other shot firer is about to fire that other shot.

(4) No shot firer shall fire or attempt to fire more than four shots at one time by fuse except by means approved by the Minister for that purpose.

(5) Where any shot is to be fired by fuse the shot firer shall ensure that—

(*a*) no naked light or person who is smoking is directly above, or within four feet in any other direction of, any shot hole, explosive or detonator;

(*b*) all surplus explosives are removed from the vicinity of the shot hole before a light is brought near to it for the purpose of lighting the fuse.

Infusion shot firing

39. (1) No shot firer shall fire a shot by the infusion method unless he has satisfied himself by taking all reasonable precautions that—

(*a*) the shot is in a shot hole which, immediately before he fires the shot, is filled with water, and

(*b*) the infusing apparatus used is so secured in the shot hole, or is so constructed, that it is not likely to be blown out by the shot.

(2) No shot firer shall fire a shot by the infusion method unless the explosives and detonators used for the purpose are each of a type approved by the Minister for use when firing shots by that method.

Warning and shelter

40. In every case where a shot may blow through into another place the person who is about to fire the shot shall cause due warning to be given to all persons in that place, and he shall after firing the shot cause notice to be given to them that the period of danger is ended.

41. (1) Any person proposing to fire a shot shall before firing determine the danger zone likely to be created.

(2) No person shall fire any shot unless he has—

(*a*) at each entrance to that danger zone either posted a sentry or placed an appropriate fence conspicuously marked with the words 'danger' and 'shot firing';

(*b*) ensured that all persons have withdrawn from that zone or have taken proper shelter; and

(*c*) himself taken proper shelter.

42. (1) No person who has been posted as a sentry in pursuance of regulation forty-one shall leave the place where he was posted until the person who so posted him has personally directed him to do so.

(2) No person shall pass a danger sign exhibited for the purpose of shot firing without the authority of the shot firer or trainee shot firer concerned, or shall pass a sentry who has forbidden him to do so.

Precautions after shot firing

43. (1) Every person who has fired a shot shall thereafter—

(*a*) ascertain by a personal examination whether it is safe for ordinary working to be resumed in each working place affected by that shot; and

(*b*) ensure that any necessary action is taken to make each such place safe for such working.

(2) Where a round of shots has been fired the person who fired the round—

(*a*) shall not make that examination, if it was a round of six shots or less, before the expiry of five minutes or, in any other case, before the expiry of ten minutes;

(*b*) shall in the course of his examination examine for sockets in the face, for any explosive remaining in any such socket and, if he has reason to think that any shot may not have completely exploded, for any unexploded charge in the material brought down.

PART VIII

SHOT FIRING—ADDITIONAL PROVISIONS FOR CROSS MEASURE DRIFTS

44. (1) Nothing in paragraph (2) of regulation seventeen or in paragraph (3) of regulation nineteen shall make it unlawful for a shot firer, in preparing to fire a round of shots in a cross measure drift, to prime the cartridges to be used in firing that round at a place which is at least one hundred and fifty feet away from the face, provided that—

(a) the place has been appointed for that purpose by the manager; and

(b) the shot firer has been appointed in writing by the manager to prime cartridges at a place other than a face.

(2) Such a shot firer, in the circumstances mentioned in the preceding paragraph, shall—

(a) immediately he has removed a detonator from a detonator case for the purpose of priming a cartridge, so twist together the leads of the detonator as to cause a short circuit;

(b) immediately he has primed each cartridge, place the cartridge in a box provided for the purpose by the owner of the mine;

(c) immediately after all the cartridges required for the round have been primed and placed in a box or boxes as aforesaid, securely lock every such box;

(d) ensure that thereafter every such box remains locked until the cartridges are required immediately for charging the shot holes; and

(e) charge the shot holes as soon as it is practicable to do so in accordance with Part VII of these regulations.

(3) No shot firer in complying with the requirements of sub-paragraph (b) of the last preceding paragraph shall put detonators of different periods of delay in the same compartment of a box.

(4) No shot firer shall begin priming the cartridges in the circumstances mentioned in paragraph (1) of this regulation unless he is satisfied on reasonable grounds that the shot holes to be charged therewith will be ready to be charged as soon as he has finished priming the cartridges.

(5) It shall be the duty of the manager to ensure that every such box as is referred to in paragraph (2) of this regulation is—

(a) of stout construction;

(b) fitted with a lock;

(c) divided into separate compartments; and

(d) so constructed and maintained that its contents are protected from shock and when it is closed it is impossible for any detonator or the leads of any detonator contained in the box to touch any metal part thereof which is exposed outside the case or is in contact with any other metal part so exposed.

(6) Any shot firer to whom any such box as is referred to in paragraph (2) of this regulation has been issued shall retain the key thereof in his own possession throughout the period during which he is on duty.

PART IX

SHOT FIRING—ADDITIONAL PROVISIONS FOR MINES IN WHICH ONLY PERMITTED EXPLOSIVES MAY BE USED

Shot firer's maximum number of shots

45. (1) For each shot firer firing shots or supervising the firing of shots in the regular course of his employment in any mine or part of a mine in which no explosives, other than permitted explosives, may be used, the manager shall from time to time fix the maximum number of shots which he may fire or permit to be fired under his supervision in any one hour and in any one shift, and shall at all times ensure that the number for the time being so fixed shall, in each case, be one which is consistent with the requirements of safety:

Provided that the numbers so fixed shall not apply to shots fired in a round of more than six shots.

(2) If the manager proposes to fix a maximum exceeding ten for any one shift for a shot firer who is a deputy assigned to a district for that shift he shall give to the inspector for the district notice thereof in such form* as may be specified by the Minister.

(3) If an inspector is of opinion that the firing of more than ten shots in a shift by or under the supervision of a shot firer referred to in a notice given under the last preceding paragraph is inconsistent with the requirements of safety, he may within fourteen days of the receipt of that notice serve on the manager a notice requiring him not to fix a number for that shot firer exceeding a number specified therein, and any such notice shall, if it is so specified therein, become operative forthwith.

(4) If an inspector is of opinion that any maximum number of shots fixed by the manager for any shot firer is inconsistent with the requirements of safety, he may serve on the manager a notice requiring him to reduce that number to a number not exceeding that specified in the notice:

Provided that an inspector shall not serve a notice under this paragraph in relation to a number of which notice was given under paragraph (2) unless there has been a material change in the circumstances since the date of that notice.

(5) The provisions of Part XV of the Act† with respect to references upon notices served by inspectors shall apply to a notice served under either of the two last preceding paragraphs and the relevant ground of objection to such a notice shall be that the firing by or under the supervision of the shot firer in question of the maximum number of shots fixed or proposed to be fixed will not be inconsistent with the requirements of safety.

46. (1) The manager shall give notice to each shot firer of each maximum fixed under the last preceding regulation in relation to him and shall record each such maximum in a book‡ provided by the owner of the mine for the purpose.

(2) No shot firer shall in any one hour or in any one shift fire or permit to be fired under his supervision a greater number of shots than the permitted maximum notified to him under the preceding paragraph:

Provided that those numbers shall not apply to shots fired in a round of more than six shots.

---

*M. & Q. Form No. 242.

†See Section 170 of the 1954 Act.

‡M. & Q. Form No. 243.

Restrictions on shot firing where inflammable gas is present

47. (1) If any determination of firedamp content made in pursuance of Part II of the Coal and Other Mines (Ventilation) Regulations 1956,* at any point in any part of a mine shows a firedamp content exceeding one and a quarter per cent, the manager shall take such steps as are necessary for securing that no person fires a shot in that part of the mine on the return side of that point during the period described in paragraph (4) of this regulation.

(2) If any deputy to whom a deputy's district is assigned in a mine in which the use of lamps or lights, other than permitted lights, is unlawful finds at any place a firedamp content exceeding one and a quarter per cent or can see at any place in the general body of the air an indication of gas on the lowered flame of a safety-lamp, he shall ensure—

(*a*) that no shot is fired or shot hole charged in his district on the return side of that place during the period described in paragraph (4) of this regulation; and

(*b*) if the air in question will ventilate any part of any other deputy's district, that the deputy in charge thereof is informed of the facts.

(3) A deputy to whom such information is given shall ensure that no shot is fired or shot hole charged in any part of his district ventilated by air which has been found to contain inflammable gas as aforesaid during the period described in paragraph (4) of this regulation.

(4) Any prohibition imposed by this regulation shall continue as regards any place until the senior official on duty at the mine has satisfied himself that the firedamp content at the place at which it was found does not exceed one and a quarter per cent and has authorised the resumption of shot firing.

(5) The manager shall forthwith give to the inspector for the district notice of any occasion on which shot firing is required to be suspended by this regulation by virtue of a firedamp content at any place exceeding one and a quarter per cent unless such content was caused by the temporary derangement of the ventilation.

Restrictions on certain shots

48. If the face of any cross measure drift in a part of a mine in which no explosives, other than permitted explosives, may be used—

(*a*) contains a seam of coal more than twelve inches thick, or

(*b*) is in waste more than twelve inches thick or is known to have approached within fifteen feet of any waste,

no shot firer shall, in that drift, use any delay detonator, unless

(i) all the detonators and explosives used in the round in question are of a type approved by the Minister for the purposes of this regulation; or

(ii) in the circumstances referred to in paragraph (*a*) of this regulation, the following conditions are fulfilled, that is to say—

---

*See page 317.

(A) any dust which can be raised in the air in any part of the drift which is within three hundred feet of the face thereof contains not less than seventy-five per cent of incombustible matter;

(B) the face of the drift has been fixed by the manager under regulation six of the Coal and Other Mines (Ventilation) Regulations 1956* as a suitable point for the determination of the firedamp content in that drift and, notwithstanding any different intervals which may apply by virtue of paragraph (1) of regulation seven of those regulations, firedamp determinations are made at that point, so far as practicable while operations are being carried out in the drift, at intervals not exceeding twenty-four hours by means of apparatus approved by the Minister under sub-paragraph (*a*) of paragraph (1) of regulation four of those regulations; and

(C) where the round of shots includes any shot fired in coal, the estimated period of delay between the first and last shots of the round calculated by reference to the markings on the detonators does not exceed 0·75 seconds; or

(iii) in the circumstances referred to in paragraph (*b*) of this regulation, an inspector by notice served on the manager has consented thereto.

49. In a mine in which the use of lamps or lights, other than permitted lights, is unlawful or in any part of a mine being a part in which safety-lamps are for the time being in use by way of temporary precaution, no person shall fire a shot—

(*a*) in the roof of any longwall working between the coal face and the waste; or

(*b*) in that waste:

Provided that the provisions of paragraph (*a*) of this regulation shall not apply in the case of a shot fired for the sole purposes of ripping the roof of a dummy gate by means of explosives and detonators of types approved for that purpose by the Minister.

Precautionary examinations

50. (1) The provisions of this regulation shall apply to every mine in which the use of lamps or lights, other than permitted lights, is unlawful and to every part of a mine being a part in which safety-lamps are for the time being in use by way of temporary precaution.

(2) No person shall fire a shot unless he has carried out with respect to it an examination for general safety and tests for the presence of inflammable gas in accordance with the following provisions of this regulation. Every such test for inflammable gas shall be made with a locked flame safety-lamp of a type approved† by the Minister for the purpose of deputies' inspections, a

---

*See page 318.

†See page 225.

methanometer of a type approved by the Minister or other apparatus of a type approved by the Minister for the purpose.

(3) No person shall fire a shot or charge a shot hole if on any such test made with respect to it he finds a percentage of inflammable gas exceeding one and a quarter or he can see an indication of gas on the lowered flame of a safety-lamp.

(4) If shots are to be fired singly in succession in coal along a longwall face, the person who is to fire the shots shall arrange them in groups of not more than six and shall fire all the shots in any such group so far as practicable without interruption for duties other than shot firing.

(5) Any person who intends to fire shots in one or more rounds or groups in any area shall—

(*a*) before shot firing in that area is begun carry out an examination for general safety and test for the presence of inflammable gas over the whole of that area and the approaches thereto;

(*b*) immediately before the first shot hole of any round or group is charged, test for gas—

(i) in every accessible place within thirty feet of each of the two shot holes in the round or group which are farthest apart;

(ii) at the mouth of each shot hole in the round or group; and

(iii) if the shots are to be fired at a face and there is waste in the vicinity, throughout that part of the workings which is between the face and the waste and between those two shot holes;

(*c*) immediately before firing any round or any shot in a group, test for gas in the vicinity of each shot hole and at the edge of any waste opposite.

(6) Any person who intends to fire a single shot otherwise than as one of a group shall—

(*a*) immediately before the shot hole is charged, carry out an examination for general safety and test for gas—

(i) in the vicinity and at the mouth of the shot hole;

(ii) if the shot hole is in a longwall face, throughout every accessible place within, if the shot hole is not within sixty feet of the end of the face, thirty feet from the shot hole, or, if it is within sixty feet of the end of the face, sixty feet therefrom;

(*b*) immediately before firing, test for gas in the vicinity of the shot hole and at the edge of any waste opposite.

Preparation and charging of shot holes

51. Unless an inspector by notice served on the manager consents thereto, no person shall charge a shot hole in any coal face in a part of a mine in which no explosives, other than permitted explosives, may be used unless the coal has been holed or sheared to a depth greater than the depth of the shot hole:

Provided that this regulation shall not apply to a shot hole in anthracite or to any shot hole in a cross measure drift, or where the shot is to be fired by the infusion method or in pursuance of sub-paragraph (*c*) (ii) of paragraph (1) of regulation sixty-three or sub-paragraph (*c*) (ii) of paragraph (1) of regulation sixty-six.

52. (1) In a mine in which the use of lamps or lights, other than permitted lights, is unlawful and in any part of a mine being a part in which safety-lamps are for the time being in use by way of temporary precaution, any person drilling a shot hole in coal or in a ripping and finding a break along or across it which exceeds one-eighth of an inch in width shall mark the hole concerned in a distinctive manner. No person shall charge any shot hole so marked.

(2) In any such mine or part of a mine no person shall charge any shot hole in coal or in a ripping unless he has tested, with the break detector with which he is provided, for breaks running along or across it and has satisfied himself that no such break exceeding one-eighth of an inch in width exists.

(3) The provisions of the preceding paragraphs of this regulation shall not apply in any case where the shot in question is to be fired by the infusion method.

53. (1) No person other than a shot firer or trainee shot firer shall charge any shot hole in a part of a mine in which no explosives, other than permitted explosives, may be used:

Provided that nothing in this paragraph shall make it unlawful for any person in a cross measure drift or a shaft in the course of being sunk to insert in a shot hole any part of the charge, not being a primer cartridge, if he has been appointed in writing by the manager so to do, and, in so doing, he is working under the close personal supervision of a shot firer.

(2) No person shall stem any such shot hole unless he is a shot firer or is doing so under the supervision of a shot firer.

54. (1) No person shall charge a shot hole in a part of a mine in which no explosives, other than permitted explosives, may be used with an aggregate weight or length of explosive exceeding the maximum specified on any cartridge forming part of the charge.

(2) No person shall use in any such part of a mine—

(*a*) any detonator except an electric detonator with a copper tube;

(*b*) except in a cross measure drift or in a shaft in the course of being sunk any delay detonator unless—

(i) if the round in question is being fired otherwise than by the infusion method, all the explosives and detonators used to fire the round are of a type approved by the Minister for the purposes of this sub-paragraph;

(ii) the estimated period of delay between the first and last shots of the round calculated by reference to the markings on the detonators does not exceed 0·1 seconds; and

(iii) in the case of shots fired in a ripping, there is not, in the same seam, a coal face which is more than eighteen feet but less than four hundred and fifty feet from the ripping.

55. In a mine in which the use of lamps or lights, other than permitted lights, is unlawful and in any part of a mine being a part in which safety-lamps are for the time being in use by way of temporary precaution, no person shall—

(*a*) begin to charge any shot hole in under-cut coal or in a roof ripping within three hundred feet of a coal face unless he has inserted a plug of sand or clay or other similar non-inflammable material at the back of the hole; or

(*b*) charge any shot hole in a roof ripping within sixty feet of the face otherwise than with sheathed explosive;

except where the shot in question is to be fired by the infusion method.

PART X

SHOT FIRING—ADDITIONAL PROVISIONS FOR SHAFTS AND STAPLE-PITS

56. No person shall take any explosive into a shaft or staple-pit for use therein unless it is immediately required for charging a shot hole.

Primer cartridges

57. No person other than a shot firer or trainee shot firer shall take a primer cartridge fitted with a detonator into a shaft in the course of being sunk and no shot firer or trainee shot firer shall take such a cartridge so fitted into such a shaft otherwise than in a thick felt bag or other receptacle suitable for protecting it from shock.

Detonators

58. No person shall fire a shot in a shaft or staple-pit except by means of an electric detonator.

Precautions before firing

59. (1) No person shall couple a shot firing cable to a detonator in a shaft or staple-pit provided with winding apparatus unless—

(*a*) the kibble is conveniently placed for men in the shaft or staple-pit to enter it; and

(*b*) he has satisfied himself that the person operating the winding apparatus is ready to raise the kibble.

(2) No person shall couple a shot firing cable to shot firing apparatus for the purpose of firing any shot in a shaft or staple-pit unless all persons who may be affected are in a place of safety.

Precautions after firing

60. No person, other than the shot firer and any trainee shot firer concerned, shall enter a staple-pit after a shot has been fired therein until the examination referred to in paragraph (1) of regulation forty-three has been carried out:

Provided that on such an examination the person who fired the shot may be accompanied by not more than two competent persons as assistants.

PART XI

MISS-FIRES

A. Single shots

Meaning of 'single-shot miss-fire'

61. (1) For the purposes of this Part of these regulations, all shots fired by fuse shall be deemed to be single shots.

(2) A shot being fired as a single shot shall be treated as a miss-fire (in these regulations referred to as a 'single-shot miss-fire'), if it fails to explode, in the case of a shot being fired—

(*a*) by fuse, after the shot firer has withdrawn after once lighting or attempting to light the fuse; or

(*b*) electrically, after the person attempting to fire the shot, having been unsuccessful in doing so, has followed the procedure described in paragraph (3) of this regulation.

(3) The said procedure is that the person who attempted to fire the shot shall—

(*a*) disconnect from the shot firing apparatus the removable handle or key and the shot firing cable;

(*b*) after waiting five minutes, examine the cable and connections for any defect, and remedy any defect so found;

(*c*) make a further attempt to fire the shot, for which purpose he may use shot firing apparatus of a type approved by the Minister for multi-shot firing with the explosives concerned, not being apparatus approved only for use in a cross measure drift or shaft in the course of being sunk.

Single-shot miss-fires—general precautions

62. In the event of a single-shot miss-fire, no person shall approach the shot hole until, if the shot is being fired—

(*a*) by fuse, there have elapsed, from the lighting of the fuse or the attempt to light it, not less than thirty minutes; or

(*b*) electrically, the removable handle or key and the shot firing cable have been disconnected from the shot firing apparatus, and there have elapsed, from the last attempt to fire the shot, not less than five minutes.

Single-shot miss-fires—remedial action

63. (1) In the event of a single-shot miss-fire, the shot firer or trainee shot firer concerned shall ensure that—

(*a*) the procedure described in paragraph (2) of this regulation is complied with; or

(*b*) in a case where the shot was being fired otherwise than by the infusion method, the stemming is removed with water, an additional primer inserted in the shot hole with proper stemming, and the shot then duly fired otherwise than by the infusion method; or (*c*) in a case where the shot was being fired by the infusion method, the infusion tube is removed and either—

(i) an additional primer is inserted in the shot hole, the infusion tube replaced, and the shot then duly fired by the infusion method; or

(ii) an additional primer of the same explosive, or of a type approved for the purpose of this paragraph by the Minister, is inserted in the shot hole with proper stemming, and the shot then duly fired otherwise than by the infusion method:

Provided that, in a case where, in the opinion of the shot firer or trainee shot firer concerned, to insert a second primer in a shot hole in accordance with sub-paragraph (*b*) or sub-paragraph (*c*) of this paragraph without removing a cartridge already in the shot hole would over-charge the shot hole, a cartridge may be removed from the shot hole, by means of a device approved for the purpose by the Minister, immediately after the stemming or the infusion tube, as the case may be, has been removed and before the second primer is inserted.

(2) The said procedure is as follows—

(*a*) a shot hole shall be drilled not nearer to the shot hole containing the miss-fire than twelve inches, and, so far as is practicable, parallel to, and of equal depth to, that shot hole;

(*b*) if the shot hole containing the miss-fire also contains a detonator, the leads or fuse thereof shall be attached by a string to the shot firing cable, or to some distinctive marker;

(*c*) a shot shall be duly fired in the shot hole drilled as aforesaid;

(*d*) if the miss-fire is not dislodged, the procedure herein described shall be repeated.

(3) A primer of a type approved by the Minister for the purpose of sub-paragraph (*c*) (ii) of paragraph (1) of this regulation, or for the purpose of sub-paragraph (*c*) (ii) of paragraph (1) of regulation sixty-six, may be inserted in a shot hole in accordance with either of the said sub-paragraphs notwithstanding that it is of a different diameter from that of the cartridges already in the shot hole or that it contains explosive of a different description from that already in the shot hole.

B. Shots in a round

Circuit not continuous

64. (1) If, when the circuit of a round is tested in pursuance of paragraph (7) of regulation thirty-seven, it is found not be continuous, the person who has made the test shall comply with the following procedure, that is to say, he shall—

(*a*) examine the shot firing cable and connections for defects (after disconnecting the cable from the shot firing apparatus, if the testing device formed part of it);

(*b*) remedy any defect so found; and

(*c*) subject to the provisions of the said paragraph (7), test the circuit again for continuity.

(2) If the circuit passes the last mentioned test successfully, the provisions of this Part of these regulations shall not apply in relation to that round, unless one or more of the shots fails to explode when fired.

(3) If the circuit does not pass the said test successfully, the shot firer or trainee shot firer concerned shall, by tests for continuity (which shall be subject to the provisions of paragraph (7) of regulation thirty-seven), determine the faulty shot or shots.

Miss-fires by broken continuity or after firing

65. (1) A shot being fired electrically in a round shall be treated as a miss-fire if—

(*a*) by the tests under paragraph (3) of regulation sixty-four, it is found to be a faulty shot (any such shot being in these regulations referred to as a 'miss-fire in a round by broken continuity'); or

(*b*) when the round is fired, it fails to explode, whether or not all other shots in the round have exploded, (any such shot being in these regulations referred to as a 'miss-fire in a round after firing').

(2) Whenever, in the event of any miss-fire in a round by broken continuity or miss-fire in a round after firing, any shot forming part of the round is, for the purposes of remedial action under regulation sixty-six or regulation sixty-seven, required to be fired singly, it may be fired by means of the shot firing apparatus used for firing the round.

Remedial action

66. (1) In the event of a miss-fire in a round by broken continuity, the shot firer or trainee shot firer concerned shall ensure that either—

(*a*) the procedure described in paragraph (2) of this regulation is complied with; or

(*b*) in a case where the round in question was being fired otherwise than by the infusion method, the stemming is removed with water, an additional primer inserted in the shot hole with proper stemming, and the round duly connected up, tested and fired otherwise than by the infusion method; or

(*c*) in a case where the round in question was being fired by the infusion method, the infusion tube is removed and either—

(i) an additional primer is inserted in the shot hole, the infusion tube replaced, and the round then duly connected up, tested and fired by the infusion method; or

(ii) an additional primer of the same explosive, or of a type approved for the purpose of this paragraph by the Minister, is inserted in the shot hole with proper stemming, and the round then duly connected up, tested and fired:

Provided that, in a case where, in the opinion of the shot firer or trainee shot firer concerned, to insert a second primer in a shot hole in accordance with sub-paragraph (*b*) or sub-paragraph (*c*) of this paragraph without removing a cartridge already in the shot hole would over-charge the shot hole, a cartridge may be removed from the shot hole, by means of a device approved for the purpose by the Minister, immediately after the stemming or the infusion tube, as the case may be, has been removed and before the second primer is inserted.

(2) The said procedure is as follows—

(*a*) the leads of the detonator of the miss-fire shall be attached by a string to the shot firing cable, or to some distinctive marker;

(*b*) the other shots in the round (excluding, where delay detonators are being used, any shot having a longer period of delay) shall be duly connected up, tested and fired, as provided in these regulations;

(*c*) if the miss-fire becomes dislodged, and if there are any shots having a longer period of delay, they shall be duly connected up, tested and fired;

(*d*) if it has not become dislodged—

(i) if there are any shots having a longer period of delay, they shall be fired in turn, in increasing order of delay (in each delay period, the shot which is nearest to the miss-fire being fired first); and

(ii) in any other case, it shall be treated as a single-shot miss-fire.

67. (1) In the event of a miss-fire in a round after firing—

(*a*) no person shall approach the shot hole unless the removable handle or key and the shot firing cable have been disconnected from the shot firing apparatus; and

(*b*) the person who fired the round shall at the expiry of the appropriate period specified in regulation forty-three make a personal examination as provided in that regulation, whether or not any shot in the round has exploded.

(2) If there were more than one miss-fire, the person who fired the round shall connect them in series and fire them as a round as provided in these regulations.

(3) If there was one miss-fire only, or if one or more miss-fires, fired as a round in pursuance of paragraph (2), fails or fail to explode, the shot firer or trainee shot firer concerned shall fire the miss-fire, or each of the miss-fires, as the case may be, singly.

(4) Any miss-fire, fired singly as aforesaid and failing to explode, shall be treated as a single-shot miss-fire.

68. (1) Whenever, in pursuance of any provision of this Part of these regulations relating to any round of shots, any shot in the round is fired while one or more shots already charged remain unexploded, the person firing the shot shall, in the course of his examination made in pursuance of regulation forty-three, ascertain whether any such shot has been dislodged.

(2) The provisions of regulation seventy-one shall apply to the recovery and disposal of the detonator and charge of any shot so dislodged.

C. All miss-fires

69. No person shall attempt to remove any part of the charge from the shot hole of any shot which is to be treated as a miss-fire except—

(*a*) a cartridge or part of a cartridge which is protruding out of the shot hole as a result of the firing of a shot or round of shots; or

(*b*) in accordance with the proviso to paragraph (1) of regulation sixty-three or the proviso to paragraph (1) of regulation sixty-six.

70. In the case of any shot which is to be treated as a miss-fire or any round of shots of which the circuit has been found not to be continuous, if the shot firer concerned leaves the working place before the shot or shots have been fired, or after the detonator and cartridges have been dislodged and before the provisions of the next following regulation have been complied with, he shall—

(*a*) cause notice of the circumstances to be given to the deputy in charge of the district; and

(*b*) ensure that sufficient fences and danger notices are erected to warn any person approaching the place.

71. Whenever any miss-fire is dislodged by the firing of another shot there shall be made under the supervision of the person who fired that shot or an official of the mine before any person resumes work and before any further shot is fired at or near that place a search for the detonator (if any) and the charge thereof and if any detonator or cartridge is not found all mineral so dislodged shall be conveyed out of the mine separately from any other mineral and under the like supervision.

72. In the event of any miss-fire, the person who attempted to fire the shot in question shall, before leaving the mine, report the circumstances thereof to the senior official on duty at the mine, and shall record the fact of the miss-fire in his daily record of shots.*

PART XII

APPARATUS AND EXPLOSIVES FOR KILLING HORSES

73. (1) Nothing in Parts III to XI of these regulations except regulation thirteen shall apply to such apparatus or such cartridges of explosive as are approved by the Minister for use in mines for destroying horses.

(2) No person shall take or use below ground in any mine for any other purpose any such apparatus or cartridge.

74. The manager of every mine shall ensure that horse killing apparatus is—

(*a*) kept in the custody of a competent person appointed by him and used only by that person or under his close personal supervision;

(*b*) cleaned and examined immediately after use on any occasion.

*M. & Q. Form No. 241.

75. (1) The manager of every mine shall ensure that cartridges for horse killing are issued from the explosives store only to a person appointed to have custody of horse killing apparatus and in a case or box with a lock provided by the owner of the mine.

(2) No person shall put any cartridge for horse killing into a receptacle containing any other kind of explosive or a detonator.

(3) Every person having a case or box of cartridges for horse killing shall keep it separate from any other receptacle containing explosive or detonators and shall keep it locked except for the purposes of the following paragraph.

(4) No person shall remove any cartridge for horse killing from its case or box below ground until it is required for immediate use.

76. (1) In any mine in which the use of lamps or lights, other than permitted lights, is unlawful or in any part of a mine being a part in which safety-lamps are for the time being in use by way of temporary precaution, no person shall fire a shot with horse killing apparatus unless immediately before firing a competent person has made tests for the presence of inflammable gas throughout every accessible place within thirty feet of the place where the shot is to be fired and it has been found safe for the firing of that shot.

(2) Every such test shall be made with a locked flame safety-lamp of a type approved by the Minister for the purpose of deputies' inspections, a methanometer of a type approved by the Minister or other apparatus of a type approved by the Minister for the purpose.

(3) No person shall fire a shot with horse killing apparatus if on any such test made with respect to that shot there has been found a firedamp content exceeding one and a quarter per cent or an indication of gas on the lowered flame of a safety-lamp has been seen at any place.

APPROVED SPECIFICATIONS AND MANNER OF TESTING

FOR PURPOSES OF THE COAL MINES (EXPLOSIVES) REGULATIONS 1961

BREAK DETECTOR

The design of break detector described below is approved for the purposes of Regulation 21 (1) (*c*):

1. *General*

A straight stiff rod or tube, made of hard brass, steel, aluminium alloy, or other material of similar rigidity and durability, with a flat prong at one end, which forms an integral part of it or is securely attached to it, and which is made of, or tipped with, hard wearing metal.

2. *Dimensions*

Length of rod or tube—at least four feet six inches, or six inches longer than the depth of the deepest shot hole in which the detector is to be used, whichever is the greater.

Diameter of rod or tube—not more than half inch.

Length of prong—not less than three-quarters inch, not more than one inch, from the centre of the rod or tube.

Width and thickness of prong at tip—not more than three thirty-second inch.

Note—

(1) *The specified design requirements are intended to ensure that the break detector is suitable for detecting any break of over one-eighth inch in width (Regulation* 52 (2) *of the Coal Mines (Explosives) Regulations,* 1961). *In order that such longitudinal breaks can be found, the prong should not only have a limiting width at the tip of three thirty-second inch or less (as specified) but should also taper steeply so that the point will drop sufficiently far into the break. This means that the width of the prong at the base must be kept sufficiently small.*

(2) *If a hollow tube, instead of a solid rod, is used, there is no objection to filling it with a core of wood. Soft metal, such as copper, is unsuitable, because it soon becomes bent and worn. One method of forming the detector prong is to turn over and shape a suitable length of a steel rod and then to coat the tip with a hard-wearing alloy, while a duralumin rod, for example, will require the fitting of a separate prong of steel tipped with hard-wearing alloy.*

(3) *The break detector may incorporate a scraper, preferably attached at the opposite end from the detector prong. It is desirable that the scraper attachment should not comprise more than half a disc, so as to minimise the risk of its mis-use for charging or stemming.*

SHOT FIRING CABLE

1. Shot firing cable conforming to the following specifications is approved for the purposes of Regulation 21 (2):

2. Cable to be used solely for single-shot firing shall be—

(*a*) twin core cable comprising two stranded copper conductors each of which has a cross-sectional area of not less than 0·0009 square inches;

(*b*) effectively insulated throughout its length for a voltage which is not less than the voltage at which it is expected to operate;

(*c*) so constructed as to resist, so far as is reasonably practicable, wear and rough usage;

(*d*) as respects the outer covering thereof coloured yellow.

3. Cable to be used for single-shot or multi-shot firing shall be—

(*a*) either—

(i) twin core cable comprising two stranded copper conductors each of which has a cross-sectional area of not less than 0·0015 square inches; or

(ii) single core cable comprising a stranded copper conductor having a cross sectional area of not less than 0·003 square inches;

(*b*) effectively insulated throughout its length for a voltage not less than fifteen hundred volts, being a voltage which is applied thereto for periods of five seconds;

(*c*) so constructed as to resist, so far as is reasonably practicable, wear and rough usage;

(*d*) as respects the outer covering thereof (except in the case of cable having an iron or steel wire covering) coloured white.

4. The approval is subject to the following conditions:—

(*a*) no cable shall be used for multi-shot firing in a mine in which the use of lamps or lights, other than permitted lights, is unlawful or in any part of a mine being a part in which safety-lamps are for the time being in use by way of temporary precaution unless it is free from joints and repairs other than joints and repairs which have been properly made and either vulcanised or moulded;

(*b*) no cable with an iron or steel wire covering shall be used for firing shots except in a shaft in the course of being sunk;

(*c*) single core cable of the type specified in paragraph 3 of this approval shall not be used for firing single shots except where the single shot is a miss-fire in a round.

APPROVED MANNER OF TESTING OF ELECTRIC MULTI-SHOT FIRING APPARATUS

The manner of testing shown below is approved, for the purposes of Regulation 26(*b*), as the testing for the electric multi-shot firing apparatus specified. These tests supersede those given in previous issues of this volume.

The 'M.E.6' Mark I Six-Shot Exploder (Electric Shot Firing Apparatus Approval No. 18).

(*a*) *Type of Tester*

The 'Six-Shot Fusehead Tester'.

(*b*) *Description of Tester*

A device comprising six metal clips, each designed to hold a 'Testex' low tension fusehead in a vertical position, a fine wire is arranged to be close to or touching each of the fuseheads, and a non-inductive resistor of such a value as to equate the total resistance of the circuit, including the six fuseheads, to that of a normal shot firing circuit. These items are connected in series between the two terminals of the tester and together form the testing circuit. The fine wire is such that it will be ruptured by the firing of any of the fuseheads.

(*c*) *Method of use of Tester*

A 'Testex' fusehead is placed in each clip, and the fine wire arranged to be close to or in contact with each of the fuseheads. The exploder should be connected to the testing device and the continuity of the circuit checked by means of the indicator built into the exploder. If this indication is satisfactory the exploder is then operated by means of the firing key. The operation is successful if, after operation of the firing key, all six fuseheads have fired and the wire has ruptured. The exploder shot firing ability is deemed to be adequate provided ten consecutive operations are completed successfully.

N.B.—When using exploders approved under Electric Shot Firing Apparatus Approval No. 18, the firing key should be rotated as quickly as possible.

(B) The Beethoven Dynamo Condenser Type Mark II 100-Shot Exploder (Electric Shot Firing Apparatus Approval No. N/1).

(*a*) *Type of Tester*

A bridge wire type of fusion tester comprising a built-in resistor and a reel of 0·0016 inch diameter Iridio Platinum wire.

(*b*) *Description of Tester*

A device for attachment directly to the exploder terminals, having two spring-loaded post terminals so as to provide a fixed distance which is bridged by the fuse wire provided on the small reel attached to the tester. A 150 ohms resistor is built into the tester and connected between one of the exploder attachment points and one of the spring-loaded terminal posts. The testing circuit thus comprises the 150 ohm resistance and a fixed length of the fuse wire.

(*c*) *Method of use of Tester*

The test must be made by a competent person appointed by the manager of the mine. The tester shall be attached firmly to the terminals of the exploder and the wire provided used to bridge the space between the two spring-loaded terminals. The handle shall be inserted into the exploder and turned until the neon indicator glows steadily when the turning of the handle must stop and the firing button must be pressed. The handle must then be removed from the exploder.

The exploder is not in satisfactory order, unless, after each of ten consecutive attempts, as detailed above, the wire has ruptured and no longer connects the two terminal posts.

(C) The Beethoven Dynamo Condenser Mark IIA 100-Shot Exploder (Electric Shot Firing Apparatus Approval No. L/3).

(*a*) *Type of Tester*

A bridge wire type of fusion tester comprising a built-in resistor and a reel of 0·0016 inch diameter Iridio Platinum wire.

(*b*) *Description of Tester*

A device for attachment directly to the exploder terminals, having two spring-loaded post terminals so as to provide a fixed distance which is bridged by the fuse wire provided on the small reel attached to the tester. A 135 ohms resistor is built into the tester and connected between one of the exploder attachment points and one of the spring-loaded terminal posts. The testing circuit thus comprises the 135 ohm resistance and a fixed length of the fuse wire.

(*c*) *Method of use of Tester*

As detailed in paragraph (B) (*c*) above.

(D) (i) The Schaffler Type 350 25-Shot Exploder (Electric Shot Firing Apparatus Approval No. L/2).

(ii) The Schaffler Type 750 100-Shot Exploder (Electric Shot Firing Apparatus Approval No. L/1).

(*a*) *Type of Tester*

A modified 6-shot exploder tester, the modification being in the case of the Schaffler Type 350 25-shot Exploder an increase in the built-in series resistor from 10 ohms to 60 ohms, and in the case of the Schaffler Type 750 100-shot Exploder an increase in the built-in series resistor to 240 ohms, this latter resistor being available at a different terminal from the 60 ohms resistor.

(*b*) *Description of Tester*

A device incorporating six metal clips, each designed to hold a 'Testex' low tension fusehead in a vertical position. A fine wire is arranged to be close to or touching each of the fuseheads, this wire being in series with a built-in non-inductive resistor of such a value as to equate the total resistance of the circuit, including the six fuseheads, to that of a normal shot firing circuit. The fuseheads, fine wire, and non-inductive resistor are all connected in series between the appropriately labelled pair of terminals on the tester, one pair being labelled '25 shots' and the other pair '100 shots'. A further pair of terminals is labelled 'Ohmmeter'. The fine wire is such that it will be ruptured by the firing of any one of the fuseheads.

(*c*) *Method of use of Tester*

The test must be made by a competent person appointed by the manager of the mine. A 'Testex' fusehead shall be inserted into each of the six clips of the tester and the wire provided drawn into position above the fuseheads and clamped at both ends in the terminals provided. An ohmmeter shall be connected to the ohmmeter terminals of the tester, a check made that the resistance is between 7 and 12 ohms. The ohmmeter shall then be disconnected. The exploder shall be connected to the pair of terminals appropriate to test that type of exploder and the lid of the tester closed as far as possible. The firing button of the exploder shall be pressed.

The exploder is not in satisfactory order, unless, after each of ten consecutive attempts, as detailed above, all six fuseheads have fired and the wire has ruptured and no longer connects the two terminal posts.

(E) (i) The 'M.E. 12' Mark II Exploder (Electric Shot Firing Apparatus Approval No. P.20).

(*a*) *Type of Tester*

The M.E. 12 Mk. II Exploder Fusehead Tester.

(*b*) *Description of Tester*

A device incorporating a two-position (GO and NO-GO) selector switch, a comb of twelve metal clips each designed to hold a 'Testex' low tension fusehead in a vertical position, a fine wire is arranged to be close to or touching each of the fuseheads, this wire being connected in series with either

(i) a 30 ohm non-inductive resistor when the selector switch is turned to the 'NO-GO' position, or

(ii) a 10 ohm non-inductive resistor when the selector switch is turned to the 'GO' position.

(*c*) *Method of use of Tester*

The test must be made by a competent person appointed by the manager of the mine. A 'Testex' fusehead shall be inserted into each of the twelve clips of the tester and the wire provided drawn into position immediately above and in contact with the fuseheads and clamped at both ends in the clamps provided. The exploder shall be connected to the terminals of the tester and the lid closed; the switch on the tester turned to the 'GO' position and the continuity of the firing circuit checked. This is satisfactory if the amber-coloured indicator lamp on the exploder is lit. The switch shall then be turned, first to the 'NO-GO' position, and the exploder operated by means of the removable firing key, then to the 'GO' position and the exploder operated by means of the removable firing key.

The exploder is not in satisfactory order unless, after each of five consecutive tests, as detailed above, following the 'NO-GO' operation no fusehead has fired and the wire has not ruptured, and following the 'GO' operation all twelve fuseheads have fired and the wire has ruptured.

(ii) *Alternative method of test*
Oscilloscope and Resistance Test of the M.E. 12 Mk. II Exploder

(*a*) *Type of Tester*

Oscilloscope with optional camera attachment.

(*b*) *Description of test apparatus*

This shall consist of apparatus as described under Method A or Method B below. The oscilloscope, which may be different for the alternative methods of test, shall be suitably calibrated to measure accurately pulse time in the range of 3 to 6 milliseconds and voltage indicating output current in the range of 1·2 to 1·6 amperes.

Method A

Resistors of 30, 1 and 10 ohms shall be connected in series as a load on the exploder, the 10 ohms resistor being shorted out as required by a shorting switch, and an oscilloscope with calibrated amplifier shall be connected across the 1 ohm resistor. The resistances shall not vary by more than 5% from the above figures.

Method B

Resistors of 30 and 10 ohms shall be connected in series as a load on the exploder, the 10 ohms resistor being shorted out as required by a shorting switch, and an oscilloscope shall be connected across the 30 ohms resistor. The resistances shall not vary by more than 5% from the above figures.

(*c*) *Method of use of test apparatus*

The test must be made by a competent person appointed by the manager of the mine. The exploder shall be connected in turn to non-inductive resistors either of 31 and 41 ohms (Method A) or of 30 and 40 ohms (Method B) to check the exploder test circuit. This test circuit is satisfactory if the amber coloured lamp on it, in either method, is lit with the lower value resistor and is not lit with the higher value resistor. The exploder shall then be connected to a non-inductive resistance load either of 31 ohms (Method A) or of 30 ohms (Method B) and the oscilloscope shall be connected as described in Methods A or B above. The exploder shall then be operated by means of the removable firing key and the output wave-form of the exploder observed either visually or photographically. The exploder is in satisfactory order if the output wave-form observed shows the output current to be in the range of 1·2 to 1·6 amperes and the output pulse time to be in the range of 3·7 to 5 milliseconds.

THE COAL MINES
(CARDOX AND HYDROX) REGULATIONS 1956

S.I. 1956 No. 1942

PART I

Application

1. The provisions of these regulations shall apply to the maintenance, preparation for use and use of blasting materials and devices known as 'cardox shells' and 'hydrox shells' (hereinafter referred to collectively as 'shells') and materials for the priming and filling thereof, at every mine of coal and in these regulations 'mine' means such a mine.

PART II

Preparation, maintenance, carriage and custody of shells and equipment

2. (1) The manager of every mine shall ensure that no shell is filled or primed with an initiator on the surface at the mine except in a place appointed by him for the purpose.

(2) The manager shall ensure that no such place is used for any other purpose and that adequate means for extinguishing any fire are provided at every such place and, in the case of a place at which hydrox shells are filled or primed, that—

(*a*) no inflammable materials other than those required for filling or priming shells are allowed to be thereat;

(*b*) it is kept cool and dry; and

(*c*) there is no smoking thereat.

3. No person shall fill or prime below ground in a mine any shell other than a shell of a type approved by the Minister for filling and priming below ground.

4. (1) The manager of every mine at which shells are filled or primed shall appoint such number of competent persons and make such arrangements as to secure that no shell is filled or primed thereat except by or under the supervision of such a person.

(2) No shell filled or primed otherwise than at the mine shall be taken below ground at any mine other than a shell filled or primed in pursuance of arrangements approved by an inspector by notice served on the manager of the mine.

Notice of approved fillings

5. (1) There shall be provided in the covered accommodation provided in pursuance of section one hundred and thirty-five of the Act and there shall be kept posted at each place on the surface appointed by the manager for the filling or priming of shells a notice specifying the weight and type of filling approved by the Minister and the type of initiator so approved for use with each type of shell used at the mine.

(2) No person shall fill or prime any shell at a mine otherwise than with the appropriate filling and initiator specified in such a notice.

Periodic examination of shells

6. (1) The manager of every mine in which shells are used shall make and ensure the efficient carrying out of arrangements to secure that—

(*a*) every shell in use and the fittings thereof are examined by a competent person appointed for that purpose by him at intervals, in the case of a shell which has been filled below ground since the last examination thereof, not exceeding thirty days, and, in any other case, not exceeding ninety days to ascertain whether there has been any significant change in the outer diameter of the shell and the condition of the screw threads with which the firing head engages the shell;

(*b*) no shell is subjected to heat treatment or machining by any person other than the manufacturer thereof or in pursuance of arrangements approved by an inspector by notice served on the manager.

(2) Any person who has made such an examination shall enter a report thereof in a book* provided for the purpose by the owner of the mine.

Conveyance of shells and materials for filling and priming them

7. The manager of every mine in which shells are used shall take such steps as may be necessary for securing that shells cannot fall out of any vehicle in which they are being conveyed at the mine or out of any cage or carriage in a shaft or outlet thereat and that any vehicle in which shells are being conveyed is distinctively marked to indicate its contents.

8. (1) No person shall take below ground materials for filling or priming shells unless he is a person authorised so to do by the manager of the mine.

(2) No person shall take or convey below ground materials for filling or priming shells, other than carbon dioxide in a cylinder, except in a stoutly constructed box which is—

(*a*) water-proof;

(*b*) so constructed and maintained that when closed no electric charge applied to any part of the outside thereof could be conducted to the contents;

(*c*) distinctively marked to indicate its contents; and

(*d*) closed and locked:

Provided that a box need not comply with sub-paragraph (*a*) and (*b*) if the materials therein are placed in a bag of such construction that the purposes thereof are achieved.

(3) Every person in charge of such a box shall ensure that it is not deposited at any time elsewhere than in a place of safety.

(4) Every person in charge of such a box shall, if at the end of his shift it contains any materials for filling or priming shells, return it to a place appointed by the manager of the mine for the purpose.

---

*M. & Q. Form No. 229.

(5) No person below ground shall unlock or open any such box or take any material out of it unless a person appointed by the manager to fire shells requires to check the quantity of the contents or the material is required immediately for filling or priming a shell or the act in question has been authorised by a deputy or other official of the mine.

9. (1) Subject to the following provisions of this regulation the manager of any mine in which shells are used may as respects that mine or any part thereof make a scheme for the conveyance in bulk of materials for filling or priming shells (herein referred to as 'a scheme of transit') whereby such materials packed on the surface in boxes complying with paragraph (2) of the last preceding regulation may be conveyed in a special carriage to one or more reserve stations in that mine or part of the mine or to the working face.

(2) Every scheme of transit shall contain provisions for securing safety with respect to each of the following matters—

(*a*) the location, construction and marking of each reserve station and the custody of the keys thereof;

(*b*) the design and construction of the special carriage;

(*c*) supervision of and precautions to be taken during the transit of the carriage;

(*d*) supervision of any materials for filling or priming shells at a reserve station;

(*e*) if such materials are to be taken in bulk to any working face, the manner of so doing;

(*f*) the maximum quantity of such materials to be at any reserve station at any time;

(*g*) the control of the issue of such materials from any reserve station;

(*h*) the return of such materials to a reserve station or other place appointed by the manager.

(3) Every scheme of transit shall contain provisions to ensure that except in pursuance of a provision of the scheme, no material for filling or priming shells shall while being conveyed in bulk be taken nearer to a working face (not being only a place in a road at which ripping or work of repair is in progress) than the reserve station nearest to that face.

(4) A scheme of transit may impose duties and prohibitions on persons employed at the mine and those persons shall comply therewith. It shall be the duty of the manager of the mine to secure that the provisions of any scheme of transit for that mine are executed and enforced.

(5) If an inspector is of opinion with respect to a scheme of transit that the provisions contained therein in pursuance of paragraph (2) of this regulation are not adequate to secure safety, he may serve on the manager of the mine a notice stating that he is of that opinion, specifying the nature of the provision which in his opinion ought to be made and requiring the manager to amend the scheme

accordingly, and any such notice shall, if it is so specified therein, become operative forthwith.

(6) The provisions of Part XV of the Act* with respect to references upon notices served by inspectors shall apply to a notice served under the last preceding paragraph, and the relevant ground of objection shall be that the provisions contained in the scheme of transit in pursuance of paragraph (2) of this regulation are adequate to secure safety.

(7) The person in charge of the materials for filling or priming shells at any reserve station shall ensure that any such materials remaining thereat at the end of his period of duty are either delivered by him to a person appointed to have charge of them during the immediately following shift or are returned to a place appointed by the manager of the mine for the purpose.

(8) The manager of every mine at which a scheme of transit is in operation shall ensure that a copy thereof is provided in the covered accommodation provided in pursuance of section one hundred and thirty-five of the Act and that a copy thereof is supplied to each person employed at the mine who is appointed by the manager to fire shells.

10. (1) The manager of every mine in which shells are used shall ensure that the total quantity of materials for filling and priming shells (whether or not contained in shells) below ground in the mine does not at any time exceed the quantity estimated to be required for use during the period of twenty-four hours next following.

(2) The manager of every mine in which shells are used shall make and ensure the efficient carrying out of arrangements to secure that any filled shell which remains unused at the end of a firing shift is returned to an appropriate place appointed by him for the purpose.

Appointment and qualifications of persons to fire shells

11. No person shall fire a shell in any mine unless he has been appointed to do so by the manager of that mine and is a person who is, or is qualified to be appointed, a shot firer at that mine.

Electric shot firing apparatus and cable

12. No person shall fire a shell in a mine except by means of electric shot firing apparatus and cable, both being provided by the owner of the mine and being of specifications approved by the Minister—

(*a*) if the shells are to be fired in a round, for multi-shot firing;

(*b*) in any other case, for single-shot firing.

13. A person appointed to fire shells who is in charge of any electric shot firing apparatus—

(*a*) shall retain the removable handle or key in his own possession throughout the period while he is on duty;

*See Section 170 of the 1954 Act.

(*b*) shall not place the removable handle or key in position in the apparatus until he is about to fire a shell; and

(*c*) shall remove it from the apparatus immediately after firing each shell.

14. If any electric shot firing apparatus appears to be defective, the person in charge of it shall not use it further but shall cause it to be returned to the surface forthwith and shall report the circumstances to the manager in writing.

15. Nothing in these regulations shall be deemed to exclude the application to electric shot firing apparatus or cable used for firing shells of regulations twenty-six and twenty-seven of the Coal Mines (Explosives) Regulations 1961.*

External firing wires

16. No person shall connect any external firing wire to any shell at a mine until it is necessary to do so for the purpose of firing the shell.

Charging shot holes with shells

17. (1) No person shall insert a shell into a hole for firing unless he has satisfied himself by taking all reasonable precautions that the hole is so placed as to be safe for the firing of a shell, and so drilled as to enable the shell to be inserted without using undue force.

(2) No person shall press any shell into a hole for firing if it cannot be inserted without the use of undue force.

Firing shells

18. (1) No person shall fire any shell unless he has satisfied himself by taking all reasonable precautions that—

(*a*) it is in a hole so placed as to be safe for firing and there has been no contravention of the last preceding regulation in connection therewith; and

(*b*) measures of a kind directed by the manager of the mine have been taken to ensure that the shell is not ejected in a dangerous manner on firing.

(2) Unless an inspector by notice served on the manager consents thereto, no person shall fire a shell in any coal face unless the coal has been holed or sheared to a depth greater than the depth of the hole.

19. (1) No person shall fire a shell or a round of shells unless he has carried out with respect to it immediately before firing an examination for general safety and tests for the presence of inflammable gas in any accessible place within thirty feet of a shot hole or any of them.

(2) Every such test for inflammable gas shall be made with a locked flame safety-lamp of a type approved by the Minister for the purpose of deputies' inspections, a methanometer of a type approved by the Minister or other apparatus of a type approved by the Minister for the purpose.

*See page 16.

(3) No person shall fire a shell if on any such test made with respect to it he finds a percentage of inflammable gas exceeding one-and-a-quarter per cent or he can see an indication of gas on the lowered flame of a safety-lamp.

20. Where a round of shells is to be fired the person about to fire them shall ensure that they are connected in series.

21. (1) No person shall use any cable for firing shells if its length is less than sixty feet.

(2) Any person about to fire a shell shall take care to prevent the shot firing cable from making contact with any other cable or electric apparatus.

(3) No person other than the person who is to fire the shell shall couple any shot firing cable to any shell or to shot firing apparatus.

(4) No person about to fire a shell shall couple a shot firing cable to the shot firing apparatus unless the cable has already been coupled by him to the shell or shells.

(5) No person shall fire a round of shells unless he has tested the circuit for continuity by means of a testing device approved by the Minister and has found it to be satisfactory. No person shall make any such test unless all persons in the vicinity have withdrawn to a place of safety and he himself has taken proper shelter.

Warning and shelter

22. In every case where the firing of a shell may result in blowing through into another place the person firing the shell shall cause due warning to be given to all persons in that place, and he shall after firing the shell cause notice to be given to them that the period of danger is ended.

23. (1) Any person about to fire a shell shall determine the danger zone likely to be created.

(2) No person shall fire a shell unless he has—

(*a*) at each entrance to that danger zone either posted a sentry or placed an appropriate fence conspicuously marked with the words 'danger' and 'shot firing';

(*b*) ensured that all persons have withdrawn from that zone or have taken proper shelter; and

(*c*) himself taken proper shelter.

24. (1) No person who has been posted as a sentry by a person about to fire a shell shall leave the place where he was posted unless personally directed so to do by that person.

(2) No person shall pass a danger sign exhibited for the purposes of these regulations without the authority of the person firing the shell or shall pass a sentry who has forbidden him to do so.

Precautions after shot firing

25. (1) Every person who has fired a shell shall—

(*a*) ascertain by personal examination whether it is safe for ordinary working to be resumed in each working place affected by that shot; and

(*b*) ensure that any necessary action is taken to make each such place safe for such working.

(2) Where a round of shells has been fired the person firing them shall not make that examination before the expiry of five minutes.

Miss-fires

26. If any shell fails to fire, the person attempting to fire the shell—

(*a*) shall not himself approach nor allow any other person to approach the shell during the interval of ten minutes after such attempt;

(*b*) before approaching or allowing any other person to approach the shell shall disconnect the removable handle or key and the cable from the shot firing apparatus;

(*c*) shall then examine the cable and connections for any defect;

(*d*) if he leaves the working place while the shell remains there shall cause notice of the miss-fire to be given to the deputy in charge of the district and ensure that sufficient fences and danger notices are erected to notify the miss-fire to any person approaching the place.

27. If any shell fails to fire, no person shall attempt to remove it from its hole until any external firing wire has been disconnected from it.

Record of firing

28. Each person appointed to fire shells shall keep a record of all shells fired by him on each shift of his in a book* provided by the owner of the mine for that purpose.

Exemptions

29. The Chief Inspector of Mines, if he is satisfied that the application of any provision of these regulations is inappropriate in relation to any mine or part thereof, may by notice served on the manager of that mine exempt it or a part thereof from the application of that provision.

Interpretation

30. (1) In these regulations the following expressions have the meanings hereby respectively assigned to them, that is to say—

'the Act' means the Mines and Quarries Act 1954;

'deputy' has the meaning assigned thereto in the Coal and Other Mines (Managers and Officials) Regulations 1956;†

'mine' has the meaning assigned thereto in regulation one;

*M. & Q. Form No. 230.

†See page 188.

'scheme of transit' has the meaning assigned thereto in regulation nine;

'shell' has the meaning assigned thereto in regulation one.

(2) Expressions to which meanings are assigned by the Act or by these regulations shall (unless the contrary intention appears) have the same meanings in any document issued under the provisions of these regulations.

(3) The Interpretation Act 1889 shall apply to the interpretation of these regulations as it applies to the interpretation of an Act of Parliament.

Commencement and citation

31. These regulations shall come into operation at the commencement of the Act and may be cited as the Coal Mines (Cardox and Hydrox) Regulations 1956.

THE COAL MINES
(COMPRESSED AIR BLASTING SHELLS) REGULATIONS 1960

S.I. 1960 No. 1114

Commencement and citation

1. These regulations shall come into operation on the first day of August, nineteen hundred and sixty, and may be cited as the Coal Mines (Compressed Air Blasting Shells) Regulations 1960.

Interpretation

2. (1) In these regulations the expressions 'mine' and 'shell' have the meanings assigned thereto in regulation three.

(2) The Interpretation Act 1889 shall apply to the interpretation of these regulations as it applies to the interpretation of an Act of Parliament.

Application

3. The provisions of these regulations shall apply to the use of any blasting device comprising a chamber into which air is charged at high pressure and from which that air is suddenly released (hereinafter referred to as a 'shell') at every mine of coal, and in these regulations 'mine' means such a mine.

Exemptions

4. An inspector may by notice served on the manager of a mine exempt the mine or part thereof, or any thing or class of things thereat, from the application of any provision of these regulations if he is satisfied that the safety of persons employed at the mine will not be prejudiced in consequence of the granting of the exemption.

Appointment and qualifications of persons to discharge shells

5. No person shall discharge any shell in a mine unless he has been appointed to do so by the manager of that mine and is a person who is, or is qualified to be appointed, a shot firer at that mine.

Charging holes with shells

6. No person shall insert a shell into a hole unless he has satisfied himself by taking all reasonable precautions that the hole is so placed that the discharge of the shell will not endanger any person, and so drilled as to enable the shell to be inserted without using undue force.

Key to control valve

7. No shell shall be charged with air except through a control valve which is so constructed that it cannot be operated except by a removable key designed especially for the purpose.

8. The person appointed to discharge any shell shall retain in his possession the key to the control valve thereof throughout the period during which he is on duty.

Procedure before discharge

9. (1) No person shall discharge a shell in either a mine in any part of which the use of lamps or lights, other than permitted lights, is unlawful, or any part of a mine, being a part in which safety lamps are for the time being in use by way of temporary precaution, unless he has carried out immediately before the discharge tests for the presence of inflammable gas—

(*a*) at the mouth of the hole in which the shell has been placed; and

(*b*) in every accessible cavity in the roof in the vicinity of the hole:

Provided that where a person discharges a group of shells, not exceeding six in number, in succession and as rapidly as is practicable by operating separate but adjacent control valves, that person may make all the tests required to be made by this paragraph in respect of each shell in the group immediately before he commences to discharge the group of shells.

(2) Every test made pursuant to the preceding paragraph shall be made with a locked flame safety-lamp of a type approved by the Minister for the purpose of deputies' inspections, a methanometer of a type approved by the Minister or other apparatus of a type approved by the Minister for the purpose.

(3) No person shall discharge a shell if on any such test made with respect to it he finds a percentage by volume of inflammable gas exceeding one and a quarter or he can see an indication of gas on the lowered flame of a safety-lamp.

10. No shear disc, shear pin or similar thing shall be—

(*a*) used in connection with any shell unless it has been provided for such use by the owner of the mine;

(*b*) fitted into a shell below ground until the shell is about to be inserted into a hole;

(*c*) so fitted below ground by any person other than a person appointed to discharge a shell or a person being trained for that purpose and acting under the supervision of such a person.

Warning and shelter

11. In every case where the discharge of a shell may result in a blowing through into another place, the person about to discharge the shell shall cause due warning to be given to all persons in that place, and he shall after discharging the shell cause notice to be given to them that the period of danger is ended.

12. (1) Any person about to discharge a shell shall determine the danger zone likely to be created.

(2) No person shall discharge a shell unless he has—

(*a*) at each entrance to that danger zone either posted a sentry or placed an appropriate fence conspicuously marked with the words 'danger' and 'shot firing';

(*b*) ensured that all persons have withdrawn from that zone or have taken proper shelter; and

(*c*) himself taken proper shelter.

13. (1) No person who has been posted as a sentry by a person about to discharge a shell shall leave the place where he was posted unless personally directed to do so by that person.

(2) No person shall pass a danger sign exhibited for the purposes of the last preceding regulation without the authority of the person discharging the shell or shall pass a sentry who has forbidden him to do so.

Precautions after discharging a shell

14. Every person who has discharged a shell shall—

(*a*) ascertain by personal examination whether ordinary working can be safely resumed in each working place affected by that discharge; and

(*b*) ensure that any necessary action is taken to make each such place safe for such working.

Failure to discharge

15. If any shell fails to discharge, no person shall approach it until the person who attempted to discharge it has released the compressed air contained therein by means of the control valve connected therewith, and is satisfied that such air has been released.

Cleaning and lubrication

16. No person shall use any inflammable oil or any inflammable grease for cleaning or lubricating any shell.

THE STRATIFIED IRONSTONE, SHALE AND FIRECLAY MINES (EXPLOSIVES) REGULATIONS 1956*

S.I. 1956 No. 1943

Arrangement of Regulations

PART I

Application

1. Except where the application thereof is further expressly limited, these regulations shall apply to every mine of stratified ironstone, shale or fireclay, and in these regulations 'mine' means (except in regulation three and where further expressly limited) such a mine.

PART II

Appointment and qualification of shot firers and persons appointed to fire shots by fuse

2.—(1) No person shall fire a shot in any mine other than a person appointed to be a shot firer by the manager of that mine (any person so appointed being hereinafter referred to as a 'shot firer'):

Provided that any person appointed by the manager to fire shots in the mine by means of safety fuse other than safety fuse capped with a detonator (hereinafter referred to as a 'person appointed to fire shots by fuse') may do so by that means.

(2) No shot firer shall fire a shot in any mine by means of a delay detonator or in a round of more than six shots unless he is appointed so to do by the manager, and no shot firer shall be so appointed unless he has during not less than five shifts been employed in connection with the firing of such shots under the close personal supervision of a shot firer authorised to fire such

*Certain words, which are used in these Regulations in a special sense which is defined in Regulation 56, appear too frequently to be footnoted separately. It is advisable, therefore, to read the definitions before studying any provision, and particularly one in which any of the following words occur: 'cross measure drift', 'detonator', 'explosive', 'round', 'safety fuse' or 'sheathed explosive'.

shots who was not then supervising any other person for the purposes of this paragraph. The manager shall include a record of any such appointment in the record of the appointment of that shot firer kept in pursuance of section one hundred and thirty-four of the Act.

Qualification of shot firers

3. No person shall be qualified to be appointed or to be a shot firer unless—

(*a*) he has attained the age of twenty-one years; and

(*b*) he has had not less than three years practical experience below ground in one or more mines in which coal, stratified ironstone, shale or fire-clay was in the course of being worked, including employment for not less than eighteen months in one or more of the following, namely—

(i) getting or cutting any of those minerals;

(ii) ripping in a roadhead;

(iii) setting or withdrawing supports at or building packs at a face from which any of those minerals was in the course of being worked;

(iv) drilling shot holes at a face from which any of those minerals was in the course of being worked;

(v) for not more than six months, repairing or enlarging roads or driving cross measure drifts;

(vi) in the case of a master sinker or a deputy whose district consists of a shaft in the course of being sunk, sinking operations.

PART III

Storage, issue and conveyance of explosives and detonators

4. —(1) The manager of a mine shall not permit any explosive, detonator or safety fuse to be stored thereat except in a place on the surface appointed by him for the purpose (hereinafter referred to as 'an explosives store').*

(2) The manager of every mine in which explosives are used shall appoint at least one place, which shall be situate conveniently near the top of each shaft or outlet normally used by workmen, as a place for the deposit of explosives and detonators brought out of the mine, and may appoint a place (other than an explosives store) for the issue thereof.

(3) The manager of every mine in which explosives are used shall appoint such number of competent persons and make such arrangements as to secure that a competent person is in charge of each explosives store and place appointed for the purposes of the last preceding paragraph whenever explosives or detonators are to be issued or returned thereat.

5. No person shall cap safety fuse with a detonator at any place at a mine except at a workshop used in connection with an explosives store in pursuance of section forty-seven of the Explosives Act 1875.

Control of issue of detonators

6.—(1) All detonators at an explosives store or at a place appointed in

*See Memorandum on Storage of Explosives at Mines, page 107.

pursuance of paragraph (2) of regulation four shall be in the sole charge of the manager of the mine except—

(*a*) during a shift for which the manager has appointed a competent person to have charge of that store or place;

(*b*) during any other period, in any case in which there is no means of entry to that store or place otherwise than through a doorway or doorways having a door or doors which can be securely locked and the manager has made such arrangements as to secure that that door is or those doors are kept securely locked throughout that period.

(2) No person shall be in possession of any detonator at any place at a mine other than an explosives store or a place appointed for the storage, issue or deposit of explosives except a shot firer to whom the detonator has been issued for use or a person authorised in writing by the manager of the mine so to be and save as aforesaid no person shall issue or take any detonator from such a store or place.

Conveyance and care of detonators

7.—(1) No person shall take any detonator below ground in a mine except in a securely locked detonator case provided by the owner of the mine:

Provided that nothing in this paragraph shall prevent a primer cartridge fitted with a detonator being taken into a shaft in the course of being sunk for use therein.

(2) No person shall put a detonator into a detonator case if it would then contain a delay detonator as well as a detonator which is not a delay detonator.

(3) No person shall put a delay detonator into a detonator case unless the detonator is clearly marked with a number which indicates the period of delay.

(4) The manager of every mine in which detonators are used shall ensure that no detonator case is issued for use in the mine unless it is so constructed and maintained that when the case is closed it is impossible for any detonator or the leads of any detonator contained in the case to touch any metal part thereof which is exposed outside the case or is in contact with any other metal part so exposed.

8.—(1) Any shot firer to whom a detonator case has been issued shall—

(*a*) retain the key of the case in his own possession throughout the period during which he is on duty;

(*b*) ensure that, apart from any check sheet for recording shots fired by him, nothing except detonators is in it;

(*c*) ensure that at any time at which it is not on his person it is in a safe place and, unless he remains in the immediate vicinity, in a securely locked box; and

(*d*) if at the end of his period of duty it contains any detonator, return it to the appropriate place on the surface appointed for the storage or deposit of explosives.

(2) No shot firer shall remove a detonator from a detonator case unless it is required immediately for charging a shot hole.

Conveyance and care of explosives

9. No person shall take any explosive below ground in any mine unless it is in the form of a cartridge.

10.—(1) Except in pursuance of the next following regulation, no person shall take any explosive below ground in any mine unless it is in a closed canister stoutly constructed and containing not more than five pounds of explosive:

Provided that nothing in this paragraph shall prevent a primer cartridge fitted with a detonator being taken into a shaft in the course of being sunk for use therein.

(2) No person shall put anything other than explosives into a canister provided for the purpose of taking explosives below ground in a mine.

(3) Every person having any canister of explosives in his possession or control shall ensure that it is not deposited at any time elsewhere than in a place of safety, and in particular if at the end of his period of duty the canister contains any explosive shall return it to the appropriate place on the surface appointed for the storage or deposit of explosives or, if he received it from a reserve station established for the purposes of a scheme of transit, to that reserve station or to a person and at a place appointed by the manager for the purposes of that scheme.

(4) No person below ground shall unlock or open any canister of explosives or take any explosive from any canister unless the shot firer or person appointed to fire shots by fuse (as the case may be) concerned requires to check the quantity of the explosives or the explosive is required immediately for charging a shot hole or the act in question has been authorised by a deputy or other official of the mine.

Conveyance of explosives in bulk

11.—(1) Subject to the following provisions of this regulation the manager of any mine may as respects that mine or any part thereof make a scheme for the conveyance of explosives in bulk (herein referred to as 'a scheme of transit') whereby explosives packed at an explosives store in securely locked canisters of any size may be conveyed in a special carriage to one or more reserve stations in that mine or part of the mine or to the working face.

(2) Every scheme of transit shall contain provisions for securing safety with respect to each of the following matters—

(*a*) the location, construction and marking of each reserve station and the custody of the keys thereof;

(*b*) the design and construction of the special carriage;

(*c*) supervision of and precautions to be taken during the transit of the carriage;

(*d*) supervision of any explosives at a reserve station;

(*e*) if explosives are to be taken in bulk to any working face, the manner of so doing;

(*f*) the maximum quantity of explosives to be at any reserve station at any time;

(*g*) the control of the issue of explosives from any reserve station;

(*h*) the return of explosives to a reserve station or other place appointed by the manager.

(3) Every scheme of transit shall contain provisions to ensure that—

(*a*) the quantity of explosives conveyed into the mine in pursuance thereof at any time together with any quantity so conveyed already in the mine does not exceed the quantity estimated to be required for use during the period of twenty-four hours next following;

(*b*) except in pursuance of a provision of the scheme, no explosive shall while being conveyed in bulk be taken nearer to a working face (not being only a place in a road at which ripping or work of repair is in progress) than the reserve station nearest to that face.

(4) A scheme of transit may impose duties and prohibitions on persons employed at the mine and those persons shall comply therewith. It shall be the duty of the manager of the mine to secure that the provisions of any scheme of transit for that mine are executed and enforced.

(5) If an inspector is of opinion with respect to a scheme of transit that the provisions contained therein in pursuance of paragraph (2) of this regulation are not adequate to secure safety, he may serve on the manager of the mine a notice stating that he is of that opinion, specifying the nature of the provision which in his opinion ought to be made and requiring the manager to amend the scheme accordingly, and any such notice shall, if it is so specified therein, become operative forthwith.

(6) The provisions of Part XV of the Act with respect to references upon notices served by inspectors shall apply to a notice served under the last preceding paragraph, and the relevant ground of objection shall be that the provisions contained in the scheme of transit in pursuance of paragraph (2) of this regulation are adequate to secure safety.

(7) The person in charge of the explosives at any reserve station shall ensure that any explosives remaining thereat at the end of his period of duty are either delivered by him to a person appointed to have charge of them during the immediately following shift or are returned to the explosives store.

(8) The manager of every mine at which a scheme of transit is in operation shall ensure that a copy thereof is provided in the covered accommodation provided in pursuance of section one hundred and thirty-five of the Act and that a copy thereof is supplied to each deputy, shot firer and person appointed to fire shots by fuse employed at the mine.

PART IV

Equipment, apparatus and material for firing shots

Equipment of a shot firer

12. Each shot firer who is to fire shots by means of electric shot firing apparatus shall be provided by the owner of the mine with the necessary cable of a specification approved* by the Minister—

(*a*) if shots are to be fired in a round, for multi-shot firing; or

(*b*) in any other case, for single-shot firing:

*See page 65.

Provided that nothing in this regulation shall restrict the use of any shot firing cable which was in use for firing shots, or was required to be delivered under a contract made, before the commencement of these regulations.

Apparatus and material for firing shots

13. No person shall fire a shot in any mine by means of electric shot firing apparatus or cable not provided by the owner of the mine.

14. No shot firer shall fire a shot by means of electric shot firing apparatus other than apparatus of a specification approved* by the Minister—

(*a*) (in the case of electric shot firing apparatus not in use within the period of six months immediately following the date of commencement of these regulations) after the expiration of that period; or

(*b*) (in any other case) after the expiration of two years from the date of commencement of these regulations.

15. A shot firer who is in charge of any electric shot firing apparatus—

(*a*) shall retain the removable handle or key in his own possession throughout the period while he is on duty;

(*b*) shall not place the removable handle or key in position in the apparatus until he is about to fire a shot; and

(*c*) shall remove it from the apparatus immediately after firing each shot.

16.—(1) If any electric shot firing apparatus appears to be defective, the shot firer in charge of it shall not use it further but shall cause it to be returned to the surface forthwith and shall report the circumstances to the deputy in charge of the district and in writing to the manager.

(2) If any electric shot firing apparatus approved for multi-shot firing fails to fire all the shots in any properly connected round at one operation, it shall be deemed to be defective for the purposes of the last preceding paragraph but it may be used to fire the shots in that round in accordance with the provisions of regulation forty.

17. It shall be the duty of the manager of every mine in which electric shot firing apparatus is used to make and secure the efficient carrying out of arrangements to ensure that—

(*a*) all such apparatus is thoroughly cleaned and overhauled at intervals not exceeding three months by the manufacturer thereof or by a competent person appointed for that purpose by the manager;

(*b*) all multi-shot firing apparatus designed for firing a round of not more than six shots is tested at the surface at intervals not exceeding seven days in a manner approved* by the Minister in respect of apparatus of that type;

(*c*) if in connection with the firing of a round of shots by means of any apparatus described in the last preceding paragraph any of the shots fails to explode after firing, that apparatus is tested at the surface in such a manner before it is again taken below ground;

---

*See page 103.

(*d*) no apparatus described in paragraph (*b*) is taken or used below ground unless on the last previous test thereof it was found to be in satisfactory order; and

(*e*) the date of each cleaning and overhaul and the result of each test carried out in pursuance of this regulation is entered in a book* provided for the purpose by the owner of the mine.

Misuse of equipment

18.—(1) No person shall open or tamper with any electric shot firing apparatus below ground.

(2) No person shall use shot firing cable for any purpose other than shot firing.

PART V

Shot firing—all mines

Drilling and cleaning shot holes

19.—(1) No person shall drill a shot hole or any part thereof with a drill of which the diameter does not exceed by at least one eighth of an inch the diameter of any cartridge to be inserted in that shot hole.

(2) No person shall for the purpose of testing, charging or stemming any shot hole use any tool other than a tool, made wholly of wood, suitable for the purpose.

20.—(1) No person shall begin to charge any shot hole unless it is thoroughly cleaned out.

(2) No person shall use compressed air to clean out any shot hole unless he ensures that the giving off of any dust is minimised.

Charging shot holes

21.—(1) No person shall charge a shot hole unless he is—

(*a*) a shot firer;

(*b*) a person doing so under the supervision of a shot firer; or

(*c*) a person appointed to fire shots by fuse.

(2) No person shall charge a shot hole, and no shot firer shall permit a shot hole to be charged, before it is necessary to do so for the purpose of firing a shot.

(3) No person shall begin to charge any shot hole unless he has satisfied himself by taking all reasonable precautions that it is so placed and drilled as to be safe for the firing of a shot.

(4) Except in the case of shots to be fired in one round or of a relieving shot fired in pursuance of the provisions of any scheme for the time being in force at the mine in pursuance of regulation forty-two for the purposes of a miss-fire, no person shall charge a shot hole (in the case of longwall working) within ninety feet of a charged shot hole or (in any other case) in the same face as a charged shot hole.

---

*M. & Q. Form No. 221.

(5) No person shall charge a shot hole to be fired as one of a round in a cross measure drift, heading or ripping or in a shaft or staple-pit until all shot holes for that round have been completely drilled.

22.—(1) No shot firer or person appointed to fire shots by fuse (as the case may be) shall permit more than one canister of explosives to be open at any one time for the charging of shot holes by him or (in the case of a shot firer) under his supervision.

(2) No person shall charge a shot hole—

(*a*) otherwise than with a complete cartridge or complete cartridges; or

(*b*) with cartridges of different diameters or of explosives of different descriptions.

(3) No person shall press any cartridge into a shot hole if it cannot be inserted without the use of force.

(4) Any person charging a shot hole shall to the best of his judgment ensure that it is not overcharged having regard to the task to be performed.

23.—(1) Except as may be provided in any scheme for the time being in force at the mine in pursuance of regulation forty-two, no person shall insert a detonator into a shot hole if that hole already contains a detonator.

(2) No shot firer shall fire a shot by means of a detonator and fuse other than safety fuse capped with a detonator at a workshop in accordance with regulation five.

(3) No shot firer shall use any detonator in firing a round of shots electrically in any mine unless it is a low tension detonator or a delay detonator.

(4) No shot firer shall use a delay detonator unless it is clearly marked with a number which indicates the period of delay.

(5) Where a delay detonator is to be used and the charge is to consist of more than one cartridge, the person charging the shot hole shall insert the primer cartridge first with the detonator at the back of the hole.

24.—(1) Any person charging a shot hole shall ensure that it is stemmed with sufficient suitable and non-inflammable stemming to prevent a blown out shot.

(2) Except where a device for pneumatic stemming approved* by the Minister is being used, no person shall insert any tool not made entirely of wood into a shot hole containing explosive.

25.—(1) No person shall remove any stemming from any charged shot hole otherwise than by means of water.

(2) No person shall pull out any detonator lead from any charged shot hole.

(3) No person shall remove any explosive from any charged shot hole except a cartridge of explosive which is protruding out of the mouth of the hole.

Firing shots

26.—(1) No shot firer or person appointed to fire shots by fuse (as the case may be) shall fire any shot unless (except in the case of a shot being fired by him

*There are no current approvals.

in accordance with the provisions of a scheme described in the proviso to the next following paragraph and for the time being in force) he has satisfied himself by taking all reasonable precautions that it is in a shot hole so placed and drilled as to be safe for the firing of a shot and is charged and stemmed in accordance with the provisions of these regulations.

(2) Subject to the provisions of the last preceding paragraph, each shot firer or person appointed to fire shots by fuse (as the case may be) shall unless prevented by circumstances beyond his control fire every shot which has been charged by him or (in the case of a shot firer) under his supervision:

Provided that in any case in which there is for the time being in force in the mine a scheme made by the manager and approved by an inspector specifying a procedure whereby any shot may be fired by a shot firer or person appointed to fire shots by fuse (as the case may be) who did not charge that shot or (in the case of a shot firer) supervise the charging thereof, shots may be fired in accordance with the provisions of that scheme.

(3) The manager of every mine at which there is for the time being in force a scheme described in the proviso to the last preceding paragraph shall ensure that a copy thereof is provided in the covered accommodation provided in pursuance of section one hundred and thirty-five of the Act and that a copy thereof is supplied to each shot firer and person appointed to fire shots by fuse employed at the mine.

27. The manager shall make and secure the efficient carrying out of arrangements to ensure that a daily record is kept, in a book* provided by the owner of the mine, either—

(*a*) by the deputy in charge of every district, in respect of the number of shots fired, and the quantity of explosives and number of detonators (if any) used, in that district on each shift of his; or

(*b*) by each shot firer and each person appointed to fire shots by fuse, in respect of the number of shots fired, and the quantity of explosives and number of detonators (if any) used, by him on each shift of his.

Firing shots electrically

28.—(1) Where a round of shots is to be fired by means of electric shot firing apparatus, the shot firer shall ensure that—

(*a*) the detonators are connected in series;

(*b*) no additional wire is used for connecting any detonator leads to each other.

(2) No shot firer shall use any cable for firing shots if its length is less than—

(*a*) sixty feet when a single shot is being fired otherwise than in a shaft in the course of being sunk;

(*b*) two hundred and ten feet when a round of shots is being fired otherwise than in a shaft in the course of being sunk;

(*c*) six hundred feet when a single shot or a round of shots is being fired in a shaft in the course of being sunk.

*M. & Q. Form No. 222.

(3) A shot firer who is about to use shot firing cable shall ensure that it is not in, and cannot make, contact with any other cable or electric apparatus.

(4) No person other than a shot firer shall couple any shot firing cable to any detonator or to shot firing apparatus.

(5) No shot firer shall couple a shot cable to shot firing apparatus for the purpose of firing a shot unless the cable has already been coupled by him to the detonator or detonator circuit.

(6) No shot firer shall fire any round of shots by means of electric shot firing apparatus unless he has tested the circuit for continuity by means of a testing device approved* by the Minister and has found it to be satisfactory. A shot firer shall not make any such test unless all persons in the vicinity have withdrawn to a place of safety, and he himself has taken proper shelter:

Provided that a shot firer shall not be required to make any such test before firing a round of less than five shots if there is for the time being in force in relation to the mine or the part thereof in which the round is to be fired an exemption from that requirement granted by an inspector by notice served on the manager.

Firing of shots by fuse

29.—(1) No shot firer or person appointed to fire shots by fuse shall fire a single shot by fuse other than safety fuse not less than three feet in length or any shot in a round by fuse other than safety fuse not less than four feet in length.

(2) Not more than one shot firer or person appointed to fire shots by fuse shall charge shot holes or fire shots by means of fuse at any one time in any working place or at any working face which does not exceed one hundred and fifty feet in length, and not more than one shot firer shall permit shot holes to be charged at any one time in any working place or at such working face.

(3) At any working face exceeding one hundred and fifty feet in length no shot firer or person appointed to fire shots by fuse shall fire any shot by means of fuse within one hundred and fifty feet of another charged shot hole unless he has satisfied himself that no other shot firer or person appointed to fire shots by fuse is about to fire that other shot.

(4) Except where a round of shots is fired—

(*a*) by means of fuse lit by a length of plastic igniter cord of a type and description approved† by the Minister; or

(*b*) by other means approved‡ by the Minister of firing a round of shots by means of fuse;

no shot firer or person appointed to fire shots by fuse shall attempt to fire more than four shots at one time by means of fuse.

(5) Where any shot is to be fired by means of fuse the shot firer or person appointed to fire shots by fuse shall ensure that—

(*a*) no naked light or person smoking is directly above, or within four feet in any other direction of, any shot hole, explosive or detonator;

---

*There are no current approvals.
†See page 105.
‡No other means have been approved.

(*b*) all surplus explosives are removed from the vicinity of the shot hole before a light is brought near to it for the purpose of lighting the fuse.

Warning and shelter

30. In every case where a shot may blow through into another place the person about to fire that shot shall cause adequate warning to be given to all persons in that place, and he shall after firing the shot cause notice to be given to them that the period of danger is ended.

31.—(1) Any person proposing to fire a shot shall before firing determine the danger zone likely to be created.

(2) No person shall fire any shot unless he has—

(*a*) at each entrance to that danger zone either posted a sentry or placed an appropriate fence conspicuously marked with the words 'danger' and 'shot firing';

(*b*) ensured that all persons have withdrawn from that zone or have taken proper shelter; and

(*c*) himself taken proper shelter.

32.—(1) No person who has been posted as a sentry by a shot firer or person appointed to fire shots by fuse (as the case may be) shall leave the place where he was posted until directed so to do by the person who posted him in person.

(2) No person shall pass a danger sign exhibited for the purpose of shot firing without the authority of the shot firer or person appointed to fire shots by fuse (as the case may be) concerned, or shall pass a sentry who has forbidden him to do so.

Precautions after shot firing

33.—(1) After the firing of any shot the person who fired it or (if any arrangements described in paragraph (3) of this regulation are for the time being in force in the mine) a deputy acting in accordance with those arrangements shall—

(*a*) ascertain by a personal examination whether it is safe for ordinary working to be resumed in each working place affected by that shot; and

(*b*) ensure that any necessary action is taken to make each such place safe for such working.

(2) Where a round of shots has been fired—

(*a*) that examination shall not be made, if the round was a round of six shots or less, before the expiry of five minutes or, in any other case, before the expiry of ten minutes, from the firing of the round;

(*b*) the person making the examination shall in the course thereof examine for sockets in the face, for any explosive remaining in any such socket and, if he has reason to think that any shot may not have completely exploded, for any unexploded charge in the material brought down.

(3) Arrangements in writing made by the manager and approved by an inspector may provide that, after the firing of every shot, the person who

fired it shall not comply with paragraph (1) of this regulation but shall, at each entrance to the danger zone determined in pursuance of paragraph (1) of regulation thirty-one, leave placed an appropriate fence conspicuously marked as specified in paragraph (2) of that regulation, that the requirements of the said paragraph (1) of this regulation shall be fulfilled, in the course of the making in pursuance of regulation twelve of the Coal and Other Mines (Managers and Officials) Regulations 1956* of the next pre-shift inspection of the deputy's district in which the shot was fired, by the deputy for the time being in charge of that district, and for matters ancillary and supplemental thereto.

(4) No person other than a deputy acting in accordance with arrangements made in pursuance of the last preceding paragraph or a person acting with the authority of such a deputy shall remove any fence left so placed.

(5) The manager of every mine at which there are for the time being in force arrangements described in paragraph (3) of this regulation shall ensure that a copy thereof is provided in the covered accommodation provided in pursuance of section one hundred and thirty-five of the Act and that a copy thereof is supplied to each deputy, shot firer and person appointed to fire shots by fuse employed at the mine.

PART VI

Shot firing—additional provisions for shafts and staple-pits

34. No person other than a shot firer shall fire a shot in a shaft or staple-pit.

35. No person shall take any explosive into a shaft or staple-pit for use therein unless it is immediately required for charging a shot hole.

Primer cartridges

36. No person other than a shot firer shall take a primer cartridge† fitted with a detonator into a shaft and no shot firer shall take such a cartridge into a shaft otherwise than in a thick felt bag or other receptacle suitable for protecting it from shock.

Detonators

37. No shot firer shall fire a shot in a shaft or staple-pit except by means of an electric detonator.

Precautions before firing

38.—(1) No shot firer shall couple a shot firing cable to a detonator in a shaft or staple-pit provided with winding apparatus unless—

(*a*) the kibble is conveniently placed for men in the shaft or staple-pit to enter it; and

(*b*) he has satisfied himself that the person operating the winding apparatus is ready to raise.

(2) No shot firer shall couple a shot firing cable to shot firing apparatus for the purpose of firing any shot in a shaft or staple-pit unless all persons who may be affected are in a place of safety.

---

*See page 180.

†See also provisos to Nos. 7 (1) and 10 (1) of these Regulations.

Precautions after firing

39. No person shall enter a shaft or staple-pit after a shot has been fired therein until it has been inspected by the deputy in pursuance of regulation fifteen or paragraph (4) of regulation thirty-two of the Coal and Other Mines (Managers and Officials) Regulations 1956.*

PART VII

Miss-fires

Meaning of miss-fire

40.—(1) A shot shall be treated as a miss-fire if it fails to explode, in the case of a shot being fired—

(*a*) by fuse, after the shot firer or person appointed to fire shots by fuse (as the case may be) has withdrawn after once lighting or attempting to light the fuse; or

(*b*) electrically, and either as a single shot or in a round, after the shot firer, having attempted unsuccessfully to fire the shot, has followed the procedure described in paragraph (2) of this regulation.

(2) The said procedure is that the shot firer shall—

(*a*) disconnect from the shot firing apparatus the removable handle or key and the shot firing cable;

(*b*) after waiting five minutes, examine the cable and connections for any defect, and remedy any defect so found;

(*c*) make a further attempt to fire the shot (for which purpose, in the case of a shot being fired as a single shot in any part of a mine to which Part VIII of these regulations applies, he may, notwithstanding the provisions of regulation forty-seven, use shot firing apparatus of a specification approved by the Minister for multi-shot firing with all explosives).

General precautions

41.—(1) In the event of a miss-fire, no person shall approach the shot hole until, if the shot is being fired—

(*a*) by fuse, there have elapsed, from the lighting of the fuse or the attempt to light it, not less than thirty minutes; or

(*b*) electrically, the shot firer has disconnected the removable handle or key and the shot firing cable from the shot firing apparatus, and there have elapsed, from the last attempt to fire the shot, not less than (in the case of a miss-fire in a round of more than six shots) ten minutes or (in any other case) five minutes.

(2) No person shall attempt to remove any part of the charge from the shot hole of any shot which is to be treated as a miss-fire except a cartridge of explosive which is protruding out of the mouth of the hole.

(3) In the case of any shot which is to be treated as a miss-fire, the shot firer or person appointed to fire shots by fuse (as the case may be) concerned shall—

(*a*) if he leaves the working place before the completion of the appropriate

---

*See page 182.

procedure specified in any scheme in force in pursuance of regulation forty-two—

(i) cause notice of the miss-fire to be given to the deputy in charge of the district; and

(ii) ensure that sufficient fences and danger notices are erected to warn any person approaching the place; and

(*b*) before leaving the mine, report the circumstances of the miss-fire to the deputy in charge of the district.

(4) The fact of any miss-fire shall be recorded, in the daily record kept in pursuance of regulation twenty-seven*,—

(*a*) in any case in which the deputy for the district in which the miss-fire has occurred is responsible for the keeping of the said record, by that deputy; or

(*b*) in any other case, by the shot firer or person appointed to fire shots by fuse (as the case may be) concerned.

Schemes for remedial action

42.—(1) The manager of every mine in which explosives are used shall ensure that there shall be at all times in force a scheme specifying the procedure to be followed in the event of a miss-fire and (if shots are fired electrically in the mine) in the event of an unsatisfactory result of a test made in pursuance of paragraph (6) of regulation twenty-eight, and any such scheme shall contain provisions for securing the safety of all persons in the vicinity.

(2) The manager of every mine at which such a scheme is in force shall ensure that a copy thereof is provided in the covered accommodation provided in pursuance of section one hundred and thirty-five of the Act and that a copy thereof is supplied to each shot firer and person appointed to fire shots by fuse employed at the mine.

(3) If an inspector is of opinion with respect to any such scheme that the provisions contained therein are not adequate to ensure the taking of proper remedial action in the event of a miss-fire or an unsatisfactory result of a test made in pursuance of paragraph (6) of regulation twenty-eight, or to ensure the taking of proper safety precautions, he may serve on the manager of the mine a notice stating that he is of that opinion, specifying the nature of the provision which in his opinion ought to be made and requiring the manager to amend the scheme accordingly and any such notice shall, if it is so specified therein, become operative forthwith.

(4) The provisions of Part XV of the Act with respect to references upon notices served by inspectors shall apply to a notice served under the last preceding paragraph and the relevant ground of objection to such a notice shall be that the provisions contained in the relevant scheme are adequate to ensure the taking of proper remedial action or the taking of proper safety precautions (as the case may be).

*M. & Q. Form No. 222.

PART VIII

Miscellaneous additional provisions—mines in which locked safety-lamps are used

Application of Part VIII

43. Except where the application thereof is further expressly limited, this Part of these regulations shall apply to every part of a mine being a part in which the use of lamps or lights other than permitted lights is unlawful.

Issue and use of detonators

44. No person shall issue for use in, and no person shall take into or use in, part of a mine to which this Part of these regulations applies—

(*a*) (except in the case of a mine of fireclay) any detonator other than an electric detonator with a copper tube;

(*b*) any delay detonator having a period of delay exceeding five seconds.

Parts of mines in which only explosives approved by the Minister may be used

45. No person shall, within fifteen feet of any waste below ground in any part of a mine to which this Part of these regulations applies, being waste in which there is not constantly produced ventilation adequate for the purposes specified in subsection (1) of section fifty-five of the Act, use any explosive other than explosive of a type and description approved by the Minister for use in places hazardous by reason of the presence or possibility of inflammable gas or of combustible dust.

Additional qualifications—shot firers and persons appointed to fire shots by fuse

46. Without prejudice to the generality of Part II of these regulations, no person shall, with respect to any part of a mine to which this Part of these regulations applies, be qualified to be appointed or to be a shot firer or person appointed to fire shots by fuse unless he has within the last preceding five years obtained a certificate* that he was then able to make accurate tests for inflammable gas (so far as is practicable with a flame safety-lamp) being a certificate granted—

(*a*) by a university or university college; or

(*b*) by a school, college or institution maintained or assisted by a local education authority; or

(*c*) in any other manner approved for the purpose by an inspector.

Shot firing apparatus

47. Without prejudice to the generality of regulation two, no person shall fire a shot in any part of a mine to which this Part of these regulations applies except by means of electric shot firing apparatus, and after the expiration of two years from the date of commencement of these regulations no person shall fire a shot by means of any such apparatus unless it is of a specification approved by the Minister—

(*a*) if shots are to be fired in a round, for multi-shot firing with all explosives; or

(*b*) in any other case, for single-shot firing with all explosives:

---

*M. & Q. Form No. 291.

Provided that if an inspector is of opinion in any case that it is expedient to allow the firing of a number of shots in a round for which no multi-shot firing apparatus has been approved, he may by notice served on the manager of the mine authorise the use therefor of electric shot firing apparatus specified in the notice.

Sheathed explosives

48. No person shall take into or use in any part of a mine to which this Part of these regulations applies any explosive having been sheathed explosive from which any part of its external sheath has been removed, and no person shall therein remove from any sheathed explosive any part of its external sheath.

Precautionary examinations

49.—(1) No person shall fire a shot in any part of a mine to which this Part of these regulations applies unless he has carried out with respect to it an examination for general safety and tests for the presence of inflammable gas in accordance with the following provisions of this regulation. Every such test for inflammable gas shall be made with—

(*a*) a locked flame safety-lamp—

(i) (in the case of a mine of shale) of a type approved by the Minister;

(ii) (in the case of any other mine) of a type approved by the Minister for the purpose of deputies' inspections; or

(*b*) a methanometer of a type approved by the Minister; or

(*c*) other apparatus of a type approved by the Minister for the purpose.

(2) No person shall fire a shot or charge a shot hole in any such part of a mine if on any such test made with respect to it he finds a percentage of inflammable gas exceeding one and a quarter per cent. or he can see an indication of gas on the lowered flame of a safety-lamp.

(3) If a person intends to fire a shot in any such part of a mine he shall—

(*a*) immediately before the shot hole is charged, carry out an examination for general safety and test for the presence of inflammable gas—

(i) in the vicinity and at the mouth of the shot hole;

(ii) throughout every accessible place within thirty feet thereof;

(*b*) immediately before firing, test for the presence of inflammable gas in the vicinity of the shot hole and at the edge of any waste opposite.

Use of safety fuse with attached igniter in mines of shale

50. Notwithstanding anything in regulation forty-four or forty-seven, if an inspector is of opinion that it is expedient to allow the firing of shots in any part of a mine to which this Part of these regulations applies, being a mine of shale, by means of safety fuse ignited by means of an igniter contained in a tube and attached to the fuse in such manner as to form a completely closed chamber, he may by notice served on the manager—

(*a*) exempt that part of the mine from the application of the said regulation forty-four; and

(*b*) authorise the firing of shots therein by those means.

PART IX

Apparatus and explosives for killing horses

51.—(1) Nothing in Parts II to VIII of these regulations except regulation four shall apply to such apparatus or such cartridges of explosives as are approved by the Minister for use in mines for destroying horses.

(2) No person shall take or use below ground in any mine for any other purpose any such apparatus or cartridge.

52. The manager of every mine shall ensure that horse killing apparatus is—

(*a*) kept in the custody of a competent person appointed by him and used only by that person or under his close personal supervision;

(*b*) cleaned and examined immediately after use on any occasion.

53.—(1) The manager of every mine shall ensure that cartridges for horse killing are issued from the explosives store only to a person appointed to have custody of horse killing apparatus and in a case or box with a lock provided by the owner of the mine.

(2) No person shall put any cartridge for horse killing into a receptacle containing any other kind of explosive or a detonator.

(3) Every person having a case or box of cartridges for horse killing shall keep it separate from any other receptacle containing explosive or detonators and shall keep it locked.

(4) No person shall remove any cartridge for horse killing from its case or box below ground until it is required for immediate use.

54.—(1) In any part of a mine, being a part in which the use of lamps or lights, other than permitted lights, is unlawful, no person shall fire a shot with horse killing apparatus unless immediately before firing he or a superior official of the mine has made tests for the presence of inflammable gas throughout every accessible place within thirty feet of the place where the shot is to be fired and it has been found safe for the firing of that shot.

(2) Every such test shall be made with a locked flame safety-lamp of a type approved by the Minister for the purpose of deputies' inspections, a methanometer of a type approved by the Minister or other apparatus of a type approved by the Minister for the purpose.

(3) No person shall fire a shot with horse killing apparatus if on any such test made with respect to that shot there has been found a firedamp content exceeding one and a quarter per cent or an indication of gas on the lowered flame of a safety-lamp has been seen at any place in the general body of the air.

PART X

General

Exemptions

55. The Chief Inspector of Mines if he is satisfied that the application of any provision of these regulations is inappropriate in relation to any mine or part thereof may by notice served on the manager of that mine exempt it or a part thereof from the application of that provision.

Interpretation

56.—(1) In these regulations the following expressions have the meanings hereby respectively assigned to them, that is to say—

'the Act' means the Mines and Quarries Act 1954;

'cross measure drift' includes any drift driven otherwise than in stratified ironstone, shale, fireclay or (in relation only to regulation three) coal or otherwise than for the purpose of getting stratified ironstone, shale, fireclay or (in relation only to regulation three) coal therefrom;

'deputy' and 'deputy's district' have the meanings assigned thereto in the Coal and Other Mines (Managers and Officials) Regulations 1956;

'detonator' includes safety fuse capped with a detonator;

'explosive' does not include a detonator;

'explosives store' has the meaning assigned thereto in paragraph (1) of regulation four;

'firedamp content' means the percentage of inflammable gas present in the general body of the air;

'mine' has the meaning assigned thereto in regulation one;

'person appointed to fire shots by fuse' has the meaning assigned thereto in paragraph (1) of regulation two;

'round', in relation to shots, means a number of shots fired—

(*a*) electrically in series, either simultaneously or by means of delay detonators; or

(*b*) by fuse, by means of apparatus approved for firing a number of shots by fuse simultaneously; or

(*c*) where the number does not exceed four, by fuses lighted at the same time;

'safety fuse' means fuse consisting of gun powder protected either by not less than three coverings of thread or by not less than two coverings of thread and one of tape or gutta-percha, being of such a quality that the rate of burning does not vary more than ten seconds above or below the rate of thirty seconds for each foot of fuse;

'scheme of transit' has the meaning assigned thereto in paragraph (1) of regulation eleven;

'sheathed explosive' means explosive covered by an external sheath of incombustible material spread evenly over the sides of the cartridge, and includes explosive in any type of cartridge certified by the Minister to be equivalent in safety to sheathed explosive;

'shot firer' has the meaning assigned thereto in paragraph (1) of regulation two.

(2) In these regulations any reference to the use of explosive includes the charging of a shot hole therewith.

(3) Expressions to which meanings are assigned by the Act or by these regulations shall (unless the contrary intention appears) have the same meanings in any document issued under the provisions of these regulations.

(4) The Interpretation Act 1889 shall apply to the interpretation of these regulations as it applies to the interpretation of an Act of Parliament.

Commencement and citation

57. These regulations shall come into operation at the commencement of the Act and may be cited as the Stratified Ironstone, Shale and Fireclay Mines (Explosives) Regulations 1956.

APPROVED SPECIFICATIONS AND MANNER OF TESTING

FOR PURPOSES OF THE STRATIFIED IRONSTONE, SHALE AND FIRECLAY MINES (EXPLOSIVES) REGULATIONS, 1956

SHOT FIRING CABLE

Shot firing cable conforming to the following specifications is approved for the purposes of Regulation 12 of the Stratified Ironstone, Shale and Fireclay Mines (Explosives) Regulations 1956:

Cable to be used solely for single-shot firing shall be—

(*a*) twin core cable comprising two stranded copper conductors each of which has a cross-sectional area of not less than 0·0009 sq. inches;

(*b*) effectively insulated throughout its length for a voltage which is not less than the voltage at which it is expected to operate;

(*c*) so constructed as to resist, so far as is reasonably practicable, wear and rough usage;

(*d*) as respect the outer covering thereof coloured yellow.

Cable to be used for single-shot or multi-shot firing shall be—

(*a*) either—

(i) twin core cable comprising two stranded copper conductors each of which has a cross-sectional area of not less than 0·0015 sq. inches; or

(ii) single core cable comprising a stranded copper conductor having a cross-sectional area of not less than 0·003 sq. inches;

(*b*) effectively insulated throughout its length for a voltage not less than fifteen hundred volts, being a voltage which is applied thereto for periods of five seconds;

(*c*) so constructed as to resist, so far as is reasonably practicable, wear and rough usage;

(*d*) as respects the outer covering thereof (except in the case of cable having an iron or steel wire covering) coloured white.

The approval is subject to the following conditions:—

In any mine in which the use of lamps or lights, other than permitted lights, is unlawful:—

(*a*) no cable shall be used for multi-shot firing unless it is free from joints and repairs other than joints and repairs which have been properly made and either vulcanised or moulded;

(*b*) no cable with an iron or steel wire covering shall be used for firing shots except in a shaft in the course of being sunk;

(*c*) single core cable of the type specified in paragraph 3 of this approval shall not be used for firing a single shot except where there has previously been an unsuccessful attempt to fire the shot in a round.

APPROVED MANNER OF TESTING OF ELECTRIC MULTI-SHOT FIRING APPARATUS

The manner of testing shown below is approved, for the purposes of Regulation 17(*b*), as the testing for the electric multi-shot firing apparatus specified.

The 'M.E. 6' Mark I Six-Shot Exploder (Electric Shot Firing Apparatus Approval No. 18).

(*a*) *Type of Tester*

The 'Six-Shot Fusehead Tester'.

(*b*) *Description of Tester*

A device comprising six metal clips, each designed to hold a 'Testex' low tension fusehead in a vertical position, a fine wire is arranged to be close to or touching each of the fuseheads, and a non-inductive resistor of such a value as to equate the total resistance of the circuit, including six fuseheads, to that of a normal shot firing circuit. These items are connected in series between the two terminals of the tester and together form the testing circuit. The fine wire is such that it will be ruptured by the firing of any of the fuseheads.

(*c*) *Method of use of Tester*

A 'Testex' fusehead is placed in each clip, and the fine wire arranged to be close to or in contact with each of the fuseheads. The exploder should be connected to the testing device and the continuity of the circuit checked by means of the indicator built into the exploder. If this indication is satisfactory the exploder is then operated by means of the firing key. The operation is successful if, after operation of the firing key, all six fuseheads have fired and the wire has ruptured. The exploder shot firing ability is deemed to be adequate provided ten consecutive operations are completed successfully.

N.B.—When using exploders approved under Electric Shot Firing Apparatus Approval No. 18, the firing key should be rotated as quickly as possible.

PLASTIC IGNITER CORD

The type of plastic igniter cord described below is approved for the purposes of Regulation 29(4) (*a*):

Plastic igniter cord shall consist of:

(*a*) an extruded cord of plastic core composition containing embedded filaments of metal or other material of suitable tensile strength, and protected on the outside by a thin layer of plastic or other suitable material, or

(*b*) an extruded tube of plastic core composition enclosing strands of black-powder igniter wick with or without textile yarns or metal filaments, and protected on the outside by a thin layer of plastic or other suitable material.

MEMORANDUM ON THE STORAGE OF EXPLOSIVES AT MINES

1. Under the Mines and Quarries Act 1954, the Coal Mines (Explosives) Regulations 1961 and the Stratified Iron-stone, Shale and Fireclay Mines (Explosives) Regulations 1956, all explosives used at a mine to which the Act applies must be provided by the owner of the mine and a suitable place above ground must be provided for the storage of the explosive. A suitable place has also to be provided conveniently near the entrance of the mine, for the storage of the unused explosive which the workmen are required to bring out at the end of each shift. The storage place should be at a safe distance from a shaft, engine-house or other vital point.

2. In making provision for the storage of explosive, the mine owner or manager has to comply with the requirements of the Explosives Acts 1875 and 1923, and the orders made under those Acts, and this memorandum is designed to explain briefly the nature of those requirements and the methods by which the storage accommodation required can be provided to suit the varying circumstances of different mines.

There are three ways in which explosive in sufficient quantity for mining purposes may be kept—

(*a*) in premises registered with the Local Authority;*

(*b*) in a 'store' licensed by the Local Authority;*

(*c*) in a magazine licensed by the Secretary of State.

3. Method (*a*) can be adopted where small quantities of explosive only are in store at any one time, and is often a suitable way of providing storage for unused explosive brought out of the mine when the main store is not conveniently near the mine entrance. The amount of explosive kept in this way (Mode A)† must not exceed 200lb. of gunpowder, or 60lb. of other explosive or of mixed explosives. The conditions to be observed are contained in Section 22 of the Act and Order in Council No. 16 which should be consulted, but the main provisions are as follows:

The place of storage must be registered with the Local Authority and (if explosive other than gunpowder is kept) the manager or other responsible person having charge of the premises must hold a certificate from the Police that he is a fit person to keep the explosives. If gunpowder and/or safety fuse is acquired a licence must be obtained from the Police in accordance with the Control of Explosives Order 1953 (S.I. 1953, No. 1598).

The storage place (Mode A)† must be a building substantially constructed of brick, stone, iron or concrete or an excavation made in solid rock, earth, or mine refuse not liable to ignition. It must be entirely appropriated‡ to the keeping of explosive and must be detached from a dwelling-house. It must also be situated at a safe distance (say 15 yards, or less if suitable protection intervenes) from any highway, street, public thoroughfare or public place, but there are no further requirements as to the distances to be maintained between the storage place and other buildings and works in the vicinity.

The precautions mentioned in paragraphs (vii), (x) and (xii) of the summary of main requirements as to licensed stores given at the end of this memorandum must be observed.

---

*See note on Local Authorities on page 108.

†For an appreciation of the difference between Registered Premises under Modes A and B see H.M.S.O. Summary VI, relating to Premises Registered for Mixed Explosives.

‡Very small quantities, however, viz., up to 50lb. of gunpowder or 15lb. of other explosive or of mixed explosives, may be kept in a building not so appropriated, provided they are kept in a substantial receptacle properly closed and secured and exclusively appropriated to the purpose under Mode B.

4. Method (*b*) provides for larger quantities, and includes five different kinds of 'Stores', named Divisions A, B, C, D and E. The quantity of explosive that may be kept in each class of store is as follows:

Division A	150lb.	of general explosive*
,, B	300lb.	,, ,,
,, C	1,000lb.	,, ,,
,, D	2,000lb.	,, ,,
,, E	4,000lb.	,, ,,

The conditions which apply to these stores are contained in Order in Council No. 6 of 27 November, 1875, as amended by the Store for Explosives Orders 1951 and 1953 (S.I. 1951 No. 1163 and S.I. 1953 No. 1197), and a summary of them is given at the end of this memorandum.

5. The most important requirements which mine owners have to consider is that which provides that all stores shall be placed at certain distances from other buildings and works. An important modification in these distances, however, is often of material assistance to mine owners in cases where the surface space at the mine is restricted. By the Stores for Explosives Order 1951 it is provided that in the case of stores licensed before 1st July, 1952, the distances may, in the case of a store of Divisions C, D and E, be reduced by half provided the protected work is in the occupation of the licensee and is completely screened from the store by a natural or artificial mound of earth, or other suitable material not less than three feet thick at the height of the eaves of the store. Further, it is provided by the same Order that the distance between a store in any of the four divisions and a mineral railway or private railway or tramway line worked by the occupier need not be more than 75 feet, if the door or doors of the store be closed and secured when and so long as any locomotive driven by steam is within 150 feet of the store. By the Stores for Explosives Order 1953 further concessions in safe distances are allowed for stores with protective mounds existing before 1951.

6. In cases where larger quantities than those mentioned above are required or where, owing to special local circumstances, it is impracticable to find a suitable place for a store, it will be necessary to provide a magazine under licence of the Secretary of State (i.e., Method (*c*)). In the first instance, it is advisable to communicate with Her Majesty's Inspectors of Explosives, Home Office, London, S.W.1., who will be prepared to consider the special requirements of each case and to recommend such conditions to suit the circumstances as may safely be entertained. The quantity of explosive that may be kept in a magazine is limited only by the provisions of the licence.

Workmen's filled canisters may be kept in any place of storage provided as above.

Local Authorities

England and Wales

The Town Council is the Local Authority in any—

(*a*) County Borough.

(*b*) Quarter Sessions Borough (other than a County Borough) having over 10,000 inhabitants according to the Census of 1881.

(*c*) Borough having over 10,000 inhabitants according to the Census of 1881, for which a special Order has been made under Section 68 of the Explosives Act.

*General Explosive means an explosive of Classes 1, 2, 3 and 4 and of the 2nd and 3rd Divisions of Class 6 of the Home Office list of Authorised Explosives published by H.M.S.O.

Elsewhere the Local Authority is the County Council which has, however, a power of delegation under the Act to—

(*a*) a Committee of its own body;

(*b*) an Urban or Rural District Council;

(*c*) the Justices in Petty Sessions.

The Councils of County Boroughs have the same power of delegation as County Councils.

Scotland

In any Royal or Parliamentary Burgh the Local Authority is the Magistrates and Town Council.

Elsewhere the Local Authority is the County Council which has, however, power of delegation to a joint Committee of its own body and of any Town Councils within the County.

In Duns and Govan, for which a special Order has been made under Section 112 of the Act, the Police Commissioners are the Local Authority.

SUMMARY OF THE MAIN REQUIREMENTS AS TO LICENSED STORES

(i) The store must be licensed by the Local Authority, in the name of the occupier, for mixed explosives.

(ii) The licence must be renewed annually.

(iii) The store must not be situated below ground in any mine, quarry or tunnel, or other underground place in which any persons are employed, or in any place opening into, from, or out of such mine, quarry, tunnel or underground place, or in communication therewith.

(iv) All buildings and places adjoining each other and occupied together are deemed to be one store, and must accordingly be included in one licence.

(v) The following distances must be maintained from the store:

Protected Works of Class 1

Dwelling-house.
Shop.
Room, of any kind.
Workshop, of any kind.
*Mineral or private railway, whether or not worked by steam.
Furnace or kiln or fire.
Magazine for explosive.
Store for explosive.
Registered premises.
} In occupation of licensee, or with consent in writing of occupier.

Highway, public footpath, or promenade or open place of resort for the public, or for persons engaged in any trade or business.

Protected Works of Class 2

Dwelling-house.
Shop.
Room, of any kind.
Workshop, of any kind.
Railway, whether or not worked by steam.
Furnace or kiln or fire.
Magazine for explosive.
Store for explosive.
Registered premises.
} Without the consent of the occupier.

Factory of any kind.
Buildings in care of Minister of Public Buildings and Works.
Place of public worship.
Educational establishments.

*The store shall not be required to maintain a greater distance than 75 feet from a mineral or private railway worked by the licensee, provided that the door or doors of the said store be kept closed and secured when and so long as any locomotive driven by steam is within a distance of 150 feet of the store. 'Mineral or private railway' includes a tramway or incline. (S.I. 1951 No. 1163.)

Protected Works of Class 1

Canal or navigable water.
Dock, river-wall or sea-wall.
Pier or jetty.
Reservoir.

Protected Works of Class 2

Hospital or like institution.
Court of Justice.
Theatre, cinema, covered market or other covered building where persons are accustomed to assemble.
Government or local government buildings.

Store belonging to	Distances from Protected Works of Class 1*	Distances from Protected Works of Class 2
Division A . .	75 feet	85 feet
Division B . .	75 feet	130 feet
*Division C . .	146 feet	292 feet
*Division D . .	230 feet	460 feet
*Division E . .	352 feet	704 feet

(vi) Detonators must be kept effectively separated from other explosive. If a considerable quantity of detonators is required they may be kept in an annexe to the store which will be regarded as part of the store (the annexe should be of the same construction as the store and at least a few feet away from it); or in a place registered in accordance with the method first mentioned in the memorandum (the colliery office may be registered for the purpose (Mode B)† if the gross weight of the detonators does not exceed 15lb. and the detonators are kept in a locked box or drawer exclusively appropriated to the purpose; see footnote on page 107). For a few hundred detonators, however, a cupboard in the porch of the store, so arranged that it cannot be opened unless the inner door of the store is closed, may be allowed. For weights of detonators, see table at the end of this summary.

(vii) When any explosive which is liable to be dangerously affected by water is kept, due precautions must be taken to exclude water from the store. It is very necessary to keep all explosives and detonators dry, or loss of efficiency and miss-fires will probably result.

(viii) The store must be well and substantially built of brick, stone, iron, steel or concrete, or excavated in solid rock, earth or mine refuse not liable to ignition, and so made and closed as to prevent unauthorised persons having access thereto, and to secure it from danger from without. Its construction must also be substantial and such as to render it not liable to unlawful entry, or to danger from accident or from evilly disposed persons; accordingly, it should be provided with doors of $\frac{1}{4}$ inch steel plate fitted with at least two strong steel mortice locks, not padlocks, for new stores or the equivalent degree of protection for old stores.

(ix) If licensed under Divisions C, D or E, and made otherwise than by excavation, the store must have attached a sufficient lightning conductor.

*In the case of stores licensed before 1st July, 1952, when the 'protected work' is in the occupation of the licensee, and is completely screened from the store by a natural or artificial mound of earth or other suitable material not less than three feet thick at the height of the eaves of the store, the distances may be reduced by one-half. (S.I. 1951 No. 1163.) By the Stores for Explosives Order 1953 further concessions in safe distances are allowed for stores with protective mounds existing before 1951.

†For an appreciation of the difference between Registered Premises under Modes A and B see H.M.S.O. Summary VI, relating to Premises Registered for Mixed Explosives.

(x) The interior of the store, and the benches, shelves and fittings therein must be so constructed or so lined or covered as to prevent the exposure of any iron or steel, and the detaching of any grit, iron, steel or similar substance in such manner as to come into contact with the explosive. This provision can best be complied with by lining the store with wood or other suitable material. A wooden lining will be easier to keep clean if painted or varnished, and will last much longer if the planks are thus treated on both sides before being placed in position. The floor must be of wood or asphalt free from grit. Nails should be preferably of copper, brass or zinc; but if iron nails are used, they should be countersunk and puttied over. All exposed ironwork in the building should be efficiently covered with wood, leather or zinc, or should be thickly painted.

(xi) All tools and implements used in the store must be of wood, copper, brass or some soft metal or material, or be covered with some safe and suitable material.

(xii) The interior, benches, shelves and fittings of the store must, so far as is reasonably practicable, be kept free from grit and otherwise clean.

(xiii) Due provision must be made by the use of suitable shoes or otherwise for preventing the introduction into the store of grit or of any exposed iron or steel. At every store there should be a visible boundary, formed by a step or by a vertical 'footboard' (about four inches high), or otherwise, beyond which dirty or iron-nailed boots should never pass, except directly into over-boots of leather, rubber or other suitable material made without any iron; and these over-boots should in their turn never be placed outside the 'clean' boundary (the word 'clean' being here used in a technical sense, implying the exclusion of all grit), or be deposited where they can take up grit. Over-boots made very large (so as easily to take in the whole boot and lower part of the trousers) are more convenient than those which necessitate removing the ordinary boots, or which entail trouble and delay in putting on.

(xiv) Due provision must be made by the use of suitable working clothes without pockets, searching, or by some of such means for preventing the introduction into the store of fire, matches, or any substance or article likely to cause explosion or fire, or any iron, or steel, or grit. (N.B.—The use of an artificial light of such construction, position or character as not to cause any danger of fire or explosion is permitted, e.g., an approved electric safety-lamp or dust-tight electrical installations which conform to the Home Office specification may be used—see paragraph 3 (*b*) of the Home Office memorandum on Electric Light and Power in Factories and Magazines for Explosives).

This important provision can best be satisfied by requiring the storekeeper to wear a pocketless magazine suit, and forbidding other persons to enter. But as this is not always practicable or convenient, the storekeeper should be required not only habitually to search his own pockets, but also the pockets of any other persons who may enter the store, in order to detect and remove therefrom any dangerous articles, among which may be included a pipe, as this is sometimes placed in the pocket before it has been properly extinguished.

(xv) No person may smoke in any part of the store.

(xvi) No person under the age of 18 may be employed in or enter the store except in the presence and under the supervision of some person of the age of 21 or upwards, and no person under the age of 16 may be employed in the store.

(xvii) No repairs are to be executed to or in any part of the store, except after the store has, so far as is practicable, been cleaned by the removal of all explosive and the thorough washing out of the store.

(xviii) The store is to be used only for the keeping of explosive and receptacles, tools or implements for work connected with the keeping of such explosive.

(xix) A warning notice to trespassers, worded in the statutory form of Section 77 of the Explosives Act 1875 must be kept conspicuously posted up.

Weights of Detonators

Size of Detonator	Gross Weight per 1,000 Detonators	Remarks
No.	lb.	
3	3.19	Not much used
3a	3.31	Not much used
4	3.62	Not much used
5	4.23	Common sizes
6	4.95	Common sizes
6½	5.50	Common sizes
7	7.06	Common sizes
8	8.66	Common sizes
9	9.76	Not much used
10	10.86	Not much used

FIRE AND RESCUE

THE COAL AND OTHER MINES (FIRE AND RESCUE) REGULATIONS 1956

S.I. 1956 No. 1768

Arrangement of Regulations

PART I

Application

1. Except where otherwise expressly provided, Part II of these regulations shall apply to every mine of coal, stratified ironstone, shale or fireclay, Part III thereof to mines of those minerals in which or in part of which the use of lamps or lights, other than permitted lights, is unlawful, and Part IV thereof to every mine of coal, stratified ironstone, shale or fireclay, other than a mine at which not more than ten persons are employed below ground, and in these regulations 'mine' shall be construed accordingly.

PART II

Fire precautions and equipment

2. (1) No highly inflammable material shall be stored below ground in any mine except in a fireproof room, compartment or box.

(2) At any mine newly opened after the sixteenth day of December, nineteen hundred and eleven, being a mine at which more than thirty persons are employed below ground, no building or structure at the top of any shaft or outlet shall be made of or comprise any inflammable material likely to cause danger from fire to any person so employed.

(3) No engine-room or motor-room constructed after the sixteenth day of December, nineteen hundred and eleven, below ground in any mine shall be made of or comprise any inflammable material likely to cause danger from fire to any person employed in the mine.

3. It shall be the duty of the manager of every mine to secure the provision of suitable and sufficient means of extinguishing fire at each of the following places, that is to say—

(*a*) at the top of and at every entrance to a shaft or outlet, being a place in the construction of which inflammable material is used;

(*b*) in every engine-room, motor-room or boiler gallery, being a place in the construction of which inflammable material is used; and

(*c*) at any place at which inflammable material is stored.

4. It shall be the duty of the manager of every mine to secure the provision and readiness for immediate use in case of fire of a sufficient supply of suitable dust or sand in suitable containers at an appropriate place in relation to every electric motor, which is not portable apparatus for the purposes of the Coal and Other Mines (Electricity) Regulations 1956*, transformer and switchgear installed at the mine.

5. It shall be the duty of the manager of every mine, other than a mine which is naturally wet throughout and at which not more than thirty persons are employed below ground or a mine of stratified ironstone, to secure the provision and readiness for immediate use in case of fire of—

(*a*) an adequate supply of water; or

(*b*) sufficient portable fire extinguishers and a sufficient supply of suitable dust or sand; and

(*c*) appropriate equipment for conveying and using the water, dust or sand in that case;

at appropriate places in relation to each working face and along any length of road below ground, being a length which is a main intake airway or a main return airway for the purposes of the Coal and Other Mines (Ventilation) Regulations 1956.†

6. (1) It shall be the duty of the manager of every mine, other than a mine at which less than one hundred persons are employed below ground, to secure the provision and readiness for immediate use in case of fire below ground of adequate supplies of water and efficient means for delivering it promptly at adequate pressure and in adequate volume to every place in the mine at which persons work otherwise than occasionally or for short periods or which persons going to or from their working places ordinarily pass, being in either case a place at which fire is liable to occur.

(2) Except in so far as provision is made in pursuance of the last preceding paragraph to deliver water through pipelines and hose extensions to every place at which it is required to be available, provision shall be made for delivery from tanks or barrels by portable manual pumps.

7. Where at any mine machinery for cutting or getting mineral is in use at a working face at which an ignition of gas has been, or having regard to the nature of the strata is liable to be, produced by such machinery, it shall be the duty of the manager to secure that—

(*a*) the machine is provided with effective means to prevent such ignition; or

(*b*) a portable fire extinguisher or supply of suitable dust or sand in a suitable container is carried on the machine; or

---

*See page 19.

†See page 317.

(*c*) if owing to the height of the working it is impracticable to carry such an extinguisher or such a container on the machine, portable fire extinguishers or supplies of suitable dust or sand in suitable containers are provided at suitable intervals along the face and at any point at which an airway, which as regards the face is an intake airway, meets the face.

8. No fire extinguisher which is liable when operated to give off poisonous gas shall be provided below ground whether in pursuance of these regulations or otherwise.

9. (1) It shall be the duty of the manager of every mine to make and ensure the efficient carrying out of arrangements—

(*a*) whereby all equipment provided in pursuance of this Part of these regulations is inspected by competent persons appointed by him at intervals not exceeding thirty days; and

(*b*) for the discharge and refilling of each fire extinguisher to ensure that it is maintained in good working order.

(2) Every person making such an inspection shall make a full and accurate report thereon to the manager in writing.

10. It shall be the duty of the manager of every mine, other than a mine at which less than one hundred persons are employed below ground, to make arrangements to secure a proper organisation of persons for combating any outbreak of fire and such arrangements shall include fire drills.

PART III*

Precautions in case of outbreak or suspected outbreak of fire

11. (1) Without prejudice to the generality of section seventy-nine of the Act if in any mine there appears any smoke or other sign indicating that a fire has or may have broken out below ground at any place, the persons in charge of any parts of the mine likely to be affected by such a fire, by products of combustion thereof or by any explosion resulting therefrom, shall cause all persons employed at any place likely to be so affected to leave it:

Provided that in any case in which it appears to the person in charge of the part of the mine from which that sign emanates that there exists no immediate danger persons may remain there for the purpose of preventing danger from arising.

(2) Where on any occasion persons have been caused to leave any place in pursuance of the provisions of the last preceding paragraph, no person shall thereafter be permitted to enter it until after examination thereof it is reported safe for him to do so either by the manager or an under-manager of the mine and by two members of the panel appointed for the mine under section one hundred and twenty-three of the Act or, if they do not concur, by an inspector:

Provided that nothing in this paragraph shall be taken to prohibit a person from entering any place for the purpose of saving life, ascertaining the condition

*For application of this Part see Regulation 1.

of that place, ascertaining or taking any measures that it is necessary to take for the purpose of rendering it safe or ascertaining the effectiveness of such measures:

Provided also that the concurrence of two members of the said panel shall not be required if such persons are not available within a reasonable period after the manager or an under-manager of the mine has informed the person for the time being nominated to receive notices under subsection (1) of section one hundred and sixteen of the Act of the occurrence.

(3) Any report under the last preceding paragraph shall be a full and accurate report* signed by the persons making it and the position of the fire or suspected fire shall, if possible, be indicated by means of a plan. A copy of any such report shall forthwith be posted at the pithead.

(4) If on any occasion it is ascertained that fire has broken out at any place the following parts of the mine shall be deemed for the purposes of paragraph (1) of this regulation to be affected, that is to say, all parts of the seam in which the fire exists and all parts of any other seam reached from an entrance below ground to a shaft or outlet being an entrance from which the first mentioned seam is reached:

Provided that a part of the mine other than that in which the fire exists shall be deemed not to be affected if it is protected against the spread thereto of any explosion by means† approved by the Minister for the purposes of this regulation, and a seam other than that in which the fire exists shall be deemed not to be affected if it is naturally wet throughout.

(5) If on any occasion a fire is being dammed off all parts of the mine below ground shall be deemed for the purposes of paragraph (1) of this regulation to be affected, and until the work is completed no person shall be permitted to go below ground except for the purposes of that work or otherwise for securing the safety of the mine.

(6) If on any occasion it is ascertained that fire has broken out at any place measures shall be taken to render harmless any coal dust in accessible parts of the mine contiguous to the fire.

PART IV‡

Rescue

Central rescue stations

12. (1) It shall be the duty of the owner of every mine—

(*a*) to provide, maintain and conduct in accordance with the following provisions of this Part of these regulations a central rescue station to provide facilities for the conduct of operations for rescue and other necessary work at that mine after an explosion or a fire, or in an atmosphere which is or may be irrespirable, thereat; or

---

*M. & Q. Form No. 261.

†No means for this purpose have yet been approved.

‡For application of this Part see Regulation 1.

(*b*) to make arrangements to ensure that there are available to that mine such facilities provided by a central rescue station so maintained and conducted,

being a station situate within fifteen miles of the entrance to the mine or such greater distance not exceeding twenty miles as an inspector may authorise by notice served on the owner.

(2) An inspector may by notice served on the owner of a mine exempt him from the preceding provisions of this regulation with respect to that mine—

(*a*) if the inspector is satisfied that there are in force effective arrangements for the conduct of operations for rescue at that mine independently of a central rescue station; or

(*b*) if the mine is situate more than fifteen miles from such a central rescue station then existing and the inspector is satisfied that it would be unreasonable that the owner should be required to provide such a central rescue station; or

(*c*) if the inspector is satisfied that the owner has unsuccessfully made reasonable efforts to conclude such arrangements as are referred to in sub-paragraph (*b*) of the last preceding paragraph and that it would be unreasonable that he should be required to provide such a central rescue station.

(3) The owner of every mine to which paragraph (1) of this regulation applies shall ensure that it is in telephonic communication with the central rescue station the facilities of which are available to that mine.

(4) Without prejudice to the generality of section one hundred and seventy-six of the Act, to an authority or exemption given under this regulation there may be attached conditions requiring the provision at the mine of rescue equipment other than or in excess of that specified in these regulations.

Superintendents of and instructors at central rescue stations

13. (1) Every central rescue station shall be under the immediate control of a competent superintendent being a person who has been fully trained in rescue work and who, unless he was so employed before the first day of January, nineteen hundred and twenty-nine, has had not less than five years' practical experience of work below ground in a mine.

(2) There shall be employed at every central rescue station instructors competent to train rescue workers.

(3) Arrangements shall be made to ensure that an instructor is present at and appointed to take charge of a central rescue station at any time when the superintendent is not present thereat.

(4) The number of instructors employed at a central rescue station at which a permanent rescue corps is maintained shall not be less than two, and, if the total number of persons employed below ground at the mines to which the facilities of that station are available exceeds fifteen thousand, shall not be less than three.

(5) The number of instructors employed at a central rescue station at which a permanent rescue corps is not maintained shall not be less than two, and, if the total number of rescue brigades required by these regulations to be maintained at the mines to which the facilities of that station are available exceeds fifty, shall not be less than three, and, if the total number of such rescue brigades exceeds one hundred, shall not be less than four.

(6) For the purposes of the two last preceding paragraphs, a superintendent who undertakes the training of rescue workers may be included as an instructor.

Permanent rescue corps

14. (1) At any central rescue station at which a permanent rescue corps is maintained that corps shall consist of not less than six men fully trained in rescue work exclusive of the superintendent and of the person appointed to take charge of the station when the superintendent is not present thereat.

(2) One or more members of the corps shall be trained to act as captain thereof.

(3) The members of the corps shall be continuously employed at and in residence at the central rescue station:

Provided that an inspector by notice served on the superintendent of the station may authorise members of the corps to reside not more than half a mile from the station so long as suitable means of summons from that residence to the station are provided.

Rescue workers to act with permanent rescue corps

15. (1) It shall be the duty of the manager of every mine at which not less than one hundred persons are employed below ground and to which the facilities of a central rescue station are available, being a station at which a permanent rescue corps is maintained, to appoint men who are employed at that mine and have a good general knowledge thereof and who have been fully trained in rescue work to co-operate with the corps in work and practice on the following scale, that is to say—

where not more than five hundred persons are employed below ground at the mine, not less than one man;

where more than five hundred but not more than one thousand persons are so employed, not less than two men;

where more than one thousand but not more than fifteen hundred persons are so employed, not less than three men;

where more than fifteen hundred persons are so employed, not less than four men.

(2) The manager of every mine to which the last preceding paragraph applies and at which more than one such man has been appointed, shall endeavour to ensure that at no time are they both or all employed below ground simultaneously otherwise than in rescue work or practice.

Rescue brigades

16. (1) It shall be the duty of the manager of every mine to which the facilities of a central rescue station are available, being a station at which a permanent rescue corps is not maintained, to organise and maintain rescue brigades on the following scale, that is to say—

where not more than five hundred persons are employed below ground at the mine, not less than one brigade;

where more than five hundred but not more than two thousand persons are so employed, not less than two brigades;

where more than two thousand persons are so employed, three brigades:

Provided that—

(*a*) the preceding provisions of this paragraph shall not apply as respects a mine at which less than one hundred persons are employed below ground if arrangements are in force whereby a brigade from another mine will be made available promptly in case of need; and

(*b*) mines of which the surface entrances to all the shafts and outlets for the time being in use lie within a circle having a radius of two miles may be treated together as one mine if the managers have made arrangements therefor and served notice thereof on the inspector for the district.

(2) The manager of every mine to which this regulation applies shall appoint not less than five men fully trained in rescue work and employed at that mine to each brigade and shall appoint one of them captain.

(3) The manager of every mine to which this regulation applies shall endeavour to ensure that at no time are—

(*a*) in the case of a mine at which one rescue brigade is maintained, all the members of that brigade; or

(*b*) in the case of a mine at which more than one rescue brigade is maintained, members of both or all the brigades;

employed below ground simultaneously, otherwise than in rescue work or practice.

Communication with rescue workers

17. The manager of every mine to which either of the two last preceding regulations applies, shall make effective arrangements for summoning every person appointed thereunder from his residence in case of need.

Saving

18. In any prosecution for a contravention of regulation fifteen or regulation sixteen it shall be a defence to prove that the manager has made reasonable efforts to induce appropriate persons to be trained in rescue work and that the failure to comply fully was due to an insufficiency of persons able and willing to acquire the requisite qualification.

Qualifications of rescue workers

19. No person shall be selected for training in rescue work with a view to appointment as a member of a permanent rescue corps, as a rescue worker to co-operate at a mine with such a corps or as a member of a rescue brigade at a mine unless—

(*a*) he is certified by a registered medical practitioner after thorough examination to be fit to undertake rescue work and to be free from any organic disease or weakness;

(*b*) he has had not less than two years' practical experience of work below ground in a mine; and

(*c*) he is the holder of a certificate of proficiency in first aid granted by a society or body* approved by the Minister for the purpose.

20. No person shall for the purposes of these regulations be deemed to be fully trained in rescue work unless he has attended one or more courses of instruction and practice therein at a central rescue station, being courses complying with a scheme approved† by the Minister, and has been certified by the superintendent of that station to be efficient and able to undertake rescue work with breathing apparatus.

21. No person shall be qualified to be appointed or to be a member of a permanent rescue corps, a rescue worker to co-operate at a mine with such a corps or a member of a rescue brigade at a mine unless he has within the last preceding twelve months—

(*a*) been certified by a registered medical practitioner after thorough examination to be fit to undertake rescue work and to be free from any organic disease or weakness; and

(*b*) attended a course of instruction and practice in rescue work, being a course including practices with breathing apparatus in a hot and irrespirable atmosphere and complying with a scheme approved† by the Minister for such courses for maintaining efficiency.

Records at central rescue stations

22. There shall be kept at every central rescue station a record of every person attending a course of instruction and practice in rescue work thereat including the date and character of each practice and the condition of each man after each practice and, if anything abnormal is observed in the condition of any man, whether it is considered to be due to any defect in any apparatus used by him.

Equipment at central rescue stations

23. At every central rescue station there shall be provided and maintained in readiness for immediate use the following equipment, that is to say—

(*a*) twenty complete suits of breathing apparatus of a type approved by the Minister with means of supplying sufficient oxygen or liquid air to enable such apparatus to be used for forty-eight hours and means of charging such apparatus;

(*b*) four smoke helmets or other apparatus serving the same purpose, being helmets or apparatus of a type approved by the Minister, with not less than one hundred and twenty feet of tubing for each;

---

*See list of approved societies and bodies on page 150.

†See page 129.

(*c*) four sets of reviving apparatus, not being apparatus of a forced breathing type, each with a cylinder or cylinders capable of supplying not less than twenty cubic feet of oxygen;

(*d*) a first aid box of a type approved* by the Minister;

(*e*) twenty electric safety-lamps and six flame safety-lamps;

(*f*) cages of small birds for testing for noxious gas;

(*g*) a motor vehicle of adequate capacity;

(*h*) two portable signalling devices; and

(*i*) means for training persons to test for inflammable gas with a flame safety-lamp.

Rescue equipment at mines

24. It shall be the duty of the manager of every mine, other than a mine at which less than one hundred persons are employed below ground, to secure the provision and readiness for immediate use thereat of the following equipment, that is to say—

(*a*) a smoke helmet or other apparatus serving the same purpose, being a helmet or apparatus of a type approved by the Minister with not less than one hundred and twenty feet of tubing;

(*b*) a set of reviving apparatus, not being apparatus of a forced breathing type, with a cylinder or cylinders capable of supplying not less than twenty cubic feet of oxygen;

(*c*) one electric safety-lamp and one flame safety-lamp for each man fully trained in rescue work and employed at that mine; and

(*d*) two small birds for testing for noxious gas.

Breathing apparatus

25. (1) Subject to any exemption given by an inspector by notice served on the manager, breathing apparatus shall not be kept at any mine but shall be obtained as required for rescue work or training thereat from a central rescue station.

(2) Every suit of breathing apparatus kept at a central rescue station, or at a mine in pursuance of an exemption given under the last preceding paragraph, shall be adjusted and tested at the times and in the manner specified in the first schedule hereto and the results thereof shall be recorded in accordance with those provisions.

(3) No oxygen cylinder shall be used for re-charging breathing apparatus unless a part of the contents has been analysed and found to contain not less than ninety-eight per cent of oxygen. A record shall be kept of the result of every such analysis.

(4) No suit of breathing apparatus shall be used below ground in any mine unless as soon as may be before use it has been tested for leakage by immersion in the manner specified in the first schedule hereto and found safe except—

(*a*) upon a practice in air which is not irrespirable; or

*See page 131.

(*b*) in a case in which subjection to such a test would prejudice an attempt to save life and the apparatus has been tested immediately before use for leakage by mouth suction.

(5) Without prejudice to the operation of sections one hundred and sixteen and one hundred and seventeen of the Act, on the happening of any accident or occurrence at a mine likely to require the use of breathing apparatus, the manager shall inform by the quickest means available the inspector for the district and the person for the time being nominated to receive notices under subsection (1) of section one hundred and sixteen of the Act.

Signals for use in rescue work

26. In rescue work and training therefor the signals specified in the second schedule hereto and no other shall be used for the purposes specified in relation thereto.

Accommodation for rescue workers at mines

27. (1) It shall be the duty of the manager of every mine to secure the provision on the surface thereat of a suitable room with sufficient accommodation for any persons who may be engaged in rescue work or practice. That room shall be near to a shaft or outlet normally used by persons employed below ground at the mine and shall be adequately heated and lighted and kept clean and properly maintained.

(2) At every mine at which not less than one hundred persons are employed below ground the said room, if not permanently separated from accommodation used for any other purpose, shall be so arranged that it can readily be so separated. The equipment provided in pursuance of these regulations at that mine shall be kept therein.

(3) The manager of every mine shall appoint a responsible person to be in charge of the room provided in pursuance of this regulation.

Plans

28. It shall be the duty of the manager of every mine to keep at the mine or at such other place as may be approved by an inspector a sufficient number of sets of plans, in a form suitable for use by rescue workers, of the workings of the mine, so that at any time there are plans for each part of the mine showing clearly and accurately up to a date not more than three months past the extent of the workings, the airways and the direction of the air current therein and all principal doors, stoppings, air crossings and regulators and telephone stations by means of the signs specified in the third schedule hereto.

Inspection of equipment, &c.

29. It shall be the duty of the owner of every mine to which the facilities of a central rescue station are available to make arrangements for the inspection at intervals not exceeding six months by the superintendent of the station or an instructor nominated by him of the accommodation and equipment provided thereat for rescue work and training. Such arrangements shall ensure that on any such inspection the superintendent or his nominee shall be accompanied by an official of the mine and that any defect or deficiency disclosed thereby is promptly reported to the manager of the mine.

Provisions relating to conduct of rescue work

30. (1) It shall be the duty of the manager of every mine to make rules allotting to competent persons the duties to be performed by them on any occasion on which rescue work is about to be or is being carried out at that mine.

(2) Such rules shall include provisions to ensure that on any such occasion, at any time when the manager is not himself performing those functions, a competent person is in charge on the surface to secure that—

(*a*) no person enters any shaft or outlet for the purpose of going to a part of the mine affected, unless he is duly authorised so to do;

(*b*) the name of every person going below ground or returning above ground at the mine is recorded in writing;

(*c*) teams of rescue workers are organised and, where such a team is not a permanent rescue corps or a rescue brigade, a captain thereof is appointed;

(*d*) suits of breathing apparatus are tested in accordance with paragraph (4) of regulation twenty-five; and

(*e*) such other steps as can be taken on the surface to regulate and facilitate the rescue work are taken.

31. On any occasion on which rescue work is about to be or is being carried on in any mine, no person shall go below ground for the purpose of going to a part of the mine affected unless authorised so to do.

32. (1) On any occasion on which rescue work is about to be or is being carried on in any mine, no person shall be authorised to go below ground for any purpose which may involve the use of breathing apparatus unless he is a person for the time being qualified to be a member of a permanent rescue corps, a rescue worker to co-operate at a mine with such a corps or a member of a rescue brigade at a mine.

(2) On any such occasion no person shall be permitted to engage in a second or subsequent spell of work involving the use of breathing apparatus unless he has been medically examined since the preceding spell of work and is found fit to undertake it.

33. (1) On any occasion on which rescue work is to be carried out in a mine in an atmosphere which is or may be irrespirable, there shall be organised as soon as may be a base or bases (hereinafter referred to as a 'fresh air base') in respirable air but as near to the places in which the work has to be carried out as appears safe.

(2) Whenever any persons are engaged in rescue work beyond the fresh air base there shall, so far as is practicable, be stationed thereat—

(*a*) two persons including a person competent to test and maintain breathing apparatus and other rescue equipment and a person holding a certificate of proficiency in first aid granted by a society or body approved* by the Minister for the purpose;

*See list of approved societies and bodies on page 150.

(*b*) a team of rescue workers ready for immediate service and equipped with breathing apparatus; and

(*c*) a set of reviving apparatus, a stretcher and a cage of birds.

(3) Telephonic communication shall, if practicable, be established and maintained between any fresh air base and the surface of the mine or an entrance below ground to a shaft or outlet.

34. (1) On any occasion on which rescue work is to be carried out in a mine, no team of rescue workers shall go beyond a fresh air base, or where an appropriate fresh air base has not been established shall go below ground, unless the captain has been given clear instructions where the team is to go and what it is to attempt by the person in charge at the fresh air base or on the surface, as the case may be, and if breathing apparatus is to be used, has assured himself that that apparatus has been tested in accordance with paragraph (4) of regulation twenty-five.

(2) Unless the captain of such a team is personally familiar with the route to be taken, he shall not proceed without a plan of the relevant part of the mine made in pursuance of regulation twenty-eight and on which that route is clearly marked.

35. (1) It shall be the duty of the captain of any rescue team engaged in rescue work in any mine to devote himself to the direction of the team and to secure its safety, and accordingly he shall not engage in manual work.

(2) Without prejudice to the generality of the foregoing, the captain of a team so engaged shall examine the state of the roof and sides of any place to be entered or passed by the team and he shall not permit the team to pass any place which appears to him insecure or except where it is necessary so to do in an attempt to save life to pass through any passage less than two feet high and three feet wide.

(3) If visibility is obscured by smoke, the captain of a rescue team shall secure that a life-line is taken in from the fresh air base or another place at which the air is respirable and that no member of the team moves out of reach of that line or, if that is not practicable, shall ensure that any road branching from a route is fenced off before the junction is passed.

(4) If visibility is not obscured by smoke, the captain of a rescue team when passing any junction shall see that the route is clearly indicated by means of arrows or other suitable marks.

36. The captain of any rescue team which is to use breathing apparatus in the course of any rescue work at any mine shall make sure that each such apparatus is working properly immediately before the team enters an atmosphere which is or may be irrespirable and shall in the case of such apparatus in which compressed oxygen is used read the pressure of oxygen at intervals not exceeding twenty minutes.

37. On any occasion on which a fire is being dammed off, there shall be kept available at or near the place two suits of breathing apparatus and persons qualified to use them under regulation thirty-two or two smoke helmets and persons competent to use them.

PART V

Interpretation

38. (1) In these regulations the following expressions have the meanings hereby respectively assigned to them, that is to say—

'the Act' means the Mines and Quarries Act 1954;

'fresh air base' has the meaning assigned thereto in regulation thirty-three;

'fully trained in rescue work' has the meaning assigned thereto in regulation twenty;

'mine' has the meaning assigned thereto in regulation one.

(2) The Interpretation Act 1889 shall apply to the interpretation of these regulations as it applies to the interpretation of an Act of Parliament.

FIRST SCHEDULE

(Regulation 25)

Adjustment and testing of breathing apparatus

1. In the case of breathing apparatus by which a uniform delivery of oxygen is provided, the reducing valve shall be so adjusted as to deliver not less than two litres of oxygen per minute.

2. A competent person shall as respects every suit of breathing apparatus at intervals not exceeding thirty days—

(*a*) thoroughly examine its general condition giving particular attention to any delicate or perishable part thereof;

(*b*) test it for leakage by complete immersion in water (other than of any liquid air pack which would thus be damaged) when fully distended under pressure and examine it closely for leakage;

(*c*) measure the pressure at which any automatic relief valve discharges;

(*d*) in the case of apparatus in which compressed oxygen is used, measure the pressure in the oxygen cylinder thereof; and

(*e*) in the case of such apparatus, measure by a flow meter the rate of delivery of oxygen and, in a case in which that rate can be adjusted by the wearer, measure that rate over the whole range of the adjustment.

3. No flow meter shall be used for the purposes of any test under the last preceding paragraph unless it has been tested for accuracy within the preceding six months.

4. No suit of breathing apparatus from which any leakage is found shall be deemed safe.

5. There shall be kept at every central rescue station, and at any mine at which any breathing apparatus is kept in pursuance of an exemption given by an inspector, a record of all tests carried out in pursuance of this schedule.

SECOND SCHEDULE

(Regulation 26)

Code of Signals

Electric Signalling	Signal	Signalling between Members of a Brigade	Signal
'Distress' or 'Help wanted' .	ONE ring	'Distress' or 'Help wanted' .	ONE hoot
(If NO ANSWER is given to a call, 'Distress' is to be understood)			
'Not understood' or 'Repeat the Message'	TWO rings	Halt	TWO hoots
'No'	THREE rings	Retire	THREE hoots
'Yes' or 'All right' or 'All's well'	FOUR rings	Advance	FOUR hoots
To 'ring up'. To 'ring off' . .	FIVE rings	To call attention	FIVE hoots

THIRD SCHEDULE

(Regulation 28)

Code of Signs

Brick, stone or concrete stoppings, constructed in the manner described in regulation 21 (2) of the Coal and Other Mines (Ventilation) Regulations 1956 . . . .

Brick, stone or concrete stoppings, other than the above

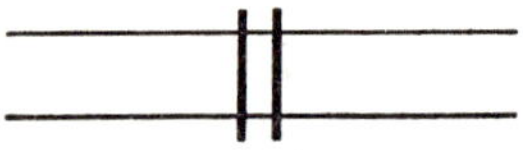

Fire dams or seals . . . .

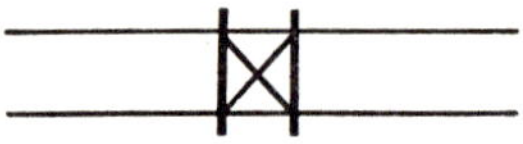

Doors . . . .

Regulators . . . .

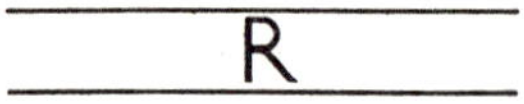

Air crossings, explosion proof . . . .

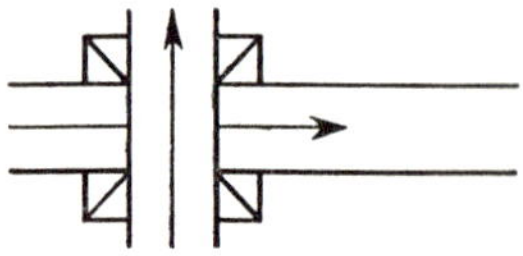

THIRD SCHEDULE

(Regulation 28) *Code of Signs—continued*

Air crossings other than the above . . . . . .

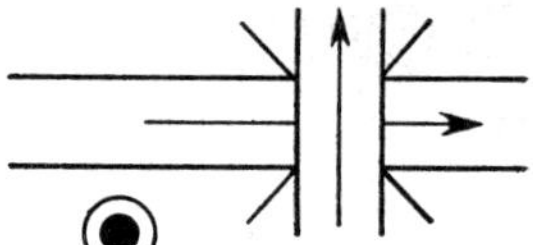

Telephones . . . .

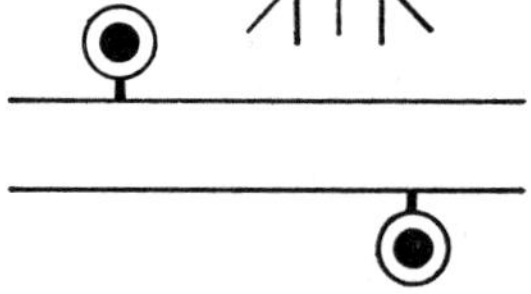

Underground ambulance station (in red) . . . . .

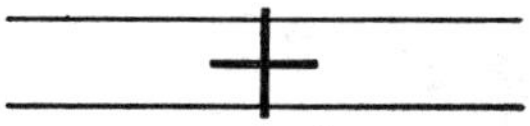

Direction of air current 

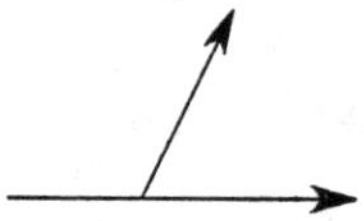

Intake airways—Blue. Return airways—Red.

APPROVED SPECIFICATIONS FOR THE PURPOSES OF THE COAL AND OTHER MINES (FIRE AND RESCUE) REGULATIONS 1956

Schemes for Instruction and Practices in Rescue Work

The schemes of instruction and practice in rescue work detailed below are approved for the purposes of regulations 20 and 21 (*b*):

Course of Initial Instruction and Practice (*Regulation 20*)

The course of instruction and practices shall be as follows:

(*a*) Instruction as to—

(i) the general methods of dealing with underground fires and the recovery of mines after fires and explosions;

(ii) the construction, use, repair, maintenance and testing of the type or types provided of breathing apparatus and of smoke helmets or other apparatus serving the same purpose;

(iii) the use of methods and apparatus of reviving men;

(iv) the properties and detection of the noxious and inflammable gases which may be found in mines;

(v) the taking of gas samples in irrespirable atmospheres;

(vi) the reading of mine plans;

(vii) the conduct of rescue work detailed in the said regulations and the code of signals contained in the second schedule to the said regulations.

(*b*) Practices—

Not less than 12 practices for each man with breathing apparatus and in addition not less than two for each man with smoke helmets or other apparatus serving the same purpose, in each case under conditions so devised as to represent those likely to be encountered in underground operations requiring the use of such apparatus.

The practices shall be carried out as follows:

(i) Rescue Brigades—as far as possible by each brigade as such, i.e., by all members of the brigade, at one and the same time.

(ii) Permanent Rescue Corps—by at least five members at one and the same time.

(iii) Men from Mines to act with Permanent Rescue Corps. Not more than eight men or less than five men shall take part in any part in any practice, but if five men do not attend on any occasion the number may be made up by members of the permanent rescue corps. So far as practicable the same five men shall practice together as one brigade.

(*c*) The practices with breathing apparatus shall take place in ordinary air and shall progress gradually until practices can be carried out in a hot and irrespirable atmosphere.

(*d*) The practices with breathing apparatus shall comprise the following operations:

(i) the repeated raising and lowering of a weight of 56lb. to and from a height of six feet by means of a rope and pulley;

(ii) walking continuously at a fair pace for half-an-hour;

(iii) building and removing temporary stoppings of stone, brick, sandbags, brattice cloth or other materials, and carrying the materials required for such operations over a distance of at least ten yards;

(iv) removing debris in confined spaces as representing the clearing of a fall of roof;

(v) setting timber or other roof supports;

(vi) carrying, pushing or pulling on a stretcher a live person or dummy body weighing 150lb. along the length of a gallery, and through an opening two feet high by three feet wide and four yards along;

(vii) the rapid establishment of communication.

All practices required by this part of this schedule shall last at least two hours except on occasion when, in the opinion of the instructor, it is desirable in the interests of safety to curtail the practice. At some of the practices the breathing apparatus shall be worn continuously for two hours.

Further Instruction and practice after initial training (*Regulation 21* (*b*))

(*a*) Instruction

Revision of all subjects included in the course of instruction and practice specified in Part I of this Schedule.

(*b*) Practices

(i) Rescue Brigades and Men from Mines to act with Permanent Rescue Corps.—Practices with breathing apparatus at least one in each quarter and at least six in each year, of which at least two shall take place in mines, and the remainder in a hot and irrespirable atmosphere.

(ii) Permanent Rescue Corps.—In addition to regular practices at the Central Rescue Station, practices with breathing apparatus underground in a mine at least one in each quarter and at least six in each year. Members who are not employed regularly underground in mines shall have six further practices underground in mines each year, making 12 practices in all.

Where possible mine practices shall include work in low and constricted roadways.

All practices required by this part of this schedule shall last at least two hours except on occasion when, in the opinion of the instructor, it is desirable in the interests of safety to curtail the practice. At some of the practices the breathing apparatus shall be worn continuously for two hours.

FIRE AND RESCUE

First Aid Box

A first aid box containing equipment described below is approved for the purposes of Regulation 23(*d*):

1 set of splints
12 triangular bandages
24 roller bandages of various sizes
36 sterilised dressings of assorted sizes
2 rolls of cotton wool—1 lb. each
1 packet of surgical lint—1 lb.
2 rolls adhesive tape
1 eye bath
1 tube of suitable eye cream
6 tubes of antiseptic cream
2 small boxes of safety pins
1 pair of small scissors
1 tourniquet (one 2½″ rubber bandage may be substituted).

FIREDAMP DRAINAGE

THE COAL MINES

(FIREDAMP DRAINAGE) REGULATIONS 1960

S.I. 1960 No. 1015

Commencement and citation

1. These regulations shall come into operation on the first day of July, nineteen hundred and sixty, and may be cited as the Coal Mines (Firedamp Drainage) Regulations 1960.

Interpretation

2. (1) In these regulations the following expressions have the meanings hereby respectively assigned to them, that is to say—

'borehole' has the meaning assigned thereto in regulation five;

'calorimeter room' has the meaning assigned thereto in regulation twelve;

'firedamp' means any inflammable mixture of gases, or any inflammable gas, naturally occurring in a mine;

'firedamp drainage' means the collecting of firedamp in a mine before it has been diluted by any ventilation therein and its safe disposal;

'firedamp drainage system' includes any system of firedamp drainage other than one which consists merely of a pipe placed in a roadside pack for the purpose of collecting firedamp which has accumulated behind the pack and conveying it to a point in the road where it can be discharged safely;

'mine' has the meaning assigned thereto in regulation three;

'the Minister' means the Minister of Power.

(2) The Interpretation Act 1889 shall apply to the interpretation of these regulations as it applies to the interpretation of an Act of Parliament.

Application

3. These regulations shall apply to every mine of coal, and in these regulations 'mine' means such a mine.

Exemptions

4. An inspector may by notice served on the manager of any mine exempt the mine or part thereof, or any thing or class of things thereat, from the application of any provision of these regulations if he is satisfied that the safety of persons employed at the mine will not be prejudiced in consequence of the granting of the exemption.

Boreholes

5. (1) The manager of every mine shall ensure that before any person drills any hole required for the purpose of tapping firedamp and draining it through any firedamp drainage system (hereinafter referred to as a 'borehole') there is available a pipe in which any firedamp that may be tapped may be collected and conveyed to a point where it may be discharged safely.

(2) No person shall drill any borehole unless, as soon as the depth of the borehole renders it practicable, the borehole is drilled through a device with which the borehole may be sealed in the event of a sudden flow of firedamp from it.

(3) Before any person commences to drill any borehole in stone he shall ensure that water is flowing through the drill rods, and, after commencing to drill any such borehole and for as long as the rods continue to rotate, he shall ensure that water continues to flow through the drill rods and is flowing out of the mouth of the borehole.

6. The manager of every mine shall ensure that facilities are provided at each borehole to permit the measurement from time to time of the percentage by volume of inflammable gas in the gaseous mixture flowing through the borehole.

Stand pipes

7. The manager of every mine shall make and ensure the efficient carrying out of arrangements to secure that—

(*a*) each stand pipe forming part of a firedamp drainage system is so inserted and sealed in the borehole from which it leads that leakage of firedamp or air around the pipe is minimised; and

(*b*) no such stand pipe is joined to a pipe range by other than a flexible connection.

Pipe Ranges

8. The manager of every mine shall ensure that—

(*a*) no pipe range forming part of a firedamp drainage system is installed in any shaft or outlet, being a shaft or outlet through which air enters the mine; and

(*b*) each such pipe range installed in the mine is—

(i) so designed and constructed as to permit, at suitable places along its length, samples of the firedamp flowing through it to be taken and water to be drained from it;

(ii) adequately supported; and

(iii) so painted that there is a yellow band near to every joint in the range.

9. The manager of every mine shall ensure that no pipe is connected to any pipe range through which firedamp is flowing unless it is connected in a way which will minimise the amount of air drawn into the pipe range.

Valves

10. The manager of every mine shall ensure that each valve in any firedamp drainage system is painted yellow.

Exhausters

11. The manager of every mine shall ensure that—

(*a*) no exhauster is installed in any firedamp drainage system unless—

(i) it is of a type and description approved by the Minister;

(ii) it is so constructed and installed that when it is not working firedamp will not be able to flow through the exhauster in the reverse direction to that in which it would flow if the exhauster were working; and

(iii) it and the system are so arranged that when the exhauster is not working the firedamp may be caused to by-pass the exhauster and allowed to flow freely through the system; and

(*b*) no exhauster forming part of any firedamp drainage system is used to pump firedamp unless it is connected to earth in such a manner as will ensure immediate electrical discharge without danger.

Exhauster houses and calorimeter rooms

12. (1) The manager of every mine shall ensure that—

(*a*) no exhauster is installed on the surface in any firedamp drainage system unless it is housed in a suitably constructed building or part thereof (such a building or part thereof being hereinafter referred to as an 'exhauster house') which shall be used exclusively for the purpose; and

(*b*) no electrical apparatus is installed in any exhauster house or at any place on the surface where firedamp is monitored or its heat content is ascertained (such a place being hereinafter referred to as a 'calorimeter room') unless it is of a type which the Minister has certified as being intrinsically safe or flameproof.

(2) No person shall take into or use in any exhauster house or calorimeter room any lamp or light other than a permitted light:

Provided that nothing in this paragraph shall prevent the taking into, or use in, a calorimeter room of—

(*a*) any calorimeter or device for monitoring firedamp, being a calorimeter or device which depends for its operation on a naked flame; or

(*b*) any light for the purpose of lighting any such calorimeter or monitoring device therein.

(3) After the first day of July, nineteen hundred and sixty-one, no such calorimeter or monitoring device shall be used in connection with any firedamp drainage system unless it is contained in an enclosure which is ventilated independently of the calorimeter room.

(4) No person shall open any enclosure provided pursuant to the last preceding paragraph or take into, or use in, any calorimeter room any naked light unless he has satisfied himself that it is safe to do so.

Discharge of firedamp

13. The manager of every mine shall ensure that—

(*a*) each point of discharge of every firedamp drainage system, not being a point of discharge into a utilisation plant, is, so far as is practicable, kept free from anything likely to ignite firedamp;

(*b*) each such system which discharges firedamp on the surface is fitted with a sufficient number of suitable flame traps to prevent flames from entering the system from each point of discharge on the surface;

(*c*) no such system discharges into a utilisation plant firedamp containing less than forty per cent by volume of inflammable gas;

(*d*) no such system discharges firedamp into any intake airway; and

(*e*) no such system discharges firedamp below ground except at a point of discharge which is surrounded by a fence placed at such a distance from it as will ensure that the percentage of inflammable gas in the air at each part of the fence during any discharge of firedamp at that point will not exceed two per cent by volume.

Supervision of exhausters and pressure control chambers

14. The manager of every mine in which a firedamp drainage system has been installed which contains an exhauster or a pressure control chamber or both, shall appoint and instruct in their duties competent persons to be in charge of such apparatus and shall make arrangements to secure that each piece of such apparatus when in use is in the personal charge of a person so instructed and appointed.

APPROVED SPECIFICATION FOR THE PURPOSES OF THE COAL MINES (FIREDAMP DRAINAGE) REGULATIONS 1960

Exhausters of the type described below are approved for the purposes of Regulation 11(a)(i):

Venturis made exclusively of metal, other than aluminium or magnesium, and depending for their operation on a supply of compressed air or water, or both, to the jet or jets thereof.

When installed in any firedamp drainage system this type must be electrically bonded to the pipe range with which it is connected.

FIRST AID

THE COAL AND OTHER MINES

(FIRST AID) REGULATIONS 1962

S.I. 1962 No. 1423

Arrangement of Regulations

PART I

General

Commencement and citation

1. These regulations shall come into operation on the 1st January, 1963, and may be cited as the Coal and Other Mines (First Aid) Regulations 1962.

Interpretation

2. (1) In these regulations the following expressions have the meanings hereby respectively assigned to them, that is to say—

'the Act' means the Mines and Quarries Act 1954;

'approved' means approved by the Minister of Power;

'deputy's district' has the meaning assigned thereto in the Coal and Other Mines (Managers and Officials) Regulations 1956;

'enrolled nurse' means a person enrolled in either the roll of nurses maintained for England and Wales under section 2 (1) (*b*) of the Nurses Act 1957, as amended by the Nurses (Amendment) Act 1961, or the roll of nurses maintained for Scotland under section 3 (1) of the Nurses (Scotland) Act 1951, as so amended;

'mine' has the meaning assigned thereto in regulation 3;

'registered medical practitioner' has the same meaning as is assigned to the expression 'fully registered person' in section 54 of the Medical Act 1956;

'registered nurse' means a person registered in either the general part of the register maintained for England and Wales under section 2 (1) (*a*) of the Nurses Act 1957, or the general part of the register maintained for Scotland under section 2 of the Nurses (Scotland) Act 1951.

(2) Expressions to which meanings are assigned by the Act or by these regulations shall (unless the contrary intention appears) have the same meanings in any document issued under the provisions of these regulations.

(3) The Interpretation Act 1889 shall apply to the interpretation of these regulations as it applies to the interpretation of an Act of Parliament.

Application

3. These regulations shall apply (except where the contrary is provided) to every mine of coal, stratified ironstone, shale or fireclay, and in these regulations 'mine' means such a mine.

PART II

Surface organisation

First Aid room

4. (1) The manager of every mine at which at any one time there are more than fifty persons at work shall secure the provision on the surface thereat of—

(*a*) a first aid room which shall—

(i) be so situated that it is near to, and there is easy access thereto from, a shaft or outlet normally used by persons employed below ground thereat, and that ambulances may approach it without difficulty, and that it does not communicate with any sanitary conveniences except through a ventilated space;

(ii) have a floor area of not less than one hundred and fifty square feet;

(iii) have interior surfaces which may easily be kept in a clean and dust free condition;

(iv) be fitted with a glazed, stainless steel or other suitable sink and suitable drainage therefor, and a telephone connected to the telephone system of the mine; and

(v) be easily identifiable from the outside by the prominent display of the words 'First Aid' or 'Medical Centre';

(*b*) waiting accommodation which shall—

(i) be so situated that there is convenient access to the first aid room therefrom;

(ii) be indoors; and

(iii) be furnished with seats; and

(*c*) sanitary conveniences which shall be situated near the first aid room unless there is easy access to constantly available sanitary conveniences therefrom.

(2) The manager of every mine at which a first aid room is provided pursuant to paragraph (1) of this regulation shall make and ensure the efficient carrying out of arrangements to secure that—

(*a*) the first aid room—

(i) is used exclusively for first aid or medical work;

(ii) is provided with adequate means for its heating and lighting and is kept ventilated by clean and fresh air;

(iii) is kept clean and properly maintained; and

(iv) has readily available hot and cold running water;

(*b*) the waiting accommodation provided pursuant to sub-paragraph (*b*) of the preceding paragraph—

(i) is provided with adequate means for its heating and lighting and is kept ventilated by clean and fresh air; and

(ii) is kept clean and properly maintained;

(*c*) any sanitary conveniences provided pursuant to sub-paragraph (*c*) of the preceding paragraph—

(i) are provided with adequate means for their lighting; and

(ii) are kept clean and properly maintained.

(3) In every such first aid room there shall be provided—

(*a*) a stretcher and separate facilities for its support at carrying level when loaded, blankets and hot-water bottles;

(*b*) a couch and either a bench or at least two chairs;

(*c*) splints suitable for the immobilisation of any injured limb and appropriate bandages and padding therefor;

(*d*) suitably filled sandbags in waterproof coverings, being sandbags designed to prevent the movement of broken bones;

(*e*) an adequate supply of wholesome drinking water;

(*f*) plain wound dressings and roller bandages;

(*g*) sterilized cotton wool in half ounce packets and adhesive wound dressings of an approved type*;

(*h*) approved eye ointment in a container of an approved type and size*, sterilized eye pads in separate sealed packets and a bottle suitable for washing eyes;

(*i*) a rubber bandage or pressure bandage, scissors and safety pins;

(*j*) soap, towels and a nail brush; and

(*k*) clean white aprons, coats or overalls suitable for use by persons rendering first aid.

5. The manager of every mine at which a first aid room is provided pursuant to regulation 4 (1) shall appoint persons to be in charge thereof, each of whom shall be a registered medical practitioner, a registered nurse, an enrolled nurse, or subject to regulation 18 a holder of an approved qualification in first aid†, and shall make arrangements to secure that one such person is on duty in the first aid room while the main body of workmen is entering or leaving the mine and is readily available while any person is working at the mine.

---

*See page 149.
†See page 150.

First aid accommodation at smaller mines

6. (1) The manager of every mine other than a mine referred to in regulation 4 (1) shall ensure that there is constantly available on the surface thereat or adjacent thereto a room where first aid may be rendered to persons who while employed at the mine suffer bodily injury or become ill, which room shall—

(*a*) be provided with adequate means for its heating and lighting;

(*b*) have interior surfaces which may easily be kept in a clean and dust free condition; and

(*c*) have readily available hot and cold water.

(2) The manager of every such mine shall make and ensure the efficient carrying out of arrangements to secure that the room is kept clean and properly maintained, and ventilated by clean and fresh air.

(3) In every such room or in some other suitable place there shall be provided—

(*a*) a stretcher and separate facilities for its support at carrying level when loaded, blankets and hot-water bottles;

(*b*) a couch and either a bench or at least two chairs;

(*c*) splints suitable for the immobilisation of any injured limb and appropriate bandages and padding therefor;

(*d*) suitably filled sandbags in waterproof coverings, being sandbags designed to prevent the movement of broken bones;

(*e*) an adequate supply of wholesome drinking water;

(*f*) soap, towels and a nail brush; and

(*g*) a first aid box clearly marked 'First Aid' and containing only first aid materials including the materials specified in the next following paragraph and one copy of a first aid leaflet approved* for the purpose.

(4) Each such first aid box shall contain—

(*a*) plain wound dressings of large, medium and small sizes, and roller bandages;

(*b*) sterilized cotton wool in half ounce packets and adhesive wound dressings of an approved type†;

(*c*) approved eye ointment in a container of an approved type and size†, sterilized eye pads in separate sealed packets and a bottle suitable for washing eyes; and

(*d*) a rubber bandage or pressure bandage, scissors and safety pins.

(5) The manager of every such mine shall appoint persons to be in charge of the room and equipment therein each of whom shall be, subject to regulation 18, a holder of an approved qualification in first aid‡, and shall make arrangements to secure that one such person is readily available while any person is working at the mine.

---

*M. & Q. Form No. 264.
†See page 149.
‡See page 150.

Part III

Underground organisation

7. This Part of these regulations shall not apply to—

(*a*) a mine consisting merely of a shaft or unwalkable outlet in the course of being sunk or driven; or

(*b*) a mine, other than such a mine as is described in paragraph (*a*), at which the total number of persons employed below ground is less than thirty:

Provided that an inspector, if he is of the opinion that the organisation of first aid or first aid equipment provided on the surface of any such mine as is mentioned in paragraph (*b*) of this regulation is inadequate to ensure prompt first aid treatment below ground, may by notice served on the manager thereof, require him to comply with the provisions of this Part of these regulations, and this Part of these regulations shall apply to that mine until that notice is withdrawn.

8. (1) The manager of every mine to which this Part of these regulations applies shall appoint persons for the purposes of this regulation, being persons who, subject to regulation 18, hold an approved qualification* in first aid, and shall make and ensure the efficient carrying out of arrangements to secure that—

(*a*) there is in each deputy's district on each shift one person so appointed for each fifty persons, and one such person for any person or persons not thus taken into account, in the total number of persons wholly or mainly employed in that district on that shift; and

(*b*) there is in the remainder of the mine below ground on each shift one person so appointed for each thirty persons, and one person so appointed for any person or persons not thus taken into account, in the total number of persons wholly or mainly employed therein on that shift.

(2) The arrangements mentioned in the preceding paragraph shall include in any case where the manager of a mine is unable to appoint a sufficient number of persons to enable him to comply with the provisions of sub-paragraphs (*a*) and (*b*) of that paragraph—

(*a*) the provision of facilities for the training in first aid of a sufficient number of persons and the making of reasonable efforts to induce appropriate persons to be so trained; and

(*b*) the making of reasonable efforts to induce persons with the requisite qualifications to accept the appointment, where such persons are available.

(3) In any prosecution for a contravention of the provisions of paragraph (1) of this regulation it shall be a defence to prove that the failure to comply with the provisions was due to either—

(*a*) an insufficiency of persons with the requisite qualifications; or

(*b*) an insufficiency of persons with the requisite qualifications willing to accept the appointment;

---

*See page 150.

and that the manager of the mine has made and ensured the efficient carrying out of the arrangements specified in the last preceding paragraph.

(4) There shall be provided in the covered accommodation provided in pursuance of section 135 of the Act and in the first aid room provided in pursuance of regulation 4 (1) or the room provided in pursuance of regulation 6 (1) (as the case may be) a notice stating the names of the persons for the time being appointed in pursuance of paragraph (1) of this regulation.

9. (1) The manager of every mine to which this Part of these regulations applies shall make and ensure the efficient carrying out of arrangements to secure that each person required to be in any deputy's district or in the remainder of the mine below ground by regulation 8 (1) is in charge of and has readily available to him a first aid container which shall—

(*a*) be marked with the words 'First Aid'; and

(*b*) contain only first aid materials including not less than—

(i) two large plain wound dressings;

(ii) two small plain wound dressings; and

(iii) six adhesive wound dressings of an approved type and of assorted sizes.

(2) Each person in charge of a first aid container in pursuance of the preceding paragraph shall at the end of his shift deliver it to a place appointed by the manager, and the manager shall appoint a suitable place for the purpose and shall make arrangements to secure that each first aid container so delivered at the end of a shift to such place is examined by a competent person and, where necessary, replenished by that person, before it is reissued.

First Aid stations

10. (1) The manager of every mine to which this Part of these regulations applies shall ensure that there shall be at all times in force a scheme specifying positions in the mine suitable to be used as places for the storage of first aid materials (hereinafter referred to as 'first aid stations'), and he shall ensure that first aid stations are provided at each position so specified.

(2) Each such scheme shall provide for the provision of first aid stations at appropriate positions in relation to—

(*a*) each working face and other parts of each deputy's district;

(*b*) each road in which persons travel or work, otherwise than occasionally or for short periods; and

(*c*) the pit bottom.

(3) Each such scheme or a copy thereof shall be kept at the office of the mine or at such other place as an inspector may approve.

(4) If an inspector is of the opinion that it is desirable that the scheme should be amended, he may serve on the manager a notice stating that he is of that opinion and requiring him to make such amendment to the scheme as may be specified in the notice.

(5) The provisions of Part XV of the Act with respect to references upon notices served by inspectors shall apply to a notice served under the last preceding paragraph, and the relevant grounds of objection shall be that compliance with any requirement sought to be imposed by, or by virtue of the notice, is wholly, or to a particular extent, unnecessary, inadvisable for reasons of safety or impracticable.

11. (1) The manager shall make arrangements to secure that there are provided and maintained in good order and ready for immediate use at each first aid station—

(*a*) a suitable stretcher and blankets adequately protected against dust and dampness;

(*b*) splints suitable for the immobilisation of any injured limb;

(*c*) a suitable container, marked with the words 'First Aid' and containing appropriate bandages and padding for use with the splints, not less than six large plain wound dressings, and a rubber bandage or pressure bandage; and

(*d*) two small, clean sandbags for use when suitably filled in cases of head and neck injuries.

(2) The manager shall make and ensure the efficient carrying out of arrangements to secure that—

(*a*) a notice, clearly inscribed with the words 'First Aid Station' and prominently placed in the road in which the first aid station is situated, or from which the first aid station is accessible, indicates the position of each first aid station; and

(*b*) the position of each first aid station is marked on—

(i) the sketch of the mine provided pursuant to regulation 11 of the Coal and Other Mines (Surveyors and Plans) Regulations 1956; and

(ii) the appropriate plan provided pursuant to regulation 28 of the Coal and Other Mines (Fire and Rescue) Regulations 1956.

PART IV

Conveyance of injured or sick persons

12. The manager of every mine to which Part III of these regulations applies shall make arrangements to secure the provision below ground thereat of a wheeled carriage, suitable for underground conditions and methods of transport and for conveying an injured or sick person to the bottom of the shaft or unwalkable outlet through which such a person is to be raised to the surface, or where such a person is to be conveyed through a walkable outlet, to the surface.

13. The manager of every mine shall make arrangements to secure the provision of a suitable appliance for the safe conveyance of injured or sick persons—

(*a*) at every shaft, staple-pit or unwalkable outlet through which injured or sick persons may be carried and in which the cage or carriage is not large enough to permit of a stretcher being laid flat therein;

(*b*) at every shaft, staple-pit or unwalkable outlet through which persons are carried otherwise than in a cage or carriage;

(*c*) at every shaft, staple-pit or unwalkable outlet in the course of being sunk or driven; and

(*d*) in every mine containing workings of a gradient 1 : 5 or more.

Ambulances

14. The owner of every mine shall make such arrangements as will secure that—

(*a*) an effective motor ambulance service is available for the conveyance, where necessary, to hospitals or their homes of persons who while employed at the mine suffer bodily injury or become ill;

(*b*) there is always readily available at the mine, while any person is working thereat, a competent person whose duty it is to summon an ambulance if needed in cases of injury or illness.

PART V

Miscellaneous provisions

Maintenance of accommodation and equipment

15. The manager of every mine shall make and secure the efficient carrying out of arrangements to secure that all accommodation, equipment, materials and appliances provided in pursuance of any provision of these regulations, other than any first aid container in a person's charge in pursuance of regulation 9 (1), are inspected by a competent person appointed by him for the purpose at suitable intervals, which, in the case of any equipment, materials and appliances provided below ground in the mine, shall not exceed seven days, and which, in any other case, shall not exceed such intervals as the manager may appoint, and such competent person shall forthwith cause any defect which he discovers in any equipment or appliance to be remedied, and any materials, equipment or appliances which he discovers are missing or have been used, to be replaced.

Standard of dressings

16. Every dressing provided in pursuance of these regulations and in respect of which a standard is specified in the British Pharmaceutical Codex, including any supplement thereto, being a supplement current at the date of these regulations or approved for the purposes of this regulation, shall be of a grade or quality not lower than that standard.

Facilities and equipment

17. The provisions of these regulations with regard to the provision of facilities and equipment for the purpose of rendering first aid shall be without prejudice to the generality of section 91 (1) of the Act.

First Aid qualifications

18. (1) After the 31st December, 1964, no person who is qualified to be appointed for the purposes of regulation 5 or of regulation 6 (5) or of regulation

8 (1) solely by reason of an approved qualification in first aid* shall be appointed for any of such purposes unless he has held the approved qualification for not more than three years.

(2) After the 31st December, 1964, any person so qualified and appointed for any of such purposes shall cease to hold such an appointment when he has held his most recent qualification for a period of three years:

Provided that where it is not practicable for a person so appointed to be examined with a view to obtaining a fresh approved qualification within three months next preceding the expiration of that period, he may continue to hold that appointment until the expiration of a further period of three months or until he has been so examined whichever is the sooner.

Exemptions

19. An inspector may by notice served on the manager of any mine exempt that mine or any part thereof from the application of any provision of these regulations if he is satisfied that the comfort and health of any person who, while employed at the mine, suffers bodily injury or becomes ill, will not be prejudiced by the granting of the exemption.

Revocation

20. The Coal and Other Mines (First Aid) Regulations 1956 are hereby revoked.

---

*See page 150.

APPROVED SPECIFICATIONS FOR THE PURPOSES OF THE COAL AND OTHER MINES (FIRST AID) REGULATIONS, 1962

Adhesive Wound Dressing

The adhesive wound dressing described below is approved for the purposes of Regulations 4(3)(g), 6(4)(b) and 9(1)(b)(iii):

An adhesive wound dressing shall consist of a pad fixed to a piece of plaster, waterproof or otherwise, as centrally as possible so as to leave an adequate margin of adhesive surface all round. The pad and the margin of adhesive surface shall be protected by muslin or other suitable material for removal before use. The pad shall be either a piece of unmedicated absorbent lint or other suitable material *or* a piece of absorbent lint or other suitable material containing one or other of the following substances in not more than the strength specified:—

Boric Acid	5%
Aminacrine Hydrochloride	0·1%
Chlorhexidine Hydrochloride	0·1%
Euflavine	0·15%
Domiphen Bromide	0·15%
Bismuth Subgallate	2·5%

Each dressing shall be put up in an individual sealed pack marked clearly to indicate content.

Eye Ointment and container

The eye ointment and container described below are approved for the purposes of Regulations 4(3)(h) and 6(4)(c):

The eye ointment referred to as Sulphacetamide Eye Ointment in the British Pharmacopoeia, 1958, to contain not less than six per cent or more than ten per cent Sulphacetamide Sodium; or a Sulphacetamide Eye Ointment of similar strength in a suitable water miscible base. The Sulphacetamide Sodium shall conform to the standard prescribed in the British Pharmacopoeia, 1958.

The eye ointment shall be packed in a sterilized collapsible opaque tube with nozzle and cap. Each tube shall contain sixty grains of the ointment and shall be clearly marked "Sulphacetamide Eye Ointment". The content of Sulphacetamide Sodium shall also be clearly marked on the tube.

Qualification in First Aid

The qualifications listed below are approved for the purposes of Regulations 5, 6(5) and 8(1):

(1) The following qualifications, granted in relation to a standard or adult course in first aid:

Title of Qualifications	*Body by which issued*
Initial Certificate Advanced Certificate Proficiency Badge Certificate Proficiency Bar Certificate	The British Red Cross Society
First Year Certificate Second Year Certificate and Medallion Re-examination Certificate	St. Andrew's Ambulance Association
The Certificate Re-examination Certificate (The Voucher) Re-examination Certificate (The Medallion) Re-examination Certificate (The Medallion Label)	The St. John Ambulance Association

(2) The First Aid Certificate granted as a qualification to render first aid in mining accidents by:

The University of Birmingham
King's College in the University of Durham
The University of Leeds

GENERAL DUTIES AND CONDUCT

THE COAL AND OTHER MINES

(GENERAL DUTIES AND CONDUCT) REGULATIONS 1956

S.I. 1956 No. 1761

1. These regulations shall apply to every mine of coal, stratified ironstone, shale or fireclay, and in these regulations 'mine' means such a mine.

2. (1) Without prejudice to the generality of subsection (3) of section three of the Act, every person employed at a mine shall obey any instruction relating to safety, health or welfare given to him by any person upon whom duties are laid by any regulation, being an instruction given by that person for the purpose of the performance of those duties.

(2) No person so employed shall impede or obstruct any other person in the performance of such duties.

3. (1) No person shall enter any cage at the top of or in any shaft unless authorised to do so by the banksman or by an onsetter as the case may be.

(2) No person riding in any such cage shall—

(*a*) interfere with or attempt to open the gates thereof; or

(*b*) attempt to leave such cage until it is stationary at a landing place.

(3) Nothing in paragraph (1) or sub-paragraph (*a*) of paragraph (2) of this regulation shall apply to a person authorised in writing by the manager to transmit signals when below ground at an entrance to a shaft and when no onsetter is in attendance at that entrance.

4. (1) Except under the authority of an official of the mine or in a case of emergency no person employed in any mine shall travel below ground to or from his work by any road other than those notified by the manager for the purpose or go into any part of the mine which it is not necessary for him to enter for the purpose of his work.

(2) Except under the authority of an official of the mine no person shall pass beyond any enclosure or barrier or danger signal or open any locked door.

(3) No person shall go into any engine house except for the performance of his duties or under the authority of an official of the mine.

5. (1) Every person engaged at any working face (including a place in a road at which ripping or work of repair is in progress) or in setting or withdrawing supports shall make a careful examination of his working place at the beginning of each period of work and at appropriate times during the course of it, and in particular after any shot has been fired thereat or nearby and after any other interruption of work:

Provided that where several persons are working at a place together and one of them is in charge, it shall be sufficient for such examinations to be made by that person.

(2) Every person so engaged shall to the best of his power leave his working place at the end of his period of work in such condition as to allow work to be resumed there safely. If he is unable to do so, he shall, without prejudice to the generality of section eighty of the Act, fence off the place and report the matter forthwith to an official of the mine.

(3) Every person so engaged shall take any necessary steps to avoid interruption of the ventilation of the mine whether by accumulations of mineral, vehicles or stores.

6. (1) No person shall interfere with any machinery at a mine or operate any machinery required by or under the Act or by the manager of the mine to be operated in compliance with signals or which if not so required is capable of developing more than ten horse-power except—

(*a*) a mechanic or electrician of the mine;

(*b*) a person carrying out duties in relation thereto in pursuance of an instruction in writing by the manager;

(*c*) in emergency for the purpose of cutting off the supply of power.

(2) No person shall interfere with any electrical apparatus at a mine or operate any such apparatus which works at a voltage exceeding twenty-five except—

(*a*) an electrician of the mine;

(*b*) a person carrying out duties in relation thereto in pursuance of an instruction in writing by the manager;

(*c*) in emergency for the purpose of cutting off the supply of power.

7. No person in a mine shall brush or waft out any inflammable gas.

8. (1) No person employed below ground at a mine shall leave his working place without taking his lamp or light with him.

(2) No loose material which is burning shall be left unattended below ground otherwise than in pursuance of section seventy-nine or section eighty of the Act.

9. (1) Every person at a mine whether on the surface or below ground shall behave in an orderly manner.

(2) No person shall be at a mine in a state of intoxication or without the permission of the manager shall bring any intoxicating liquor to a mine.

(3) No person shall sleep whilst below ground in any mine or whilst in charge of any machinery or boiler upon the surface.

10. (1) In these regulations the following expressions have the meanings hereby respectively assigned to them, that is to say—

'the Act' means the Mines and Quarries Act 1954;

'banksman' and 'onsetter' have the meanings assigned thereto by the Coal and Other Mines (Shafts, Outlets and Roads) Regulations 1956;*

'electrical apparatus', 'electrician of the mine' and 'mechanic of the mine' have the meanings assigned thereto by the Coal and Other Mines (Mechanics and Electricians) Regulations 1956;†

'mine' has the meaning assigned thereto by regulation one.

(2) The Interpretation Act 1889, shall apply to the interpretation of these regulations as it applies to the interpretation of an act of Parliament.

---

*Now replaced by the Coal and Other Mines (Shafts, Outlets and Roads) Regulations 1960—see page 229.

†Now replaced by the Coal and Other Mines (Mechanics and Electricians) Regulations 1965—see page 191.

HORSES

THE COAL AND OTHER MINES

(HORSES) REGULATIONS 1956

S.I. 1956 No. 1777

Application

1. These regulations shall apply to every mine of coal, stratified ironstone, shale or fireclay, and in these regulations 'mine' means such a mine.

Age and health of horses employed below ground

2. No horse shall—

(*a*) be taken below ground at a mine unless it has attained the age of four years; or

(*b*) be taken or allowed to be below ground at a mine if it is blind.

3. No horse shall be taken below ground at a mine unless as shortly as practicable before being so taken it has been subjected to a test for the purpose of ascertaining whether it is suffering from glanders, and has been certified to be free therefrom, by a duly registered veterinary surgeon (in these regulations referred to as a 'veterinary surgeon').

4. (1) It shall be the duty of the manager of every mine to ensure that every horse employed below ground at that mine is, at intervals not exceeding twelve months, examined by a veterinary surgeon.

(2) A report of every such examination (including a certificate as to the fitness or permanent or temporary unfitness of the horse concerned for work or for work below ground at the mine, as the case may be) shall forthwith be recorded in the book* in which the record relating to that horse is required to be kept in pursuance of paragraph (1) of regulation ten of these regulations, and signed by the veterinary surgeon who made the examination.

(3) Any horse certified as aforesaid to be permanently unfit for work or for work below ground at a mine shall (if below ground) forthwith be brought to the surface.

(4) No horse certified as aforesaid to be permanently or temporarily unfit for work shall be disposed of alive otherwise than for immediate destruction or to a home of rest maintained for the reception of animals not then fit for work or to a responsible person not carrying on the business of dealing in horses.

(5) Where a horse, having been certified as aforesaid to be permanently unfit for work or for work below ground at a mine, is destroyed or otherwise disposed of, a statement of the manner of that disposal shall be recorded forthwith by a

---

*M. & Q. Form No. 265.

person appointed for the purpose by the manager in the book* in which the record relating to that horse was last required to be kept in pursuance of paragraph (1) of regulation ten of these regulations.

Carriage of horses

5. No horse shall be carried through any part of a mine on a vehicle except when it is impracticable or dangerous for it to walk because of an accident in that mine, or when the horse has been injured or is ill:

Provided that nothing in this regulation shall restrict the carrying of any horse by means of winding or haulage apparatus through a shaft or staple-pit or on an incline, being an incline too steep for that horse to walk thereon with safety.

Prohibition of riding on horses

6. No person shall ride on a horse below ground at a mine.

Periods of employment of horses

7. (1) No horse shall be allowed to be out of its stable for the purpose of work during any period—

(*a*) of twenty-four hours, during more than two shifts;

(*b*) of forty-eight hours, during more than three shifts; or

(*c*) of seven days, during more than seven shifts or for more than forty-eight hours in the aggregate:

Provided that nothing in this regulation shall restrict the working of any horse where necessary through unforseen circumstances for the purpose of—

(i) saving life;

(ii) remedying the effect of an accident; or

(iii) avoiding serious interference with ordinary work in the mine.

(2) It shall be the duty of the appropriate horse-keeper to ensure compliance with the provisions of the last preceding paragraph.

(3) For the purposes of this regulation the period of work on any day (excluding any overtime) of any person under whose charge a horse is when out of its stable shall be regarded as a shift.

Appointment and duties of horse-keepers

8. The manager of every mine shall make and secure the efficient carrying out of arrangements whereby a competent person appointed for the purpose by the manager (in these regulations referred to as a 'horse-keeper') has the care of each horse employed below ground at the mine when it is in a stable at that mine, and without prejudice to the generality of that requirement the number of horse-keepers so appointed shall not be less than one for each fifteen horses, and one for any number of horses not thus taken into account, in the total number of horses employed below ground at that mine.

*M. & Q. Form No. 265.

9. Every horse-keeper shall—

(*a*) ensure that no horse for the time being under his care leaves its stable, for the purpose of work, in an unfit condition, improperly shod or wearing harness otherwise than of a proper fit and in good condition and having a guard for the eyes; and

(*b*) forthwith after the return to its stable of any horse for the time being under his care, examine that horse and its harness, attend to any injury to that horse, and clean and groom it or cause it to be cleaned and groomed.

10. (1) In the case of every mine at which any horse is employed, there shall be kept, in a book* provided for the purpose by the owner of the mine, a record of each horse for the time being so employed.

(2) Every horse-keeper shall, with respect to every horse for the time being under his care, make a full and accurate report every day in the book provided in pursuance of the last preceding paragraph, stating in particular—

(*a*) the condition of the horse;

(*b*) the name of every person (other than the horse-keeper) who has been in charge of it;

(*c*) in any case in which it has been taken from its stable, the times at which it was taken therefrom and returned thereto;

(*d*) the nature and period of any working of that horse for any purpose specified in the proviso to paragraph (1) of regulation seven of these regulations, being working which, but for the operation of that proviso, would be prohibited by that regulation;

(*e*) the nature of any report made to or by him in pursuance of paragraph (2) of regulation fourteen or paragraph (1) of regulation fifteen (as the case may be) of these regulations, and the nature of any action known by him to have been taken as a consequence of that report; and

(*f*) any other information for which provision is made in that book.

Construction, equipment and use of stables

11. (1) The manager shall ensure that no stable below ground at a mine is used to house any horse unless—

(*a*) no part of it is in a road on which any person travels to or from his working place, vehicles (other than vehicles used for the servicing of the stable) run or conveyors are operated;

(*b*) it is provided with suitable and sufficient artificial lighting;

(*c*) it is ventilated by air which has not ventilated any working face;

(*d*) there is provided, at its return end, one loose box, of adequate size to house the largest horse for the time being in that stable, for each twenty-five horses, and one such loose box for any number of horses not thus taken into account, in the total number of horses for the time being housed in that stable;

---

*M. & Q. Form No. 265.

(*e*) there are provided one or more drinking troughs, so constructed as to be easily drained and cleaned, being adequate in aggregate length and capacity for the horses for the time being housed in that stable;

(*f*) the floor throughout is paved or of concrete; and suitable drainage is provided for every stall and loose box therein; and

(*g*) every roof, wall and partition (other than a roof, wall or partition which has been painted or is made of slate, tiles, glazed brick or iron) has been limewashed before being so used and at intervals not exceeding three months during such use.

(2) The manager shall ensure that no stall below ground at a mine is used—

(*a*) to house more than one horse;

(*b*) to house any horse, unless it is fitted with a manger.

(3) The manager shall make and secure the efficient carrying out of arrangements to ensure that every horse below ground at the mine is provided with accommodation in a stable and, except when in a loose box, in a stall of adequate size for that horse.

12. The manager of every mine at which any horses are employed below ground shall make and secure the carrying out of efficient arrangements to ensure that—

(*a*) every stable in use is cleaned daily, and kept in a sanitary condition;

(*b*) an adequate supply of clean straw or other suitable bedding is provided for the use of every horse in a stable;

(*c*) there is provided daily, and so far as practicable protected from dust and other deleterious substances before it is consumed, an adequate supply of wholesome food and wholesome drinking water for every horse for consumption while the horse is in its stable and while it is out of its stable for the purpose of working;

(*d*) every receptacle for such food and water is so far as practicable so constructed as to protect the contents from dust and other deleterious substances;

(*e*) an adequate supply of medicines, ointments and dressings of a kind suitable for horses, and suitable and sufficient apparatus for the destruction of horses requiring to be destroyed, are provided and kept readily available for use.

Duties of persons in charge of horses outside the stables

13. (1) The manager shall make and secure the efficient carrying out of arrangements to ensure that every horse below ground at the mine is, when out of its stable, under the charge of a person appointed for that purpose.

(2) Every person appointed in pursuance of the last preceding paragraph, when in charge of a horse out of its stable, shall—

(*a*) be responsible for that horse throughout the period from his taking charge of it until he returns it to a horse-keeper at its stable or otherwise disposes of it in accordance with an order given to him by an official of the mine or a horse-keeper;

(*b*) when driving it, do so carefully;

(*c*) comply with any instructions relating to the horse given to him by an official of the mine or a horse-keeper;

(*d*) in every case in which the horse is out of its stable for a period exceeding four hours, feed and water it, or cause it to be fed and watered during that period;

(*e*) unless otherwise ordered by an official of the mine or a horse-keeper, return it not later than the end of his shift to a horse-keeper at its stable;

(*f*) unless the horse is properly secured, remain with it throughout the period during which it is in his charge.

14. (1) No person shall at any time work a horse below ground at a mine if

(*a*) it is unfit;

(*b*) it is not properly shod; or

(*c*) it is wearing harness which does not fit properly or is not in good condition or is without a guard for the eyes.

(2) In any case in which a person, other than a horse-keeper, for the time being in charge of a horse below ground at a mine has reason to believe that—

(*a*) the horse is unfit, is injured, or shows any symptoms of overwork; or

(*b*) the horse is not properly shod; or

(*c*) the horse is wearing harness which does not fit properly or which is not in good condition, or is without a guard for the eyes; or

(*d*) there is any inadequacy in the supply of food or water for the horse at or near any place where it is working; or

(*e*) the horse or its harness has rubbed against the roof or sides of a road; or

(*f*) any other matter has arisen affecting or likely to affect the care or treatment of the horse;

he shall forthwith report the matter to the official under whose immediate charge he works and to a horse-keeper.

Reports of sick, injured, etc., horses

15. (1) In any case in which it comes to the notice of an official of the mine that a horse for the time being in the charge of a person who works under the immediate charge of that official, and in any case in which it comes to the notice of a horse-keeper that a horse for the time being under his care (as the case may be)—

(*a*) is unfit, is injured, or shows any symptoms of overwork; or

(*b*) bears any marks indicating ill-treatment; or

(*c*) is wearing any harness likely to cause pain or injury;

that official or that horse-keeper (as the case may be) shall forthwith make a report thereof to the manager or an under-manager.

(2) No horse with respect to which a report has been made in pursuance of the last preceding paragraph shall be worked at the mine until the manager or an under-manager so authorises.

Interpretation

16. (1) In these regulations the following expressions have the meanings hereby respectively assigned to them, that is to say—

'horse' includes pony, mule and donkey;

'horse-keeper' has the meaning assigned thereto in regulation eight;

'mine' has the meaning assigned thereto in regulation one;

'veterinary surgeon' has the meaning assigned thereto in regulation three.

(2) The Interpretation Act 1889 shall apply to the interpretation of these regulations as it applies to the interpretation of an Act of Parliament.

INRUSHES

THE COAL AND OTHER MINES

(PRECAUTIONS AGAINST INRUSHES) REGULATIONS 1956

S.I. 1956 No. 1770

1. These regulations shall apply to every mine of coal, stratified ironstone, shale or fireclay, and in these regulations 'mine' means such a mine.

2. (1) Without prejudice to the generality of section seventy-five of the Act, no working which is approaching and within one hundred and fifty feet of the surface shall be carried on in any mine, unless the manager has sufficient information about the nature of the material between the working and the surface to determine whether it may cause danger to persons working in the mine:

Provided that this paragraph shall not apply where there is another working or a disused working vertically above the working in question at a distance not less than thirty feet or five times the thickness of the seam to be worked whichever is the greater.

(2) No working shall be carried on at any place in any mine if there is evidence that within one hundred and fifty feet thereof there may be any peat, moss, sand, gravel, silt or other material that is likely to flow when wet, unless the manager of the mine has sufficient information to determine the nature, position, thickness and extent thereof.

(3) No working shall be carried on at any place in any mine if there is evidence that within one hundred and fifty feet thereof there may be any rock or stratum containing or likely to contain water (whether dispersed or in natural cavities) unless the manager of the mine has sufficient information about the nature or position thereof to determine that it is not dangerous to persons working in the mine or sufficient information about the nature, position, thickness and extent thereof to determine whether it may cause danger to such persons.

3. Without prejudice to the generality of section seventy-seven of the Act, no working which—

(*a*) is approaching and within one hundred and fifty feet of the surface; or

(*b*) is within one hundred and fifty feet of any peat, moss, sand, gravel, silt or other material that is likely to flow when wet; or

(*c*) is within one hundred and fifty feet of any rock or stratum containing or likely to contain water (whether dispersed or in natural cavities) not being rock or stratum which by reason of its nature or position is not dangerous;

shall exceed ten feet in width, unless the manager has given to the inspector for the district notice of his intention to work to a greater width and the inspector has within thirty days, by notice served on the manager, consented to that working exceeding ten feet in width.

4. Without prejudice to the generality of section seventy-seven of the Act, no working which is approaching and within one hundred and twenty feet of any place containing or likely to contain an accumulation of water or material that flows when wet or of any disused workings, not being workings which have been examined and found to be free from accumulations of water or material that flows when wet, shall exceed eight feet in width, and in respect of any such working the manager shall ensure that boreholes are at all times maintained in advance near the centre of the working of a length not less than fifteen feet and on each flank at intervals not exceeding fifteen feet.

5. The manager of every mine shall ensure that no person carries out any work, other than work necessary for the preservation of the mine or for the sinking of a shaft or the driving of an outlet from the surface, in any working in the mine within sixty feet or ten times the height of the working (whichever is the greater) of—

(*a*) any peat, moss, sand, gravel, silt or other material that is likely to flow when wet; or

(*b*) any rock or stratum containing or likely to contain water (whether dispersed or in natural cavities) not being rock or stratum which by reason of its natural position is not dangerous;

except in accordance with special regulations applicable to that mine.

6. (1) In these regulations the following expressions have the meanings hereby respectively assigned to them, that is to say—

'the Act' means the Mines and Quarries Act 1954;

'mine' has the meaning assigned thereto in regulation one.

(2) The Interpretation Act 1889 shall apply to the interpretation of these regulations as it applies to the interpretation of an Act of Parliament.

LOCOMOTIVES

THE COAL AND OTHER MINES

(LOCOMOTIVES) REGULATIONS 1956

S.I. 1956 No. 1771

Arrangement of Regulations

PART I

*Application**

1. Except where the application thereof is further expressly limited, these regulations shall apply below ground in every mine of coal, stratified ironstone, shale or fireclay, and in these regulations, except as aforesaid, 'mine' means such a mine.

PART II

Design, construction and equipment of locomotives†

2. The manager of every mine shall ensure that no locomotive runs in that mine unless it complies with the requirements of this Part of these regulations.

3. (1) Every locomotive and each of its accessories shall, so far as practicable, be constructed of non-inflammable material, and any inflammable material included therein shall be shrouded with a substantial metallic covering:

Provided that an inspector may by notice served on the manager of any mine consent to the running in that mine of a locomotive in which inflammable material is not so shrouded.

(2) In the case of every locomotive in which the motive power is generated by an internal combustion engine, that locomotive shall be so constructed that—

(*a*) no air enters the engine without first being cleaned;

(*b*) no exhaust gases are expelled from the locomotive without first being cooled and diluted; and

---

*The application of these Regulations as regards locomotives is, by the definition in Regulation 36 (1), limited to 'mechanically propelled vehicles running on rails and constructed or used for moving other vehicles'.

†Design, construction, equipment and manner of test of diesel engined locomotives is dealt with in Testing Memo. No. 12, copies of which are available from the Safety and Health Division of the Ministry of Technology.

(c) no flames or sparks are emitted from the locomotive.

(3) Every locomotive which runs in a mine or part of a mine in which the use of lamps or lights, other than permitted lights, is unlawful shall be of a type approved by the Minister:

Provided that the provisions of this paragraph shall not apply to a locomotive which runs only in lengths of road not ventilated by air that has ventilated any working face and which does not run to any place in such a length of road within nine hundred feet of a working face accessible from that length of road.

4. In the case of every locomotive in which the motive power is generated by an electric motor supplied with electricity by a storage battery (in these regulations referred to as a 'storage battery locomotive') that part of the locomotive in which the battery is carried shall be so constructed as to be capable of resisting rough usage and adequately ventilated.

5. (1) Every locomotive shall be provided with—

(*a*) brakes which can (whether or not any other device for applying them is fitted) be applied by the driver by direct mechanical action;

(*b*) means for applying sand to the rails;

(*c*) means for giving adequate audible warnings;

(*d*) a suitable portable fire extinguisher;

(*e*) a seat for the driver;

(*f*) controls so placed that the driver can simultaneously operate them and see ahead without leaning out of the locomotive; and

(*g*) a portable lamp.

(2) Every locomotive, other than a locomotive which cannot develop more than twenty-five horse power and cannot on a level road exceed a speed of eight miles per hour, shall be provided with a combined speed and mileage indicator so placed as to be easily seen by the driver when he is operating the locomotive:

Provided that the provisions of this paragraph shall not apply to a locomotive which was in use in a mine before the first day of May, nineteen hundred and forty-nine and which has not been provided with such an indicator before the commencement of the Act.

(3) Every locomotive shall be provided with a headlight with an effective range of at least two hundred feet or, in the case of a locomotive which was in use in a mine before the first day of May, nineteen hundred and forty-nine, if an inspector by notice served on the manager of the mine consents thereto, such a headlight as that with which it was equipped at that date.

PART III

Roads and tracks

Construction of tracks

6. (1) Subject to the provisions of regulation eight the manager of every mine in which any locomotive runs shall ensure that no locomotive runs in any length of road otherwise than on a track of rails being a track—

(*a*) which is ballasted and where necessary drained;

(*b*) having rails of a weight per yard of rail not less than that specified in paragraph (2) of this regulation;

(*c*) so constructed that the distance between the centres of any adjacent sleepers does not exceed—

(i) in a length of road in a mine of stratified ironstone or shale in which no locomotive exceeding three and one half tons in weight runs, three feet;

(ii) in any other length of road, two feet nine inches;

(*d*) having every rail joint secured by suitable fishplates with at least four bolts; and

(*e*) so constructed that every curve thereon is sufficiently gradual to enable any locomotive which runs thereon to do so in safety and has where necessary a raised outer rail or check rail or both of them.

(2) The minimum weight per yard of rail shall be—

(*a*) in the case of rail in a mine of coal or fireclay on which no locomotive exceeding five tons in weight runs, and which is used only for the carrying of loads other than persons or minerals, twenty-eight pounds;

(*b*) in the case of a rail in a mine of stratified ironstone or shale on which no locomotive exceeding three and one half tons in weight runs, twenty-four pounds;

(*c*) in the case of any other rail, forty pounds or, if the weight calculated as follows be greater, ten pounds with an addition of five pounds for each ton of the greatest weight on one pair of wheels of the heaviest locomotive which runs thereon.

(3) The manager of every mine in which any locomotive runs shall ensure that no locomotive runs and no vehicle is drawn by a locomotive at any place at which it may pass another locomotive or vehicle on an adjacent track unless those tracks are so laid that taking into account any swing of either locomotive or vehicle there is a clearance not less than one foot between any parts of them.

Minimum clearances

7. (1) Subject to the provisions of regulation eight the manager of every mine in which any locomotive runs shall ensure that no locomotive runs in any length of road therein which is not throughout of such height and width as to comply with the following provisions of this regulation taking into account any swing of the locomotive.

(2) The height of any such length of road shall be such that—

(*a*) in the case of a locomotive with a covered cab, there is as regards any part of the locomotive a vertical clearance not less than one foot; or

(*b*) in the case of a locomotive without a covered cab running in a mine of stratified ironstone or shale in a length of road in which any locomotive ran, or for the running in which any locomotive was required to be delivered under a contract made, before the first day of May, nineteen hundred and forty-nine, there is as regards any part of the locomotive a vertical clearance not less than one foot; or (*c*) in the case of any other locomotive, the driver can stand upright on any part of the floor of the cab.

(3) The width of any such length of road shall be such that as regards any part of a locomotive there is a horizontal clearance not less than two feet:

Provided that, at a side on which refuge holes are not provided of a length of road in which there are not more than two tracks of rails, a horizontal clearance exceeding one foot shall not be required.

Exemptions

8. An inspector, if he is satisfied that the application of any provision of either of the two last preceding regulations is not requisite for safety in relation to any mine or part thereof, may by notice served on the manager of that mine exempt it or a part thereof from that provision.

Gradients

9. The manager of every mine shall ensure that no locomotive runs therein on a gradient exceeding 1 : 15.

Inspections of rails and track

10. (1) Without prejudice to the provisions of the Coal and Other Mines (Managers and Officials) Regulations 1956* with regard to the functions of deputies in districts assigned to them and with regard to the inspection of places outside deputies' districts, the manager of every mine in which any locomotive runs shall secure that a competent person (who may be the deputy or person assigned to make such inspection) is appointed by him to be in charge of every length of road in which a locomotive runs.

(2) At intervals not exceeding twenty-four hours the person for the time being in charge of any such length of road shall inspect or supervise the inspection of that length to ascertain the condition thereof as regards—

(*a*) the state of the track and its freedom from obstructions, and

(*b*) the maintenance of the requisite height and width of the road,

and upon the completion of such an inspection shall forthwith record and sign a full and accurate report thereof in a book† provided by the owner of the mine for the purpose.

PART IV

Ventilation

Determinations of firedamp content

11. Without prejudice to the provisions of the Coal and Other Mines (Ventilation) Regulations 1956‡ where a locomotive runs in any length of road in which the use of lamps or lights, other than permitted lights, is unlawful, the manager shall make and secure the efficient carrying out of arrangements whereby determinations of the percentage of inflammable gas present in the general body of the air (in these regulations referred to as 'the firedamp content') are made in that length of road in accordance with the provisions of the three next following regulations:

---

*See page 117.
†M. & Q. Form No. 269.
‡See page 317.

Provided that an inspector, if he is satisfied that the normal firedamp content in any length of road is not such as to make regular determinations necessary, may by notice served on the manager exempt that length from the application of any provision in this Part of these regulations.

Methods for determinations

12. Determinations of the firedamp content shall be made—

(*a*) by means of apparatus of a type approved for the purpose by the Minister, by a competent person appointed for that purpose by the manager of the mine; or

(*b*) by means of samples of air taken by a competent person so appointed and analysed within four days (without taking into account any Saturday, Sunday or day of general holiday) of the taking thereof.

Places for determinations

13. (1) Determinations of the firedamp content shall be made—

(*a*) at a point at each end of every length of road in which any locomotive runs;

(*b*) at such other suitable points as may be fixed by the manager:

Provided that paragraph (*a*) shall not require any determination to be made in a length of intake airway which begins at a shaft or outlet at any place more than nine hundred feet from any working face ventilated by that airway.

(2) An inspector may, if he is of opinion that any point fixed in pursuance of sub-paragraph (*b*) of paragraph (1) of this regulation is unsuitable, serve on the manager a notice requiring him to fix some other point in substitution therefor and may serve on the manager a notice requiring determinations to be made at any other point specified in the notice in addition to those required by the preceding paragraph.

Times for determinations

14. (1) Determinations of the firedamp content shall be made at every point required by or under the last preceding regulation once in every week at the time when the firedamp content is likely to be greatest:

Provided that—

(*a*) if any determination at any such point shows a firedamp content exceeding 0·8 per cent by volume determinations shall be made at that point at intervals not exceeding twenty-four hours so long as the content is shown to exceed or to have exceeded that percentage and for the seven next following working days;

(*b*) if every determination made during a period of thirty days at any such point showed a firedamp content not exceeding—

(i) in the case of a point in a length of road not ventilated by air which has ventilated a working face, 0·2 per cent by volume;

(ii) in the case of a point in any other length of road, 0·6 per cent by volume;

it shall be sufficient to make determinations at that point at intervals not exceeding thirty days for so long as the firedamp content shown thereby does not exceed that percentage.

(2) Notwithstanding anything in the last preceding paragraph, whenever any alteration is made in the arrangements for ventilating a mine which affects or may affect substantially any length of road in which determinations of the firedamp content are required by or under this Part of these regulations to be made, a determination of the firedamp content at each point in that length shall be made as soon as any substantial effect of the alteration would be apparent.

(3) Where a determination of the firedamp content made for the purposes of these regulations is made by means of a sample of air, it shall be deemed to be made at the time and place at which the sample is taken.

Records of determinations

15. Particulars of every determination of firedamp content made in accordance with this Part of these regulations shall be recorded forthwith in a book* provided for that purpose by the owner of the mine.

16. (1) If any determination of firedamp content made in any length of road (not being a determination made by analysis of a sample of air) shows a firedamp content exceeding one and one quarter per cent by volume, or any indication of inflammable gas is seen on the lowered flame of a safety-lamp in the general body of the air, the person making that determination or the person using the lamp (as the case may be) shall forthwith inform the person in charge of the part of the mine which includes that length of road and that latter person shall after forthwith verifying the accuracy of the information so given to him forthwith discontinue the running of any locomotive in that length of road.

(2) After such discontinuance no locomotive shall be run in that length of road until the manager of the mine, being satisfied that the firedamp content therein does not exceed one and one quarter per cent by volume, so directs.

(3) If any determination of firedamp content made in any length of road by analysis of a sample of air shows a firedamp content exceeding one and one quarter per cent by volume, the manager of the mine shall forthwith upon receipt of that information ensure that no locomotive runs in that length of road until he is satisfied that the firedamp content therein does not exceed one and one quarter per cent by volume.

(4) The manager shall forthwith give to the inspector for the district notice of any discontinuance of the running of a locomotive in pursuance of this regulation.

PART V

Working and maintenance of locomotives

Drivers of locomotives

17. (1) No person shall operate any locomotive in any mine other than a person appointed by the manager of the mine to be a driver of that locomotive

*M. & Q. Form No. 270.

or of that type of locomotive (hereinafter referred to as 'an appointed driver', or a person so doing in the course of his duty in connection with the maintenance, repair or testing of that locomotive, and no appointed driver shall operate a locomotive hauling persons in vehicles unless he has attained the age of:—

(*a*) in the case of a mine of shale, eighteen years;

(*b*) in the case of any other mine, twenty-one years.

(2) A manager shall not appoint any person to be an appointed driver unless that person is the holder of a certificate that he is competent without supervision to operate a locomotive of the type in question given by a person responsible for his training in such operation.

(3) The manager shall supply to every appointed driver a copy or summary of so much of the transport rules* of the mine as affect the discharge of his duties.

18. No person for the time being operating a locomotive in a mine shall leave that locomotive unattended, otherwise than at the place where it is normally kept when not in use, unless he has ensured that it cannot be set in motion by any person prohibited by these regulations from operating it.

19. Except in accordance with the transport rules* of the mine, no person shall be on any locomotive in motion in the mine unless he is:—

(*a*) an appointed driver; or

(*b*) when the locomotive is being used in shunting operations, a person engaged in those operations; or

(*c*) a person engaged in maintaining, repairing or testing the locomotive.

20. Except during shunting operations no person shall couple next to any locomotive a vehicle containing any timber or other material of a length exceeding the length of the vehicle.

21. (1) In any mine of coal or fireclay no person shall use a locomotive for moving any vehicle otherwise than by hauling from in front, except during shunting operations.

(2) In any mine of stratified ironstone or shale no person shall use a locomotive for moving any vehicle otherwise than by hauling from in front except:—

(*a*) during shunting operations; or

(*b*) for moving a single vehicle at a place within twelve hundred feet of a working face; or

(*c*) in a length of road in which a locomotive was used for hauling material before the first day of May, nineteen hundred and forty-nine.

(3) Where in any mine of stratified ironstone or shale any vehicle is moved by a locomotive otherwise than by hauling from in front in pursuance of sub-paragraph (*c*) of the last preceding paragraph, a white light visible at a distance of two hundred feet shall be attached to the front of the vehicle or, if there is more than one, of the leading vehicle:

*See Section 37 of the 1954 Act.

Provided that nothing in this paragraph shall apply to any single vehicle so moved within twelve hundred feet of any working face.

22. A red light visible at a distance of two hundred feet shall be attached:—

(*a*) at the rear of the last vehicle of every train in a mine; and

(*b*) at the rear of every locomotive in a mine when it is not attached to a vehicle:

Provided that nothing in this regulation shall apply in any mine of stratified ironstone or shale to any train or locomotive within twelve hundred feet of any working face.

Maintenance of locomotives

23. (1) It shall be the duty of the manager of every mine in which a locomotive runs to make and secure the efficient carrying out of arrangements whereby every locomotive thereat is examined externally during every period of twenty-four hours during which the engine or motor has been run, by a competent person appointed by the manager for that purpose, and upon the completion of such an examination the person making it shall forthwith record and sign a full and accurate report thereof in a book* provided by the owner of the mine for the purpose.

(2) In relation to any locomotive in which the motive power is generated by an internal combustion engine, it shall be the duty of the manager to make and secure the efficient carrying out of arrangments whereby any protective device fitted to any exhaust opening of the engine is thoroughly cleaned, or a clean device is substituted, whenever necessary and in any event during every period of twenty-four hours during which the engine has been run or such longer period as the Minister may by notice served on the manager approve in relation to any such locomotive.

24. (1) Without prejudice to the generality of regulations six and seven of the Coal and Other Mines (Mechanics and Electricians) Regulations 1956† it shall be the duty of the manager of every mine in which a locomotive runs to ensure that a scheme for the systematic examination of plant at that mine made in pursuance of the said regulation seven provides for the thorough examination and testing‡ at intervals not exceeding seven days of every locomotive thereat. In the course of such examination and testing steps shall be taken to ensure that all parts of the locomotive requiring to be cleaned are properly clean and the brakes shall be applied:—

(*a*) when the locomotive is in motion, by direct mechanical action and by any other means provided; and

(*b*) when the locomotive is stationary and the engine or motor is not running, by any means provided other than direct mechanical action and for a period of ten minutes.

---

*M. & Q. Form No. 271.

†Replaced by regulations 9 and 10 of the Coal and Other Mines (Mechanics and Electricians) Regulations, 1965—see page 194.

‡Reports on these examinations and tests are required by No. 14 of the Mechanics and Electricians Regulations 1965, to be made on M. & Q. Forms Nos. 272 and 273.

(2) Such scheme shall provide also for the like examination and testing of the brakes forthwith after any repair or adjustment to the braking system of any locomotive.

PART VI

Additional provisions—diesel locomotives

Housing stations

25. (1) The Manager of every mine in which there is any diesel locomotive shall make and secure the efficient carrying out of arrangements whereby that locomotive is, when not in use, kept in a place appointed for that purpose by him (in these regulations referred to as a 'housing station').

(2) The manager shall ensure that every housing station—

(*a*) is provided with not less than two means of egress;

(*b*) is ventilated by a current of air sufficient to dilute and render harmless all exhaust gases emitted by any engine running therein.

(*c*) is constructed of non-inflammable material;

(*d*) has a floor of smooth concrete;

(*e*) has an inspection pit or other suitable means for making inspections from below the locomotive; and

(*f*) is provided with suitable and sufficient apparatus for combating outbreaks of fire.

Filling stations

26. (1) No person shall replenish any diesel locomotive with fuel oil in any mine except at a place appointed for that purpose by the manager (in these regulations referred to as a 'filling station').

(2) The manager shall ensure that every filling station—

(*a*) is provided with not less than two means of egress;

(*b*) is ventilated by a current of air sufficient to dilute and render harmless all gases emitted therein;

(*c*) is constructed of non-inflammable material;

(*d*) has a floor of smooth concrete surrounded by a sill;

(*e*) is provided with suitable and sufficient apparatus for combating outbreaks of fire; and

(*f*) is so equipped that the spilling of oil is minimised.

(3) Any person spilling oil in a filling station shall—

(*a*) forthwith wipe it up or cause it to be wiped up with a non-inflammable absorbent;

(*b*) forthwith thereafter deposit that absorbent, or cause it to be deposited, in a fireproof receptacle; and

(*c*) as soon as practicable take that absorbent, or cause it to be taken, to the surface.

(4) No person shall take any oil from any container in a filling station while any internal combustion engine in the filling station is running.

(5) In a mine or part of a mine which is not a safety-lamp mine or safety-lamp part of a mine, no person shall, in, or within ten yards of, any filling station, smoke or use any lamp or light other than a locked safety-lamp or an electric lamp adequately protected:

Provided that this paragraph shall not apply in relation to any filling station constructed before the first day of May, nineteen hundred and forty-nine, in any mine of stratified ironstone or of shale for any diesel locomotive which was in use before that date or was required to be delivered under a contract made before that date.

Fuel oil

27. The manager of every mine in which any diesel locomotive runs shall make and secure the efficient carrying out of arrangements whereby—

(*a*) no fuel oil is used for the generation of energy in that locomotive other than oil of a specification* approved by the Minister;

(*b*) no oil for use as aforesaid is taken below ground otherwise than in a suitable container which does not leak; and

(*c*) any such oil at any time stored below ground (otherwise than in the tanks of a locomotive)—

(i) is kept in a filling station in a suitable container which does not leak; and

(ii) does not exceed in quantity, such quantity as, together with any oil then in the tanks of locomotives for which it has been brought below ground, is likely to be consumed by those locomotives (having regard to their normal user) within the period of forty-eight hours next following.

Posting of notices in filling stations

28. The manager of every mine in which any diesel locomotive runs shall ensure that a notice is kept posted in every filling station in such characters and in such a position as to be easily seen and read by the persons resorting thereto, being a notice specifying the requirements and prohibitions of paragraphs (1), (3), (4) and (5) (if applicable) of regulation twenty-six.

Exhaust gases

29. The manager of every mine in which any diesel locomotive runs shall ensure that no such locomotive runs therein if—

(*a*) in the case of a locomotive in a mine of stratified ironstone or of shale, being a locomotive which was in use before the first day of May, nineteen hundred and forty-nine or was required to be delivered under a contract made before that date, gas emitted from its exhaust contains more than 0·4 per cent by volume of carbon monoxide or 0·15 per cent by volume of oxides of nitrogen; or

*The specification approved for this purpose is that for Class A fuels in British Standard Specification No. 209: 1947 (Fuels for Oil Engines).

(*b*) in any other case, gas emitted from its exhaust contains more than 0·2 per cent by volume of carbon monoxide or 0·1 per cent by volume of oxides of nitrogen.

30. (1) No person for the time being operating any diesel locomotive in a mine shall keep the engine running when that locomotive is stationary except—

(*a*) during brief halts while the locomotive is in use; or

(*b*) while the locomotive is being tested.

(2) If at any place in a mine in which a diesel locomotive runs there is found in the general body of the air an amount of carbon monoxide exceeding 0·005 per cent by volume, the manager shall forthwith take such steps as are necessary so to improve the ventilation at that place that that percentage of carbon monoxide is not exceeded.

(3) If at any place in a mine in which a diesel locomotive runs there is found in the general body of the air an amount of carbon monoxide exceeding 0·01 per cent by volume, the manager shall ensure that no engine of a diesel locomotive is run at that place or at any other place at which such running could affect the ventilation at the first mentioned place until it has been determined that the amount of carbon monoxide in the general body of the air at the first mentioned place does not exceed 0·005 per cent by volume.

31. (1) The manager of every mine in which any diesel locomotive runs shall make and secure the efficient carrying out of arrangements whereby samples are taken by a competent person appointed for that purpose by him and analysed in accordance with the following provisions of this regulation.

(2) At intervals not exceeding ninety days separate samples of the gas emitted from the exhaust of every diesel locomotive in use in the mine shall be taken when the engine of the locomotive is—

(*a*) developing maximum power; and

(*b*) idling with the locomotive stationary.

(3) At intervals not exceeding thirty days separate samples of the general body of the air shall be taken at places and times appointed by the manager so as to secure the detection of any harmful concentration of carbon monoxide produced by any diesel locomotive. An inspector may by notice served on the manager require him to appoint any place specified in the notice either instead of or in addition to any place already appointed by the manager.

(4) Every sample taken in pursuance of paragraph (2) of this regulation shall within four days of the taking thereof be analysed to determine the percentages of carbon monoxide and oxides of nitrogen therein and every sample taken in pursuance of paragraph (3) of this regulation shall within that period be analysed to determine the percentage of carbon monoxide therein and particulars of each such analysis shall be recorded forthwith in a book* provided for that purpose by the owner of the mine. In reckoning a period of four days for the purposes of this paragraph no account shall be taken of any Saturday, Sunday or day of general holiday.

*M. & Q. Form No. 274.

PART VII

Additional provisions—storage battery locomotives

Charging and changing of batteries

32. (1) No person shall charge or change any battery of a storage battery locomotive in any mine except at a place appointed for that purpose by the manager.

(2) The manager shall ensure that every place so appointed for charging batteries (in these regulations referred to as a 'charging station') is so arranged in relation to the ventilation that—

(*a*) the charging apparatus is on the intake side of the battery racks; and

(*b*) the air passes from the battery racks directly into an airway and does not subsequently ventilate a working face.

(3) The manager shall ensure that every charging station—

(*a*) is constructed of non-inflammable material;

(*b*) is provided with suitable and sufficient apparatus for combating outbreaks of fire;

(*c*) is so equipped that the spilling of water or electrolyte is minimised.

(4) Any person spilling any water or electrolyte on any battery in a charging station shall forthwith wipe it up or cause it to be wiped up.

(5) In a mine or part of a mine which is not a safety-lamp mine or a safety-lamp part of a mine, no person shall, in, or within thirty feet of, any charging station, smoke or use any lamp or light other than a locked safety-lamp or an electric lamp adequately protected.

Posting of notices in charging stations

33. The manager of every mine in which any storage battery locomotive runs shall ensure that a notice is kept posted in every charging station in such characters and in such a position as to be easily seen and read by the persons resorting thereto, being a notice specifying the requirements and prohibitions of paragraphs (1), (4) and (5) (if applicable) of regulation thirty-two.

PART VIII

General

34. *Nothing in these regulations shall be taken to authorise the use of any locomotive below ground without the consent of the Minister or an inspector.

Exemptions

35. The Chief Inspector of Mines, if he is satisfied that the application of any provision of these regulations (other than a provision in relation to which an express power of exemption is contained in these regulations) is not requisite for safety in relation to any mine or part thereof, may by notice served on the manager of that mine exempt it or a part thereof from the application of that provision.

---

*See also Section 83 of the 1954 Act.

Interpretation

36. (1) In these regulations the following expressions have the meanings hereby respectively assigned to them, that is to say—

'the Act' means the Mines and Quarries Act 1954;

'appointed driver' has the meaning assigned thereto in regulation seventeen;

'charging station' has the meaning assigned thereto in regulation thirty-two;

'deputy' and 'deputy's district' have the meanings assigned thereto in the Coal and Other Mines (Managers and Officials) Regulations 1956*;

'filling station' has the meaning assigned thereto in regulation twenty-six;

'firedamp content' has the meaning assigned thereto in regulation eleven;

'housing station' has the meaning assigned thereto in regulation twenty-five;

'locomotive' means a mechanically propelled vehicle running on rails and constructed or used for hauling other vehicles;

'mine' has the meaning assigned thereto in regulation one;

'storage battery locomotive' has the meaning assigned thereto in regulation four.

(2) Expressions to which meanings are assigned by the Act or by these regulations shall (unless the contrary intention appears) have the same meanings in any document issued under the provisions of these regulations.

(3) The Interpretation Act 1889 shall apply to the interpretation of these regulations as it applies to the interpretation of an Act of Parliament.

---

*See page 188.

MANAGERS AND OFFICIALS

THE COAL AND OTHER MINES

(MANAGERS AND OFFICIALS) REGULATIONS 1956

S.I. 1956 No. 1758

(As varied by the Coal and Other Mines (Managers and Officials) (Variation) Regulations 1961, S.I. 1961 No. 817, and the Coal and Other Mines (Managers and Officials) (Variation) Regulations 1962, S.I. 1962, No. 594, the Coal and Other Mines (Managers and Officials) (Variation) Regulations 1963, S.I. 1963 No. 1617, and the Coal and Other Mines (Managers and Officials) (Variation) Regulations 1966, S.I. 1966 No. 882)

Arrangement of Regulations

Part I

Application

1. These regulations shall apply to every mine of coal, stratified ironstone, shale or fireclay, and in these regulations, unless otherwise expressly provided, 'mine' means such a mine.

Part II

Miscellaneous duties of managers and under-managers

2. The manager of every mine and any under-manager thereof to the extent of his jurisdiction shall take such steps as may be necessary to secure that a sufficient supply of suitable materials and appliances is at all times readily available for ensuring compliance with all requirements imposed by or under the Act and the safety of the mine and of persons employed therein.

3. The manager of every mine and any under-manager thereof to the extent of his jurisdiction shall give attention to and cause to be carefully investigated any representation or complaint made to him by or on behalf of persons employed thereat about any matter affecting the safety or health of such persons.

4. The manager of every mine shall make and ensure the efficient carrying out of arrangements whereby a correct record of the number of persons going below ground and returning above ground is made daily by a competent person appointed by him.

5. Every under-manager of a mine to the extent of his jurisdiction and, as respects any part of a mine which is not within the jurisdiction of an under-manager, the manager thereof shall make and maintain arrangements for conferring daily on matters arising in the carrying out of their duties with the deputies of the mine and other officials having charge of operations carried on below ground:

Provided that to the extent that there are officials superior to the deputies and to such other officials it shall be sufficient for the under-manager or manager, as the case may be, so to confer with those superior officials.

6. Every under-manager of a mine to the extent of his jurisdiction and, as respects any part of a mine which is not within the jurisdiction of an under-manager, the manager thereof shall from time to time examine all parts of the mine which are required to be ventilated whether or not they are frequented by workmen employed thereat.

6A. It shall be the duty of every under-manager of a mine, with respect to each report, record or other item of information which, in pursuance of the Act or any regulation made thereunder, is entered in a book which by or by virtue of the Act is required to be provided for that purpose by the owner of the mine, and which relates to a part of the mine within his jurisdiction, either to read it himself forthwith or to secure that it is read forthwith by some other competent person and that there is promptly brought to his notice any matter disclosed by the report, record or other item of information which either is of an abnormal or unusual nature as regards the mine or, not being of such a nature, is of a kind which will or may necessitate the taking of any steps by the manager or any other person.

PART III

Underground officials superior to the deputies

7. No person shall be qualified to be appointed under subsection (1) of section thirteen of the Act, or to be, an underground official superior to the deputies but inferior to the manager and, where there is an under-manager, to the under-manager unless—

(*a*) he is the holder of a first class or second class certificate of competency valid with respect to that mine; or

(*b*) he is the holder of a deputy's certificate granted by the Minister on the recommendation of the Mining Qualifications Board, which shall, unless an Inspector by notice served on the manager of the mine consents to that person's being such an official at that mine, be a certificate valid with respect to that mine, and has had not less than one year's experience as a deputy; or

(*c*) he is the holder of a certificate given under sub-paragraph (*d*) of paragraph (1) of regulation eighteen of the Coal Mines (Officials and Inspections) General Regulations 1951 (being a certificate relating to his service as such an official before the coming into operation of that regulation).

8. (1) Every underground official superior to the deputies but inferior to the manager and, where there is an under-manager, to the under-manager shall to the extent of his jurisdiction have the duty of securing compliance with all requirements imposed by or under the Act and the safe performance of all operations.

(2) Every such official shall—

(*a*) during each shift of his confer with the deputy assigned to each district and with each other official then performing duties in or responsible for any part of the mine, being a district or part to which his jurisdiction extends;

(*b*) at the end of each shift of his give to any person succeeding to any of his duties all information he has obtained which is relevant to safety; and

(*c*) within twenty-four hours of the end of each shift of his examine and counter-sign any report made by such a deputy in relation to that shift by virtue of regulation twenty-five of these regulations.

PART IV

Deputies

General duties of deputies

9. (1) In every mine competent persons appointed by the manager as deputies shall each during his shift in the district assigned to him—

(*a*) have the immediate charge of the workmen for the time being in that district and of all operations carried on by them therein; and

(*b*) make such inspections and carry out such other duties with regard to the presence of gas, ventilation, support of roof and sides and general safety (including the health of persons working in that district) as are required by the Act or by regulations (including these regulations).

(2) Subject to the provisions of the next following paragraph, every deputy to whom a district is assigned shall devote his whole time during his shift to the duties specified in the last preceding paragraph.

(3) Paragraph (2) of this regulation shall not prevent any deputy being employed in firing shots or apply in relation to the deputy in any district—

(*a*) being a district exempted therefrom by a notice served on the manager by an inspector on the ground of the special circumstances of that district; or

(*b*) in a mine at which not more than thirty persons are employed below ground, if the number of persons at work in that district during the shift concerned does not exceed ten; or

(*c*) in any mine if the number of persons at work in that district during the shift concerned does not exceed five:

Provided that no duty shall be assigned to the deputy by virtue of this paragraph if performance of that duty would prevent the deputy carrying out the duties specified in paragraph (1) of this regulation in a thorough manner, and an inspector may serve a notice on the manager requiring that such a duty shall not be so assigned if he is of opinion that performance thereof would be likely to prevent the deputy so carrying out those duties.

(4) No deputy shall at any time perform any duty himself or allow any workman in his charge to do any work, not being a duty or work the carrying out of which is necessary for securing the safety or health of workmen employed at the mine, if so doing would prevent or delay the due carrying out of any duty or work necessary for that purpose.

Determination of deputies' districts

10. (1) The manager of every mine shall define, by means of a plan on a scale not less than six inches to one mile kept at the office at the mine or at such other place as may be approved by an inspector, the limits of each district in the mine* to be in the charge of a deputy (hereinafter referred to as 'a deputy's district') in such manner that—

(*a*) there is included within the limits of a deputy's district every place in the mine at which mineral is worked, other than a place at which mineral is worked for the purpose of repairing, restoring or enlarging a road or preparing accommodation required for the working of the mine; and

(*b*) no deputy's district is of a size which may prevent a deputy assigned thereto making the pre-shift inspections referred to in regulation twelve within a period of one-and-a-half hours if he is not interrupted in so doing.

(2) Different districts may be defined in relation to different shifts or different days of the week or both of them having regard to the nature of the work to be carried out thereon.

(3) If an inspector is of opinion that any deputy's district so defined is of a size which may prevent or prejudice the carrying out by a deputy assigned thereto of all his duties in a thorough manner, the inspector may serve on the manager a notice requiring him to reduce the size of that district.

(4) The provisions of Part XV of the Act† with respect to references upon notices served by inspectors shall apply to a notice served under the last preceding paragraph and the relevant ground of objection to such a notice shall be that the size of that deputy's district does not prevent or prejudice the carrying out by the deputy assigned thereto of all his duties in a thorough manner.

11. It shall be the duty of the manager to secure that a deputy is assigned to each deputy's district for each shift during which any workman is to go into that district.

Pre-shift inspections

12. (1) Within the period of two hours‡ immediately before the commencement of work on any shift during which workmen will enter a deputy's district,

---

*Except in relation to a shaft in the course of being sunk (see Regulation 32 (2)).

†See Section 170 of the 1954 Act.

‡See Regulation 32 (3) as regards shafts in the course of being sunk.

the deputy to whom that district is assigned for that shift or for the last preceding shift shall himself ascertain by inspection of every part of it which is required to be ventilated (hereinafter referred to as 'pre-shift inspection') the condition of every such part as regards the presence of gas, ventilation, state of roof and sides and general safety:

Provided that during any period in which workmen are continuously in the district since the last preceding pre-shift inspection it shall be sufficient for such an inspection to be made at intervals not exceeding eight hours.

(2) Every deputy making a pre-shift inspection shall have with him a locked flame safety-lamp and a locked electric safety-lamp or a locked safety-lamp combining those two, being in every case a lamp for the time being approved* by the Minister for the purpose of deputies' inspections, and he shall not use any other lamp during his inspection. This paragraph shall not apply in mines of stratified ironstone other than—

(*a*) mines in the Cleveland district; and

(*b*) mines in any part of which the use of lamps or lights, other than permitted lights, is unlawful.

(3) A deputy may be accompanied during any pre-shift inspection by one competent workman as an assistant. Such a workman shall not use during that inspection any lamp other than a locked safety-lamp of a type for the time being approved by the Minister for general use by workmen.

(4) For the purposes of this regulation as regards any deputy's district a reference to a deputy assigned thereto for the last preceding shift shall include a deputy assigned to a deputy's district which comprised that district and the deputies assigned to deputies' districts which or parts of which together comprised that district.

(5) Notwithstanding anything contained in regulation 9 (1) (b) or in the preceding paragraphs of this regulation, the manager of a mine may appoint one or more competent persons, each of whom is qualified under regulation 26 to be a deputy, and, unless an inspector by notice served on the manager of the mine consents to that person's making pre-shift inspections pursuant to this paragraph, such qualification is valid with respect to that mine to make pre-shift inspections and where a pre-shift inspection of a deputy's district is required to be made pursuant to paragraph (1) of this regulation and is made in respect of a shift by such a person in accordance with this paragraph the deputy whose duty it would otherwise be to make a pre-shift inspection in respect of that shift shall not be required himself to make such an inspection.

(6) Paragraphs (2) and (3) of this regulation shall apply to a person appointed under the last preceding paragraph as if he were a deputy.

Meeting stations

13. (1) The manager shall fix by means of a plan referred to in regulation ten a station at an entrance to every deputy's district (hereinafter referred to in relation to that district as 'the meeting station') and shall ensure that notices

---

*See page 225.

†Except in relation to a shaft in the course of being sunk (see Regulation 32 (2)).

indicating the position of every meeting station are kept posted at such suitable places and in such characters as to be easily seen.

(2) An inspector may, if he is of opinion that the position of any meeting station does not provide adequately for the safety of the workmen, serve on the manager a notice requiring him to alter the position thereof.

(3) The provisions of Part XV of the Act* with respect to references upon notices served by inspectors shall apply to a notice served under the last preceding paragraph and the relevant ground of objection to such a notice shall be that the position of the meeting station fixed by the manager provides adequately for the safety of the workmen.

14. (1) No workman shall pass beyond the meeting station of, or enter any deputy's district (except in pursuance of regulation 12) unless he is instructed to do so by the deputy assigned to that district or a district comprising or comprised in that district, or by a person appointed pursuant to regulation 12 (5) to make pre-shift inspections or he does so in pursuance of an arrangement made by the manager.

(2) No deputy or person appointed pursuant to regulation 12 (5) to make pre-shift inspections shall instruct any workman to pass beyond the meeting station or enter a district unless he has made, or is satisfied that another deputy or person appointed pursuant to regulation 12 (5) to make pre-shift inspections has made, any pre-shift inspection required by these regulations to be made before that workman commences work and he is satisfied that, having regard to any instruction he gives to that workman relating to his safety, that workman can safely enter the district.

(3) The manager shall not make arrangements for any workman to pass beyond the meeting station or enter any deputy's district (otherwise than in pursuance of the last preceding paragraph) except arrangements which will operate only when a workman will already be in the district and any such arrangements shall be subject to any instruction given by a deputy or person appointed pursuant to regulation 12 (5) to make pre-shift inspections.

Inspections during shifts

15. (1) †Every deputy to whom a deputy's district is assigned for any shift shall at least twice during that shift inspect every part of that district which is required to be ventilated to ascertain the condition thereof as regards the presence of gas, ventilation, state of roof and sides and general safety in such manner that—

(*a*) no place at which workmen are at work shall remain uninspected for more than four hours; and

(*b*) he inspects any part of the district, which has remained for a period of two hours after the pre-shift inspection without workmen being at work therein, not more than two hours before workmen are to re-enter it.

(2) Nothing in the last preceding paragraph shall require the inspection under this regulation of a development working which the manager has caused

*See Section 170 of the 1954 Act.

†See Regulation 32 (4) as regards shafts in the course of being sunk.

to be marked with a notice to the effect that work therein is for the time being discontinued.

(3) Paragraphs (2) and (3) of regulation twelve shall apply to an inspection under this regulation as they apply to a pre-shift inspection.

(4) A pre-shift inspection made during any shift may be taken into account also as an inspection made under this regulation during that shift.

Miscellaneous duties of deputies

*__16.__ Without prejudice to the generality of section thirty-three of the Act, the deputy to whom a deputy's district is assigned for any shift shall ensure that any place therein which is for the time being dangerous by reason of the presence of gas or from any other cause is so fenced off at each approach as to prevent any person from accidentally entering it and that each such fence is marked with a danger sign provided by the owner of the mine:

Provided that where a person appointed pursuant to regulation 12 (5) to make pre-shift inspections makes such an inspection of a deputy's district he shall forthwith fence off and mark any such place in the manner hereinbefore provided and shall inform the deputy to whom that district is assigned for the shift in respect of which that inspection was made, or the deputy for the last preceding shift if he is still in the district, of the nature of the danger and the fact that the place has been so fenced and marked.

17. Every deputy to whom a deputy's district is assigned for any shift shal immediately before going below ground for that shift and upon returning to the surface after it read the barometer provided in pursuance of subsection (1) of section sixty of the Act.†

18. Every deputy to whom a deputy's district is assigned for any shift shall—

(*a*) record the names of the workmen under his charge in that district during that shift; and

(*b*) take all reasonable steps to ensure that such workmen understand and carry out any duties which fall to be performed by them in order to secure compliance with all requirements imposed by or under the Act or to secure the safety or health of any person employed at the mine.

19. Every deputy to whom a deputy's district is assigned shall take all reasonable steps to ensure that—

(*a*) all machinery, apparatus and other equipment in use in that district is properly maintained; and

(*b*) no machinery, apparatus or equipment which is found by or reported to him to be in an unsafe condition is used while in that condition.

‡**20.** A deputy to whom any district is assigned (otherwise than during the temporary absence of another deputy) shall, where not less than two ways of egress therefrom or from any place therein are required under section twenty-four

*This Regulation does not apply to shafts in the course of being sunk (see Regulation 32 (5)).
†See also Regulation 25 which requires the readings to be recorded.
‡This Regulation does not apply to shafts in the course of being sunk (see Regulation 32 (5)).

of the Act, forthwith make himself acquainted with two such ways from the district and from any such place therein, and shall thereafter travel along the whole of each of them once at least in each month during which that district is assigned to him.

***21.** (1) A deputy to whom any district is assigned for any shift shall not leave that district while workmen remain in it unless he has committed the charge of those workmen to a competent person, who shall during the absence of the deputy perform the functions of the deputy, and where there is in that district a person appointed pursuant to regulation 12 (5) to make pre-shift inspections the charge of those workmen shall if practicable be committed to him.

(2) Nothing in the last preceding paragraph shall be construed as relieving the deputy from any responsibility imposed on him by or under the Act or in particular as relieving the deputy from himself making the inspections and reports required by these regulations.

Deputies' duties on conclusion of shift

***22.** Every deputy to whom a deputy's district is assigned for any shift shall at the end of that shift, unless there is any person then in that district for a succeeding shift, ensure that in that district—

(*a*) the ventilation is taking its proper course; and

(*b*) all lights are extinguished and any supply of electricity is cut off, except any light or supply of which the continuance is necessary for the safety of the mine:

Provided that if—

(i) workmen are due to arrive in that district for a succeeding shift; or

(ii) a person appointed pursuant to regulation 12 (5) to make pre-shift inspections is in that district for the purpose of making such an inspection or is due to arrive in that district for that purpose—

not more than thirty minutes after the departure of the last workman in the shift to which that deputy is assigned, this regulation shall not require the extinction of any fixed electric lights.

***23.** A deputy to whom a deputy's district is assigned for any shift shall not leave the mine at the end of that shift if any workman is due to arrive in that district for a succeeding shift within one hour after the departure of the last workman in the shift to which that deputy is assigned until he has conferred with the deputy succeeding him and has given that deputy all information in his possession necessary for the safety of persons who will be employed in the district.

23A. Every person appointed pursuant to regulation 12 (5) to make pre-shift inspections shall without prejudice to any other obligations imposed on him by the Act or these regulations confer with the deputy to whom the district of which he makes any such inspection is assigned for the shift in respect of

*See Regulation 32 (6) as regards shafts in the course of being sunk.

which that inspection is made and give to him all the information in his possession necessary for the safety of persons who will be employed in the district.

Deputies' reports

24. (1) Every person who has made a pre-shift inspection shall forthwith upon the completion thereof record and sign in a book* provided by the owner of the mine for the purpose a full and accurate report thereof which shall, except in so far as it consists of printed matter, be in his own handwriting, and which in particular shall specify—

(*a*) the condition of roof and sides and of the ventilation in the district; and

(*b*) whether or not he has found therein any inflammable or noxious gas or other source of danger and if found particulars thereof.

(2) A copy of every report made under this regulation shall be posted at the pithead not later than ten o'clock in the morning of the day following that on which the report was made and shall be kept posted there until ten o'clock in the morning of the next following day.

25. Every deputy to whom a deputy's district is assigned for any shift shall forthwith after the end of that shift record and sign in a book provided by the owner of the mine for the purpose a full and accurate report,† which shall, except in so far as it consists of printed matter, be in his own handwriting, upon the performance of all his duties during that shift, and such report shall include any information in his possession which is material to the proper working of the mine or to the safety or health of persons who may be employed in that district, and the readings of the barometer made by him in pursuance of regulation seventeen.

Qualifications of deputies

26. (1) ‡No person shall be qualified to be appointed, or to be, a deputy unless he is the holder of—

(*a*) a first or second class certificate of competency valid with respect to that mine; or

(*b*) a deputy's certificate granted by the Minister on the recommendation of the Mining Qualifications Board§ which shall, unless an inspector, by notice served on the manager of the mine consents to that person's being a deputy at that mine, be a certificate valid with respect to that mine; or

(*c*) a certificate given under subsection (2) of section fifteen of the Coal Mines Act 1911 (as amended by regulation fifteen of the Coal Mines (Officials and Inspections) General Regulations 1951), being a certificate relating to his service as a deputy before the coming into operation of that regulation; or

---

*M. & Q. Form No. 231.
†M. & Q. Form No. 232.
‡See Regulation 32 (7) as regards shafts in the course of being sunk.
§See the Board's rules relating to these certificates on page 369.

(*d*) a certificate given under sub-paragraph (*d*) of paragraph (1) of regulation eighteen of the Coal Mines (Officials and Inspections) General Regulations 1951 being a certificate relating to his service as an underground official superior to the deputies but inferior to the manager or under-manager in any mine before the coming into operation of that regulation.

(2) No person shall be qualified to be appointed, or to be, a deputy unless he has within the last preceding five years obtained a certificate *that he was then able *to make proper tests for inflammable gas*, and able in so far as concerned his hearing to carry out his duties efficiently, being a certificate granted by a university or university college or by a school, college or institution maintained or assisted by a local education authority or by another body approved† by the Minister for that purpose:

Provided that this paragraph shall not apply to a deputy at a mine of stratified ironstone other than—

(*a*) a mine in the Cleveland district;

(*b*) a mine in any part of which the use of lamps or lights, other than permitted lights, is unlawful.

(3) No person shall be qualified to be appointed, or to be, a deputy unless he has within the last preceding five years obtained a certificate of proficiency in first aid granted by a society or body approved‡ by the Minister for the purpose:

Provided that this paragraph shall not apply to a person who is the holder of a certificate referred to in sub-paragraph (c) of paragraph (1) of this regulation.

(4) The expenses incurred by a person who is employed as a deputy at a mine in obtaining a certificate described in either of the two last preceding paragraphs shall be borne by the owner of that mine.

(5) Every certificate required by the preceding provisions of this regulation to be held as a qualification by any person for the time being appointed a deputy at any mine shall be kept at the office at that mine or at such other place as may be approved by an inspector.

27. (1) If in the case of a mine at which not more than thirty persons are employed below ground the number of persons employed thereat who may be appointed deputy in accordance with the provisions of the last preceding regulation is less by reason of sickness, holidays or other temporary cause than the number for the time being requisite for the full working of the mine, nothing in that regulation shall prevent any competent persons being appointed or being deputies in that mine.

*M. & Q. Form No. 306. Notwithstanding the amendment (underlined) made by the Coal and Other Mines (Managers and Officials) (Variation) Regulations 1961 to the Coal and Other Mines (Managers and Officials) Regulations 1956 any person who obtained prior to 1st June, 1961, a certificate 'that he was able to recognise the various gas caps formed in a flame safety-lamp in atmospheres containing one and one quarter per cent by volume of inflammable gas and more, and able in so far as concerned his hearing to carry out his duties effectively' shall, so long as five years have not elapsed since the issue of the certificate be deemed to have the qualification necessary for this regulation.

†No other bodies have been approved for this purpose.

‡See page 150.

(2) Nothing in this regulation shall authorise a person appointed in pursuance thereof to be a deputy for a period exceeding three months.

(3) The manager of a mine shall give to the inspector for the district notice of the making of any appointment under this regulation in respect of that mine and of the name and address of the person appointed within seven days after the making of the appointment.

Part V

Inspections outside deputies' districts

28. It shall be the duty of the manager of every mine to secure that competent persons, each of whom is qualified under regulation 26 to be a deputy, and unless an inspector by notice served on the manager consents to that person's making the inspections specified in the next following regulation, such qualification is valid with respect to that mine, are appointed by the manager and assigned by him to make such inspections.

29. A competent person appointed under the last preceding regulation shall ascertain by inspection the condition of the following parts of the mine, in so far as they are not within any deputy's district, at the times respectively specified, that is to say—

(*a*) at the beginning of and, in addition, at least once during each shift in which a workman is to be thereat, every working place at which—

(i) mineral is worked for the purpose of repairing, restoring or enlarging a road or preparing accommodation required for the working of the mine, or

(ii) apparatus, equipment or supports are being withdrawn in preparation for the abandonment of that place, or

(iii) any other work is done, being a place which persons do not regularly pass;

(*b*) at intervals not exceeding twenty-four hours, every place which persons regularly pass; and

(*c*) at intervals not exceeding seven days, every airway and road.

30. Every person who is assigned to make an inspection required by the last preceding regulation during any shift shall immediately before going below ground for that shift and upon returning to the surface after it read the barometer provided in pursuance of subsection (1) of section sixty of the Act.

31. Every person who has made an inspection required by regulation twenty-nine during any shift shall forthwith record and sign in a book* provided by the owner of the mine for the purpose a full and accurate report thereof which shall, except in so far as it consists of printed matter, be in his own handwriting, and shall include the readings of the barometer made by him in pursuance of the last preceding regulation.

*M. & Q. Form No. 234 for reports required by Regulation 29 (*a*) and (*b*), and M. & Q. Form No. 235 for reports required by Regulation 29 (*c*).

PART VI

Special provisions relating to shafts in the course of being sunk

32. (1) In relation to a mine or part of a mine consisting of a shaft in the course of being sunk the preceding regulations shall have effect subject to the following modifications.

(2) Nothing in regulation ten or thirteen shall require a deputy's district consisting of a shaft in the course of being sunk or the meeting station in relation to such a district to be defined or fixed by means of a plan.

(3) A pre-shift inspection of such a district made in pursuance of paragraph (1) of regulation twelve (otherwise than by virtue of the proviso thereto) shall be so made as to be completed as nearly as may be immediately before the workmen are to be lowered.

(4) An inspection of such a district in pursuance of regulation fifteen shall be made whenever workmen have been withdrawn for shotfiring or any other purpose and before they are lowered again. On such an inspection the deputy may be accompanied by not more than two competent workmen as assistants.

(5) Regulations sixteen and twenty shall not apply.

(6) At the end of his shift the deputy assigned to such a district shall not be raised to the surface leaving any workmen of that shift to be raised after him, and, if his shift is to be succeeded immediately by another shift, he shall not leave the bottom of the shaft until the deputy succeeding him has been lowered thereto. Regulations twenty-one, twenty-two and twenty-three shall not apply.

(7) Notwithstanding anything in paragraph (1) of regulation twenty-six a person shall be qualified to be appointed, and to be, a deputy if—

(*a*) he has attained the age of twenty-five years;

(*b*) he has had not less than five years' practical experience in the sinking of shafts;

(*c*) he holds the certificates required by paragraphs (2) and (3) of that regulation; and

(*d*) an inspector by notice served on the manager of the mine approves the appointment:

Provided that a deputy appointed by virtue of this paragraph shall not be assigned any district as the deputy thereof other than a district consisting of a shaft in the course of being sunk.

PART VII

Interpretation

33. (1) In these regulations the following expressions have the meanings hereby respectively assigned to them, that is to say:

'the Act' means the Mines and Quarries Act 1954;

'deputy' means a person appointed as such for the purposes of regulation nine;

'deputy's district' has the meaning assigned thereto in regulation ten;

'meeting station' has the meaning assigned thereto in regulation thirteen;

'mine' has the meaning assigned thereto in regulation one;

'pre-shift inspection' has the meaning assigned thereto in regulation twelve.

(2) Expressions to which meanings are assigned by the Act or by these regulations shall (unless the contrary intention appears) have the same meanings in any document issued under the provisions of these regulations.

(3) The Interpretation Act 1889 shall apply to the interpretation of these regulations as it applies to the interpretation of an Act of Parliament.

MECHANICS AND ELECTRICIANS

THE COAL AND OTHER MINES (MECHANICS AND ELECTRICIANS) REGULATIONS 1965

S.I. 1965 No. 1559

Arrangement of Regulations

PART I

General

Commencement and Citation

1. These regulations shall come into operation on 23rd August 1965 and may be cited as the Coal and Other Mines (Mechanics and Electricians) Regulations 1965.

Interpretation

2.—(1) In these regulations, unless the context otherwise requires, the following expressions have the meanings hereby respectively assigned to them, that is to say—

'the Act' means the Mines and Quarries Act 1954;

'deputy' has the meaning assigned thereto in the Coal and Other Mines (Managers and Officials) Regulations 1956;*

'electrical apparatus' includes electric cables and any part of any machinery, apparatus or appliance, being a part designed for the generation, conversion, storage, transmission or utilisation of electricity, but excludes any electric cable, machinery, apparatus or appliance or part thereof which is not used and is not intended to be used as, and does not form and is not intended to form, part of the equipment of a mine;

'electrical engineering staff' has the meaning assigned thereto in regulation 6;

'flexible cable' means an electric cable which is designed to be movable while in use;

'incendive sparking' means, in relation to any electrical apparatus, sparking in such circumstances that inflammable gas present in the air outside the apparatus might be ignited directly or indirectly;

'mechanical apparatus' includes any machinery, apparatus or appliance used in connection with the generation, conversion, storage, transmission or utilisation of mechanical energy and ropes, chains, permanent haulage track and rolling stock, but excludes any machinery, apparatus or appliance or part thereof which for the purposes of these regulations is electrical apparatus and anything which is not used and is not intended to be used as,

*See page 188.

and does not form and is not intended to form, part of the equipment of a mine;

'mechanical energy' means energy derived from steam, water or other fluid, wind, compressed air or gas, electricity, combustion of fuel or any other source;

'mechanical engineering staff' has the meaning assigned thereto in regulation 5;

'mine' has the meaning assigned thereto in regulation 3;

'person having supervisory duties' means, in the case of mechanical engineering staff, the mechanical engineer or the mechanic in charge, or a supervisory mechanic and, in the case of electrical engineering staff, the electrical engineer or the electrician in charge, or a supervisory electrician;

'portable apparatus' includes electrical apparatus that is designed to be moved while working;

'prime mover' means an engine or motor which provides mechanical energy;

'supervisory mechanic' has the meaning assigned thereto in regulation 5;

'supervisory electrician' has the meaning assigned thereto in regulation 6.

(2) For the purposes of ascertaining the number of prime movers or electric motors at any mine and of any provision of these regulations requiring systematic examination and testing of any mechanical or electrical apparatus, no account shall be taken of any mechanical or electrical apparatus which is surplus to ordinary requirements and which has not been issued for use or installed as a standby or which, if so issued, has been withdrawn from use for repair or otherwise and has not been re-issued.

(3) Expressions to which meanings are assigned by the Act or by these regulations shall (unless the contrary intention appears) have the same meanings in any document issued under the provisions of these regulations.

(4) The Interpretation Act 1889 shall apply to the interpretation of these regulations as it applies to the interpretation of an Act of Parliament.

Application

3. Except where the application thereof is further expressly limited, these regulations shall apply to every mine of coal, stratified ironstone, shale or fireclay, and in these regulations 'mine' means (except where further expressly limited) such a mine.

Revocation

4. The Coal and Other Mines (Mechanics and Electricians) Regulations 1956, the Coal and Other Mines (Mechanics and Electricians) (Variation) Regulations 1958 and the Coal and Other Mines (Mechanics and Electricians) (Variation) Regulations 1961 are hereby revoked.

PART II

Appointment of mechanical engineering staff and electrical engineering staff

Mechanical engineering staff

5.—(1) For every mine there shall be appointed by the manager a competent person to be the mechanical engineer or the mechanic in charge; as many competent persons as may be required to supervise the proper installation, examination, testing and maintenance of all mechanical apparatus* at the mine in accordance with the following provisions (in these regulations referred to as 'supervisory mechanics'); and as many competent persons to be craftsmen mechanics as may be required to effect such proper installation, examination, testing and maintenance as aforesaid. In relation to a mine, the mechanical engineer or mechanic in charge, the supervisory mechanics and the craftsmen mechanics are hereinafter referred to as 'the mechanical engineering staff.'

(2) In the case of any mine at which the total number† of prime movers exceeds seventy-five the manager shall ensure that, at any time when the mechanical engineer or mechanic in charge is not on duty, a supervisory mechanic is in charge at the mine whenever any prime mover is being used in the mine for any purpose specified in an instruction in writing given by the manager to the mechanical engineer or mechanic in charge and for the time being in force.

Electrical engineering staff

6.—(1) For every mine at which electricity is used there shall be appointed by the manager a competent person to be the electrical engineer or the electrician in charge; as many competent persons as may be required to supervise the proper installation, examination, testing and maintenance of all electrical apparatus* at the mine in accordance with the following provisions (in these regulations referred to as 'supervisory electricians'); and as many competent persons to be craftsmen electricians as may be required to effect such proper installation, examination, testing and maintenance as aforesaid. In relation to a mine, the electrical engineer or electrician in charge, the supervisory electricians and the craftsmen electricians are hereinafter referred to as 'the electrical engineering staff.'

(2) In the case of any mine at which the total number† of electric motors exceeds seventy-five the manager shall ensure that at any time when the electrical engineer or electrician in charge is not on duty a supervisory electrician is in charge at the mine whenever any electric motor is being used in the mine for any purpose specified in an instruction in writing given by the manager to the electrical engineer or electrician in charge and for the time being in force.

Supplementary provisions as to supervisory mechanics and electricians

7.—(1) A copy of any instruction given in pursuance of paragraph (2) of either of the two last preceding regulations and for the time being in force shall be kept at the office at the mine or at such other place as may be approved by an inspector, and if an inspector at any time so requests the manager shall send to him a copy of any such instruction.

(2) If in a case to which paragraph (2) of either of the two last preceding regulations applies an inspector is of opinion that at any time when the mechanical engineer or mechanic in charge is not on duty a supervisory mechanic, or at any time when the electrical engineer or electrician in charge is not on duty a supervisory electrician, as the case may be, ought to be in charge at the

*As defined in Regulation 2 (1).
†See also Regulation 2 (2).

mine whenever a prime mover or electric motor is being used in the mine for a purpose not specified under that paragraph, he may serve on the manager a notice requiring him to give an instruction accordingly.

(3) The provisions of Part XV of the Act* with respect to references upon notices served by inspectors shall apply to a notice served under the last preceding paragraph, and the relevant ground of objection to such a notice shall be that it is not necessary for a supervisory mechanic or a supervisory electrician, as the case may be, to be in charge at the mine whenever a prime mover or electric motor is being used in the mine for the purpose specified in the notice in order to secure the proper supervision of mechanical or electrical apparatus thereat.

8. Nothing in regulation 5 or 6 shall prevent a competent person being a member both of the mechanical engineering staff and of the electrical engineering staff, or prevent a person having supervisory duties from himself effecting any work of installation, examination, testing or maintenance of mechanical or electrical apparatus, as the case may be, without supervision by another.

PART III

Duties of mechanical engineering staff, electrical engineering staff and other persons concerned with mechanical or electrical apparatus

†**9.** It shall be the duty of the mechanical engineer or mechanic in charge in respect of mechanical apparatus, and of the electrical engineer or electrician in charge in respect of electrical apparatus, to ensure that the mechanical engineering staff or the electrical engineering staff, as the case may be, supervise or effect—

(*a*) the installation of all such apparatus at the mine;

(*b*) the examination and testing of all such apparatus before it is put into use after installation, re-installation or repair;

(*c*) the maintenance in safe working condition and in accordance with all requirements imposed by or under the Act of all such apparatus at the mine; and

(*d*) the systematic examination and testing of all such apparatus at the mine in accordance with the scheme therefor for the time being in operation.

Schemes of maintenance

†**10.**—(1) It shall be the duty of the manager of every mine to ensure that there shall be at all times in force a scheme in respect of all mechanical apparatus at the mine other than simple mechanical supports, and, if electricity is used thereat, a scheme in respect of all electrical apparatus thereat, being a scheme providing for the systematic examination and testing of all mechanical apparatus

*See Section 170 of the 1954 Act.

†See also Nos. 19 and 71 (1) of the Shafts Outlets and Roads Regulations 1960, No. 24 of the Locomotives Regulations 1956 and No. 9 of the Steam Boilers Regulations 1956 pages 235, 249, 170 and 272, which are expressed to be without prejudice to the generality of these two Regulations.

or electrical apparatus, as the case may be, at the mine to ensure proper maintenance thereof.

(2) Any such scheme shall specify the intervals (which may be different for different apparatus and parts of apparatus) within which all mechanical or electrical apparatus, as the case may be, must be examined and tested and the nature of the examination and testing to be carried out on each occasion, and the manner in which the results of every examination and test made pursuant to such a scheme are to be recorded.

(3) The scheme for each mine or copies thereof shall be kept at the office at the mine or at such other place as may be approved by an inspector.

(4) If an inspector is of opinion that amendment of a scheme is necessary to ensure the proper maintenance of any mechanical or electrical apparatus at the mine or to secure the keeping of proper records thereof, he may serve on the manager a notice requiring him to remedy the defect.

(5) The provisions of Part XV of the Act* with respect to references upon notices served by inspectors shall apply to a notice served under the last preceding paragraph and the relevant ground of objection to such a notice shall be that the scheme already ensures the proper maintenance of all mechanical or electrical apparatus at that mine, or the keeping of proper records thereof, as the case may be.

(6) Every record of any test or examination made pursuant to any such scheme, or a copy of such record, shall, until the expiration of three years after such test or examination, be kept at the office at the mine or at such other place as may be approved by an inspector and be open to inspection by, or by a person authorised in that behalf in writing by, any person employed at the mine.

(7) In this regulation 'simple mechanical supports' means hydraulic props or friction props for the support of the roof or side of any place in the mine not being supports which are advanced and set to the roof by mechanical energy, and 'prop' includes chock.

11.—(1) Persons, other than the mechanical engineering staff and the electrical engineering staff, may be instructed in writing by the manager of the mine to carry out such duties relating to—

(*a*) the installation, examination, testing or maintenance of mechanical or electrical apparatus; or

(*b*) the operation of any machinery or electrical apparatus;

as may be specified in the instruction being duties for which they are competent.

(2) No person shall be instructed under paragraph (1) (*a*) of this regulation to carry out any duty for which technical knowledge and experience are necessary to avoid danger except under such degree of supervision by one of the mechanical engineering staff or electrical engineering staff, being a person having supervisory duties, as may be appropriate having regard to the nature of the work and the knowledge and experience of the person concerned.

*See Section 170 of the 1954 Act.

(3) No person shall commence or do any work upon any conductor, or in proximity to an exposed conductor, being in either case a conductor in a circuit in which the voltage exceeds twenty-five, unless one of the electrical engineering staff has ensured that the conductor has been made dead and has taken any necessary steps by earthing or otherwise to ensure that it will remain dead whilst the work in question is being carried out:

Provided that the provisions of this paragraph shall not apply to—

(*a*) the cleaning of a commutator or slip-rings, if the electrical engineer or electrician in charge has taken any necessary steps to ensure that the voltage between no two brushes of the apparatus being cleaned will exceed six hundred and fifty whilst the cleaning is in progress;

(*b*) work on, or in proximity to, telephone and signalling apparatus or a conductor in or connected to apparatus which is such that, by reason of the inherent nature of the apparatus, it is impracticable for the conductor to be made dead whilst the work in question is being carried out;

(*c*) the use of any electrical instrument, other than a test lamp, for testing a circuit on the surface of the mine where the test is being made in a workshop or on a circuit which forms part of an electric winding apparatus;

(*d*) the use of any electrical instrument for testing insulation resistance or conductance;

(*e*) the removal or insertion of lamps in a lighting circuit.

(4) No person shall remove or insert a lamp in a lighting circuit unless the lamp-holder has been made dead—

(*a*) by one of the electrical engineering staff; or

(*b*) if the lamp-holder is neither at a place within nine hundred feet of a working face accessible from that place, nor at a place hazardous by reason of the presence or possibility of inflammable gas, by one of the electrical engineering staff or by a person instructed under paragraph (1) of this regulation whose duties include the making dead of electric lighting circuits in the mine.

12.—(1) No person whose duties include the operation of any portable electrical apparatus supplied with electricity by means of a flexible trailing cable shall at any time either leave that apparatus while it is working or leave the working place (except for the purpose of cutting off the supply of electricity to the cable) without ensuring that the cable has been made dead, unless his instructions expressly authorise him to do so.

(2) A person whose duties include the operation during his shift of any electrical apparatus supplied with electricity by means of a flexible trailing cable shall ensure, before using that cable during that shift, that so much of it as is accessible is examined, and subsequently ensure that any further parts which become accessible are examined and shall not use any cable which is thus found to be damaged or defective.

13.—(1) Without prejudice to the generality of section 80 of the Act a member of the mechanical engineering staff, in respect of mechanical apparatus, a member of the electrical engineering staff, in respect of electrical apparatus, or a person instructed under regulation 11 shall stop forthwith the use of any such apparatus which it appears to him in the course of his duties may be in a dangerous condition by reason of some mechanical or electrical defect or abnormality, and cut off the supply of mechanical energy thereto or make dead the circuit or part of a circuit in which it is connected, as the case may be, and take any other necessary action to avoid danger. Unless in the case of a person instructed under regulation 11 his duties include the repair of the defect and he has repaired it, that apparatus shall not be used again at the mine until one of the mechanical engineering staff or the electrical engineering staff, as the case may require, is satisfied that it is safe to do so.

(2) Without prejudice to the generality thereof the provisions of the last preceding paragraph shall apply in any case in which incendive sparking* occurs in any electrical apparatus below ground in any part of a mine in which inflammable gas, although not normally present, is likely to occur in quantities sufficient to indicate danger.

(3) Without prejudice to the generality of section 80 of the Act a member of the mechanical engineering staff, in respect of mechanical apparatus, a member of the electrical engineering staff, in respect of electrical apparatus, or a person instructed under regulation 11 shall report forthwith to an official of the mine anything which it appears to him in the course of his duties may affect the safe use of any such apparatus, and which it is not part of his duties to prevent or remedy.

14.—(1) Every member of the mechanical engineering staff being a person having supervisory duties and every member of the electrical engineering staff being such a person shall record in books† provided by the owner of the mine—

(*a*) any action taken by him or under his supervision in pursuance of regulation 13;

(*b*) a report of any defect revealed by any examination or test of any mechanical or electrical apparatus made pursuant to regulation 9, being an examination or test carried out or supervised by him or reported to him, and of the action taken to remedy such defect;

(*c*) any other information for which provision is made in such a book.

(2) Without prejudice to the generality of regulation 13, every craftsman mechanic and every craftsman electrician, and every person instructed under regulation 11 shall forthwith report any defect revealed by any examination or test carried out by him, in the case of mechanical apparatus to a member of the mechanical engineering staff being a person having supervisory duties, and in the case of electrical apparatus to a member of the electrical engineering staff being such a person.

*As defined in Regulation 2 (1).
†The relevant M. & Q. Forms are No. 267 for mechanical plant, and No. 268 for electrical plant. See also the footnotes to Nos. 19 and 71(1) of the Shafts, Outlets and Roads Regulations 1960 No. 24 of the Locomotives Regulations 1956 and No. 9 of the Steam Boilers Regulations 1956.

PART IV

Qualifications of persons having supervisory duties

Mechanical engineers or mechanics in charge, and electrical engineers or electricians in charge

15.—(1) No person shall be qualified to be appointed or to be the mechanical engineer or mechanic in charge or the electrical engineer or electrician in charge for a mine of coal, shale or fireclay, being a mine at which—

(i) the total number of prime movers is not less than seventy-five; or

(ii) there is for the time being in force a direction given by an inspector by notice served on the manager of the mine, being a direction given on the ground that the nature of the mechanical apparatus or the electrical apparatus or both, as the case may be, at the mine or the conditions in which that apparatus is used thereat increase the risk of danger, that this paragraph shall apply to the mine unless—

(*a*) he is at least twenty-five years of age, and is the holder, as the case may be, of a mechanical engineer's certificate or electrical engineer's certificate, being a certificate valid with respect to that mine; or

(*b*) he is the holder of a service certificate showing that—

(i) during a period of at least eighteen months between 1st January 1957 and 1st January 1959 he had been, as the case may be, the mechanical engineer or mechanic in charge for a mine at which the total number of prime movers exceeded seventy-five or the electrical engineer or the electrician in charge for a mine at which the total number of electric motors exceeded seventy-five; or

(ii) during a period of at least two years between 1st October 1954 and 1st January 1959 he had been, as the case may be, the mechanical engineer or mechanic in charge for such a mine or the electrical engineer or electrician in charge for such a mine.

(2) No person shall be qualified to be appointed or to be the mechanica engineer or mechanic in charge or the electrical engineer or electrician in charge for a mine of coal, shale or fireclay to which the preceding paragraph does not apply, unless—

(*a*) he is at least twenty-three years of age and is the holder, as the case may be, of a mechanical engineer's certificate or electrical engineer's certificate or a mechanic's certificate class I or electrician's certificate class I, being in any case a certificate valid with respect to that mine; or

(*b*) he is the holder of a service certificate showing that during a period of at least six months between 1st April 1955 and 31st December 1955 he had been, as the case may be—

(i) the mechanical engineer or mechanic in charge for a mine at which the total number of prime movers exceeded ten or in which a prime mover capable of developing more than ten horse-power was used at or within thirty feet of a working face; or

(ii) the electrical engineer or electrician in charge for a mine at which the total number of electric motors exceeded ten or in which an electric motor was used at or within thirty feet of a working face.

(3) No person shall be qualified to be appointed or to be the mechanical engineer or mechanic in charge or the electrical engineer or electrician in charge for a mine of stratified ironstone unless—

(*a*) he is at least twenty-three years of age, and is the holder, as the case may be, of—

(i) a mechanical engineer's certificate or electrical engineer's certificate being a certificate valid with respect to all mines or any class of mine; or

(ii) a mechanic's certificate class I or electrician's certificate class I, being a certificate valid with respect to mines of coal, shale or fireclay; or

(*b*) he is qualified in accordance with paragraph (1) (*b*) of this regulation to hold a corresponding appointment at a mine of coal, shale or fireclay; or

(*c*) he was before 1st January 1959 qualified in accordance with paragraph (2) (*b*) of this regulation to hold a corresponding appointment at a mine of coal, shale or fireclay; or

(*d*) he is the holder of a service certificate showing that during a period of at least six months between 1st April 1961 and 31st December 1961 he had been, as the case may be—

(i) the mechanical engineer or mechanic in charge for a mine of stratified ironstone at which the total number of prime movers exceeded ten or in which a prime mover capable of developing more than ten horse-power was used at or within thirty feet of a working face; or

(ii) the electrical engineer or electrician in charge for a mine of stratified ironstone at which the total number of electric motors exceeded ten or in which an electric motor was used at or within thirty feet of a working face.

Supervisory mechanics and supervisory electricians

16.—(1) No person shall be qualified to be appointed or to be a supervisory mechanic for a mine of coal, shale or fireclay unless he is the holder of—

(*a*) a mechanical engineer's certificate or a mechanic's certificate, being a certificate valid with respect to that mine; or

(*b*) (i) a certificate granted by a person authorised in that behalf by the Minister showing that during a period of at least six months between 1st October 1955 and 31st December 1956 he had been the mechanical engineer or mechanic in charge for a mine or had performed responsible or supervisory duties in connection with the installation, examination, testing and maintenance of mechanical apparatus at a mine at which the total number of prime movers exceeded ten or in which a prime mover capable of developing more than ten horse-power was used at or within thirty feet of a working face; and

(ii) a certificate as to his knowledge of the elementary principles of mechanical engineering granted by the Minister on the recommendation of the Mining Qualifications Board, or a certificate granted under regulation 12 (2) (*b*) (ii) of the Coal Mines (Mechanics and Electricians) General Regulations 1954.*

(2) No person shall be qualified to be appointed or to be a supervisory electrician for a mine of coal, shale or fireclay unless he is the holder of—

(*a*) an electrical engineer's certificate or an electrician's certificate, being a certificate valid with respect to that mine; or

(*b*) a service certificate showing that during a period of at least six months between 1st October 1954 and 31st December 1955 he had been the electrical engineer or electrician in charge for a mine or an electrician for a mine at which the total number of electric motors exceeded ten or in which an electric motor was used at or within thirty feet of a working face.

Supervisory mechanics and supervisory electricians to be in charge

17. No supervisory mechanic for a mine of coal, shale or fireclay or supervisory electrician for a mine of coal, shale or fireclay shall be qualified to be in charge at such a mine, being a mine at which—

(i) the total number of prime movers is not less than seventy-five; or

(ii) there is for the time being in force a direction given by an inspector by notice served on the manager of the mine, being a direction given on the ground that the nature of the mechanical apparatus or the electrical apparatus or both, as the case may be, at the mine or the conditions in which the apparatus is used thereat increase the risk of danger, that this paragraph shall apply to the mine

when the mechanical engineer or mechanic in charge, or the electrical engineer or electrician in charge, as the case may be, is not on duty unless—

(*a*) he is at least twenty-three years of age and is the holder of such a certificate as is described in regulation 15 (2) being a certificate prescribed by that paragraph as a qualification for appointment as the mechanical engineer or mechanic in charge or the electrical engineer or electrician in charge, as the case may be, for a mine to which that paragraph relates; or

(*b*) he is the holder of a service certificate, signed by the manager of the relevant mine not later than 31st July 1961, showing that on at least ninety working days between 1st January 1956 and 30th April 1961 he took charge at such a mine, being a mine at which the total number of prime movers or electric motors, as the case may be, exceeded seventy-five, when the mechanical engineer or the mechanic in charge or the electrical engineer or electrician in charge, as the case may be, was not on duty.

Exceptions and exemptions

18.—(1) Nothing in regulations 15 and 16 shall apply to a person having supervisory duties at a mine—

(*a*) at which the total number of prime movers or electric motors does not exceed ten and in which no prime mover capable of developing

*S.I. 1954 No. 594.

more than ten horse-power or, as the case may be, electric motor is used at or within thirty feet of a working face; or

(*b*) at which not more than fourteen persons are employed below ground, unless there is for the time being in force a direction given by an inspector by notice served on the manager of the mine, being a direction given on the ground that the nature of the mechanical apparatus or the electrical apparatus or both, as the case may be, at the mine or the conditions in which that apparatus is used thereat increase the risk of danger, that such persons having supervisory duties as may be specified in such notice should be qualified to hold a corresponding appointment in a mine of the same class to which neither sub-paragraph (*a*) nor sub-paragraph (*b*) of this paragraph applies.

(2) An inspector may by notice served on the manager of any mine exempt it from the application of any provision contained in the three last preceding regulations.

19. Without prejudice to the generality of section 88 of the Act, it shall be the duty of the manager of every mine of stratified ironstone to secure that no person who has not been employed in work below ground in any mine to which the Act applies is employed in the mechanical engineering staff or electrical engineering staff in the first-mentioned mine in work below ground unless for at least the first twenty working days of his employment below ground he is throughout every period during which he is so employed accompanied by a deputy, an official of the mine superior to the deputies, or one of the mechanical engineering staff or electrical engineering staff, being a person appointed for the purpose by the manager in pursuance of section 13 of the Act who is competent to give instruction in safe methods of working and travelling below ground in a mine.

20. In this Part of these regulations—

'mechanical engineer's certificate', 'mechanic's certificate', 'electrical engineer's certificate' and 'electrician's certificate' mean certificates so entitled granted by the Minister on the recommendation of the Mining Qualifications Board* and expressed to be valid with respect to all mines or to mines of a specified class or description and, unless the context otherwise requires, 'mechanic's certificate' and 'electrician's certificate' include such certificates class I or class II;

'service certificate' means a certificate on the form provided for the purpose by the Minister signed by the manager of the mine at which the appointment referred to therein has been held and, within fourteen days of signature, authenticated by the owner of that mine or a representative of the owner superior to the manager.

---

*See the Board's rules relating to these certificates on page 349.

MEDICAL EXAMINATIONS

THE MINES (MEDICAL EXAMINATIONS) REGULATIONS 1964

S.I. 1964 No. 209

Commencement and Citation

1. These regulations shall come into operation on 1st October 1964, and may be cited as the Mines (Medical Examinations) Regulations 1964.

Interpretation

2.—(1) In these regulations the following expressions have the meanings hereby respectively assigned to them, that is to say—

'the Act' means the Mines and Quarries Act 1954;

'approved doctor' has the meaning assigned thereto in regulation 5;

'medical examinations book' has the meaning assigned thereto in regulation 8;

'the Medical Examinations Regulations of 1956' means the Coal Mines (Medical Examinations) Regulations 1956; and

'the Miscellaneous Mines Regulations' means the Miscellaneous Mines (General) Regulations 1956.

(2) Expressions to which meanings are assigned by the Act or by these regulations shall (unless the contrary intention appears) have the same meanings in any document issued under the provisions of these regulations.

(3) The Interpretation Act 1889 shall apply to the interpretation of these regulations as it applies to the interpretation of an Act of Parliament.

Revocation

3. The Medical Examinations Regulations of 1956 and regulation 70 of the Miscellaneous Mines Regulations are hereby revoked.

Application

4. These regulations shall apply to every mine of every class.

Medical Examination of young persons and the giving of certificates

5.—(1) The owner of every mine shall make arrangements for the medical examination at the expense of the owner by an approved doctor of every young person when first employed or about to be so employed, before or within thirty days after the first employment of that young person at the mine:

Provided that this paragraph shall not apply in relation to a young person who—

(*a*) has been medically examined pursuant to this paragraph in connection with employment at another mine;

(*b*) has been medically examined pursuant to the Medical Examinations Regulations of 1956 and to whom there was issued pursuant thereto a certificate which specified that he was fit for employment at a mine; or (*c*) has been medically examined pursuant to regulation 70 of the Miscellaneous Mines Regulations and has been certified fit for employment at a mine.

(2) The owner of every mine shall make arrangements for the medical examination at the expense of the owner by an approved doctor of every young person employed at the mine who has been medically examined pursuant to the Medical Examinations Regulations of 1956 and to whom a certificate pursuant to those regulations has been issued which specifies that a further examination of that young person is requisite, before or within thirty days after the date so specified for such further examination.

(3) The owner of every mine shall make arrangements for the medical examination at the expense of the owner by an approved doctor of every young person employed at the mine who has already been medically examined pursuant to either of the two preceding paragraphs, before or within thirty days after the expiry of the last certificate given pursuant to the next following paragraph in respect of that young person.

(4) The arrangements mentioned in the three preceding paragraphs shall provide for the approved doctor to give a certificate of the result of the examination by making and signing an entry thereof in the medical examinations book* provided by the owner of the mine.

(5) Such certificate may state whether in the opinion of the approved doctor the young person is—

(*a*) fit for employment at a mine;

(*b*) unfit for employment at a mine in a capacity or in work specified in such certificate; or

(*c*) unfit for employment at a mine,

and if in the opinion of the approved doctor further examination is requisite within a period less than a year the certificate may specify such period.

(6) The arrangements mentioned in paragraphs (1), (2) and (3) of this regulation shall provide for the approved doctor, if required by the young person examined, to give to him a copy of the certificate† and other entries in the medical examinations book in respect of the examination made pursuant to such arrangements.

(7) A certificate given in pursuance of this regulation shall—

(*a*) expire if a period within which further examination is requisite is specified pursuant to paragraph (5) of this regulation upon the expiration of that period and in any other case twelve months after the date of the examination in respect of which the certificate was given; and

(*b*) be revoked by the giving of any further certificate given pursuant to these regulations in respect of the same young person.

(8) For the purpose of these regulations 'an approved doctor' means a fully registered medical practitioner who is approved by the Minister for the purposes of these regulations.

---

*M. & Q. Form No. 312.
†M. & Q. Form No. 313.

Notices

6.—(1) The owner of a mine shall give notice to every young person employed or to be employed at the mine, for whose medical examination arrangements are required by the last preceding regulation to be made, requiring him to attend the approved doctor by whom he is to be examined and specifying the date and time and place at which the young person is to attend for such medical examination.

(2) The date specified in such notice shall be—

(*a*) in the case of a young person to be examined pursuant to regulation 5 (1) before or within thirty days after the commencement of his employment;

(*b*) in the case of a young person to be examined pursuant to regulation 5 (2) before or within thirty days after the date specified in the certificate therein mentioned for further examination; and

(*c*) in any other case before or within thirty days after the expiry of the certificate given in respect of the previous medical examination of that young person pursuant to these regulations.

(3) When any such notice as is mentioned in paragraph (1) of this regulation is given the owner of the mine shall give to the approved doctor, by whom the young person is to be examined, notice thereof including the name, date of birth and residence of that young person, and, in the case of a medical examination other than the first such examination of that young person pursuant to these regulations, particulars of the last certificate given in respect of that young person, unless the book containing such certificate is to be produced to the approved doctor at the time when that young person is to be examined, and in such case the notice shall state that such book is to be so produced and the page thereof upon which such certificate appears.

(4) Every notice required to be served pursuant to this regulation shall be in writing and shall be served on the young person or the approved doctor as the case may be not less than four days before the date specified in such notice on which that young person is to attend for examination.

Prohibition on employment of certain young persons

7.—(1) No young person, for whose medical examination arrangements are to be made pursuant to regulation 5, shall be employed at a mine after the last date upon which such medical examination ought to take place pursuant thereto, until a certificate in respect of such examination has been given.

(2) No young person shall be employed at any mine or employed in any capacity or in any work at a mine, if there is in force a certificate given in respect of that young person pursuant to these regulations stating that he is unfit for any employment at a mine, or for employment in that capacity or in that work, as the case may be:

Provided that a young person may be so employed for a period not exceeding fourteen days from the giving of such certificate if it appears that the nature of his unfitness is such that his continued employment for that period will not be prejudicial to the health and safety of that young person or of any other person.

Medical examinations book and information

8. The owner of every mine shall provide a book* (in these regulations referred to as a 'Medical examinations book') in which shall be entered particulars of every notice given to a young person to attend for any medical examination and every certificate given after such examination, and in any case in which the employment of a young person is terminated in pursuance of regulation 7 the date of termination and the reason therefor.

9. The manager of any mine shall, if so requested by the owner or manager of any other mine, send to him any information with respect to any young person as such owner or manager may reasonably require to enable him or them to comply with these regulations with respect to the employment of that young person at that other mine, being information recorded in pursuance of regulation 5 of the Medical Examinations Regulations of 1956 or otherwise, in the register of young persons kept in pursuance of section 131 of the Act, or recorded in pursuance of these regulations in the medical examinations book.

*M. & Q. Form No. 312.

REFEREES

THE MINES AND QUARRIES

(REFERENCES) RULES 1956

S.I. 1956 No. 1784

Form and service of counter-notice

1. Every counter-notice served by a person (hereinafter referred to as an 'objector') under subsection (2) of section one hundred and seventy of the Act (being a counter-notice demanding a reference upon a notice served by an inspector on him) shall—

(*a*) be in the form specified in the first schedule to these rules or as near thereto as circumstances will admit; and

(*b*) be served in duplicate on the inspector who served the notice upon which a reference is demanded (that inspector being hereinafter referred to as 'the inspector') within the period of twenty-one days from the date of service of that notice;

and in these rules 'counter-notice' means a counter-notice which complies with the requirements of this rule.

Application for selection of referee

2. Every inspector on whom has been served a counter-notice shall, as soon as may be and in any event within the period of twenty-one days from the date of service thereof, apply to the nominated selector for the selection of a referee and forward with the said application a copy of that counter-notice and a copy of the notice upon which a reference is demanded.

Statement of grounds of objection

3. (1) Every objector shall serve in duplicate upon the inspector a statement specifying every ground of objection to the notice upon which a reference is demanded, being a relevant ground of objection for the purposes of subsection (4) of the said section one hundred and seventy of the Act, and the facts and contentions relied on in support of that ground (that statement being hereinafter referred to as 'the objection statement').

(2) Every objection statement shall be served upon the inspector within the period of twenty-one days from the date of service of the relevant notice or within such longer period (if any) as may be agreed or ordered under rule fourteen.

(3) In any case in which the inspector is of opinion that the service of an objection statement is unnecessary for the purposes of the reference he shall serve on the objector a notice to that effect and the preceding provisions of this rule shall not apply to that reference.

Reply to objection statement

4. (1) Every inspector upon whom in pursuance of paragraph (2) of rule three an objection statement has been served shall serve upon the objector a statement (hereinafter referred to as 'the reply') specifying the facts and contentions relied on in rebuttal of the objection statement.

(2) Every reply shall be served upon the objector as soon as may be after service of the relevant objection statement and in any event either within the period of twenty-one days from the date of that service or within such longer period (if any) as may be agreed or ordered under rule fourteen.

Appointment of referee and notification to parties to reference

5. In every case in which the nominated selector selects two or more persons to be referee on a reference he shall appoint one of them to preside over the reference.

6. Forthwith after the appointment of a referee on any reference the nominated selector shall notify the parties to that reference of the referee's name and address.

Furnishing of documents to the referee

7. Forthwith after—

(*a*) the service of a notice in pursuance of paragraph (3) of rule three or the service of the reply in pursuance of paragraph (2) of rule four; or

(*b*) receipt of the notification of the name and address of the referee;

(whichever of (*a*) and (*b*) is the later) the inspector shall send to the referee a copy of the notice served by him in pursuance of paragraph (3) of rule three or a copy of the objection statement and a copy of the reply, as the case may be.

Hearing of reference

8. (1) Without prejudice to the provisions of paragraph (*a*) of rule eleven, as soon as may be after rule seven has been complied with the referee shall determine a date, time and place for the hearing of the reference and notify the parties to the reference of the date, time and place so determined and may notify, or require any party to the reference to notify, in such manner as he thinks fit, the date, time and place so determined to any person appearing to him to be affected by the notice upon which a reference has been demanded or any association or body representative of any such person.

(2) Forthwith after any party to the reference, being the owner or manager of the relevant mine or the owner or a manager of the relevant quarry (as the case may be), has been notified in pursuance of paragraph (1) of this rule, that party shall take such steps as may be necessary to secure that notice of the date, time and place so notified is kept posted at that mine or quarry at all times at which persons are employed thereat during the period until the quashing or confirmation of the notice upon which a reference has been demanded, in such characters and in such positions as to be easily seen and read by the persons employed thereat, and in the form specified in the second schedule to these rules or as near thereto as circumstances will admit.

9. No objector shall (except in a case in which a notice under paragraph (3) of rule three has been served on him), on the hearing of a reference, be entitled without the consent of the referee to raise, or adduce evidence with respect to, any ground of objection to the relevant notice other than a ground of objection specified in the relevant objection statement.

10. In every case in which the nominated selector has selected two or more persons to be referee on a reference—

(*a*) every decision on the reference of a majority of those persons present and voting shall be the decision of the referee;

(*b*) in any case in which on the reference the votes of those persons present and voting are equally divided, the person presiding over the reference shall have a second or casting vote.

Powers of the referee

11. The referee shall, for the purposes of any reference, have power—

(*a*) to dispose of any outstanding matter on the reference and in particular any matter in any case in which any party to the reference has failed to comply with any of the preceding rules or in which any party to the reference fails to appear at the hearing;

(*b*) to enter and inspect any mine or quarry affected by the relevant notice;

(*c*) (so far as appears to him to be reasonable having regard to the desirability of quashing or confirming the relevant notice as soon as may be) to adjourn the reference from time to time and from place to place; and

(*d*) subject to the provisions of the Act and of these rules, to regulate the procedure on the reference.

Payment of costs

12. The referee may make such orders as he thinks fit respecting the payment of the costs of the reference (including the payment of his remuneration and allowances).

Remuneration of the referee

13. The amount of the remuneration and allowances to be paid to a referee upon a reference shall be determined by the Minister with the approval of the Treasury.

Extensions of time

14. (1) In any case in which provision is made in these rules for such extension of any period of time as may be agreed or ordered under this rule, the period specified in that provision may, upon the application of any party to the reference, be extended—

(*a*) by agreement in writing by the other party or parties (as the case may be) to the reference; or

(*b*) in default of such agreement—

(i) (in any case in which application for the extension is made before the appointment of a referee) by order of the nominated selector;

(ii) (in any other case) by order of the referee.

(2) Every application for an extension of time shall be made in writing by the person seeking the extension to the person or persons empowered at the time of the making of that application to agree to or order that extension, and any such agreement or order may be reached or made although the application for the same is not made until after the expiration of the period of time in relation to which an extension is sought.

Interpretation

15. (1) In these rules the following expressions have the meanings hereby respectively assigned to them, that is to say—

'the Act' means the Mines and Quarries Act 1954;

'counter-notice' has the meaning assigned thereto in rule one;

'inspector' has the meaning assigned thereto in rule one;

'objection statement' has the meaning assigned thereto in rule three;

'objector' has the meaning assigned thereto in rule one;

'parties to the reference' means, in relation to any reference, the inspector who served the relevant notice and the person or persons who served the relevant counter-notice or counter-notices (as the case may be);

'referee' means, in relation to any reference, the person or persons to whom a notice stands referred in pursuance of a selection or direction by the nominated selector under subsection (2) of section one hundred and seventy of the Act;

'reference' means a reference under section one hundred and seventy of the Act; and

'reply' has the meaning assigned thereto in rule four.

(2) Expressions to which meanings are assigned by the Act or by these rules shall (unless the contrary intention appears) have the same meanings in any document issued under the provisions of these rules.

(3) The Interpretation Act 1889 shall apply to the interpretation of these rules as it applies to the interpretation of an Act of Parliament.

Commencement and citation

16. These rules shall come into operation at the commencement of the Act and may be cited as the Mines and Quarries (References) Rules 1956.

FIRST SCHEDULE Rule 1

MINES AND QUARRIES ACT 1954.

THE MINES AND QUARRIES (REFERENCES) RULES 1956.

COUNTER-NOTICE

DEMANDING A REFERENCE UPON A NOTICE

IN THE MATTER OF
THE MINES AND QUARRIES
ACT 1954, AND IN THE
MATTER of a question

BETWEEN (Name of objector)..Objector

and

(Name of inspector)..Inspector

To the Inspector

TAKE NOTICE that the above-named objector being {the owner / the manager / a manager}*

of ....{mine / quarry}*

in pursuance of subsection (2) of section one hundred and seventy of the Mines and Quarries Act, 1954, hereby demands a reference upon a notice relating to that {mine / quarry}* served under ....†

upon him by the above-named inspector on the..................day of....................
19 , being a notice to which apply the provisions of Part XV of the said Act with respect to references upon notices.

The address for service of the objector is...

Dated.................................19 .

(Signed)................................

SECOND SCHEDULE Rule 8

MINES AND QUARRIES ACT 1954.

THE MINES AND QUARRIES (REFERENCES) RULES 1956.

NOTICE

OF REFERENCE UPON A NOTICE SERVED BY AN INSPECTOR

IN THE MATTER OF
THE MINES AND QUARRIES
ACT 1954, AND IN THE
MATTER of a question

BETWEEN (Name of objector) ....Objector

and

(Name of inspector)..Inspector

TAKE NOTICE—

(1) THAT the above-named objector, being {the owner / the manager / a manager}* of....................
.... {mine / quarry}* in pursuance of subsection (2) of section one hundred and seventy of the Mines and Quarries Act 1954, has demanded a reference upon a notice relating to that {mine / quarry}* served under.................†

*Delete as inapplicable.

†Insert number of the section of the Act or title of the regulations and number of the regulation (as the case may be) under which notice was served.

upon him by the above-named inspector on the...........day of................., 19 , being a notice to which apply the provisions of Part XV of the said Act with respect to references upon notices;

(2) THAT the name(s) and address(es) of the person(s) selected to be referee on the references { is / are }..

(3) THAT the referee has determined that the reference shall be heard on the ....day of..............................., 19 , at (*insert time*)................... at (*insert place*)...

*(4) THAT the objection statement and the reply thereto relating to the notice upon which a reference has been demanded may be inspected at.............................

....

....

Dated..19 .

(Signed)..

TO ALL PERSONS AFFECTED BY THE ABOVE-MENTIONED NOTICE

*Omit paragraph in any case in which a notice has been served under paragraph (3) of rule 3.

THE MINES AND QUARRIES (DRAFT REGULATIONS) RULES 1956

S.I. 1956, No. 2018

PART I

Proceedings preliminary to inquiries

1. As soon as may be after the appointment by the Lord Chancellor of a person or persons to hold an inquiry (such a person or persons being in these rules referred to as a 'tribunal') the tribunal shall publish or cause to be published in such manner as it thinks fit for the purpose of notifying persons likely to be affected by the draft regulations, and send or cause to be sent by post to the Minister and to every person who duly made an objection with respect to a provision of the draft regulations, a notice specifying—

(*a*) the name of every member of the tribunal and of any person appointed to preside over the inquiry (such a person being in these rules referred to as 'the president');

(*b*) an address to which all communications for the tribunal shall be sent.

2. (1) The tribunal may, if it thinks fit for the purpose of facilitating the just, expeditious and economical disposal of the inquiry, include in the notice published and sent under the last preceding rule or in a notice subsequently so published and sent notice of the date on which and the place and time at which there shall be held a meeting for the purposes hereinafter specified in this rule (such a meeting and any resumed meeting after an adjournment thereof being in these rules referred to as a 'meeting for directions').

(2) If a meeting for directions is so ordered, every person desiring to appear at the inquiry in pursuance of sub-paragraph (*c*) of paragraph eighteen of Part III of the Second Schedule to the Act shall at that meeting make application either in person or by counsel, solicitor or agent for the opinion of the tribunal or (if there are two or more members of the tribunal) of the president whether or not that person is affected by the relevant draft regulations and the opinion of the tribunal or the president (as the case may be) thereupon shall be recorded by the tribunal and announced to the applicant.

(3) Any person entitled to appear at an inquiry in pursuance of paragraph eighteen of Part III of the Second Schedule to the Act may, either in person or by counsel, solicitor or agent, make such representations to the tribunal at the relevant meeting for directions as he thinks fit relating to the directions to be given by the tribunal in pursuance of paragraph (4) of this rule.

(4) At any meeting for directions, the tribunal may give such directions as to the future course of the inquiry as appear best adapted to secure the purposes aforesaid and in particular, but without prejudice to the generality thereof—

(*a*) the tribunal may direct that evidence of any fact or opinion shall be given at the inquiry in such manner as may be specified by the direction;

(*b*) the tribunal may direct that any person entitled to appear at the inquiry who desires to produce thereat any plans, photographs, models, statistics or results of experiments shall, not later than ten days before the inquiry, afford to every other person so entitled an opportunity of inspecting those plans, photographs, models or documents or a copy thereof and of agreeing to the admission thereof at the inquiry without further proof;

(*c*) the tribunal shall endeavour to secure that the persons entitled to appear at the inquiry make all admissions for the purposes of the inquiry and all agreements as to the conduct thereof which ought reasonably to be made by them;

(*d*) the tribunal may give such directions as it thinks necessary or expedient as to the order in which objections or representations shall be considered at the inquiry and as to the order in which persons appearing at the inquiry shall be heard; and

(*e*) the tribunal may direct the date on which and time at which the inquiry shall be held.

3. In any case in which a meeting for directions is not ordered by the tribunal, it shall be published or cause to be published in such manner as it thinks fit for the purpose of notifying persons likely to be affected by the draft regulations and send or cause to be sent by post to the Minister and to every person who duly made an objection with respect to a provision of the draft regulations, a notice specifying the date on which and time at which the inquiry shall be held.

Part II

Inquiries

4. At and for the purposes of every inquiry—

(*a*) the tribunal may enter and inspect any premises occupied by any person entitled to appear at the inquiry, being premises which would be affected by the relevant draft regulations (if made);

(*b*) the tribunal may vary or revoke any order made or direction given by it at the relevant meeting for directions and may (so far as appears to it to be appropriate) make any order or give any direction which it could have made or given at such a meeting;

(*c*) the tribunal may (so far as appears to it to be reasonable having regard to the desirability of making a report to the Minister as soon as may be) adjourn the inquiry from time to time; and

(*d*) subject to the provisions of the Act and of these rules, the tribunal may regulate the procedure at the inquiry.

5. No person shall at an inquiry be entitled without the consent of the tribunal—

(*a*) to raise, or adduce evidence relating to, any ground of objection not specifically stated in an objection duly made with respect to a provision of the relevant draft regulations; or (*b*) to ask for, or adduce evidence relating to, any omission, addition or modification not asked for in such an objection.

6. In every case in which the Lord Chancellor has appointed a tribunal consisting of two or more persons—

(*a*) every decision of a majority of those persons present and voting shall be the decision of the tribunal;

(*b*) in any case in which the votes of those persons present and voting are equally divided, the president shall have a second or casting vote.

PART III

General

Interpretation

7. (1) In these rules the following expressions have the meanings hereby respectively assigned to them, that is to say—

'the Act' means the Mines and Quarries Act 1954;

'inquiry' means an inquiry under Part III of the Second Schedule to the Act;

'meeting for directions' has the meaning assigned thereto in rule two;

'president' has the meaning assigned thereto in rule one;

'tribunal' has the meaning assigned thereto in rule one.

(2) Expressions to which meanings are assigned by the Act or by these rules shall (unless the contrary intention appears) have the same meanings in any document issued under the provisions of these rules.

(3) The Interpretation Act 1889 shall apply to the interpretation of these rules as it applies to the interpretation of an Act of Parliament.

Application to Scotland

8. Where any draft regulations referred for inquiry and report apply to Scotland only, for references in these rules to the Lord Chancellor there shall be substituted references to the Lord President of the Court of Session.

Commencement and citation

9. These rules shall come into operation at the commencement of the Act and may be cited as the Mines and Quarries (Draft Regulations) Rules, 1956.

SAFETY-LAMPS

THE COAL AND OTHER MINES

(SAFETY-LAMPS AND LIGHTING) REGULATIONS 1956

S.I. 1956 No. 1765

Arrangement of Regulations

PART I

Application

1. These regulations shall apply to every mine of coal, stratified ironstone, shale or fireclay, and in these regulations, unless otherwise expressly provided, 'mine' means such a mine.

PART II

Provision and maintenance of safety-lamps and firedamp detectors

Arrangements for examination of safety-lamps and firedamp detectors before and after use

2. (1) It shall be the duty of the manager of every mine in which or in part of which the use of lamps or lights, other than permitted lights,* is unlawful to appoint competent persons and to make and ensure the efficient carrying out of arrangements to secure the examination of safety-lamps and appliances (whether or not safety-lamps) for detecting the presence of inflammable gas (hereinafter referred to as 'detectors') in accordance with the provisions of this regulation.

(2) The manager shall make and ensure the efficient carrying out of arrangements to secure that no safety-lamp or detector is taken for use below ground in such a mine unless—

(*a*) since last in use it has been thoroughly examined above ground by a competent person appointed by him and has been found by that person to be in safe working order; and

(*b*) it is securely locked.

*This expression, as used here and subsequently in these Regulations, has the meaning defined in Section 182 (1) of the 1954 Act.

Such arrangements shall provide for the keeping of a record of the person by whom any safety-lamp or detector is so taken on any occasion.

(3) The manager shall make and ensure the efficient carrying out of arrangements to secure the examination by a competent person appointed by him of every safety-lamp or detector upon its return to the lamp room after use. If the competent person upon such an examination finds any lamp or detector to be damaged he shall forthwith record the nature of the damage in a book* provided for that purpose by the owner of the mine.

(4) Without prejudice to the generality of paragraph (2), the examination thereunder of every flame safety-lamp with a self-contained re-lighting contrivance shall include the taking apart of the lamp, thorough cleaning of all parts and the testing of the re-lighting contrivance. After reassembly the re-lighting contrivance shall not be operated unnecessarily.

3. (1) The manager of every safety-lamp mine† shall make and ensure the efficient carrying out of arrangements to secure that every safety-lamp being taken below ground by a person employed at the mine (other than an official of the mine) is examined by a deputy or other competent person appointed by the manager before or as soon as practicable after it is taken into the mine to ascertain that it is in safe working order and properly locked.

(2) The manager of every mine in which there is a safety-lamp part† shall make and ensure the efficient carrying out of arrangements to secure the like examination of every safety-lamp being taken into a safety-lamp part of the mine at a place appointed by him for the purposes of this paragraph.

Bulbs for electric safety-lamps

4. It shall be the duty of the manager of every mine to ensure that every bulb used in an electric safety-lamp of a type for the time being approved by the Minister for general use by workmen is a bulb—

(*a*) of a type approved by the Minister and marked in a manner specified‡ by the Minister in or in relation to that approval;

(*b*) where the safety-lamp is of a type the approval for which contains provisions relating to the characteristics of any bulb to be used therein, in conformity with those provisions.

Cap lamps for persons employed in haulage

5. Any safety-lamp provided for personal use by a person ordinarily employed in haulage operations shall be an electric cap lamp, and there shall be provided therewith a proper fitting for carrying that lamp.

Maintenance of lighting performance

6. It shall be the duty of the manager of every mine to make and ensure the efficient carrying out of arrangements to secure the maintenance of the lighting

---

*M. & Q. Form No. 214.

†This expression, as used here and subsequently in these Regulations, has the meaning defined in Section 182 (1) of the 1954 Act.

‡The manner of marking is described in Test Memo. No. 1 (Test and Approval of Safety-Lamps).

performance of safety-lamps used in the mine, being lamps of a type the approval for which specifies the lighting performance thereof, and in particular so that if an inspector selects from lamps of such types returned to the lamp room after use on any shift and not upon examination in pursuance of paragraph (3) of regulation two found to be damaged a sample comprising not less than fifty lamps or one-half of the number of lamps returned after that shift (whichever is the less) and after external cleansing determines the mean spherical candle-power of any cap lamps and the maximum horizontal candle-power of other lamps in that sample it shall in the case of at least half of those lamps be not less than sixty per cent of the performance specified in the relevant approval, or, if another percentage (not exceeding seventy five per cent) is specified* in an order made by the Minister, that other percentage thereof.

General duties of persons with safety-lamps

7. Every person to whom a locked safety-lamp is issued for use in a mine shall before taking it below ground examine it externally and assure himself that it is locked and in safe working order and shall also examine it from time to time while in the mine to assure himself that it remains in safe working order.

8. No person shall unlock or open any safety-lamp or detector below ground in a safety-lamp mine or safety-lamp part of a mine or have in his possession below ground in any such mine or part of a mine any contrivance for unlocking or opening any safety-lamp or detector.

9. No person shall place a safety-lamp or detector on its bottom in a mine unless it is necessary to do so for the safe performance of any work in which that person is engaged or unless he is authorised to do so by the manager, and no person working in a mine with a pick, hammer or other such tool shall swing it within two feet of a safety-lamp or detector (other than a cap lamp which he is wearing).

10. If any safety-lamp is damaged in a mine the person using it shall forthwith carefully extinguish the light.

11. Every person to whom a safety-lamp or detector is issued for use in a mine shall on the completion of his shift return it to the lamp room.

PART III

Re-lighting safety-lamps underground

12. The provisions of this Part of these regulations shall apply to safety-lamp mines and safety-lamp parts of mines.

13. (1) No person, except a competent person appointed by the manager for the purpose at a place appointed by the manager as a lamp station, shall re-light below ground any flame safety-lamp other than a lamp with a self-contained re-lighting contrivance.

*No other percentage has yet been specified for this purpose.

(2) No contrivance for re-lighting a flame safety-lamp (other than a contrivance contained in a lamp) shall be kept below ground otherwise than at such a lamp station, and no person shall have any such contrivance in his possession below ground, other than a contrivance at such a lamp station.

(3) Any such contrivance for re-lighting a flame safety-lamp shall be so constructed, maintained and used as to prevent the emission of flame or a spark.

14. (1) The manager shall not appoint as a lamp station any place in a road which as regards any working face is a return airway, or any place in any part of the mine in which inflammable gas although not normally present is likely to occur in a quantity sufficient to indicate danger.

(2) It shall be the duty of the manager to secure that at or near every lamp station there is kept posted a notice indicating its position in such characters and in such a place as to be easily seen.

15. (1) No person other than an inspector, a manager, an under-manager, a deputy, a shot firer, a person carrying out an inspection under Part VII of the Act* or a person as to whom the manager is satisfied that he is capable of using a re-lighting contrivance safely and who is authorised by the manager in writing so to do, shall take any flame safety-lamp with a self-contained re-lighting contrivance into any mine or part of a mine to which this Part of these regulations applies.

(2) A person having a flame safety-lamp with a self-contained re-lighting contrivance shall at all times while he is below ground retain the key for operating the contrivance in his possession.

16. (1) No person shall re-light any flame safety-lamp below ground (either at a lamp station or by means of a self-contained re-lighting contrivance) unless he has examined it and found it to be undamaged. Any person who has so re-lighted a safety-lamp shall forthwith again examine it and unless he finds it to be securely locked and in safe working order shall not allow it to be used or to remain lighted.

(2) A person having a flame safety-lamp with a self-contained re-lighting contrivance shall not attempt to re-light it at any place at which there is reason to suspect the presence of inflammable gas.

Part IV

General lighting and permitted lights

Places at which general lighting is to be provided

17. (1) It shall be the duty of the manager of every mine to secure the provision and maintenance of suitable and sufficient lighting at the following places below ground at all times when any persons are working thereat or walking therethrough going to or from their working places at the beginning or end of a shift, that is to say—

(*a*) such entrances to each shaft or outlet and such sidings provided in relation thereto as are regularly used;

*i.e., an inspection on behalf of persons employed.

(*b*) the top and bottom of every incline on which vehicles are moved by gravity operated rope haulage apparatus other than apparatus which is advanced with the working of a face;

(*c*) every siding, landing, passbye, junction and off-take, every place at which vehicles are regularly coupled or uncoupled or regularly attached to or detached from a haulage rope and every place at which vehicles are regularly filled mechanically;

(*d*) every room or place made to house and containing any engine or motor.

(2) Lighting provided in pursuance of this regulation shall be so arranged as to minimise glare or eyestrain.

(3) Nothing in the preceding provisions of this regulation shall require the provision of lighting at any place ventilated by air none of which has ventilated a working face and within one hundred and fifty feet of a working face, or at any other place within nine hundred feet of a working face being in either case a place accessible from the face in question:

Provided that an inspector may serve on the manager of a mine a notice requiring him to secure the provision and maintenance of suitable and sufficient lighting at any place specified in the notice at which such lighting would be required but for the preceding provisions of this paragraph and which is not within thirty feet of such a working face.

(4) Nothing in the preceding provisions of this regulation shall require the provision of lighting in a mine at which not more than ten persons are employed below ground and an inspector may by notice served on the manager exempt any mine at which not more than thirty persons are employed below ground from those requirements.

18. (1) Subject to the following provisions of this regulation and to the provisions of the Coal and Other Mines (Electricity) Regulations 1956,* electric lights supplied with electricity from a source of electric power external to the lighting unit are hereby authorised to be used at the following places in mines in which the use of lamps or lights, other than permitted lights, is unlawful (either throughout or in any part) that is to say—

(*a*) in any length of road ventilated by air none of which has ventilated a working face except within one hundred and fifty feet of a working face accessible from that length of road;

(*b*) in any length of any other road except within nine hundred feet of a working face accessible from that length of road;

(*c*) where electric power is used at a working face, in any length of road which is an intake airway as regards that face except within thirty feet of a face and in any other length of road used in connection with that face except within three hundred feet of that face;

(*d*) if authorised by a notice served by an inspector on the manager, in any length of road described in the notice except within thirty feet of a working face;

and accordingly such electric lights so used are permitted lights in those mines.

*See page 19.

(2) Where electric lights are installed at any place by virtue of sub-paragraph (*c*) of the last preceding paragraph, the manager shall forthwith give notice thereof to the inspector for the district.

(3) Electricity at a voltage exceeding two hundred and fifty shall not be applied to any such lights and if the system is polyphase the neutral point shall be connected to earth or if it is not polyphase the mid-voltage point shall be connected to earth:

Provided that the provisions of this paragraph shall not apply to any system of electric lighting by direct current installed in a seam in a mine before the first day of August, nineteen hundred and forty-seven.

(4) It shall be the duty of the manager to ensure that appropriate precautions are taken to prevent damage to any such electric lighting system from shot firing and that every lamp fitting is so constructed as to protect the lamp from accidental damage.

(5) In any part of a mine in which inflammable gas, although not normally present, is likely to occur in a quantity sufficient to indicate danger, no electrical apparatus, other than apparatus of a type approved by the Minister, shall be used as part of such a system in any length of road within nine hundred feet of a working face accessible from that road.

19. (1) Subject to the following provisions of this regulation and to the provisions of the Coal and Other Mines (Electricity) Regulations 1956,* an electric lighting unit operated by a generator enclosed in the unit and driven by compressed air, being a unit of a type approved by the Minister, is hereby authorised to be used in mines in which the use of lamps or lights, other than permitted lights, is unlawful (either throughout or in any part), and accordingly such a unit is a permitted light in those mines.

(2) No person shall below ground in any such mine turn on the air pressure in such a unit unless the unit is fully assembled and closed, or open any such unit unless the air pressure has been turned off.

(3) No person shall attempt to use below ground in such a mine any such unit any part of which is defective.

(4) No person other than a person appointed in writing by the manager so to do shall dismantle, repair, alter or adjust any such unit below ground in such a mine.

(5) It shall be the duty of the manager to ensure that at intervals not exceeding three months every such unit is cleaned, thoroughly overhauled and tested in a workshop appointed by the manager for that purpose. The person by whom such a test is made shall forthwith make a full and accurate report thereon in a book† provided for that purpose by the owner of the mine.

20. (1) Electric lights which are fittings of or accessories to any machinery or electrical apparatus (including signalling apparatus) and which are of a type

*See page 19.

†M. & Q. Form No. 215.

approved by the Minister are hereby authorised to be used in mines in which the use of lamps or lights, other than permitted lights, is unlawful (either throughout or in any part), and accordingly such lights are permitted lights in those mines.

(2) It shall be the duty of the manager to ensure that any such lights are maintained and tested in the manner (if any) specified in the relevant approval.

PART V

General

Lamps at places with general lighting

21. There shall be provided for every person who works at a place below ground in any mine, being a place at which there is general lighting, a portable lamp for use in emergency and every such person shall have that lamp with him whenever he is at such a place.

22. There shall be provided at every place below ground lighted by electric lights the failure of which would be likely to cause danger a safety-lamp or other proper light which shall be kept alight at all such times.

Places which are to be whitened

23. The manager of every mine shall make and ensure the efficient carrying out of arrangements to secure that the roof and sides of the following places below ground in that mine are kept whitened, that is to say—

(*a*) such entrances to every shaft or outlet and such sidings provided in relation thereto as are regularly used;

(*b*) the top and bottom of every incline on which vehicles are moved by gravity operated rope haulage apparatus, other than apparatus which is advanced with the working of a face;

(*c*) every siding, landing, passbye, junction and off-take, every place at which vehicles are regularly coupled or uncoupled or regularly attached to or detached from a haulage rope and every place at which vehicles are regularly filled mechanically except in so far as any such place is within three hundred feet of a working face in connection with which that place is used;

(*d*) every room or place made to house and containing any engine, motor, electrical transformer or switchgear:

Provided that an inspector may by notice served on the manager exempt any place from the requirements of this regulation.

Exemptions

24. The Chief Inspector of Mines if he is satisfied that the application of any provision in regulation four, five, six, seventeen, twenty-one or twenty-three of these regulations is inappropriate in relation to any mine or part thereof may by notice served on the manager of that mine exempt it or a part thereof from the application of that provision.

Interpretation

25. (1) In these regulations the following expressions have the meanings hereby respectively assigned to them, that is to say—

'the Act' means the Mines and Quarries Act 1954;

'deputy' has the meaning assigned thereto in the Coal and Other Mines (Managers and Officials) Regulations, 1956;*

'detector' has the meaning assigned thereto in regulation two;

'mine' has the meaning assigned thereto in regulation one;

'shot firer' has the meaning assigned thereto (in the case of a mine of coal) in the Coal Mines (Explosives) Regulations 1961,† or (in the case of a mine of stratified ironstone, shale or fireclay) means a person appointed to be a shot firer by the manager of the mine;

'working face' does not include a place in a road at which the work consists of ripping or work of repair.

(2) Expressions to which meanings are assigned by the Act or by these regulations shall (unless the contrary intention appears) have the same meanings in any document issued under the provisions of these regulations.

(3) The Interpretation Act 1889 shall apply to the interpretation of these regulations as it applies to the interpretation of an Act of Parliament.

*See page 188.
†See page 37.

APPROVED SPECIFICATION OF SAFETY-LAMPS FOR USE DURING INSPECTIONS BY DEPUTIES AND SHOT FIRERS

The following types of safety-lamps are approved for the purposes of No. 12 (2) of the Coal and Other Mines (Managers and Officials) Regulations 1956 No. 50 (2) of the Coal Mines (Explosives) Regulations 1961 and No. 49(1) of the Stratified Ironstone, Shale and Fireclay Mines (Explosives) Regulations 1956;

Any safety-lamp, being of a type approved by the Minister for the purposes of Section 64 (2) of the Mines and Quarries Act 1954, which is—

(*a*) a combined flame and electric lamp;

(*b*) a flame lamp fitted with a self-contained relighting device and adjustable by the user to admit air at the top of the lamp only;

(*c*) for use in conjunction with a flame lamp of a type approved as being capable of giving light throughout the shift, an electric hand lamp weighing not more than three and a half pounds, or an electric cap lamp; or

(*d*) for use in conjunction with a flame lamp of a type not approved as being capable of giving light throughout the shift, an electric hand lamp weighing not more than six and a half pounds, or an electric cap lamp; and

(*e*) in the case of an electric lamp or combined flame and electric lamp, provided with a switch.

SANITARY CONVENIENCES

THE COAL AND OTHER MINES (SANITARY CONVENIENCES) REGULATIONS 1956

S.I. 1956 No. 1776*

Application

1. These regulations shall apply to every mine of coal, stratified ironstone, shale or fireclay, and in these regulations 'mine' means such a mine.

Location and construction of sanitary conveniences

2. It shall be the duty of the manager of every mine to ensure that sanitary conveniences provided at the mine in pursuance of section ninety-four of the Act are provided—

(*a*) in or adjacent to the winding engine house;

(*b*) at such other suitable places above ground as may be requisite in order to afford to every person employed at the mine convenient access to one at least of such conveniences;

(*c*) at or adjacent to every entrance below ground to every shaft and outlet, being an entrance ordinarily used by persons for the purpose of getting to or from their working places in the mine; and

(*d*) at suitable places along any length of road below ground, being a length which is a main intake airway or a main return airway for the purposes of the Coal and Other Mines (Ventilation) Regulations 1956†, so far as may be requisite for persons normally employed at places along that length of road.

3. It shall be the duty of the manager of every mine to ensure—

(*a*) that all sanitary conveniences provided above ground at the mine are—

(i) under cover; and

(ii) so screened as to secure privacy for persons using them;

(*b*) that in any case where persons of both sexes are, or are intended to be, employed at the mine, every sanitary convenience provided above ground at the mine for the use of persons of one sex is—

(i) so placed or screened that, whatever the position for the time being of any door thereto, no part of the interior of that convenience can be seen from any place where any person of the other sex may work or pass; and

---

*The provisions of these Regulations are additional to the provisions of Section 94 of the 1954 Act.

†See page 317.

(ii) (if it adjoins a sanitary convenience provided for the use of persons of the other sex) readily approachable by a way separate from every way of approach to that other convenience; and

(*c*) that every sanitary convenience provided at the mine for the use of females is provided with a door which can be firmly secured on the inside when shut.

Equipment and cleaning of sanitary conveniences

4. The manager of every mine shall make and secure the efficient carrying out of arrangements whereby (except in the case of urinals, water-closets and conveniences so constructed and used that any deposit flows therefrom to a separate container and is therein chemically treated)—

(*a*) an adequate supply of disinfectant, dry coal dust, or other suitable substance for covering faeces is constantly provided in a suitable receptacle at every sanitary convenience at the mine;

(*b*) every sanitary convenience below ground at the mine is provided with a portable receptacle with a lid, both being made of suitable material;

(*c*) every receptacle provided in pursuance of sub-paragraph (*b*) is, at such intervals as may be necessary and in any case at intervals not exceeding seven days, emptied above ground or below ground in waste, and cleaned; and

(*d*) the contents of every such receptacle emptied below ground in any waste are forthwith disposed of in that waste in a hygienic manner.

Use of sanitary conveniences

5. (1) No person shall relieve his bowels at a mine above ground or on a road below ground otherwise than in a sanitary convenience.

(2) No person shall improperly soil or render unfit for use any sanitary convenience at a mine or any sanitary utensil or appliance provided for use at such a sanitary convenience.

(3) Every person who relieves his bowels below ground at a mine (otherwise than in a water-closet or a convenience so constructed and used that any deposit flows therefrom to a separate container and is therein chemically treated) shall forthwith cover the faeces with disinfectant, dry coal dust, or other suitable substance.

Interpretation

6. (1) In these regulations the following expressions have the meanings hereby respectively assigned to them, that is to say—

'the Act' means the Mines and Quarries Act 1954;

'mine' has the meaning assigned thereto in regulation one.

(2) The Interpretation Act 1889 shall apply to the interpretation of these regulations as it applies to the interpretation of an Act of Parliament.

SHAFTS, OUTLETS AND ROADS

(*a*) THE COAL AND OTHER MINES

(SHAFTS, OUTLETS AND ROADS) REGULATIONS 1960

S.I. 1960 No. 69

(As amended by the Coal and Other Mines (Shafts, Outlets and Roads) (Amendment) Regulations 1968, S.I. 1968 No. 1037)

Arrangement of Regulations

PART I

General

Commencement and citation

1. These regulations shall come into operation on the first day of February, nineteen hundred and sixty, and may be cited as the Coal and Other Mines (Shafts, Outlets and Roads) Regulations 1960.

Interpretation

2. (1) In these regulations the following expressions have the meanings hereby respectively assigned to them, that is to say—

'the Act' means the Mines and Quarries Act 1954;

'banksman' has the meaning assigned thereto in regulation thirty-one;

'deputy' has the meaning assigned thereto in the Coal and Other Mines (Managers and Officials) Regulations 1956*;

'kibble' includes any form of bucket, basket or barrel in which things can be raised or lowered in a shaft or staple-pit in the course of being sunk;

'locomotive' has the meaning assigned thereto in the Coal and Other Mines (Locomotives) Regulations 1956†;

'mine' has the meaning assigned thereto in regulation five;

'the Minister' means the Minister of Power;

'onsetter' has the meaning assigned thereto in regulation thirty-one;

'travelling onsetter' has the meaning assigned thereto in regulation forty-two.

(2) Any reference to a shaft or staple-pit in the course of being sunk shall (unless the contrary intention appears) include a reference to a shaft or staple-pit being driven upwards.

(3) Expressions to which meanings are assigned by the Act or by these regulations shall (unless the contrary intention appears) have the same meanings in any document issued under the provisions of these regulations.

(4) The Interpretation Act 1889 shall apply to the interpretation of these regulations as it applies to the interpretation of an Act of Parliament, and as if these regulations and the regulations hereby revoked were Acts of Parliament; and any reference in any other regulations made under the Act to any provision of the regulations hereby revoked shall be construed as a reference to the corresponding provision of these regulations.

Revocations

3. (1) The Coal and Other Mines (Shafts, Outlets and Roads) Regulations 1956, are hereby revoked.

(2) All special regulations relating to the spacing of refuge holes in roads in which a locomotive runs, being special regulations in force immediately before the coming into operation of these regulations and

(*a*) made by the Minister in pursuance of sections one hundred and forty-one, one hundred and forty-three and forty of the Act; or

(*b*) made under the Coal Mines Act 1911(a), and having effect by virtue of paragraph (a) of subsection (1) of section one hundred and ninety-one of the Act,

are hereby revoked.

Savings

4. Notwithstanding the revocation of the Coal and Other Mines (Shafts, Outlets and Roads) Regulations 1956, any authority granted by the Minister or any exemption granted by the Minister or by an inspector for the purposes of any

*See page 188.
†See page 175.

provision of those regulations shall, if in force at the coming into operation of these regulations and so far as it could have been granted by an inspector under the corresponding provision of these regulations, have effect as if it had been so granted.

PART II

Application

5. These regulations shall apply to every mine of coal, stratified ironstone, shale or fireclay, and in these regulations, unless otherwise expressly provided, 'mine' means such a mine.

PART III

Winding and haulage apparatus in shafts, staple-pits and unwalkable outlets

6. At any shaft or unwalkable outlet* which is provided at a mine for affording to persons employed below ground therein means of ingress or egress and in the case of which the vertical distance between the top of the shaft or the point at which the outlet reaches the surface, as the case may be, and the lowest entrance to the shaft or outlet exceeds one hundred and fifty feet, being a shaft or outlet at a mine at which more than thirty persons are employed below ground, the apparatus for carrying persons provided in pursuance of subsection (1) of section twenty-eight of the Act shall be mechanically operated winding apparatus* or mechanically operated rope haulage apparatus* as the case may be.

7. Where mechanically operated winding apparatus or mechanically operated rope haulage apparatus is used for carrying persons through any shaft, staple-pit or unwalkable outlet, the engine shall be firmly fixed and completely separated by a substantial partition from any other such engine which is or may be in use at the same time and also from any other machinery:

Provided that an inspector may by notice served on the manager of the mine exempt an engine from the requirements of this regulation.

8. Where mechanically operated winding apparatus or mechanically operated rope haulage apparatus, being apparatus installed at a shaft or unwalkable outlet after the fifteenth day of September, nineteen hundred and thirteen, comprises a drum shaft not less than ten inches in diameter, that drum shaft shall be bored longitudinally at the centre.

Brakes and indicator

9. (1) Where mechanically operated winding apparatus or mechanically operated rope haulage apparatus is used for carrying persons through a shaft, staple-pit or unwalkable outlet, there shall be provided one or more brakes on the drum or drum shaft being brakes which—

(*a*) if there are two cages or carriages, will hold the drum stationary when the loads are balanced and the maximum torque is applied thereto in either direction by the engine; or

---

*These expressions, which are frequently used in these Regulations, are defined in Section 182 (1) of the 1954 Act.

(*b*) if there is only one cage or carriage, will hold the drum stationary when a fully loaded cage or carriage is half way down the shaft, staple-pit or outlet and the maximum torque is applied thereto downwards by the engine:

Provided that an inspector may by notice served on the manager of the mine exempt an engine from the requirements of this paragraph.

(2) Where such apparatus is so used, there shall be provided a suitable indicator (not being merely a mark on the rope or drum) showing the position of each cage or carriage in the shaft, staple-pit or outlet. That indicator shall be so placed as to be seen easily by the person operating the engine.

(3) Where winding apparatus or rope haulage apparatus (not being mechanically operated winding apparatus or rope haulage apparatus) is installed at a shaft, staple-pit or unwalkable outlet, there shall be provided on the drum or drum shaft a locking device or brake which will hold the drum stationary when a fully loaded cage or carriage is at any point in the shaft, staple-pit or outlet.

(4) In this regulation 'drum' and 'drum shaft' shall include a sheave and sheave shaft respectively and in relation to a shaft or staple-pit in the course of being sunk 'cage' shall include a kibble.

Flanges and horns

10. Where mechanically operated winding apparatus or mechanically operated rope haulage apparatus is used for carrying persons through a shaft, staple-pit or unwalkable outlet, there shall be provided on the drum or sheave such flanges or horns and, if the drum is conical, such other devices as will prevent the rope from slipping off.

Prevention of overwinding

11.* (1) Where mechanically operated winding apparatus or mechanically operated rope haulage apparatus is ordinarily used for carrying persons through a shaft or unwalkable outlet and the speed of winding or haulage can exceed twelve feet per second, there shall be provided an effective automatic contrivance to prevent overwinding so constructed as—

(*a*) to prevent the descending cage or carriage from being landed at the lowest entrance to, or the bottom of, the shaft or unwalkable outlet at a speed exceeding five feet per second; and

(*b*) to control the movement of the ascending cage or carriage to prevent danger to any persons therein.

(2) Unless such automatic contrivance is in full and fixed engagement with the engine, it shall be fully engaged whenever persons are to be carried through the shaft or outlet, and there shall be provided an automatic indicator, in such position at the top of the shaft or outlet as to be easily seen by any person transmitting signals therefrom, showing whether or not the contrivance is so engaged.

(3) An inspector may, if he is of opinion that special circumstances subsist at any mine, by notice served on the manager thereof exempt any such winding or haulage apparatus thereat from the requirements of this regulation.

---

*This Regulation now also applies in relation to a staple-pit (see Regulation 84).

Construction of cages and carriages and apparatus ancillary thereto

12.* (1) No person shall be carried through a shaft or unwalkable outlet otherwise than in a cage or carriage which complies with the requirements of the next following paragraph except—

(*a*) for the purposes of sinking operations; or

(*b*) for the purposes of examining or repairing a shaft or outlet or any machinery or appliances therein; or

(*c*) for the purposes of accompanying animals or bulky materials that cannot be raised or lowered in such a cage or carriage; or

(*d*) in pursuance of a notice of exemption served by an inspector on the manager of the mine.

(2) Every cage or carriage which is used for carrying persons through a shaft or unwalkable outlet shall be covered in completely at the top, closed in at the two sides sufficiently to prevent persons or things projecting beyond the sides and provided with suitable gates at the ends and with a rigid bar easily reached by all persons in it.

(3) After the first day of February, nineteen hundred and sixty-one, the door or gate of every cage used for carrying persons through a shaft shall be so constructed and installed that it cannot project beyond the side or end of the cage:

Provided that an inspector may by notice served on the manager of a mine exempt any such cage thereat from the provisions of this paragraph.

13. Every cage or carriage which is used for carrying vehicles through a shaft, staple-pit or unwalkable outlet shall be provided with catches or other suitable contrivances to prevent them from falling out.

Guides

14. In every shaft and staple-pit provided with winding apparatus, being a shaft or staple-pit in the case of which the distance between the top thereof and the lowest entrance thereto exceeds one hundred and fifty feet, or being a shaft or staple-pit in the course of being sunk of a depth exceeding three hundred feet, guides shall be provided for the cage or kibble:

Provided that an inspector may by notice served on the manager of the mine exempt a shaft or staple-pit from the requirements of this regulation.

Keps

15.† (1) In every shaft keps for supporting cages when at rest shall be provided at the highest landing to which the cages are raised, may be provided at the lowest entrance to the shaft but shall not be provided at any intermediate entrance thereto.

(2) Nothing in the last preceding paragraph shall require the provision of keps in a shaft in which the cages are raised and lowered by means of the friction of a rope on a winding sheave and an inspector may by notice served on the manager of the mine exempt any other shaft from that requirement.

---

*This Regulation now also applies in relation to a staple-pit (see Regulation 84).

†This Regulation now also applies to any staple-pit in relation to which the manager has not appointed a travelling onsetter in pursuance of Regulation 42 (see Regulation 84).

(3) Keps shall be used when persons are entering or leaving a cage at a place at which they are provided.

Detaching gear

16. (1) Where mechanically operated winding apparatus is ordinarily used for carrying persons through a shaft, there shall be provided appropriate gear for detaching each cage from the rope and holding it stationary in the event of overwinding when it is ascending.

(2) An inspector may, if he is of opinion that special circumstances subsist at any mine, by notice served on the manager thereof exempt any such winding apparatus thereat from the requirements of this regulation.

Winding and haulage ropes

17. (1) No spliced rope shall be used for winding or haulage in a shaft, staple-pit or unwalkable outlet in which persons are raised or lowered:

Provided that nothing in this paragraph shall prevent the use of an endless rope in an unwalkable outlet.

(2) No rope shall be so used for more than, in the case of a rope used in a shaft or staple-pit, three and a half years, or, in the case of a rope used in an unwalkable outlet, two and a half years:

Provided that if an inspector, having regard to the condition of the rope and to the extent to which and the circumstances in which it has been used, is satisfied that it can be used for such winding or haulage for a further period without danger, he may by notice served on the manager of the mine authorise such use of that rope for a further period.

(3) No rope installed after the first day of February, nineteen hundred and sixty, shall be so used unless it is of a type which has been found to withstand a load of at least six and a half times the maximum static load which may ordinarily be suspended on that rope where a cage is raised or lowered:

Provided that an inspector may by notice served on the manager of a mine exempt any such rope thereat from the provisions of this paragraph.

Maintenance of shafts, staple-pits and unwalkable outlets and of winding and haulage apparatus used therein

18. At every mine a competent person appointed for that purpose by the manager shall at intervals not exceeding seven days, or in the case of a shaft or staple-pit in the course of being sunk, or of an unwalkable outlet in the course of being driven, twenty-four hours, examine thoroughly the state of every part of any shaft, staple-pit and unwalkable outlet through any part of which persons are carried, and shall forthwith make and sign in a book* provided for the purpose by the owner of the mine a full and accurate report of the result of the examination:

Provided that an inspector may by notice served on the manager of the mine exempt any part of a shaft, staple-pit or unwalkable outlet thereat from the provisions of this regulation.

*M. & Q. Form No. 275.

19. (1) Without prejudice to the generality of regulations six and seven of the Coal and Other Mines (Mechanics and Electricians) Regulations, 1956*, it shall be the duty of the manager of every mine to ensure that a scheme for the systematic examination of plant at that mine made in pursuance of the said regulation seven provides for the matters specified in the following paragraphs of this regulation.

(2) Provision shall be so made for the thorough examination† at intervals not exceeding twenty-four hours of the external parts of any winding or haulage apparatus (including any apparatus ancillary thereto) which is in use for carrying persons through any shaft, staple-pit or unwalkable outlet.

(3) Provision shall be so made for the examination† at intervals not exceeding thirty days of every rope used for carrying persons or loads through a shaft, staple-pit or unwalkable outlet, in the course of which examination the rope is to be thoroughly cleaned at all places particularly liable to deterioration and at other places not more than three hundred feet apart throughout its length, and at each of these places after cleaning examination is to be made of the circumference and surface condition of the rope and for any fractures of the wires.

(4) Where an automatic contrivance to prevent overwinding is provided in pursuance of regulation eleven of these regulations, provision shall be so made for testing‡ the operation thereof—

(*a*) at intervals not exceeding seven days by raising each cage or carriage so that it passes the point at which the contrivance comes into operation above the highest landing or beyond the point at which the outlet reaches the surface;

(*b*) at intervals not exceeding three months by attempting to land each cage when descending at an excessive speed.

For the purposes of sub-paragraph (*b*), the automatic contrivance may be so adjusted as to control the speed of descent at a point other than the lowest entrance to, or the bottom of, the shaft or outlet.

(5) Provision shall be so made for the thorough examination‡ of all apparatus (including any detaching hook) provided for attaching to the rope a cage, carriage or kibble ordinarily used in a shaft, staple-pit or unwalkable outlet—

(*a*) forthwith after overwinding has caused any detaching gear, or, in the case of a cage which is raised and lowered by means of the friction of a rope on a winding sheave, any braking appliance fitted in the head-frame or sump of the shaft, to operate, and

(*b*) in any case at intervals not exceeding six months.

---

*Now replaced by regulations 9 and 10 of the Coal and Other Mines (Mechanics and Electricians) Regulations 1965—see page 194.

†No. 14 of the Mechanics and Electricians Regulations 1965, requires reports to be made on such examinations. The appropriate M. & Q. Forms are:
Reg. 19 (2)—No. 276.
Reg. 19 (3)—No. 277.

‡No. 14 of the Mechanics and Electricians Regulations 1965, requires reports to be made on such examinations and tests. The appropriate M. & Q. Forms are:
Reg. 19 (4)—No. 278.
Reg. 19 (5)—No. 279.

(6) Provision shall be so made for any apparatus so used—

(*a*) in the case of any apparatus or part thereof made of steel of a type for the time being approved* by the Minister for use in a particular manner, to be subjected to such heat treatment (if any) as may be specified in the notice of approval in relation thereto and if any such treatment is so specified at intervals not exceeding the intervals so specified; or

(*b*) in any other case, to be subjected to annealing or other appropriate heat treatment at intervals not exceeding six months:

Provided that an inspector may on an application made to him in that behalf, by notice served on the manager of the mine, exempt any such apparatus or part thereof from the requirements of sub-paragraph (*b*) if he is of the opinion, having regard to the material of which such apparatus or part thereof is made, the method of construction thereof or the manner in which it is used, that it is unnecessary or impracticable to require heat treatment in relation thereto.

(7) Provision shall be so made for the dismantling, cleaning and refitting of every detaching hook so used at intervals not exceeding three months.

(8) Where the efficient operation of any such detaching hook would be affected by wear of any ancillary plate or bell, provision shall be so made for the measurement of the relevant dimensions by means of calipers or gauges at intervals not exceeding thirty days.

PART IV

Duties of persons operating winding apparatus and rope haulage apparatus in shafts, staple-pits and unwalkable outlets

20. A person operating any winding apparatus or rope haulage apparatus which is used for carrying persons through a shaft, staple-pit or unwalkable outlet shall not leave the controlling gear when the apparatus is in motion or he has any cause to believe that anyone is in the cage, carriage or kibble.

21. (1) Every person operating any such winding or rope haulage apparatus shall at least once during his shift carefully examine the external parts of the apparatus under his charge and any apparatus ancillary thereto, unless such an examination has been carried out during his shift by another person in pursuance of paragraph (2) of regulation nineteen of these regulations.

(2) After any cessation of winding or haulage exceeding two hours the person operating any such winding or rope haulage apparatus shall, immediately before lowering or raising any person, run the cage, carriage or kibble at least once between the top of the shaft, staple-pit or outlet and the lowest entrance thereto for the time being in use or the bottom thereof in order to ascertain whether all the apparatus is in order.

(3) If during the course of any such examination or test or on any other occasion a person operating any such winding or rope haulage apparatus discovers any defect likely to affect the proper working of the apparatus, he shall not put the machinery in motion again until the defect has been reported to the manager, an under-manager or the official under whose direction he works and he has been instructed to operate the machinery by one of those persons.

*See page 263.

22. Every person operating any such winding or rope haulage apparatus shall during his shift keep the apparatus under his charge cleaned and oiled, unless some other person is appointed so to do.

23. No person in charge of any winding apparatus or rope haulage apparatus with which a shaft, staple-pit or unwalkable outlet is provided shall allow it to be operated under his supervision (on an occasion to which subsection (1) of section forty-two of the Act does not apply)* by any person other than one authorised in writing by the manager so to do.

24. No person operating any such winding or rope haulage apparatus shall set the machinery in motion in pursuance of any signal transmitted to him which is indistinct or in pursuance of any series of signals which is or appears to him to be incomplete or inconsistent.

Part V

Hours of employment of winding enginemen

25. A person appointed under section forty-two of the Act may be employed at a mine for more than eight hours in any day on which his duties consist of or include the operation, when persons are carried by means thereof, of mechanically or gravity operated winding apparatus with which a shaft is provided in the circumstances and subject to the conditions specified in the three next following regulations. Such a person is in this Part of these regulations referred to as a "winding engineman".

26. (1) Where winding is carried on at a shaft by a succession of shifts a winding engineman may, for the purpose of changing shifts, be employed on one day in the week for a period not exceeding sixteen hours, or for two shifts of eight hours each, provided that in either case—

(*a*) an interval of not less than eight hours elapses between the termination of his employment in one shift and the commencement of his employment in the next;

(*b*) the period of employment does not, on the average of any three consecutive weeks, exceed eight hours per working day.

(2) Where winding is carried on at a shaft by a succession of shifts and when on any day one of the winding enginemen is prevented from attending by illness, accident or other cause, a winding engineman may be employed for not more than twelve hours on that day, or may be employed on a system of eight-hour shifts with an interval of eight hours between each shift, provided that he shall not be so employed for more than six weeks consecutively in respect of the absence of such engineman.

(3) Where winding is carried on at a shaft by a succession of shifts, but the work during some period or periods of the day is much heavier than the work during other periods, and it is desirable in the interests of safety that the winding

*Section 42 (1) applies when persons are being carried. This provision, therefore, only applies on occasion when no person is being carried.

engineman employed during the period or periods of heavier work shall not be employed for so long a time as eight hours, then if such winding engineman is employed for any less time than eight hours during the day, a winding engineman employed during the other part of the day may be employed for a corresponding time in excess of the eight hours, but not exceeding ten hours in all.

(4) Where winding is carried on at a shaft by a succession of shifts, and the winding enginemen employed at that shaft have agreed, with the consent of the manager, to be absent in turn from the end of their shift on Saturday to the commencement of their shift on Monday, each of the winding enginemen may be employed for not more than sixteen hours both on Saturday and on Sunday in not more than two weeks in any three, or for alternate shifts of sixteen hours and twelve hours and twelve hours, or on a system of eight-hour shifts:

Provided that in any case an interval of not less than eight hours elapses between the termination of the employment in one shift and the commencement of employment in the next, and provided that notice of this arrangement is affixed by the manager in the winding engine house.

27. (1) Where at any shaft one shift only of persons descends and ascends the shaft during the day, and mineral is not wound before the descent or after the ascent of that shift, a winding engineman may be employed for not more than ten and a half hours on any day at that shaft.

(2) In any mine where only two shifts of workmen are employed below ground during a day, the one a mineral-getting shift and the other a repairing shift, and mineral is not wound or got except during the hours of the mineral-getting shift, and the total output of any such mine does not exceed on the average one hundred tons of mineral per working day, a winding engineman may be employed for a period not exceeding nine hours.

(3) Where at times when no shift of men is at work in the mine it is necessary for a person to descend the mine, and a person not otherwise employed to operate the winding apparatus is employed to lower and raise such person, the person so employed may be employed for more than eight hours but not for more than twelve hours in any day.

28. In the event of any accident to the winding apparatus or other accident interfering with the lowering or raising of workmen, or in the event of any emergency requiring the continuous attendance of a winding engineman at the engine in the interests of the safety of the men or animals in or about the mine, a winding engineman may continue to be employed after the end of his shift unless and until another winding engineman regularly employed at the same shaft is available to take his place.

29. (1) It shall be the duty of the manager of every mine to fix within the limits allowed by the Act and this Part of these regulations and to specify in a notice posted in the engine room the period of employment for each day of the week of the winding enginemen or the winding engineman for each shift as the case may be.

(2) If any period of employment exceeding eight hours in any day is fixed in pursuance of any of the preceding provisions of this Part of these regulations,

reference to that provision shall be included in the notice in relation to that period of employment.

30. Every winding engineman shall on each day on which he is so employed enter in a book provided by the owner for the purpose and kept in the engine room the times at which he began and ended his employment on each shift and if he is so employed for more than eight hours in any day by virtue of the provisions of paragraph (2) of regulation twenty-six or of regulation twenty-eight, he shall enter in the book* particulars of the circumstances in which he was so employed.

PART VI

Provisions relating to carriage of persons and things through shafts

Banksmen and onsetters

31. (1) At every mine where persons are carried through a shaft the manager shall make and secure the efficient carrying out of arrangements whereby a competent person appointed by him for the purpose (hereinafter referred to as a 'banksman') is in attendance for the purpose of receiving and transmitting signals at the landing in use at the top of the shaft—

(*a*) whenever any person is about to be lowered through that shaft; and

(*b*) whenever any person who is to be raised through that shaft is below ground.

(2) At every mine where persons are carried through a shaft the manager shall make and secure the efficient carrying out of arrangements whereby whenever any person who is to be raised through that shaft is below ground a competent person appointed by him for the purpose (hereinafter referred to as an 'onsetter') is in attendance for the purpose of receiving and transmitting signals at the entrance to that shaft from which any such person is to be raised.

(3) Nothing in the last preceding paragraph shall require an onsetter to be in attendance at an entrance to any shaft when all the persons below ground who are to be raised through that shaft from that entrance are officials of the mine or persons authorised in writing by the manager to give signals.

Procedure when persons are to be lowered

32. (1) No banksman shall allow any person who is to be lowered from the top of a shaft to enter a cage for that purpose—

(*a*) unless he has transmitted to the person operating the winding apparatus and to the person defined in paragraph (4) hereof (if any) the signal......3; and

(*b*) unless he has received from the person so defined (if any) the signal......3.

(2) The banksman shall not transmit to the person operating the winding apparatus the signal to lower when any person is in the cage until he has received from the person defined in paragraph (4) hereof (if any) the signal......1.

*M. & Q. Form No. 280.

(3) In order to direct the person operating the winding apparatus to lower a cage from the landing in use at the top of the shaft when any person is therein the banksman shall transmit to him the signal......2.

(4) The person hereinbefore referred to is—

(*a*) if two cages are lowered and raised by means of the same winding apparatus and the second cage is resting at another entrance to the shaft, the onsetter or other person authorised to transmit signals in attendance at that entrance; or

(*b*) if one cage only is lowered and raised by means of the winding apparatus, the onsetter or other person authorised to transmit signals in attendance at the entrance to the shaft to which the cage is to be lowered.

Procedure when persons are to be raised

33. (1) No onsetter or other person authorised to transmit signals shall allow any person who is to be raised to the top of a shaft to enter a cage for that purpose—

(*a*) unless he has transmitted to the banksman the signal......3; and

(*b*) unless he has received from the banksman the signal......3.

(2) In order to direct the person operating the winding apparatus to raise a cage when any person is therein the onsetter or other person authorised to transmit signals shall transmit to him the signal......1.

(3) The person operating the winding apparatus shall not raise a cage in pursuance of a signal......1 given under the last preceding paragraph until he has received from the banksman the signal......2.

Signal to stop cage in motion when persons are carried

34. When the cage is in motion and any person is therein the person operating the winding apparatus shall stop the cage upon receiving the signal......1.

Signals when persons are not carried

35. In a shaft when persons are not being carried the following signals and no other shall be transmitted to require the movements specified in relation thereto, that is to say—

to raise up	1
to lower down	2
to stop when in motion	1
to raise steadily	4
to lower steadily	5.

Further signals

36. (1) In relation to a shaft to which there is more than one entrance below ground, the manager shall determine the signals to be transmitted to indicate to which entrance a cage is to be sent.

(2) In relation to any shaft, the manager may determine the signal to be transmitted to give any indication (other than one for which a signal is specified in these regulations) and no person shall transmit any signal which is not so specified or determined.

37. (1) The means provided for the transmission of the signals required by this Part of these regulations shall be such that any signal transmitted from an entrance to a shaft underground shall be transmitted simultaneously to the person operating the winding apparatus and to the banksman.

(2) There shall be provided and so placed as to be readily seen by the person operating any winding apparatus an appliance giving visual indication of every signal transmitted to that person in pursuance of the provisions of this Part of these regulations and retaining that indication until a cage is next raised or lowered.

38. No person, other than the banksman, an onsetter, an official of the mine or a person authorised in writing by the manager to transmit such signals, shall transmit any signal in any shaft.

39. There shall be kept posted at each entrance for the time being in use to every shaft, and in the place at which is operated the winding apparatus provided therefor, a notice of the signals specified in these regulations and any signals determined by the manager for transmission in that shaft.

Part VII

Provisions relating to the carriage of persons and things through staple-pits

40. After the first day of February, nineteen hundred and sixty-one,—

(*a*) there shall be provided and maintained in connection with every staple-pit provided with winding apparatus in a mine being a staple-pit in the case of which the distance between the highest and lowest entrance thereto for the time being in use exceeds fifty feet, effective means of transmitting audible and visible signals from each entrance to the staple-pit for the time being in use to the place at which the winding apparatus is operated; and

(*b*) the provisions of Part VI of these regulations shall (save as hereinafter expressly provided) apply in relation to a staple-pit as they apply in relation to a shaft.

41. Where it appears to the manager of a mine that the provisions of regulation thirty-one (which relates to banksmen and onsetters) are inappropriate in relation to any staple-pit he may with the consent of an inspector elect to make and secure the carrying out of arrangements in pursuance of the next following regulation; and where a manager has duly elected as aforesaid, the said regulation thirty-one and regulations thirty-two and thirty-three (which relate to procedure where persons are raised or lowered) shall not apply in relation to that staple-pit.

Travelling onsetters

42. Where the manager of a mine has so elected he shall make and secure the efficient carrying out of arrangements whereby a competent person appointed by him for the purpose (hereinafter referred to as a 'travelling onsetter') is in the cage, when any person is to be or is being carried therein, for the purpose of transmitting signals to the person operating the winding apparatus.

Procedure when persons are lowered

43. (1) No travelling onsetter shall allow any person who is to be lowered from the top of the staple-pit to enter a cage for that purpose unless he has transmitted to the person operating the winding apparatus the signal......3.

(2) In order to direct the person operating the winding apparatus to lower a cage from the landing in use at the top of the staple-pit when any person is therein the travelling onsetter shall transmit to him the signal......2.

Procedure when persons are raised

44. (1) No travelling onsetter shall allow any person who is to be raised to the top of the staple-pit to enter a cage for that purpose unless he has transmitted to the person operating the winding apparatus the signal......3 and has received from that person the signal......3.

(2) In order to direct the person operating the winding apparatus to raise the cage when any person is therein the travelling onsetter shall transmit to him the signal......1.

45. Paragraph (1) of regulation thirty-seven shall not apply in any case in which signals are transmitted by a travelling onsetter.

PART VIII

Signalling in roads and unwalkable outlets

Signalling in roads

46. (1) In roads in which signalling apparatus is provided the following signals and no other shall be transmitted thereby to require such movements in such cases as are specified in relation thereto, that is to say—

(*a*) in the case of mechanically operated rope haulage apparatus used for direct or main rope haulage—

to stop	1
to lower	2
to raise up	3;

(*b*) in the case of mechanically operated rope haulage apparatus used for main and tail rope haulage—

to stop	1
to haul inbye	2
to haul outbye	3
to slack out tail rope	4
to tighten tail rope	5
to slack out main rope	6
to tighten main rope	7;

(*c*) in the case of gravity operated rope haulage apparatus* (except where an endless rope is used)—

to stop	1
to lower	2;

*This expression, here and subsequently in these Regulations, has the meaning defined in Section 182 (1) of the 1954 Act.

(*d*) in the case of endless rope haulage—

to stop	1
to commence hauling	2;

(*e*) in the case of a conveyor—

to stop	1
to start	2.

(2) In any case in which persons are to be carried in vehicles moved by means of any apparatus specified in the last preceding paragraph any signal so specified requiring the vehicles to be moved shall be preceded by the signal......8.

(3) No person shall pass on foot along any part of a road in which signalling apparatus is provided and in which vehicles can be moved by means of gravity operated rope haulage apparatus (not having an endless rope) while a person authorised by the manager to transmit signals by means of that signalling apparatus is on duty thereat unless that person has transmitted the signal......4 and that signal has been acknowledged by the signal......4.

47. In relation to any road the manager may determine the signal to be transmitted to give any indication, and in particular to indicate the place from which any signal is transmitted (other than an indication for which a signal is specified in these regulations), and no person shall transmit any signal which is not so specified or determined.

Signalling in unwalkable outlets

48. In relation to any unwalkable outlet the manager of a mine—

(*a*) shall determine the signal to be transmitted to require any movement therein; and

(*b*) may determine the signal to be transmitted to give any other indication, and in particular to indicate the place from which any signal is transmitted, and no person shall, except in a case of emergency, transmit any signal which is not so determined.

Notices

49. Where vehicles are moved through an unwalkable outlet or road by means of mechanically operated or gravity operated rope haulage apparatus, there shall be kept posted, at the place at which that apparatus is operated and at suitable points on each unwalkable outlet or road through which vehicles can be so moved, a notice of the signals specified in these regulations and any signals determined by the manager for transmission in that outlet or road.

Prohibition of unauthorised signals

50. Except in a case of emergency no person other than an official of the mine or a person authorised by the manager to transmit such signals shall transmit any signal by means of any signalling apparatus provided in any unwalkable outlet or road.

PART IX

Further provisions relating to carriage of persons and things through shafts, staple-pits and unwalkable outlets

51. (1) No minerals*, equipment or materials (other than things which are required to be or are normally kept by a person in his possession) shall be carried through a shaft, staple-pit or unwalkable outlet whilst persons are being carried through it, whether in the same direction or not.

(2) Nothing in paragraph (1) of this regulation shall prevent—

(*a*) persons who are to work in a shaft, staple-pit or outlet having with them when being carried therethrough equipment or materials which they will or may require for the purposes of that work; or

(*b*) persons accompanying animals or bulky materials that cannot be raised or lowered in a cage.

(3) Where a shaft, staple-pit or unwalkable outlet is divided throughout by a substantial partition, each compartment shall for the purposes of this regulation be deemed to be a separate shaft, staple-pit or outlet, as the case may be.

(4) It shall be the duty of persons authorised by these regulations or by the manager to transmit signals in relation to the operation of the relevant winding or haulage apparatus to ensure compliance with the provisions of paragraph (1) of this regulation.

52. (1) The manager of every mine shall, in relation to each shaft, staple-pit and unwalkable outlet through which persons are carried, determine the maximum number of persons who may be carried at any one time in any cage or carriage therein and where a cage or carriage has more than one deck, on each deck thereof or, in the case of a shaft or staple-pit in the course of being sunk in any kibble.

(2) There shall be kept posted at each entrance for the time being in use to each such shaft, staple-pit or unwalkable outlet a notice specifying every number so determined.

(3) It shall be the duty of persons authorised by these regulations or by the manager to transmit signals in relation to the operation of the relevant winding or haulage apparatus to ensure that no person in excess of the number so determined enters any cage or carriage or any deck thereof or, in the case of a shaft or staple-pit in the course of being sunk, any kibble.

53.† Where an automatic contrivance to prevent overwinding is provided in pursuance of regulation eleven at any shaft or unwalkable outlet (not being a contrivance which is in full and fixed engagement with the engine) it shall be the duty of any person authorised by these regulations or by the manager to transmit signals in relation to the operation of the relevant winding or haulage apparatus to ensure that, unless he has taken steps to be assured that the contrivance is engaged, no person is permitted to enter a cage or carriage therein.

*As defined in Section 182 (1) of the 1954 Act.

†This Regulation now also applies in relation to a staple-pit (see Regulation 84).

54. Where persons are to be carried in a cage or carriage provided with gates through a shaft, staple-pit or unwalkable outlet the banksman, onsetter, travelling onsetter or other person authorised to transmit signals shall not signal the cage or carriage away until the gates are properly closed.

55. (1) The onsetter or other person authorised to transmit signals at any entrance below ground to a shaft, staple-pit or unwalkable outlet shall not begin, or allow any assistant or other person to begin, to remove or open any enclosure or barrier provided at that entrance unless a cage or carriage is stationary at that entrance or has reached such a position that the floor or a deck thereof will be stationary opposite that entrance by the time the enclosure or barrier is removed or opened.

(2) The onsetter or other person authorised to transmit signals at any entrance below ground to a shaft, staple-pit or unwalkable outlet shall replace or close any enclosure or barrier provided at that entrance (other than one operated by the cage or carriage) either before or immediately after he has signalled away therefrom a cage or carriage.

56. Where persons are to be raised through a shaft, staple-pit or unwalkable outlet from the lowest entrance thereto in a cage or carriage having more than one deck, the onsetter, travelling onsetter or other person authorised to transmit signals shall secure that the top deck is loaded first:

Provided that this regulation shall not apply in any case in which a balanced platform is used or the decks are loaded simultaneously.

PART X

Provisions for securing safety in transport roads

Travelling in transport roads

57. Nothing in paragraph (*a*) of subsection (1) of section thirty-nine of the Act shall prohibit a person passing on foot along a length of road during a period during which vehicles are moving therein—

(*a*) if there is a continuous clear space not less than two feet in width between the vehicles and one side of the road and if the maximum speed at which vehicles may run therein does not exceed ten miles per hour; or

(*b*) in the case of a mine opened before the first day of July, nineteen hundred and twelve, if the maximum speed at which vehicles may run in that length of road does not exceed three miles per hour, and if the gradient thereof nowhere exceeds 1:9 and does not exceed 1:12 for any distance exceeding three hundred feet, and if the average gradient of that length of road does not exceed 1:12, and, in a case in which there are two lines of rails in that length of road, if the space between them is kept free of obstructions.

Clearances at coupling places

58. At every place at which sets or trains consisting of three or more vehicles are coupled or uncoupled there shall be provided and maintained a continuous clear space not less than two feet in width between the vehicles standing on any rails thereat and the side of the road nearest to those rails:

Provided that this regulation shall not apply where there are two parallel lines of rails and there is a clear space not less than three feet in width between the vehicles standing on those lines.

Refuge holes

59. (1) For the purposes of section forty of the Act, the intervals which must not be exceeded between refuge holes in roads in which run vehicles moved by gravity or by mechanical power (other than locomotives) shall be—

(*a*) in the case of a length of road in which the gradient does not exceed 1:20 and in which either there is a continuous clear space not less than two feet in width between the vehicles and one side of the road or the maximum speed of the vehicles must not exceed three miles per hour, sixty feet; or

(*b*) in any other case, thirty feet.

(2) For the said purposes the intervals which must not be exceeded between refuge holes in any length of road in which a locomotive runs shall be—

(*a*) in a part of the road in which there is no gradient but which curves and with respect to which the radius of the curve measured to the centre of that part of that road—

(i) does not exceed one hundred feet—sixty feet;

(ii) exceeds one hundred feet but does not exceed two hundred feet—ninety feet;

(iii) exceeds two hundred feet but does not exceed three hundred feet—one hundred and fifty feet;

(*b*) in a part of the road which does not curve but in which there is a gradient which—

(i) does not exceed 1:80—three hundred feet;

(ii) exceeds 1:80 but does not exceed 1:50—one hundred and eighty feet;

(iii) exceeds 1:50 but does not exceed 1:30—one hundred and twenty feet;

(iv) exceeds 1:30—sixty feet;

(*c*) in a part of the road which curves and in which there is a gradient, the intervals specified in sub-paragraph (*a*) of this paragraph in relation to a part of a road having a curve with a like radius (being in each case the radius measured as specified in that sub-paragraph) or the intervals specified in sub-paragraph (*b*) in relation to a part of a road in which there is a like gradient, whichever are the lesser;

(*d*) in any other part of the road—three hundred feet.

(3) For the said purposes, and without prejudice to the provisions of the last preceding paragraph, a refuge hole shall be provided at each end of every curved part of a road in which a locomotive runs.

(4) For the said purposes the intervals which must not be exceeded between refuge holes on roads in which run vehicles moved by animals (but not vehicles moved by gravity or mechanical power) shall be seventy-five feet.

(5) For the said purposes the prescribed dimensions of refuge holes are—

(*a*) in width, three feet as nearly as may be;

(*b*) in depth, not less than four feet; and

(*c*) in height, not less than the height of the road at that place or six feet whichever is the less.

(6) Where in any length of road there is a continuous clear space not less than two feet in width between the vehicles running therein and one side of the road, every refuge hole therein shall be on that side of the road.

(7) Where in any length of road such clear space is not provided any refuge holes in a part of the road which curves shall be on the outside of the curve and, so far as is consistent with that requirement, all the refuge holes therein shall be on the same side of the road.

(8) Every refuge hole shall be—

(*a*) marked with a distinctive number;

(*b*) if necessary to make it readily visible, constantly kept whitewashed both inside and for a distance of not less than one foot round the aperture; and

(*c*) kept clean.

Transport of persons

60. (1) The manager of every mine in which trains are run for the conveyance of persons below ground shall ensure that each such train is accompanied by, and all persons therein are in the charge of, a competent person appointed by him.

(2) No person shall get on to or off such a train when it is moving or ride upon the footboard, buffer or coupling of any vehicle.

61. No person shall ride on a set or train of vehicles moved by mechanically operated or gravity operated rope haulage apparatus for the purpose of detaching vehicles from, or attaching them to, the rope if that set or train is moving at a speed exceeding three miles per hour.

62. No person shall ride on any haulage rope.

Movement of vehicles by hand

63. (1) No person when moving a vehicle by hand down a gradient exceeding 1:12 shall go down in front of the vehicle.

(2) No person shall move any vehicle by hand down an incline in circumstances in which he cannot by his own strength control it from behind unless there is provided such a contrivance as to enable him to control it from behind.

Apparatus to prevent accidents from runaway vehicles

64. (1) A sufficient supply of suitable sprags, lockers or drags shall be provided, maintained and used for the purpose of holding vehicles—

(*a*) at the top of every incline on which vehicles are moved by gravity operated rope haulage apparatus;

(*b*) at every place at which sets or trains consisting of three or more vehicles are coupled or uncoupled; and

(*c*) at suitable points on any length of road of which the gradient exceeds 1:20 and in which vehicles are moved by animals.

(2) Stop blocks or other similar contrivances shall be provided and maintained—

(*a*) at the top of every incline on which vehicles are moved by gravity operated rope haulage apparatus (not being such apparatus with an endless rope); and

(*b*) at every entrance to such an incline by which vehicles are brought on to the incline.

(3) In relation to every train by which persons are carried and which is moved by mechanically operated rope haulage apparatus (not being such apparatus with an endless rope) upon any length of road having a gradient exceeding 1:12 there shall be provided and maintained means of preventing any vehicle forming part of that train from becoming disconnected accidentally from other vehicles in the train.

(4) Nothing in this regulation shall be so construed as to affect the generality of section forty-one of the Act.

PART XI

Cappings of winding and haulage ropes

65. (1) No capped rope shall be used at any time in winding or haulage apparatus unless the capping has been made within a period of six months immediately preceding that time.

(2) No capped rope shall be so used unless the capping is of a type which has been found to withstand a load of—

(*a*) in the case of a rope used in winding apparatus, at least seven times the maximum static load which may ordinarily be borne by that capping where a cage is raised or lowered;

(*b*) in the case of a rope used in haulage apparatus for carrying persons through an outlet, at least seven times the maximum static load which may ordinarily be borne by that capping;

(*c*) in the case of a rope used in any other haulage apparatus, at least sixty per cent of the breaking strength of rope of that type.

66. No capped rope shall be used in any haulage apparatus by means of which persons are carried or in any winding apparatus unless, when the capping was made, the work was superintended by a competent person appointed for that purpose by the manager of the mine.

67. (1) No rope which has been re-capped shall be used in any haulage apparatus by means of which persons are carried or in any winding apparatus unless on the last occasion on which it was re-capped a part of the rope including the capping not less than six feet in length was cut off: so however that if at the date of any re-capping the preceding capping or re-capping was done not more than three, four or five months previously the part to be cut off need not exceed three, four or five feet respectively.

(2) Any length of rope cut off in pursuance of this regulation shall forthwith be opened up and its internal condition examined by a competent person appointed for the purpose by the manager of the mine, and the person making such an examination shall forthwith make and sign in a book* provided for the purpose by the owner of the mine, a full and accurate report of the result thereof.

68. No rope having a capping containing white metal shall be used in any winding or haulage apparatus unless—

(*a*) the capping† was made with white metal of which the melting point is not higher than 570° Fahr., and the temperature of which when poured into the socket of the capel did not exceed 685° Fahr.;

(*b*) in the length of rope which lies within the tapered part of the socket any fibre core was cut out when the capping was made and the wires were then untwisted and thoroughly cleaned; and

(*c*) the temperature of the socket of the capel was—

(i) in the case of a capel made of steel of a type for the time being approved‡ by the Minister for the purposes of this sub-paragraph, between 212° and 400° Fahrenheit; or

(ii) in any other case, as nearly as might be 212° Fahrenheit immediately before the white metal was poured into it.

69. No rope with a form of capping in which the wires at the end of the rope are bent back on the rope itself to form a cone shall be used in any haulage apparatus by means of which persons are carried or in any winding apparatus, unless—

(*a*) wedges formed by lapping with soft iron wire are placed between the rope and the wires which are bent back; and

(*b*) the length of the tapered portion of the socket of the capping is not less than eight times the diameter of the rope.

70. No round rope to which a capel is attached by rivets passing through the rope shall be used in any haulage apparatus by means of which persons are carried or in any winding apparatus.

PART XII

Additional provisions relating to shafts and staple-pits in the course of being sunk

71. (1) Without prejudice to the generality of regulations six and seven of the Coal and Other Mines (Mechanics and Electricians) Regulations 1956, § it shall

*M. & Q. Form No 281.

†The capping metal specified and the method of capping described in British Standard Specification No. 643, 1935, are advised.

‡See page 263.

§Now replaced by Regulations 9 and 10 of the Coal and Other Mines (Mechanics and Electricians) Regulations 1965—see page 194.

be the duty of the manager of every mine consisting of or comprising a shaft or staple-pit in the course of being sunk to ensure that a scheme for the systematic examination of plant at that mine made in pursuance of the said regulation seven provides for the thorough examination* at intervals not exceeding twenty-four hours of all gear by which any cradle, platform or other thing is suspended in that shaft or staple-pit.

(2) Where walling or tubbing is being carried out in a shaft or staple-pit in the course of being sunk, the manager shall make and ensure the efficient carrying out of arrangements to secure that it is thoroughly examined by a competent person appointed by him immediately before or during each shift in which work is carried out thereon, whether in the course of an inspection required by regulations or otherwise.

72. (1) Any place where a person could fall off any cradle or platform on which he works in a shaft or staple-pit in the course of being sunk shall be protected by fencing or otherwise to prevent him doing so.

(2) While any person is at work on any such cradle or platform it shall be secured to the side of the shaft or staple-pit to prevent it swinging and shall not be moved except upon the direction of the deputy for that shift or an official of the mine superior to the deputy.

(3) While any person is at work on any such cradle or platform which is constructed of two or more parts hinged together, those parts shall be securely bolted together.

73. At any shaft or staple-pit in the course of being sunk it shall be the duty of the banksman to ensure that the top of the shaft or staple-pit and any landing thereat is kept free of mineral or any other thing which might fall into that shaft or staple-pit and cause injury.

74. No engine which is not fixed shall be used for raising or lowering any person or thing in a shaft or staple-pit in the course of being sunk.

75. (1) In a shaft or staple-pit in the course of being sunk the provisions of regulations thirty-two to thirty-nine of these regulations shall not apply in relation to the determination or transmission of signals, but the following signals and no other shall be used for the purposes specified in relation thereto, that is to say—

to raise up	1
to lower down	2
to stop when in motion	1
when men are to be raised or lowered the person transmitting the signal shall transmit a preliminary signal of ..	3.

(2) In relation to any shaft or staple-pit in the course of being sunk the manager may determine a signal to be transmitted to give any indication (other than one for which a signal is specified in this regulation) and no person shall transmit any signal which is not so specified or determined.

*No. 14 of the Mechanics and Electricians Regulations 1965, requires reports to be made on these examinations. The appropriate form is M. & Q. Form No. 282.

(3) No person other than the banksman, an official of the mine or a person authorised in writing by the manager to transmit such signals shall transmit any signal in any shaft or staple-pit in the course of being sunk.

76. (1) When anything is to be raised or lowered in any kibble through any shaft or staple-pit in the course of being sunk, it shall be the duty of the deputy for that shift or the banksman or other person authorised to transmit signals in relation thereto, as the case may be, to ensure that it is properly loaded and in particular that—

(*a*) no mineral* projects above the rim;

(*b*) tools, equipment or other materials for use or used in the mine are not loaded together with mineral;

(*c*) when things which project above the rim are carried, they are securely fastened to the bow or chains supporting the kibble;

(*d*) nothing capable of causing injury is adhering to the outside of the kibble;

(*e*) when the kibble is being raised, it is in line with the pulleys and carefully steadied.

(2) When anything is to be lowered otherwise than in a kibble through a shaft or staple-pit in the course of being sunk, it shall be the duty of the banksman or other person authorised to transmit signals in relation thereto to ensure that it is safely slung.

77. No person shall ride on the edge of a kibble when being raised or lowered thereby.

78. The person operating any winding apparatus at a shaft or staple-pit in the course of being sunk—

(*a*) when lowering the kibble, shall stop it eighteen feet above the point to which it is being lowered and shall not lower it further until he has received another signal to lower down;

(*b*) when raising the kibble, shall stop it four feet above the point from which it is being raised and shall not raise it further until he has received another signal to raise up.

79. If a shaft or staple-pit is being sunk through any rock or stratum containing or likely to contain water (whether dispersed or in natural cavities) there shall be provided and maintained as a means of escape from the bottom of the shaft or staple-pit to the surface or to some other place of safety, in any case in which more than ten persons are employed below ground at any one time, at least four ladders and, in any other case, at least two ladders.

PART XIII

Miscellaneous provisions

Provision of means of telephonic communication

80. (1) Where in any mine vehicles can be moved by means of rope haulage apparatus or locomotives from a point at or near an entrance to a shaft or

*As defined in Section 182 (1) of the 1954 Act.

unwalkable outlet along a road for a distance exceeding three thousand feet, effective means of telephonic communication shall be provided and maintained between the furthest point inbye to which vehicles can be so moved, that entrance to the shaft or outlet and a point above ground.

(2) Nothing in this regulation shall apply to a mine at which not more than thirty persons are employed below ground or to a mine of stratified ironstone in the Cleveland district.

Prevention of injuries through things falling down shafts or staple-pits

81. There shall be provided in every shaft and staple-pit reasonable protection for the purpose of preventing persons loading cages at entrances thereto being injured by articles falling down it.

82. (1) No person shall go into or across any uncovered space at the bottom of a shaft or staple-pit except for the purpose of working there.

(2) The manager of every mine shall ensure that no person is at work in any uncovered space at the bottom of a shaft or staple-pit (not being a shaft or staple-pit in the course of being sunk) at any time at which any cage is in motion therein.

Assignment of duties to competent persons

83. It shall be the duty of the manager to make and ensure the efficient carrying out of arrangements to secure that every inspection, examination or other thing required by these regulations to be carried out or done by a competent person appointed by him is assigned to a competent person so appointed.

Application of certain regulations to staple-pits

84. (1) After the first day of February, nineteen hundred and sixty-two, the provisions of these regulations specified in the next following paragraph shall apply in relation to a staple-pit in a mine as they apply in relation to a shaft or unwalkable outlet.

(2) Regulation eleven (which relates to overwinding), regulation twelve (which relates to the construction of cages and ancillary apparatus), regulation fifteen (which relates to keps), regulation sixteen (which relates to detaching gear) and regulation fifty-three (which relates to the prevention of overwinding):

Provided that the said regulation fifteen shall not apply to any staple-pit in relation to which the manager of a mine has appointed a travelling onsetter in pursuance of regulation forty-two.

THE COAL AND OTHER MINES (HEIGHT OF TRAVELLING ROADS) REGULATIONS 1956

S.I. 1956 No. 1940

1. These regulations shall apply to every mine of coal, stratified ironstone, shale, or fireclay.

2. (1) There shall be exempted from the provisions of subsection (1) of section thirty-five of the Act (which requires to be not less than five feet six inches high throughout every length of road in a mine which is used at the beginning or end of a shift by not less than ten persons for the purpose of walking to or from their working places in the mine, being a length made after the commencement of the Act) any part of any such road which is within a distance of nine hundred feet from a working face and the height of which has been reduced by movement of the strata due to the working of that face being—

(*a*) where that face is a longwall face substantially parallel to that part of that road, a part not exceeding in length nine hundred feet or the length of that face whichever is the less; or

(*b*) in any other case, a part not exceeding four hundred and fifty feet in length:

Provided that, in a case in which the distance walked along parts of roads to which the provisions of this paragraph would apply apart from this proviso and which are less than five feet six inches high, by not less than ten persons at the beginning or end of a shift for the purpose of going to or from their working places exceeds nine hundred feet, or more than one hundred and fifty feet of that distance is along parts of roads less than four feet six inches high, the provisions of this paragraph shall not apply to those parts of those roads.

(2) The exemption of any length of road by virtue of paragraph (1) of this regulation is subject to the condition that it is maintained not less than four feet high throughout.

3. (1) For the purposes of these regulations the expression 'working face' does not include a place in a road at which only ripping or work of repair is in progress.

(2) The Interpretation Act 1889 shall apply to the interpretation of these regulations as it applies to the interpretation of an Act of Parliament.

(3) These regulations shall come into operation at the commencement of the Act and may be cited as the Coal and Other Mines (Height of Travelling Roads) Regulations 1956.

T.L.R.S.H.—R

THE COAL MINES (CLEARANCES IN TRANSPORT ROADS) REGULATIONS 1959

S.I. 1959 No. 1217

PART I

General

Commencement and citation

1. These regulations shall come into operation on the first day of August nineteen hundred and fifty-nine, and may be cited as the Coal Mines (Clearances in Transport Roads) Regulations 1959.

Interpretation

2. (1) In these regulations the following expressions have the meanings hereby respectively assigned to them, that is to say—

'the Act' means the Mines and Quarries Act 1954;

'clearance' has the meaning assigned by regulation five;

'boarding point' means, in relation to a road, any place on that road at which any person normally boards or alights from a vehicle;

'locomotive' has the meaning assigned by the Coal and Other Mines (Locomotives) Regulations 1956;

'mine' has the meaning assigned by regulation three;

'new road' has the meaning assigned by regulation four;

'old road' has the meaning assigned by regulation seven;

'road' has the meaning assigned by regulation three;

'unsettled ground' means ground within nine hundred feet of a working face measured in the plane of the working;

'working face' does not include a place at which the work consists only of ripping or work of repair; and

'working place' means, in relation to a road, any place on that road at which any person is normally employed in, or in connection with, the loading, unloading, handling or operation of any vehicle otherwise than for the purpose of or in connection with the execution of works to any part of the road at or adjacent to that place.

(2) Expressions to which meanings are assigned by the Act or by these regulations shall (unless the contrary intention appears) have the same meanings in any document issued under the provisions of these regulations.

(3) The Interpretation Act, 1889, shall apply to the interpretation of these regulations as it applies to the interpretation of an Act of Parliament.

PART II

Application

3. Except where the application thereof is further expressly limited, these regulations shall apply in every mine of coal to any length of road therein in which any vehicle runs on rails or any conveyor is operated, and in these regulations 'mine' means such a mine and 'road' means (except where further expressly limited) such a length of road.

PART III

Clearances in New Roads

4. This Part of these regulations shall apply to every length of road described and used as specified, in relation to any length in which persons are carried in vehicles with open sides, in column 1 of Part I of the schedule to these regulations or, in relation to any other length of road, in column 1 of Part II of that schedule, being a length—

(*a*) made after the thirtieth day of April, nineteen hundred and sixty, for the purpose of being so used for any period other than a period expiring less than three years after that date; or

(*b*) enlarged after that date for the purpose of being so used for any such period as aforesaid (and which was not so used before that date).

In these regulations 'new road' means such a length of road, and any reference to a vehicle with open sides shall be construed as a reference to a vehicle which is not closed in at both sides in such a way as to prevent persons or things projecting beyond the sides of the vehicle.

5. (1) Subject to the provisions of the next following paragraph the manager of every mine shall ensure that in every new road in which any vehicle is running or any conveyor is in operation there are provided and maintained continuous clear spaces (taking into account the swing of any vehicle)—

(*a*) between any side of the road or anything supporting that side and any part of any vehicle or conveyor;

(*b*) between any parts of any vehicles on adjacent tracks of rails;

(*c*) between any parts of adjacent conveyors; and

(*d*) between any part of any conveyor and any part of any vehicle on an adjacent track of rails;

(any such continuous clear space being, in these regulations, referred to as a 'clearance') which are (subject to the provisions of regulation six of these regulations) in every case of a width not less than the appropriate clearance (if any) specified in relation to that road—

(i) in the case of a new road in which persons are carried in vehicles with open sides in column 2 of Part I of the schedule to these regulations; or

(ii) in the case of any other new road and notwithstanding anything in paragraph (4) of regulation forty-seven of the Coal and Other Mines (Shafts, Outlets and Roads) Regulations 1956*, in column 2 of Part II of that schedule.

(2) Nothing in sub-paragraph (ii) of the last preceding paragraph shall require the provision of any clearance in pursuance of that sub-paragraph in the case of a new road in relation to which the manager of a mine makes and secures the effective carrying out of arrangements to secure that no person is in that road when any vehicle is in motion therein except a person who is—

(*a*) there for the purpose of accompanying a vehicle or set of vehicles; or

(*b*) at a working place thereon.

(3) Paragraph (3) of regulation six and paragraph (3) of regulation seven of the Coal and Other Mines (Locomotives) Regulations 1956†, shall not apply in relation to any new road in which a locomotive runs.

Working places and boarding points

6. (1) The Manager of every mine shall ensure that there is provided and maintained at every working place and boarding point in a new road a clearance of a width not less than—

(*a*) where it is a length of road in unsettled ground and no persons are carried in vehicles with open sides therein—two feet; or

(*b*) in any other case—two and a half feet.

(2) Regulation forty-six of the Coal and Other Mines (Shafts, Outlets and Roads) Regulations, 1956‡ shall not apply to any place to which paragraph (1) of this regulation applies.

PART IV

Clearances in Old Roads

7. This Part of these regulations shall apply to every length of road described and used as specified, in relation to any length in which persons are carried in vehicles with open sides, in column 1 of Part I of the schedule to these regulations or, in relation to any other length of road, in column 1 of Part II of that schedule, not being a length to which Part III of these regulations applies, and in these regulations 'old road' means such a length of road.

8. (1) If, with respect to any old road in a mine, an inspector is of opinion that it is necessary that any clearances therein should be widened in order to avoid danger to persons employed in the mine, he may serve on the manager of the mine a notice specifying that road and requiring the manager to execute, before the expiration of such period beginning with the date on which the notice becomes operative (being a date not earlier than the first day of May, nineteen hundred and sixty) as may be specified therein, such works to that road as may be necessary to secure that the clearances therein are (subject to the provisions of

*Now replaced by regulation 59(6) of the Coal and Other Mines (Shafts, Outlets and Roads) Regulations 1960—see page 247.

†See pages 165 and 166.

‡Now replaced by Regulation 58 of the Coal and Other Mines (Shafts, Outlets and Roads) Regulations 1960—see page 245.

regulation nine of these regulations) in every case of a width not less than the appropriate clearance (if any) specified in relation to that road in column 2 of Part I or Part II (as the case may require) of the schedule to these regulations.

(2) The provisions of Part XV of the Act* with respect to references upon notices served by inspectors shall apply to a notice of requirement under the last preceding paragraph and either of the following shall be a relevant ground of objection to such a notice, namely—

(*a*) that the execution of the said works is not necessary in order to avoid danger to persons employed in the mine;

(*b*) that it is not practicable for the said works to be executed before the expiration of the period specified in the notice.

(3) Paragraph (3) of regulation six and paragraph (3) of regulation seven of the Coal and Other Mines (Locomotives) Regulations 1956†, shall not apply in relation to any old road in which a locomotive runs, being a road with respect to which a notice served under the provisions of paragraph (1) of this regulation has become operative.

Working places and boarding points

9. After the thirty-first day of July, nineteen hundred and sixty-four, the provisions of regulation six of these regulations shall apply to every working place and boarding point in an old road as if it were a working place or boarding point in a new road.

PART V

Miscellaneous Provisions

Notices

10. The manager of every mine shall ensure that in every road which is used by persons on foot there shall be kept posted at each end of the road and at such other place therein as may be requisite to avoid danger, in such characters and in such positions as to be easily seen and read by those persons, notices stating the position in the road of any clearance provided in pursuance of these regulations and indicating any point at which the position of the clearance changes.

11. (1) Without prejudice to the provisions of section thirty-six of the Act and subject to the provisions of paragraph (2) of this regulation, nothing in these regulations shall require the provision of any clearance in accordance with the requirements of these regulations at any place in a road at which there has occurred a sudden decrease howsoever caused, or a gradual decrease caused by workings in a different plane, of a clearance provided in accordance with those requirements.

(2) The provisions of paragraph (1) of this regulation shall apply only—

(*a*) during such period immediately following the said occurrence as might reasonably have been expected in all the circumstances to be required in order to secure that the clearance is restored to a width not less than the appropriate width specified in these regulations; and

---

*See Section 170 of the 1954 Act.
†See pages 165 and 166.

(*b*) where there is no reasonable ground for apprehending that the running of the vehicles or the operation of the conveyor, as the case may be, on any occasion would result in bodily injury to persons or animals using the road.

Exemptions

12. An inspector, if he is satisfied that the application of any provision of these regulations is not requisite for safety or is inappropriate in relation to any mine or part thereof, may by notice served on the manager of that mine exempt it or a part thereof from the application of that provision.

SCHEDULE

Part I

Clearances in roads in which persons are carried in vehicles with open sides

Column 1	Column 2 Clearances					
Description and usage of length of road	Clearance on one side of road (being a side on which refuge holes are not provided)		Clearance on the other side of road (being a side on which refuge holes (if any) are provided)		Clearance between vehicles on adjacent tracks, or between a conveyor and any vehicle on an adjacent track (as the case may be)	
	Length of road in unsettled ground	Length of road not in unsettled ground	Length of road in unsettled ground	Length of road not in unsettled ground	Length of road in unsettled ground	Length of road not in unsettled ground
	Feet	Feet	Feet	Feet	Feet	Feet
Any length of road in which there is a single track of rails on which persons are carried in vehicles moved otherwise than by hand or by animal traction	2	2	2	2	—	—
Any length of road in which there are two adjacent tracks of rails on each of which persons are carried in vehicles moved otherwise than by hand or by animal traction	2	2	2	2	2	2
Any length of road in which there are two adjacent tracks of rails on one of which (but not on the other) persons are carried in vehicles moved otherwise than by hand or by animal traction	1	1	2	2	2	2
Any length of road in which persons are carried in vehicles moved by animal traction	1	1	2	2	1	1

PART II
Clearances in other roads

Column 1	Column 2 Clearances					
Description and usage of length of road	Clearance on one side of road (being a side on which refuge holes are not provided)		Clearance on the other side of road (being a side on which refuge holes (if any) are provided)		Clearance between vehicles on adjacent tracks, or between a conveyor and any vehicle on an adjacent track or between two adjacent conveyors (as the case may be)	
	Length of road in unsettled ground	Length of road not in unsettled ground	Length of road in unsettled ground	Length of road not in unsettled ground	Length of road in unsettled ground	Length of road not in unsettled ground
	Feet	Feet	Feet	Feet	Feet	Feet
Any length of road in which mechanically or gravity operated rope haulage apparatus is used	—	1	1½	2	—	1
Any length of road in which any locomotive runs	—	1	2	2	—	1
Any length of road in which run vehicles moved by animal traction	—	1	1½	2	—	1
Any length of road in which run vehicles moved by hand	—	1	—	1	—	1
Any length of road in which a single conveyor is operated	1	1½	2	2	—	—
Any length of road in which a double conveyor is operated	1	1½	1	1½	2	2
Any length of road in which a single conveyor is operated and in which, beside the conveyor, is a track of rails on which vehicles run: (a) (if the average gradient does not exceed 1 : 5) ...	2	2	—	1	—	1
or (b) whatever the gradient: either	1	1½	2	2	—	1
or	1	1½	—	1	2	2

STEEL: TYPE APPROVED FOR THE PURPOSES OF REGULATIONS 19(6)(*a*) AND 68(*c*)(i) OF THE COAL AND OTHER MINES (SHAFTS, OUTLETS AND ROADS) REGULATIONS 1960, AS AMENDED BY THE COAL AND OTHER MINES (SHAFTS, OUTLETS AND ROADS) (AMENDMENT) REGULATIONS 1968, THE APPROVED MANNER OF USE AND THE SPECIFIED MAXIMUM INTERVALS FOR SPECIFIED HEAT TREATMENT

For the purposes of Regulation 19(6)(*a*), as amended, steel of the type specified in paragraph (1) below has been approved for use in the particular manner specified in paragraph (2) below. The type of heat treatment is described in paragraph (3) below and the intervals in paragraph (4) below have been specified as the maximum intervals for annealing or subjecting to heat treatment as described any apparatus or part thereof made of such steel.

Type of steel

(1) Steel of the type having the chemical composition specified for '1·5% manganese steel' in the British Standard Specification 2772: Part 2:1956 and having the mechanical properties specified in Table 4 of that specification or, if the ruling section* is greater than the appropriate limiting ruling section* specified in that table, the properties specified in the following table:—

Property	Bars, billets and forgings		
	Normalised or Normalised and Tempered	Hardened and Tempered	
	Limiting ruling section		
	Over 6″	Over 6″	Over 4″–6″
Tensile strength tons/sq. in., min.	28	28	31
Yield stress tons/sq. in., min.	17	18	20
Elongation per cent, min.	30	25	27
Izod impact value ft. lb., min.	45	40	45

**Note:* For the meaning of the terms 'ruling section' and 'limiting ruling section' reference should be made to the British Standard Specification referred to in paragraph 1 of this schedule.

Particular Manner of Use

(2) The steel shall be used to make apparatus or part thereof (including a detaching hook) provided for attaching to the rope a cage, carriage or kibble ordinarily used in a shaft, staple-pit or unwalkable outlet of a mine, being apparatus or part thereof

which, when new, (*a*) has a factor of safety of at least ten in relation to the maximum static load which may ordinarily be borne by it, and (*b*) is shown by test to be capable of withstanding without any permanent deformation a proof load equal to two and a half times the beforementioned maximum load.

Heat Treatment

(3) The heat treatment shall be stress relieving consisting of raising the temperature of the apparatus or part thereof to between 610°C and 650°C followed by slow cooling.

Maximum Intervals for Heat Treatment

(4) Where the apparatus or part thereof is used in connection with:—

(*a*) a cage, carriage or kibble which is in use in a shaft, staple-pit or unwalkable outlet and does not land at any landing or entrace where baulks or keps are provided ... ... 7 years;

(*b*) a cage, carriage or kibble which is in use in a shaft, staple-pit or unwalkable outlet and lands at any landing or entrance when baulks or keps are provided ... ... 5 years;

(*c*) a kibble which is in use in a shaft sinking ... ... 4 years.

Steel of the type having the chemical composition specified for '1·5% manganese steel' in the British Standard Specification 2772: Part 2: 1956 has been approved for the purposes of Regulation 68(*c*)(i).

SIDINGS

THE COAL AND OTHER MINES

(SIDINGS) REGULATIONS 1956

S.I. 1956 No. 1773

Application

1. These regulations shall apply, at every mine of coal, stratified ironstone, shale or fireclay, in relation to any railway line above ground which is deemed by virtue of subsection (3) or (5) of section one hundred and eighty of the Act to form part of the mine, being a line (except in regulation two) of a gauge not less than four feet eight and one-half inches. In these regulations 'mine' and 'line' means such a mine and such a line respectively.

Transport of persons

2. (1) The manager of every mine at which trains are run on a line for the conveyance of workmen shall ensure that each such train is accompanied by, and all persons therein are in the charge of, a competent person appointed by him.

(2) No person shall get on to or off such a train when it is moving or ride upon the footboard, buffer or coupling of any vehicle forming part thereof.

Points and signal wires

3. It shall be the duty of the manager of every mine to ensure—

(*a*) that any points rod or signal wire installed for use in connection with a line, being a points rod or signal wire so positioned as to be a source of danger to persons employed at that mine, is sufficiently covered or otherwise guarded; and

(*b*) that every ground lever for the operation of points on any line at the mine, being a line constructed after the tenth day of June, nineteen hundred and eleven, is so installed that any person moving that lever is, when so doing, clear of any traffic on any adjacent line, and that that lever is—

(i) so installed that it can be moved only in directions as nearly as may be parallel to the track of rails nearest to that lever; or

(ii) of such a shape and so installed as to minimise obstruction to persons employed at the mine.

Provision of equipment and safety devices

4. It shall be the duty of the manager of every mine to ensure that there are provided in relation to every line—

(*a*) sufficient coupling poles or other suitable mechanical appliances for the purpose of coupling and uncoupling vehicles;

(*b*) where requisite, sufficient pointed wooden sprags (each of a length not exceeding three feet) and sufficient scotches; and

(*c*) on every self-acting incline, that is to say an arrangement in which vehicles are pulled or intended to be pulled up a line by other vehicles moving by gravity down another line, such safety devices as are necessary to prevent the occurrence of accidents likely to cause bodily injury to persons, being accidents caused by the running away of such vehicles, and, at the top of each of those lines, stop-blocks.

Operation of points

5. (1) Every person who operates points on a line by holding them in position shall, before leaving those points, satisfy himself that they are in the proper position which they are intended to resume when not so held.

(2) Every person who moves a throw-over lever which operates points on a line shall, before leaving that lever, satisfy himself that it is in the proper position in which, having regard to the safe operation of any traffic on the lines concerned, it should be placed.

Movement of vehicles

6. The manager of every mine shall make and secure the efficient carrying out of arrangements whereby (except in the case of a vehicle being moved by a railway company) no vehicle is moved on a line otherwise than under the charge of a competent person appointed by the manager for that purpose.

7. No person shall move a vehicle, and no person in charge of a vehicle shall allow it to be moved, on a line by means of a prop or pole unless there is no other practicable method of moving the vehicle.

8. No person shall couple or uncouple any vehicle in motion in circumstances in which it is practicable to use a coupling pole or other suitable mechanical appliance for that purpose except by means of such a pole or appliance.

9. In every case in which any person employed at a mine is or might be exposed to risk of injury by reason of the movement on a line of two or more other vehicles pushed by a locomotive, the person in charge of those other vehicles shall—

(*a*) accompany or precede the leading vehicle, watch the line ahead of it, and give any warning which may be requisite for the purpose of minimising that risk; or

(*b*) ensure that that vehicle is accompanied or preceded by a person charged by him with the duty of watching the line ahead of it and giving any warning which may be requisite for the purpose aforesaid; or

(*c*) make and secure the efficient carrying out of any other arrangements whereby that risk is minimised.

10. In every case in which the movement of a vehicle on a line would be likely to endanger the safety of any person employed at the mine, that movement shall not be made unless appropriate warning has been given to that person by the person in charge of that vehicle.

11. The manager of every mine shall make and secure the efficient carrying out of arrangements whereby no locomotive or train is, during any period between one hour after sunset and one hour before sunrise, or in a fog, moved on a line at a part of the mine through which persons pass on foot or at which persons work, being a part at which there is not for the time being sufficient fixed artificial lighting, unless a suitable warning light is fixed to the leading end of that locomotive or train or that end is accompanied or preceded by a person carrying such a light.

12. Every driver in charge of a locomotive on a line, or a person preceding that locomotive on foot, shall, on approaching any level crossing ordinarily used by persons employed at the mine to cross that line, any curve of the line round which it is not possible to see from the locomotive or any other place at which the safety of any person employed at the mine is likely to be endangered by reason of the movement of the locomotive, give sufficient and timely warning of the approach of that locomotive, being a warning audible to persons for the time being at or near that level crossing, curve, or place (as the case may be).

13. No person shall move or attempt to move a vehicle on a line by pushing a buffer thereof.

14. (1) No person shall ride on any buffer of a vehicle in motion on a line (not being a vehicle forming part of a train with respect to which regulation two applies) unless there is a secure hand-hold easily reached by any person riding on that buffer, and no person shall stand on that buffer unless there is also a secure footplace thereon.

(2) No person shall be carried along by a vehicle on a line by riding on a pole, prop or other similar appliance.

Stationary vehicles

15. No person in charge of a vehicle at a mine shall leave it, or allow it to be left, on an incline described in paragraph (*c*) of regulation four, unless the vehicle is properly secured.

16. The manager of every mine shall make and secure the efficient carrying out of arrangements whereby in every case in which, for the purpose of affording passage across a line, a space is left between two vehicles stationary on one track of rails, that space is not less than fifteen feet in width.

17. It shall be the duty of the person in immediate charge of the carrying out to any vehicle on a line of any operation of repair to ensure that, in every case in which the safety of a person engaged in that operation might be endangered as a result of the movement of a vehicle, a danger signal is displayed at or near each end of the vehicle under repair or (if that vehicle for the time being forms part of a train of vehicles) of that train (as the case may be), being an end which might be struck or moved by another vehicle.

Restrictions on passage of persons on foot

18. No person shall pass immediately in front of any vehicle moving on a line under screens at a mine, or between any vehicles so moving:

Provided that nothing in this regulation shall apply to the person in charge of that vehicle or those vehicles (as the case may be).

19. No person shall cross a line by passing underneath any vehicle thereon if by so doing his safety might be endangered by traffic.

Stacking of material beside lines

20. The manager of every mine shall make and secure the efficient carrying out of arrangements whereby, in every case in which any material is placed (otherwise than on ground ordinarily used for the stocking of material) at a distance less than three feet from the track of rails of a line and any person employed at the mine is required in the course of his duty to pass on foot over that material or between it and the line, that material is so placed in such manner that—

(*a*) every such person can so pass without being exposed to risk of injury by traffic on that line; and

(*b*) if that material extends (whether continuously or not) for a distance exceeding sixty feet measured parallel with that line, there are provided at intervals not greater than sixty feet adequate spaces or recesses in that material.

Minimum age for locomotive drivers and shunters

21. (1) No person who has not attained the age of eighteen years shall be employed at a mine for the purpose of driving a locomotive on a line.

(2) No person who has not attained the age of sixteen years shall be employed in relation to a line as a shunter.

Interpretation

22. (1) In these regulations the following expressions have the meanings hereby respectively assigned to them, that is to say—

'the act' means the Mines and Quarries Act 1954;

'line' has the meaning assigned thereto in regulation one;

'locomotive' means a mechanically propelled vehicle running on a track of rails and constructed or used for moving other vehicles;

'mine' has the meaning assigned thereto in regulation one.

(2) The Interpretation Act 1889 shall apply to the interpretation of these regulations as it applies to the interpretation of an Act of Parliament.

SMOKING MATERIALS

THE MINES

(MANNER OF SEARCH FOR SMOKING MATERIALS) ORDER 1956

S.I. 1956 No. 2016

1. Every search made in pursuance of the said section sixty-six of the Act at any mine shall be made in the manner following, that is to say—

(*a*) the search shall be made by a person appointed for the purpose in writing by the manager of the mine (that person being hereinafter referred to as 'the searcher');

(*b*) in the case of a search of any person employed or about to be employed on a shift, the search shall be made in the presence of not less than two other persons so employed or about to be so employed;

(*c*) in making the search the searcher shall observe the proprieties and shall cause to the person being searched no more inconvenience than may be necessary for the purpose of making an efficient search;

(*d*) the searcher shall—

(i) feel for any such article as is mentioned in subsection (1) of the said section sixty-six of the Act by handling the clothing of the person being searched (including the inside of any pockets), and, if after so doing he has reason to believe or suspect that any such article is in the possession of that person, examine that clothing;

(ii) examine any other article which that person has with him.

2. (Revocation of Order of 21st May, 1912.)

3. (1) The Interpretation Act 1889 shall apply to the interpretation of this order as it applies to the interpretation of an Act of Parliament.

(2) This order shall come into operation at the commencement of the Act and may be cited as the Mines (Manner of Search for Smoking Materials) Order 1956.

STEAM BOILERS

THE COAL AND OTHER MINES

(STEAM BOILERS) REGULATIONS 1956

S.I. 1956 No. 1772*

Application

1. These regulations shall apply to every mine of coal, stratified ironstone, shale or fireclay, and in these regulations 'mine' means such a mine.

Safety valves, steam gauges and water gauges

2. Every steam boiler, whether separate or one of a range, at a mine shall be provided with—

(*a*) a suitable safety valve; and

(*b*) a suitable steam gauge and a suitable water gauge to show respectively the pressure of steam and the height of water in that boiler.

3. Every water gauge attached to any steam boiler at a mine shall be provided with a suitable covering or guard unless it is so constructed as to be as safe to persons working or passing near-by as it would be if so protected.

4. No person shall alter the setting of any safety valve attached to any steam boiler at a mine except with the authority of the official under whose immediate charge the boiler minder works, and no weight shall be used on a safety valve which works with weights other than a weight constructed for that purpose.

Determination and indication of maximum steam pressure

5. The manager of every mine shall, in relation to each steam boiler for the time being in use, or intended to be used, at the mine, determine the maximum pressure to which steam may be generated at pressure in that boiler and have that pressure marked upon the steam gauge in a distinctive colour.

Appointment and duties of boiler minders

6. The manager of every mine shall make and secure the efficient carrying out of arrangements whereby every steam boiler for the time being in use at the mine is in the charge of a competent person appointed by him for that purpose (in these regulations referred to as a 'boiler minder').

7. Every boiler minder shall, with respect to every steam boiler for the time being in use at the mine and in his charge,—

(*a*) from time to time during the course of each day inspect externally that boiler and all its fittings and attachments, and forthwith report to the official under whose immediate charge he works any patent defect of that boiler or of those fittings or attachments;

*The provisions of these Regulations are additional to the provisions of Section 84 (1) of the 1954 Act.

(*b*) maintain the level of water in that boiler as nearly as practicable at the proper working level;

(*c*) if the level of water in that boiler falls below, and he is unable to raise that level to, the proper working level, forthwith—

(i) lower the dampers;

(ii) damp down the fire;

(iii) (if it is necessary further to reduce the consumption of water) draw the fire; and

forthwith thereafter report to the official under whose immediate charge he works the facts and the nature of the action taken by him in pursuance of sub-paragraphs (i), (ii) and (iii) of this paragraph; and

(*d*) ensure that the pressure to which steam is generated in that boiler does not exceed the maximum pressure determined by the manager in pursuance of regulation five.

Cleaning of boilers

8. The manager of every mine shall make and secure the efficient carrying out of arrangements whereby every steam boiler for the time being in use at the mine is cleaned out at intervals not exceeding three months by a competent person appointed for that purpose by the manager.

9. (1) Without prejudice to the generality of regulations six and seven of the Coal and Other Mines (Mechanics and Electricians) Regulation 1956,* it shall be the duty of the manager of every mine to ensure that a scheme for the systematic examination of plant at that mine made in pursuance of the said regulation seven provides that every steam boiler at a mine shall—

(*a*) be examined internally, as far as the construction thereof will permit, by a competent person appointed for that purpose by the manager, forthwith after every cleaning of that boiler carried out in pursuance of the last preceding regulation; and

(*b*) be examined thoroughly at intervals not exceeding fourteen months by a competent person so appointed.

(2) In every case in which a boiler inspection company or association has been appointed by the manager of a mine to make an examination of a steam boiler in pursuance of provisions of a scheme for the systematic examination of plant at that mine, being provisions included in that scheme in pursuance of sub-paragraph (*b*) of the last preceding paragraph, there shall, within fourteen days of the completion of the examination, be made in, or attached to, a book† provided for the purpose by the owner of the mine a report signed by the person who made the examination and countersigned by the chief engineer or other officer of similar status of the company or association.

*Now replaced by regulations 9 and 10 of the Coal and Other Mines (Mechanics and Electricians) Regulations, 1965—see page 194.

†M. & Q. Forms Nos. 288 and 289. A report must also be made on M. & Q. Form No. 287 on the internal examination required by Regulation 9(1)(a).

General

10. (1) In these regulations the following expressions have the meanings hereby respectively assigned to them, that is to say—

'the Act' means the Mines and Quarries Act 1954;

'boiler minder' has the meaning assigned thereto in regulation six;

'mine' has the meaning assigned thereto in regulation one.

(2) Nothing in these regulations shall apply to any steam boiler forming part of a locomotive belonging to and used by a railway company.

(3) Expressions to which meanings are assigned by the Act or by these regulations shall (unless the contrary intention appears) have the same meanings in any document issued under the provisions of these regulations.

(4) The Interpretation Act 1889 shall apply to the interpretation of these regulations as it applies to the interpretation of an Act of Parliament.

SUPPORT

THE COAL AND OTHER MINES (SUPPORT) REGULATIONS 1966

S.I. 1966 No. 881

Arrangement of Regulations

PART I

General

Commencement and citation

1. These regulations shall come into operation on the 1st October, 1966, and may be cited as the Coal and Other Mines (Support) Regulations 1966.

Interpretation

2.—(1) In these regulations, unless the context otherwise requires, the following expressions have the meanings hereby respectively assigned to them, that is to say—

'the Act' means the Mines and Quarries Act 1954;

'approved' in relation to a prop, bar or other device to be used for purposes of support, means complying with a specification approved by the Minister of Power for such a prop, bar or device for use at a place where an armoured conveyer is used, and where a provision of these regulations so requires, complying with a specification approved by the Minister for the purpose of that provision, whether or not approved for other purposes of this definition;

'armoured conveyor' does not include any conveyor designed to be readily dismantled for the purpose of being moved forward;

'bar' includes girder;

'face working' in relation to a working face at which supports are systematically withdrawn means all that part of the mine between the face and the front line of the packs, if any, or the last row of supports for the time being maintained whichever is farther from the face and in relation to a working face at which supports are not systematically withdrawn means all that part of the mine between the face and a line parallel to it and twelve feet distant from it;

'mechanical energy' has the same meaning as it has for the purposes of the Coal and Other Mines (Mechanics and Electricians) Regulations 1965;*

'mine' has the meaning assigned thereto in regulation 5;

'powered support' has the meaning assigned thereto in regulation 16;

'prop' includes hydraulic chock and friction chock; and

'working face' does not include a place at which the work consists only of ripping or work of repair.

*See page 192.

(2) Expressions to which meanings are assigned by the Act or by these regulations shall (unless the contrary intention appears) have the same meanings in any document issued under the provisions of these regulations.

(3) The Interpretation Act 1889 shall apply to the interpretation of these regulations as it applies to the interpretation of an Act of Parliament.

Exemptions

3. An inspector may by notice served on the manager of any mine exempt that mine or any part thereof from the application of any provision of these regulations if he is satisfied that the safety of persons employed at the mine will not be prejudiced in consequence of the granting of the exemption.

Revocation

4. The Coal and Other Mines (Support) Regulations 1956 are hereby revoked.

PART II

Application

5. These regulations shall apply to every mine of coal, shale or fireclay, and in these regulations 'mine' means such a mine.

PART III

General provisions relating to the setting of supports

Props

6.—(1) Any person setting a prop to support the roof or side of any place in a mine shall set it securely and on a proper foundation.

(2) If it appears to any person whose duties include the setting of props in any part of a mine that any prop in that part of the mine has become

(*a*) broken or defective, he shall forthwith replace that prop; or

(*b*) unstable, he shall forthwith replace or make stable that prop:

Provided that if such person is unable to comply with the preceding provisions of this paragraph he shall forthwith report the condition of such broken, defective or unstable prop to the person for the time being in charge of that part of the mine.

(3) It shall be the duty of the person for the time being in charge of any part of a mine to take all reasonable steps to ensure that any prop therein which becomes broken or defective is forthwith replaced and that any prop therein which becomes unstable is forthwith replaced or made stable.

Use of lids

7.—(1) Any person setting a prop in a mine shall insert between the top of the prop and the roof or bar* above it, so as to cover the whole of the top of the prop, a suitable wooden lid of adequate thickness, and where there is no bar

*This expression, as used here and subsequently in these Regulations, has the meaning given in Regulation 2 (1).

above the prop the lid shall be of a width not less than the largest dimension of the top of the prop and of a length not less than twice that dimension.

(2) Nothing in the last paragraph shall require the use of a lid above—

(*a*) a prop set under a wooden bar; or

(*b*) a prop set under any bar other than a wooden bar, being

(i) an approved prop; and

(ii) a prop which is fitted with an approved friction cap, or which, by means provided with the prop or the bar, engages with the bar under which it is set so that movement of the prop relative to the bar is prevented while it is so engaged; or

(*c*) a prop set for the purpose of inducing a roof break; or

(*d*) a rigid steel prop fixed to a girder in any place not in a face working or roadhead; or

(*e*) a wooden prop set under a corrugated steel bar in any place where the working height does not, or does not generally, exceed two feet six inches; or

(*f*) an approved prop fitted with an approved bar slide head; or

(*g*) a prop having a top the smallest dimension of which is not less than nine inches.

Chocks

8.—(1) Any person building a chock which is to form part of a system of support in a mine shall build it on a proper foundation and make it tight to the roof.

(2) No person shall include as a main member in such a chock timber other than timber which has flat bearing surfaces where it is in contact with any other main member, otherwise than in a chock which is intended to be left in a pack or in the waste.

Packs

9. Any person building a pack which is to form part of a system of support in a mine shall so far as is practicable make it tight to the roof over its whole area and, wherever a pack is being built by hand or by hand tools, shall build the walls thereof on a proper foundation and fill it with debris.

Arch girders

10. Every arch girder to be set to support the roof or sides of any place in a mine shall be set on a proper foundation and made tight to the roof and sides of the place and shall be so fixed by ties or struts to its neighbours as to secure and maintain its stability.

Part IV

Provisions relating to systematic support at faces and roadheads

Application and interpretation of this part of these regulations

11.—(1) In this part of these regulations 'place', except where that expression is further expressly limited, means every place in a face working* and

*This expression, as used here and subsequently in these Regulations, has the meaning given in Regulation 2 (1).

every place in a roadhead throughout the following distance from the face in that roadhead or, where the road passes beyond a face to which it leads, from that face, that is to say—

(*a*) in the case of a roadhead at an advancing face in which the roof is ripped within thirty feet outbye from the face, throughout the distance between the face and such of the following points as is farthest therefrom, that is to say—

(i) such ripping or, if there is more than one, such ripping farthest from the face; or

(ii) the front line of the last completed roadside pack; or

(iii) where the last completed roadside pack is nearer to the face than the last completed pack on the other side of the road, the front line of such last mentioned pack; or

(*b*) in the case of such a roadhead in which the roof is not so ripped, throughout the distance of thirty feet outbye from the face; or

(*c*) in the case of a roadhead at a retreating face, throughout the width of the face working.

(2) Regulations 12 to 14 shall not apply in relation to any place at which the systematic support of the roof is provided by means of powered supports.

Props at face workings and roadheads where armoured conveyors are used*

12.—(1) At every place where any armoured conveyor is used, not being a place in a roadhead where arch girders are used for the support of the roof, the system of support of the roof shall include the use of props and support rules† in relation thereto shall specify the intervals not to be exceeded between adjacent rows of props, between adjacent props in the same row and between the front row of props and the face, which intervals shall be such as to enable regulation 14 (2) to be complied with.

(2) At every place where any armoured conveyor is used and persons do not pass or work between such conveyor and the face, otherwise than occasionally or for short periods, not being a place in a mine or part of a mine in respect of which there is in force a direction given by an inspector by notice served on the manager of the mine that this paragraph shall not apply, being a direction given on the grounds referred to in paragraph (8) of this regulation, the intervals specified by the support rules at which props shall be set shall not in the following cases exceed those specified in relation thereto, that is to say—

(*a*) the interval between adjacent rows of props shall not exceed three feet six inches;

(*b*) the interval between the front row of props and the face shall not exceed six feet six inches;

(*c*) where the support rules specify an interval between the front row of props and the face not exceeding six feet, the interval between adjacent

*This expression, as used here and subsequently in these Regulations, has the meaning given in Regulation 2(1).

†The expression 'support rules', here and subsequently in these Regulations, should be read in relation to Section 54 of the 1954 Act.

props in the same row shall not exceed five feet or a distance equal to seven feet less the interval so specified between adjacent rows of props at that place, whichever is the less; and

(*d*) where the support rules specify an interval between the front row of props and the face exceeding six feet, the interval between adjacent props in the same row shall not exceed four feet six inches or a distance equal to six feet six inches less the interval so specified between adjacent rows of props at that place, whichever is the less.

(3) At every place where any armoured conveyor is used and the last preceding paragraph does not apply, the intervals specified by the support rules at which props shall be set shall not in the following cases exceed those specified in relation thereto, that is to say—

(*a*) the interval between adjacent rows of props shall not exceed four feet;

(*b*) the interval between adjacent props in the same row shall not exceed three feet six inches; and

(*c*) the interval between the front row of props and the face shall not exceed three feet:

Provided that support rules may—

(i) specify that while the conveyor is being advanced the interval between adjacent rows of props for a distance along the face of not more than ninety feet may exceed four feet but shall not exceed seven feet;

(ii) if the width of any machine used for cutting or loading mineral requires a greater interval than three feet between the front row of props and the face at any place, specify in relation to that place an interval not exceeding three feet six inches.

(4) All props used as part of a system of support specified in compliance with either of the two preceding paragraphs shall be approved props.

(5) In relation to any place where any armoured conveyor is used, and where, by reason of an irregularity in the condition of the floor or roof or in the working height at that place the approved props supplied for use there are ineffective to keep that place secure, support rules may, notwithstanding the last foregoing paragraph, specify the use of props not approved until the condition of the floor or roof or the working height as the case may be enables approved props once more to be used:

Provided that if props not approved are in use pursuant to this paragraph for more than seven days consecutively at any face, notice thereof shall be given by the manager of the mine to the inspector for the district.

(6) At any place where a machine is used which shears mineral to a depth exceeding fifteen inches at a single cut, the props to support the roof exposed at that place by such cut shall be set before the machine is permitted to approach within ninety feet of that place on its next cut.

(7) At any place where a machine is used which cuts and loads mineral and at the same time makes a cut into the face thereby exposed, preparatory to cutting and loading at the next operation of the machine at that place, the distance specified by the support rules pursuant to paragraph (2)(*b*) of this regulation

shall be such that the distance between the front row of props and the back of the cut shall not exceed six feet six inches except over a length of sixty feet from the machine, measured in the direction opposite to the machine's direction of travel.

(8) A direction may be given by an inspector pursuant to paragraph (2) of this regulation on the ground that the system of work at that mine or part of the mine requires men to pass or work between the conveyor referred to in that paragraph and the face to a greater extent than is necessary, or on the ground that precautions which could be taken for securing the safety of such men are not being taken.

(9) The provisions of Part XV of the Act with respect to references upon notices served by inspectors shall apply to a notice containing a direction that paragraph (2) of this regulation shall not apply to a mine or part of a mine and the relevant grounds of objection shall be that the system of work does not expose men to danger or that all practicable precautions are taken for securing their safety.

Props at face workings and roadheads where armoured conveyors are not used

13.—(1) At every place not being a place where any armoured conveyor is used or a place in a roadhead where arch girders are used for the support of the roof, the system of support shall include the use of props, and support rules in relation thereto shall specify the intervals not to be exceeded between adjacent rows of props, between adjacent props in the same row and between the front row of props and the face, which intervals shall, in relation to any place to which regulation 14 applies, be such as to enable paragraph (2) of that regulation to be complied with.

(2) The intervals specified pursuant to the last preceding paragraph, in relation to any place at a longwall face or in a roadhead at a longwall face, shall not in the following cases exceed those specified in relation thereto, that is to say—

(*a*) the interval between adjacent rows of props shall not exceed four feet, or, in a place in which bars are used not being a place in a roadhead and the interval between adjacent bars in each row does not exceed four feet, six feet;

(*b*) the interval between adjacent props in the same row shall not exceed four feet; and

(*c*) the interval between the front row of props and the face at any place at which filling or loading has been completed shall not exceed three feet.

(3) The intervals specified pursuant to paragraph (1) of this regulation, in relation to any place at a face other than a longwall face or in a roadhead at a face other than a longwall face, shall not in the following cases exceed those specified in relation thereto, that is to say—

(*a*) the interval between props measured in a direction at right angles to the face shall not exceed four feet;

(*b*) the interval between the front row of props and the face at any place at which filling or loading has been completed shall not exceed three feet.

Bars at face workings and roadheads

14.—(1) At every place where machinery is used for cutting, conveying or loading mineral and at every place in a roadhead not being a place at which arch girders are included in the system of support of the roof, the system of support shall include the use of bars throughout the length and width of that place to be set above every prop therein included in the system of support specified in compliance with either of the last two preceding regulations as the case requires.

(2) The intervals between adjacent bars in the same row shall not exceed four feet, except where the support rules require the front row of bars to be set approximately half a bar's length nearer the face than the last row to have been set and each bar in the front row is set at an approximately equal distance from the bars on either side of it in such last row, and in any such case the intervals between adjacent bars in the same row shall not exceed five feet.

(3) The system of support specified in compliance with the foregoing provisions—

(*a*) need not include the use of bars in any place, not being a place in a roadhead, where the working height does not, or does not generally, exceed two feet and where the sum of the interval specified by the support rules between adjacent props in the same row and the interval so specified between adjacent rows of props does not exceed seven feet;

(*b*) may permit an interval not exceeding one foot between the ends of bars in adjacent rows in any place where an overcutting machine has been used; and

(*c*) need not include the use of bars above props set in any place, not being a place in a roadhead, which is farther from the face than the front line of the packs.

(4) The ends of the bars in the front row shall extend to within one foot, or, where any armoured conveyor is used and persons do not pass or work between such conveyor and the face, otherwise than occasionally or for short periods, and such bars are approved bars, eighteen inches, from the face.

(5) Every bar set in any place shall be supported by at least two props: Provided that where approved coupled bars are used—

(i) any such bar may be supported by one support only provided it is connected to another such bar similarly supported; and

(ii) any such bar in the front row may be supported in cantilever.

(6) In any case where support rules permit the use in any place of slide bars every such bar shall be supported by at least two props each of which has an approved bar slide head and gives direct and effective support to the roof at any time when such bar is being slid forward.

Arch girders in roadheads

15. Where the system of support of the roof at any place in a roadhead includes the use of arch girders, the support rules with respect to that place shall specify the interval not to be exceeded between adjacent arch girders, which shall not exceed four feet.

16.—(1) At any place where the systematic support of the roof is provided by supports which are advanced and set to the roof by mechanical energy (in these regulations referred to as 'powered supports'), the support rules shall specify the intervals not to be exceeded between adjacent supports and between the front vertical members of such supports and the face.

(2) At any place where any armoured conveyor is used all powered supports used as part of a system of support specified in compliance with the preceding paragraph shall be approved powered supports.

(3) Powered supports shall not be used as part of a system of support at any place at which any armoured conveyor is used—

(*a*) if persons pass or work between such conveyor and the face, otherwise than occasionally or for short periods; or

(*b*) if there is in force a direction in respect of that place given by an inspector by notice served on the manager of the mine that this paragraph shall apply, being a direction given on the grounds referred to in paragraph (9) of this regulation

unless all powered supports so used at that place are approved for the purpose of this paragraph.

(4) In relation to any place where any armoured conveyor is used, and where by reason of an irregularity in the condition of the floor or roof or in the working height at that place the powered supports supplied for use there are ineffective to keep that place secure, support rules may, notwithstanding paragraph (2) of this regulation or anything contained in regulation 12, specify the use of props not approved until the condition of the floor or roof or the working height as the case may be enables approved powered supports once more to be used or approved props to be used:

Provided that if props not approved are in use pursuant to this paragraph for more than seven days consecutively at any face, notice thereof shall be given by the manager of the mine to the inspector for the district.

(5) Any person whose duties include the setting of powered supports shall ensure that any such support when set is secure and if it appears to any such person that any such support is defective he shall forthwith report the condition thereof to the person for the time being in charge of that part of the mine.

(6) It shall be the duty of the person for the time being in charge of any part of a mine to take all reasonable steps to ensure that any powered support at any place therein which becomes defective is as soon as practicable repaired or replaced and that all necessary steps are forthwith taken to ensure that the roof at that place is effectively supported.

(7) At any place where a machine is used which shears mineral to a depth exceeding fifteen inches at a single cut, the powered supports at that place shall be advanced to support the roof exposed at that place by such cut before the machine is permitted to approach within ninety feet of that place on its next cut.

(8) At any place where a machine is used which cuts and loads mineral and at the same time makes a cut into the face thereby exposed, preparatory to cutting and loading at the next operation of that machine at that place, the distance

specified by the support rules as not to be exceeded between the front vertical members of the powered supports and the face shall be such that the distance between such members and the back of the cut shall not exceed six feet six inches except over a length of sixty feet from the machine, measured in the direction opposite to the machine's direction of travel.

(9) A direction may be given by an inspector pursuant to paragraph (3) of this regulation on the ground that the system of work at that mine or part of the mine requires men to pass or work between the conveyor referred to in that paragraph and the face to a greater extent than is necessary, or on the ground that precautions which could be taken for securing the safety of such men are not being taken.

(10) The provisions of Part XV of the Act* with respect to references upon notices served by inspectors shall apply to a notice containing a direction that paragraph (3) of this regulation shall not apply to a mine or part of a mine and the relevant grounds of objection shall be that the system of work does not expose men to danger or that all practicable precautions are taken for securing their safety.

Rippings

17. In any case in which the roof of any roadhead or advancing place is ripped, the support rules shall include, in addition to other provisions required by these regulations to be included therein which may apply to such case—

(*a*) provision for the setting of one or more bars or other supports as near as practicable to the ripping lip so as to provide effective support for the roof adjacent to the ripping lip, and where such provision includes the use of bars such rules shall include provision for each such bar to be supported by a prop at either end thereof and if the length of any such bar exceeds four feet, by props at intervals not exceeding four feet throughout the length thereof;

(*b*) provision for the roof newly exposed by such ripping to be forthwith effectively supported;

(*c*) provision for the face of the ripping to be effectively supported; and

(*d*) provision as to the greatest length along the roadhead or advancing place in which the roof may be ripped at any one stage before supports are set to make the roof exposed by such ripping secure.

Temporary supports

18.—(1) At any place where any armoured conveyor is used and persons do not pass or work between such conveyor and the face, otherwise than occasionally or for short periods, support rules in relation thereto shall require the setting of at least one temporary prop within three feet of every place where any person passes or works if such place is more than three feet in front of the front row of props or other supports:

Provided that if at any such place approved powered supports fitted with cantilever bars approved for the purpose of this paragraph are used, the support rules may specify the use of at least one such bar within three feet of every place where any person passes or works, instead of temporary props.

*See Section 170 of the 1954 Act.

(2) At any place to which the foregoing paragraph does not apply, being a place at a longwall face, support rules in relation thereto shall require the setting as soon as may be during the process of filling or loading—

(i) where mineral is worked on the front, of temporary props in a row not more than three feet in advance of the front row of props and at intervals between adjacent props in such row of temporary props not exceeding the interval at which the props in the front row are set;

(ii) where mineral is worked on the buttock, of temporary props at intervals not exceeding three feet measured parallel to the face from the last prop in the row of props then in the course of being set or from the last temporary prop as the case may be.

(3) At any place at which mineral is worked, being a place to which neither of the two foregoing paragraphs apply but at which the work does not consist solely of ripping, the support rules in relation thereto shall include provision for the roof newly exposed by the working of that mineral in advance of the last support to have been set to be forthwith effectively supported by props or other suitable supports and where the system of support specifies the use of props and bars, such provision shall specify the setting of temporary props not more than three feet in advance of the last support to have been set and at intervals between adjacent props in a row of temporary props not exceeding four feet.

Holing props and sprags

19.—(1) During holing at any working face holing props, sprags or other suitable supports shall, unless in the cases hereinafter specified the support rules relating thereto otherwise provide, be set forthwith at such intervals not exceeding six feet as may be specified in such support rules and such props, sprags or other supports shall not be removed until the mineral holed is about to be taken down.

(2) In any case where any armoured conveyor is used at any working face and persons do not pass or work between such conveyor and the face, otherwise than occasionally or for short periods, the support rules may dispense with the setting of such holing props, sprags or other suitable supports as aforesaid.

(3) In any case where the mineral being holed is unstable by reason of its nature or of the strata in which it is found, the support rules may provide for the setting of holing props, sprags or other suitable supports as aforesaid at such time during the cycle of operations as shall be specified in such support rules.

Postponement of setting or removal of supports

20.—(1) Nothing in the foregoing regulations shall prevent provision being made in support rules for the postponement of the setting or for the removal of—

(*a*) any prop in any place where all props used as part of the system of support are approved props and, if coupled bars are used as part of that system all such bars at that place are bars approved for the purposes of this paragraph, in so far as the setting or maintenance of such prop would prevent the operation, advancing or turning of, or the making of room for, any mineral cutter, power loader or conveyor;

(*b*) any bar which would be in the intended path of travel of an overcutting machine and would have to be removed to enable the machine to operate.

(2) The postponement of the setting or removal of any prop or bar as aforesaid shall be for as short a period as is practicable.

(3) Where provision is made in pursuance of paragraph (1)(*a*) of this regulation for the postponement of the setting, or for the removal, of any prop, provision shall be made for the continued support of the roof by bars which shall be single bars greater in length than the distance between the props at that place, or where that distance does not exceed seven feet, coupled bars.

(4) Every such single bar shall be supported by at least one prop at each end thereof, and every such coupled bar shall be supported by at least one prop:

Provided that one coupled bar in any line of such bars need not be so supported if that bar is connected at each end to another such bar supported by at least one prop.

Part V

Miscellaneous Provisions

21. If any fall of roof or side displaces, breaks or renders ineffective any support at any place where any person has to pass or work, it shall be the duty of the person for the time being in charge of that part of the mine forthwith to ensure that any roof or side exposed thereby or adjacent thereto is, if necessary, dressed and is secured by supports, and that any such dressing and securing is done before any work of clearing debris is begun, other than such work of clearing debris as is necessary for the setting of the supports:

Provided that if such person is unable to comply with the preceding provisions of this regulation he shall ensure that no person passes or works there except in accordance with directions given by the manager.

Control of strata by packing

22.—(1) Where, in accordance with the system of work at any face working, packs are used for the purpose of controlling the general movement of strata in the mine, support rules shall specify—

(*a*) the distance not to be exceeded at any place between the face and the front line of the packs built for that purpose opposite the face;

(*b*) the minimum width of every such pack;

(*c*) the maximum distance between adjacent packs built for that purpose.

(2) Where packs are used for the purpose of controlling the general movement of strata in the mine, each operation by which such packs are built shall be completed before the width of roof exposed by the working of mineral at any place, since the completion of the last preceding operation by which such packs were built at that place, exceeds a distance to be specified by support rules and the distance so specified shall not exceed seven feet.

23.—(1) Where, in accordance with the system of work at any face working supports are withdrawn from the waste or from under the roof adjoining the waste, support rules shall provide for the setting and maintenance of supports at intervals specified therein for the purpose of preventing the breaking of the roof overriding the supports at that face, and occurring otherwise than in the waste.

(2) Notwithstanding anything contained in these regulations, supports may be withdrawn in accordance with the system of work at any face working from the area in advance of the waste for a distance not exceeding five feet in advance of the front line of the pack bounding that waste, if no material for the building of any pack is to be obtained from any place from which supports have been withdrawn, and if support rules applicable thereto include, in addition to other provisions required by these regulations to be included therein which may apply to such case, provision for the setting of support in advance of the packs for the purpose of preventing the breaking of roof from overriding the supports in front of the packs.

Form of support rules

24. Support rules with respect to every mine shall comprise such plans and sections or diagrams of every system of support to be provided as to make the particulars of each system readily understood by all persons who are to be engaged in carrying out that system.

SURVEYORS AND PLANS

THE COAL AND OTHER MINES

(SURVEYORS AND PLANS) REGULATIONS 1956

S.I. 1956 No. 1760

Arrangement of Regulations

PART I

Application

1. These regulations shall apply to every mine of coal, stratified ironstone, shale or fireclay, and in these regulations 'mine' means such a mine.

PART II

Qualifications and duties of surveyors

2. (1) No person shall be qualified to be appointed or to be the surveyor for a mine unless he is the holder of—

(*a*) a surveyor's certificate granted by the Minister on the recommendation of the Mining Qualifications Board* or

(*b*) a certificate which was a surveyor's certificate for the purposes of the Coal Mines (Surveyors and Plans) General Regulations 1952.†

(2) No person shall be qualified to be appointed or to be the surveyor for a mine, other than a mine at which not more than thirty persons are employed below ground, or a mine of fireclay, unless (in addition to holding such a certificate) he has had not less than three years' experience in work relating to surveys of mines, including making mine surveys and preparing plans and sections of mines therefrom, since the grant to him of such a certificate.

3. (1) It shall be the duty of the surveyor for a mine to prepare or supervise the preparation of all plans, drawings and sections of the mine which are required by Part III of these regulations to be kept.

---

*See the Board's rules relating to these certificates on page 347.

†S.I. 1952 No. 1846.

(2) It shall be the duty of the surveyor for a mine to establish the accuracy as regards any matters which may involve substantial error or danger of any such plans, drawings and sections of the mine which have not been prepared by him or to ensure that such accuracy is established by a person who is qualified to be appointed the surveyor for that mine.

4. (1) It shall be the duty of the surveyor for a mine to ensure that working papers recording all observations or calculations which were necessarily made for the preparation or checking of any plans, drawings or sections kept by the manager by virtue of Part III of these regulations are signed by the person making them and are preserved.

(2) Where any such papers are not kept at the office at the mine or a place approved by an inspector, it shall be the duty of the surveyor for the mine to make such arrangements as will ensure that upon his ceasing to be the surveyor or upon the abandonment of the mine all such papers are transferred to the owner of the mine or to a person nominated by the owner.

PART III

*Working plans**

†**5.** It shall be the duty of the manager of every mine to keep at the office at the mine or at such other place as may be approved by an inspector plans and sections in accordance with the following provisions of this Part of these regulations.

6. (1) In the case of any mine, plans and sections of the workings of which are made after the commencement of these regulations or have been made after the fifteenth day of December, nineteen hundred and fifty-two, and in the case of every mine after the thirty-first day of December, nineteen hundred and sixty-two, there shall be kept as aforesaid—

(*a*) a separate plan for each seam being worked in the mine showing at any times clearly and accurately the workings in that seam and all shafts, outlets, drifts or staple-pits driven from or to it up to a date not more than three months past and up to a point not more than three hundred feet from their actual positions at any time; and

(*b*) in respect of every mine, other than a mine of stratified ironstone, such sections of the seams being worked in the mine as may be necessary to show any substantial variation in the thickness or character thereof, and so far as practicable such sections of the strata sunk or driven through in the mine or proved by boring as may be necessary to enable the relation between those seams to be determined at any place within the boundaries of the mine; or

(*c*) in respect of every mine of stratified ironstone, a section of the strata sunk or driven through, or, if that is impracticable, a section of every seam being worked in the mine, and in every case any additional section

*See also the Coal and Other Mines (Working Plans) Rules 1956, page 293.

†See also Regulation 3.

of any seam that may be necessary to show any substantial variations in the thickness or character thereof.

(2) An inspector may on account of special circumstances existing at any mine by notice served on the manager thereof exempt it from the requirement that a separate plan be kept for each seam for as long as the workings in each seam are shown on a plan and are clearly distinguished by the use of different colours or otherwise.

7. In the case in which and for the period during which the provisions of the last preceding regulation do not apply, there shall be kept as aforesaid—

(*a*) a plan showing at any time clearly and accurately the workings in the mine up to a date not more than three months past; and

(*b*) a section of the strata sunk or driven through or, if that is impracticable, a section of every seam being worked in the mine.

8. (1) Plans kept in pursuance of either of the two last preceding regulations shall show as clearly and accurately as is practicable the position of—

(*a*) any workings of the mine which are disused or abandoned; and

(*b*) any workings of any other mine (whether abandoned or not);

being workings within the boundaries of the mine or within three hundred and seventy-five feet outside any boundary (measured from any point on the boundary in a straight line on any plane) and being workings which are or are likely at any stage to be at a depth differing from the depth of workings to which the plans relate by not more than one hundred and twenty feet or which are likely at any time to contain an accumulation of water dangerous to persons working in the mine.

(2) The position of any such workings which are not disused or abandoned shall be shown up to a date not more than three months past.

9. (1) In addition to the plans and sections required by regulation six or seven there shall be kept as aforesaid at every mine a plan showing the system of ventilation in the mine and in particular the general direction of the flow of the ventilation, the points at which the quantity of air passing is measured and the principal devices for regulating the flow of the ventilation.

(2) On any such plan every airway which as regards any working face is an intake airway and which is not as regards any working face a return airway shall be coloured blue, and every airway which as regards any working face is a return airway and which is not as regards any working face an intake airway shall be coloured red.

(3) If an inspector is satisfied as regards any mine that the information required by paragraph (1) of this regulation cannot be shown fully and clearly on a plan, he may by notice served on the manager of the mine authorise the keeping in substitution therefor of such a drawing as will show the information fully and clearly.

PART IV

Geological map and sketch of the mine

10. The manager of every mine shall keep at the office at the mine or at such other place as may be approved by an inspector a geological map of the district in which the mine is situate, being a map on a scale of six inches to a mile or, if a map on so large a scale is not available, a map on the nearest scale which shows the boundaries of superficial and drift deposits.

11. The manager of every mine shall provide in the covered accommodation provided in pursuance of section one hundred and thirty-five of the Act a sketch of the mine showing the main roads and means of egress from each part of the mine to the surface and the telephone stations below ground.

PART V

*Abandonment plans**

12. (1) In the event of the abandonment of a mine or seam in a mine or of the expiration of the period of twelve months from the time at which the mine or a seam in a mine was last worked for the purpose of getting minerals or products of minerals, the person who is the owner of the mine at the time of the happening of that event shall within three months thereafter send to the inspector for the district the plans, drawings and sections of those workings required to be kept by virtue of regulation six or seven (where such plans, drawings and sections are no longer required by regulation five to be kept at the mine or a place approved by an inspector) or an accurate copy thereof or of so much thereof as is shown by virtue of those workings, being a copy prepared by or made under the supervision of the surveyor for that mine or the person who was the surveyor when the mine was last worked or if such a person is not available a person who is qualified to be appointed surveyor for that mine.

(2) In a case in which the provisions of the last preceding paragraph apply to any mine by virtue only of the expiration of the period of twelve months from the time at which the mine or the seam therein was last worked for the purpose of getting minerals or products of minerals, an inspector may, if he is of opinion that compliance with the requirements of that paragraph is unnecessary having regard to the circumstances and to the plans, drawings and sections thereof kept at the office at the mine or at such other place as is approved by an inspector, by notice served on the owner of the mine exempt him from the obligation imposed by that paragraph by virtue of the happening of that event.

(3) In the event of the abandonment of a mine the person who is the owner of the mine at the time of the abandonment shall send to the inspector for the district with the plans, drawings and sections referred to in paragraph (1) of this regulation all working papers relating to those plans, drawings and sections required to be preserved by regulation four or accurate copies thereof.

13. The owner of a mine to whom the provisions of paragraph (1) of the last preceding regulation apply shall ensure that every plan sent to the inspector in pursuance of that paragraph is endorsed with a certificate that no further work has been carried out at the mine which would affect the accuracy of the plan being a certificate given by—

(*a*) the manager of the mine or the person who was the manager when the mine was last worked; or

*See also the Coal and Other Mines (Abandonment Plans) Rules 1956, page 297.

(*b*) a person appointed by the owner for the purpose of securing the fulfilment in relation to that mine of statutory responsibilities of the owner being a person who can so certify from his own knowledge.

14. (1) The owner of a mine to whom the provisions of paragraph (1) of regulation twelve apply shall ensure that there is endorsed on or attached to every plan sent to the inspector in pursuance of that paragraph a report of the surveyor for that mine or the person who was the surveyor when the mine was last worked or, if such a person is not available, a person who is qualified to be appointed surveyor for that mine or a person who is or was employed at that mine and is the holder of a certificate specified in paragraph (1) of regulation two.

(2) Such report shall indicate the extent to which the person making it can certify the accuracy and completeness of the plan as at the date when the mine or the seam in question was last worked, the steps taken by him to ensure such accuracy and completeness and the reason for any qualification made by him and may include any information which he considers desirable for the promotion of safety.

PART VI

General

15. The Interpretation Act 1889 shall apply to the interpretation of these regulations as it applies to the interpretation of an Act of Parliament.

THE COAL AND OTHER MINES (WORKING PLANS) RULES 1956

S.I. 1956 No. 1782

Application

1. The provisions of these rules shall apply to plans of workings in mines kept in pursuance of Part III of the Coal and Other Mines (Surveyors and Plans) Regulations 1956.* In these rules such a plan kept in pursuance of regulation six is referred to as 'a new plan' and such a plan kept in pursuance of regulation seven is referred to as 'an old plan'.

Scale of plans

2. Every plan to which these rules apply shall be on a scale of not less than 1/2500.

Correlation with Grid

3. Every new plan shall be orientated to and correlated with the Ordnance Survey National Grid and marked with squares corresponding to the kilometre squares shown on Ordnance Survey sheets on the scale 1/2500.

Variations in level

4. (1) Every new plan shall indicate variations in level from an assumed datum ten thousand feet below Ordnance Datum—

(*a*) on every length of road which is a main intake airway or a main return airway for the purposes of the Coal and Other Mines (Ventilation) Regulations 1956†; and

(*b*) so far as they can be ascertained, on the outline of any disused or abandoned workings shown on the plan;

at horizontal intervals not exceeding three hundred feet and at any such intermediate points as are necessary to indicate any substantial change in gradient within such an interval.

(2) Every old plan shall indicate variations from Ordnance Datum or from a datum below Ordnance Datum specified on the plan on such appropriate roads in the mine and at such places thereon as to indicate the gradients and any substantial change of gradient, being variations of ten feet or multiples of ten feet.

Gradient of seam

5. (1) Every new plan shall, so far as their position can be ascertained, be marked with contour lines indicating the level of the floor of the workings in every part of the seam which is being worked, being the level relative to the assumed datum ten thousand feet below Ordnance Datum as follows, that is to say—

(*a*) if the gradient of the seam at no place exceeds 1:3, such lines shall show vertical variations at intervals not exceeding fifty feet; or

---

*See page 288.

†See page 317.

(*b*) if the gradient of the seam exceeds 1:3 at any place, such lines shall show the vertical variations of multiples of ten feet being not less than fifty feet nor more than one hundred and fifty feet.

In every case the vertical variation represented by any consecutive contour lines shall be the same throughout the plan and the lines shall be marked with the level relative to the assumed datum.

(2) In the case of any new plan where the level of the floor of the workings in a seam shown thereon does not change by more than fifty feet, the plan shall show the direction and rate of dip of the seam.

(3) Every old plan shall show the general direction and rate of dip of the strata.

Faults

6. Every plan to which these rules apply shall show the position, direction, extent and vertical throw, so far as they can be ascertained, of any known fault or other displacement of the seam (in the case of a new plan) or each seam (in the case of an old plan) and any known washout, roll, igneous intrusion or mineral vein affecting such seam.

Manner of showing other workings

7. On every plan to which these rules apply workings shown in pursuance of regulation eight* of the Coal and Other Mines (Surveyors and Plans) Regulations 1956, shall be shown in outline.

External dangers to workings

8. If there is any evidence that within one hundred and fifty feet of any working in a mine there may be—

(*a*) any rock or stratum containing or likely to contain water (whether dispersed or in natural cavities) which might constitute a danger to persons in the mine;

(*b*) any peat, moss, sand, gravel, silt or other material that is likely to flow when wet;

the plan of that working shall record the nature, position, thickness and extent thereof as accurately as possible and shall also record such particulars, so far as they are available, of any such rock, stratum or material within the boundaries of the mines or within three hundred and seventy-five feet outside any such boundary.

Water dams

9. Every new plan shall show, so far as they can be ascertained, the position and the dimensions of any water dam which may affect workings in the seam.

Position and level of shafts, etc.

10. (1) Every plan to which these rules apply shall show, so far as they can be ascertained, the position of and the level at the top and bottom of every shaft, outlet, drift or staple-pit giving access to the workings to which the plan relates and the level of every entrance giving access thereto from those workings.

---

*See page 289.

(2) Every new plan shall show, so far as they can be ascertained, the position and the level at the top and bottom of every borehole sunk from or driven to the surface or from one seam to another which may provide evidence relevant to the workings to which the plan relates.

Boundaries

11. Every plan to which these rules apply shall show the boundaries to which it is intended that the workings shown thereon should extend.

Correlation

12. Every new plan shall indicate—

(*a*) the direction of the National Grid North;

(*b*) the assumed datum level; and

(*c*) the date on which it was commenced.

General

13. The Interpretation Act 1889 shall apply to the interpretation of these rules as it applies to the interpretation of an Act of Parliament.

14. These rules shall come into operation at the commencement of the Act and may be cited as the Coal and Other Mines (Working Plans) Rules 1956.

THE COAL AND OTHER MINES (ABANDONMENT PLANS) RULES 1956

S.I. 1956 No. 1783

1. Any copy of a plan sent to an inspector by virtue of regulation twelve* of the Coal and Other Mines (Surveyors and Plans) Regulations 1956, shall be on a scale not less than the plan of which it is a copy.

2. Any plan or copy of a plan sent to an inspector by virtue of that regulation shall show (so far as they can be ascertained) as regards the mine or seam abandoned or disused—

(*a*) the position of any pump in use below ground immediately before the mine or that seam was abandoned or was last worked for the purpose of getting minerals or products of minerals and the quantity of water being pumped by each such pump;

(*b*) any variation in level on the boundaries of the workings from Ordnance Datum or from the datum below Ordnance Datum used for the purposes of the plan;

(*c*) the position and extent of any area known to be water-logged; and

(*d*) the position and, so far as practicable, the dimensions and method of construction of any water dam and the pressure of water being retained by it immediately before the mine or that seam was abandoned or was last worked for the purpose of getting minerals or products of minerals.

3. The Interpretation Act 1889 shall apply to the interpretation of these rules as it applies to the interpretation of an Act of Parliament.

4. These rules shall come into operation at the commencement of the Act and may be cited as the Coal and Other Mines (Abandonment Plans) Rules 1956.

*See page 290.

TIPS

THE MINES AND QUARRIES (NOTIFICATION OF TIPPING OPERATIONS) REGULATIONS 1969

S.I. 1969 No. 1141

1.—(1) These regulations may be cited as the Mines and Quarries (Notification of Tipping Operations) Regulations 1969 and shall come into operation on 1st September, 1969.

(2) The Interpretation Act 1889 shall apply to the interpretation of these regulations as it applies to the interpretation of an Act of Parliament.

2. Every class and description of mines and quarries are hereby prescribed for the purposes of section 4(1) and (2) of the Mines and Quarries (Tips) Act 1969.

TRAINING

THE COAL MINES (TRAINING) REGULATIONS 1967

S.I. 1967 No. 82

Arrangement of Regulations

PART I

General

Commencement and citation

1. These regulations shall come into operation on 1st February 1967 and may be cited as the Coal Mines (Training) Regulations 1967.

Interpretation

2.—(1) In these regulations the following expressions have the meanings hereby respectively assigned to them, that is to say—

'the Act' means the Mines and Quarries Act 1954;

'deputy's district' has the meaning assigned thereto in the Coal and Other Mines (Managers and Officials) Regulations 1956,*

'electrical apparatus' and 'electrical engineering staff' have the meanings respectively assigned thereto in the Coal and Other Mines (Mechanics and Electricians) Regulations 1965;†

'instructor' means a person appointed by the manager of a mine in pursuance of section 13 of the Act who is competent to give instruction and supervision in the performance of the work in which instruction and supervision are being given, who is required to devote his whole time to giving instruction and supervision, and who does not himself assist in the performance of the work in which he is giving instruction and supervision otherwise than for the purpose of demonstration;

'mechanical apparatus' and 'mechanical engineering staff' have the meanings respectively assigned thereto in the Coal and Other Mines (Mechanics and Electricians) Regulations 1965;†

'mine' has the meaning assigned thereto in regulation 3;

'supervising workman' means a workman appointed by the manager of a mine in pursuance of section 13 of the Act who is skilled in the performance of the work in which instruction and supervision are being given;

'training district' has the meaning assigned thereto in regulation 16(1)(*c*)(ii);

'work for coal production' means any work performed within thirty feet of a face at which coal is got, being work which comprises getting of coal,

*See page 188.

†See page 191.

filling or loading of coal for removal from that face, building or stowing of packs, formation or enlargement of roadways, setting or withdrawing supports, shifting of conveyors, drilling of coal or stone (other than the drilling of any borehole required for the purpose of tapping firedamp and draining through any firedamp drainage system), infusion of water into coal prior to shot firing or cutting, or shot firing, but does not include work performed at a roadhead by a person employed on the haulage, or in handling or filling tubs or as a conveyor engine attendant.

(2) Expressions to which meanings are assigned by the Act or by these regulations shall (unless the contrary intention appears) have the same meanings in any document issued under the provisions of these regulations.

(3) The Interpretation Act 1889 shall apply to the interpretation of these regulations as it applies to the interpretation of an Act of Parliament.

Application

3. These regulations shall apply to every mine of coal, and in these regulations, unless otherwise expressly provided, 'mine' means such a mine.

Revocation

4. The Coal Mines (Training) Regulations 1956, the Coal Mines (Training) (Variation) Regulations 1957 and the Coal Mines (Training) (Variation) Regulations 1960 are hereby revoked.

Exemptions

5. An inspector may by notice served on the manager of a mine exempt that mine or any part thereof or any person employed thereat from the application of any of the provisions of these regulations if he is satisfied that neither the training of any person who is receiving training at that mine nor the safety of persons employed at the mine will be prejudiced by the granting of that exemption.

Defences in legal proceedings

6. Where in any legal proceedings it is alleged that a person was so employed in work below ground in any mine that one or more of the provisions of these regulations has been contravened, it shall be a defence to prove—

(*a*) that he was so employed for the purpose of saving life or dealing with circumstances arising out of an accident; or

(*b*) that owing to unforeseen circumstances his employment was urgently required to prevent serious interference with the safe working of the mine and that he was sufficiently qualified and experienced to be so employed.

PART II

Training and Supervision

Training for employment in work below ground

7. Without prejudice to the generality of section 88 of the Act, it shall be the duty of the manager of every mine to secure that, subject to the provisions of regulation 14 of these regulations, no person who has not been employed in work below ground in any mine to which the Act applies is employed in the first-mentioned mine in work below ground (otherwise than for the purposes of the training hereinafter mentioned) unless—

(*a*) he has received such training as is described in the next following regulation being (except in the case of a person who has received such training before attaining the age of sixteen) training received as nearly as may be immediately before he is first employed in that mine in work below ground; and

(*b*) there has been issued by a training officer for a mine or other person responsible for superintending the giving of training under such a scheme as is mentioned in the next following regulation, being in either case a person who has superintended the giving to him of the whole or part of that training, a certificate in such form* as the Minister may direct that he has received that training.†

8. The training referred to in the last foregoing regulation is training which is given in accordance with a scheme described in the next following regulation and which, unless otherwise expressly provided in that scheme,—

(*a*) is given during the working hours in which the person receiving such training could lawfully be employed at a mine;

(*b*) comprises adequate instruction in safe and efficient methods of working below ground; and

(*c*) in the case of a person who has not attained the age of eighteen years when he begins such training, extends for at least fifty days, and in any other case, extends for at least twenty days.

9.—(1) The scheme mentioned in the last foregoing regulation is a scheme containing the particulars specified in paragraph (3) of this regulation, and in the case of a scheme under which any person is to be trained who has not attained the age of eighteen years when he begins such training, is approved by the Minister.

(2) No such scheme as aforesaid shall be submitted to the Minister for his approval except after consultation with a local education authority in regard to the subjects in which there are to be classes wholly or partly provided by that authority, the conduct of such classes and any physical education to be so provided.

(3) Every such scheme shall specify the manner in which the training is to be carried out and, in particular, shall specify the subject matter of, and the time to be allotted to, the classes, the practical instruction and the physical education of which such training is comprised, the places and times at which they are to be given, the nature of the accommodation and equipment to be provided for them and the arrangements for securing the effective co-ordination of the classes and the practical instruction.

---

*M. & Q. Form No. 223.

†See other provisions about the certificate in Regulation 20 (1) and (2).

Training for employment in work for coal production

10.—(1) Without prejudice to the generality of section 88 of the Act, it shall be the duty of the manager of every mine to secure that, subject to the provisions of regulation 14 of these regulations, no person who has not been employed in work for coal production in any mine is employed in work for coal production in the first-mentioned mine (otherwise than for the purposes of receiving training in accordance with the following provisions of this regulation) unless—

(*a*) he had prior to the coming into force of these regulations received such training as was specified by regulation 5 of the Coal Mines (Training) Regulations 1956 (which specified requirements for training persons prior to their employment at a coal face) and there has been issued by a training officer for a mine who has superintended the giving of the whole or part of that training a certificate in such form as the Minister may direct that he has received such training and is competent to be employed at a coal face;

(*b*) he had at the coming into force of these regulations begun to receive such training as was specified by regulation 5 of the Coal Mines (Training) Regulations, 1956 and has thereafter completed a period of such training for employment at a coal face not being less than one hundred days, and there has been issued by a training officer for a mine who has superintended the giving of the whole or part of that training a certificate in such form* as the Minister may direct that he has received such training and is competent to be employed in work for coal production;† or

(*c*) he has received such training as is described in the following paragraphs and there has been issued by a training officer for a mine who has superintended the giving of the whole or part of that training a certificate in such form‡ as the Minister may direct that he has received such training and is competent to be employed in work for coal production.†

(2) The training mentioned in paragraph (1)(*c*) of this regulation shall be training which is given in accordance with a scheme approved by the Minister and shall comprise—

(*a*) basic training for work for coal production, being training in operations specified in such scheme, under the close personal supervision of an instructor§ or supervising workman,§ at a place defined by the manager of the mine pursuant to the next following paragraph, for a period specified in such scheme in relation to every class of person to receive training pursuant to that scheme and which, unless otherwise expressly provided in that scheme, shall not end before the person receiving training attains the age of eighteen and shall not be less than one hundred days; and

*M. & Q. Form No. 315. (This form was not printed as it was only required for a transitionary period. The Minister directed the form of words to be used and N.C.B. reproduced the form themselves).

†See other provisions about the certificates in Regulation 20 (1) and (2).

‡M. & Q. Form No. 224.

§These expressions as used here and subsequently in these Regulations, have the meanings given in Regulation 2 (1).

(*b*) improvership in work for coal production, being training in operations specified in such scheme for a period commencing after the end of the period mentioned in sub-paragraph (*a*) of this paragraph being a period which shall be specified in every such scheme in relation to every class of person to receive training pursuant to that scheme and which, unless otherwise expressly provided in that scheme, shall not be less than forty days.

(3) The manager of a mine shall define in writing any place which is to be used at the mine for purposes of basic training for work for coal production in accordance with any scheme made pursuant to the last foregoing paragraph and shall give to the inspector for the district notice of the commencement or termination, as the case may be, of the use of any such place for those purposes within seven days thereof. No place shall be used for such purposes if an inspector by notice served on the manager objects thereto.

(4) The manager of a mine shall ensure that—

(*a*) no supervising workman supervises at any one time more than one person receiving basic training in work for coal production under this regulation in any operation, and that no instructor supervises at any one time more than such number of persons receiving training under this regulation in any operation as may be specified in relation to that operation in the scheme made pursuant to paragraph (2) of this regulation under which such persons are receiving training;

(*b*) no work is performed at a place wholly used for purposes of training for employment for work for coal production when training is in progress, except by a person being trained, an instructor, a supervising workman, an official of the mine or any other person duly authorised to perform that work at that place by the manager or by an official of the mine.

(5) In any case in which a quantity of work is assigned to be done in any period of employment—

(*a*) by one or more persons receiving instruction from an instructor; or

(*b*) by a supervising workman and the person whom he is supervising, or either of them,—

the manager of the mine shall ensure that that quantity is not more than can reasonably be done in that period by the person or persons to whom that quantity is assigned nor more than can be adequately supervised by that instructor or supervising workman, as the case may be, having regard to the experience of the person or persons receiving training and the amount of supervision or instruction required.

(6) Neither the wages of any person who is receiving basic training for work for coal production pursuant to paragraph (2)(*a*) of this regulation, nor the wages of any instructor or supervising workman whose duties include the supervision of any such person, shall in whole or part be calculated according to the amount of mineral gotten or the quantity of work done by persons receiving instruction or by the supervising workman or person receiving supervision or both of them:

Provided that—

(i) the wages of such a supervising workman who is employed at a place which is part of a coal production face for the time being used for training purposes may be determined by division of a payment in respect of the total amount of mineral gotten from that and the other parts of that face between persons employed at the other parts and the supervising workman if it is customary for the wages of persons employed at that face to be so determined;

(ii) the wages of an instructor or a supervising workman may include a sum paid in respect of completion of a quantity of work assigned to be done which complies with the provisions of the last foregoing paragraph.

Training for employment in work on coal getting machines

11.—(1) Without prejudice to the generality of section 88 of the Act, it shall be the duty of the manager of every mine to secure that no person shall be employed in operating any type of coal getting machine in that mine, who has not been employed in operating a machine of that type in any mine, unless—

(*a*) he has been employed in work for coal production other than operating a coal getting machine for a period of not less than six months after completing the training specified in the last foregoing regulation; and

(*b*) he has received such training as is necessary to enable him safely to operate a machine of the type in question and there has been issued by a training officer for a mine who has superintended the whole or part of that training a certificate in such form* as the Minister may direct that he has received such training and is competent to be employed in operating a machine of that type.†

(2) In this regulation 'coal getting machine' means any mechanical apparatus or electrical apparatus used at a coal face for cutting or moving coal, not being only a conveyor, but does not include a machine held in the hand.

Supervision of persons working below ground

12.—(1) Without prejudice to the generality of section 88 of the Act, it shall be the duty of the manager of every mine to secure that, subject to the provisions of regulation 14 of these regulations, no person who has not been employed in work below ground in any mine to which the Act applies is employed in the first-mentioned mine in work below ground (other than work for coal production) unless for at least the first twenty working days of his employment below ground he is employed under the close personal supervision of an instructor or supervising workman.

(2) Subject to the provisions of the next following paragraph, every instructor or supervising workman exercising supervision for the purpose of this regulation shall be nominated for duty by the manager of the mine or a training officer for that mine on his behalf and given notice in such form‡ as the Minister may

*M. & Q. Form No. 318.

†See other provisions about the certificate in Regulation 20 (1) and (2).

‡M. & Q. Form No. 225.

direct, by the manager of the mine or, as the case may be, a training officer for that mine, of the persons to be supervised and the nature of the work to be performed.*

(3) An instructor or supervising workman may be nominated for duty by an official of the mine where owing to unforeseen circumstances it appears to him expedient so to do to avoid any interruption in the employment under supervision of any person in pursuance of paragraph (1) of this regulation and, in any such case, the instructor or supervising workman shall be notified by the official of the mine of the person to be supervised and the nature of the work to be performed. An official who nominates an instructor or supervising workman for duty under this paragraph shall forthwith give notice of the nomination to a training officer for the mine and no instructor or supervising workman nominated for duty under this paragraph shall by virtue of that nomination exercise supervision of any person for more than three consecutive working days.

(4) The manager of a mine shall ensure that no such supervision as aforesaid may be given by an instructor or supervising workman to more than one person at any one time unless an inspector by notice served on the manager so consents.

13. No person who is being trained in pursuance of the foregoing regulations shall be at any place at a coal face or in a roadhead unless he is accompanied by the instructor or supervising workman under whose supervision he is being trained.

Exceptions

14.—(1) Nothing in regulations 7, 10 and 12 of these regulations shall affect the employment in work below ground in a mine of any person—

(*a*) as an official of the mine;

(*b*) as a member of the mechanical engineering staff or electrical engineering staff of the mine, or a tradesman;

(*c*) as a horsekeeper;

(*d*) as the surveyor for the mine or a person solely engaged in surveying;

(*e*) as a person solely engaged in carrying out observations or making measurements or partly engaged in carrying out observations and partly in making measurements; or

(*f*) who is not normally employed below ground in a mine.

(2) Nothing in regulation 7 shall affect the employment in work below ground in any mine of any person under and in accordance with an apprenticeship scheme approved by the Minister for the purpose of this paragraph if—

(*a*) he has received such training as is described in regulation 8 of these regulations at any time before he is first so employed; or

(*b*) he has received for not less than twenty days training comprising instruction in safe methods of working and travelling below ground, practical instruction in, and demonstrations of, mining operations, and talks and discussions on subjects relating to mining operations.

---

*See other provisions about the notice in Regulation 20 (3).

(3) Nothing in the said regulation 7 shall affect the employment in work below ground in a mine of any person who is taking a course of study at an institution approved by the Minister leading to a degree or diploma so approved and who is for at least the first twenty working days of his employment below ground employed under the close personal supervision of an official of the mine or of an instructor or supervising workman by whom no supervision is given to more than one person at any one time unless an inspector by notice served on the manager so consents.

(4) Nothing in the said regulation 7 shall affect the employment in work below ground in a mine of any person who—

(*a*) has within the six months immediately before the commencement of his employment been inscribed as a teacher or student on the books of a university or training establishment outside the United Kingdom, being a university or training establishment recognised as such by the government of the country in which it is situate;

(*b*) has had not less than four months practical experience of mining below ground in one or more mines outside the United Kingdom; and

(*c*) has, to the satisfaction of the manager of the mine, a sufficient knowledge of the English language.

(5) Nothing in the said regulation 7 shall affect the employment in work below ground in a mine of any person as a person solely engaged in performing operations for the sinking of any shaft or driving of any drift from the surface of the mine if—

(*a*) he has attained the age of eighteen years; and

(*b*) he has received, during not less than five days and for not less in the aggregate than thirty hours, training comprising practical instruction in and demonstrations of such operations as aforesaid (including instruction in and demonstrations of the use of machinery, apparatus and other equipment used therein) and talks and discussions on subjects relating to those operations.

(6) Nothing in the said regulation 7 shall affect the employment in work below ground in a mine of any person who—

(*a*) has attained the age of eighteen years;

(*b*) has received such training as is described in the last foregoing paragraph; and

(*c*) has had not less than nine months experience in performing such operations as are described in that paragraph.

(7) Nothing in paragraphs (2), (4), (5) and (6) of this regulation shall affect the application of the said regulation 12 to a person to whom any of those paragraphs applies.

(8) Nothing in the said regulation 10 shall affect the employment in work for coal production in a mine of any person who—

(*a*) has within the six months immediately before the commencement of his employment been inscribed as a teacher or student on the books of a university or training establishment outside the United Kingdom, being a university or training establishment recognised as such by the government of the country in which it is situate;

(*b*) has had not less than two years practical experience of mining below ground including experience of not less than one year of work for coal production, in one or more coal mines outside the United Kingdom;

(*c*) has, to the satisfaction of the manager of the mine, a sufficient knowledge of the English language; and

(*d*) is during the whole period of his employment in work for coal production employed under the close personal supervision of an instructor or supervising workman by whom no supervision is given to more than one person at any one time unless an inspector by notice served on the manager so consents.

PART III

Instruction of young persons below the age of sixteen

15. Without prejudice to the provisions of regulation 7(*a*), and except as otherwise expressly provided in regulation 16, nothing in regulation 6 or in Part II of these regulations shall apply in relation to any male young person who has not attained the age of sixteen.

16.—(1) The instruction for the purpose of receiving which any male young person who has not attained the age of sixteen may be employed below ground in a mine shall be none other than—

(*a*) any instruction, other than practical instruction, in, or in any work connected with, mining minerals, given in any part of the mine by a competent person appointed by the manager for the purpose;

(*b*) any instruction comprised in such training as is described in regulation 8;

(*c*) in the case of any such young person who has received such training as is so described—

(i) further instruction of any kind which was or could have been given as part of that training;

(ii) instruction in safe and efficient methods of working below ground, including practical instruction in and demonstrations of mining operations, given (otherwise than at a coal face) in a deputy's district the whole of which is set aside for training purposes (hereinafter referred to as a 'training district') in the manner described in the following paragraph; or

(iii) (if the said person is employed below ground in any mine in any of the following counties, that is to say, Brecknock, Cardigan, Carmarthen, Glamorgan and Monmouth) instruction, including practical instruction, in work for coal production, given in a training district in the manner described in paragraph (3) of this regulation:

Provided that sub-paragraph (*c*)(iii) of this paragraph shall not have effect after 31st December 1969.

(2) The manager of a mine shall ensure that any instruction given to a person in pursuance of sub-paragraph (*c*)(ii) of the foregoing paragraph is given by—

(*a*) an instructor who is not for the time being instructing or supervising an aggregate of more than five persons; or

(*b*) a supervising workman who is not for the time being instructing or supervising any other person.

(3) The manager of a mine shall ensure that any instruction given to a person in pursuance of sub-paragraph (*c*)(iii) of paragraph (1) of this regulation—

(*a*) is given by an instructor or supervising workman who is not for the time being instructing or supervising any other person, unless, in relation to an instructor, an inspector by notice served on the manager so consents;

(*b*) is given during a period in which no work is being performed at the coal face except by a person being trained, an instructor, a supervising workman, an official of the mine or any other person duly authorised to perform that work at that place by the manager or by an official of the mine; and

(*c*) is (in the case of practical instruction) no more in quantity and no more arduous than is reasonable having regard to the age and experience of the person receiving it.

17.—(1) The manager of a mine shall define in writing any training district and shall within seven days of the commencement or termination (as the case may be) of—

(*a*) the use of any training district for training purposes;

(*b*) (in the case of a mine in which instruction is given to any person in pursuance of regulation 16(1)(*c*)(iii)) the use of a coal face for that purpose

give notice thereof to the inspector for the district. No training district or face (as the case may be) shall be used for any such purpose if an inspector by notice served on the manager objects thereto.

(2) No wages of any person employed in a training district during any period in which any person employed therein is receiving instruction in pursuance of this Part of these regulations shall depend directly on the amount of mineral gotten or the quantity of work done during that period.

18. No person who is below ground in a mine for the purpose of receiving instruction in pursuance of this Part of these regulations shall be at any place in the mine unless he is at all times under the close personal supervision of the instructor, supervising workman or other person whose duty it is to instruct him.

PART IV

Training of mechanics and electricians

19. Without prejudice to the generality of section 88 of the Act, it shall be the duty of the manager of every mine at which not less than thirty persons are employed to secure that no person is employed as a member of the mechanical engineering staff or electrical engineering staff of the mine unless—

(*a*) he is qualified in accordance with regulation 16 of the Coal and Other Mines (Mechanics and Electricians) Regulations 1965 to be appointed or to be a supervisory mechanic or supervisory electrician, as the case may be, for a mine of coal, shale or fireclay; or

(*b*) he has served an apprenticeship as a mechanic or electrician, as the case may be, under an apprenticeship scheme approved by the Minister and there has been issued by a training officer for a mine or a person whose appointment for that purpose has been notified to the inspector for the district, being in either case a person who has superintended the whole or part of his service under that apprenticeship, a certificate in such form* as the Minister may direct that he has duly served that apprenticeship;† or

(*c*) he has had such mechanical or electrical engineering training or experience, as the case may be, as to give him a standard of competence to carry out in a mine the duties of a mechanic or electrician at least equal to that which would be obtained by serving such an apprenticeship and there has been issued by a manager of a mine a certificate in such form‡ as the Minister may direct that he has that standard of competence as a mechanic or electrician, as the case may be.†

PART V

Certificates and notices

20.—(1) A copy of every certificate issued under regulation 7(*b*), regulation 10(1)(*b*) or (*c*), regulation 11(1)(*b*) or regulation 19(*b*) or (*c*) of these regulations, or having effect under regulation 10(1)(*a*) of these regulations shall be kept at the office at the mine at which the person to whom it relates is employed, or at such other place as may be approved by an inspector, and shall be preserved during his employment at the mine and, subject to the provisions of the next following paragraph, for twelve months thereafter.

(2) The manager of every mine shall ensure that a copy of every certificate preserved at that mine in pursuance of the foregoing paragraph and relating to a person who has ceased to be employed thereat shall be sent forthwith to the manager of the mine (if any) at which that person is next thereafter employed upon being given notice of his employment at that mine by the manager thereof.

(3) A copy of every notice given under regulation 12(2) of these regulations shall be kept at the office at the mine at which the instructor or supervising workman nominated for duty thereat in accordance with that paragraph is employed, or at such other place as may be approved by an inspector, for twelve months after it is given.

PART VI

Appointment and duties of Training Officers

21.—(1) It shall be the duty of the manager of every mine to appoint a training officer or such number of training officers as may be required to

*M. & Q. Form No. 316.
†See other provisions about the certificates in Regulation 20 (1) and (2).
‡M. & Q. Form No. 317.

superintend the training provided at the mine in pursuance of the foregoing regulations and the manager shall forthwith give notice of each such appointment to the inspector for the district.

(2) A training officer for a mine at which more than one thousand persons are employed or, where there is more than one training officer, at least one of them, shall devote his full time to his duties as training officer for that mine.

(3) The manager of a mine at which the number of persons employed is not more than one thousand shall not assign to a training officer any other duties which would prejudice the thorough performance of his duties as training officer for that mine.

(4) At any mine at which there is more than one training officer, the manager shall assign to each of them the duties to be performed by him and shall give notice to the inspector for the district of the duties so assigned to each training officer and of any change in the duties so assigned.

(5) If owing to the special circumstances of any mine it appears to an inspector expedient so to do he may by notice served on the manager require—

(*a*) that one or more training officers shall be appointed in addition to those required by the foregoing provisions of this regulation;

(*b*) that a training officer shall be appointed who is required to devote his full time to his duties as training officer at that mine;

(*c*) that a training officer who is not required to devote his full time to his duties as training officer at that mine shall devote at least such time to the performance of those duties as may be specified.

(6) A training officer shall be deemed to devote his full time to his duties notwithstanding that in addition to his duties as such he performs other duties relating to the safety of persons who are employed at the mine, or that at any time while the number of persons being trained below ground in pursuance of regulations 7 and 10 of these regulations or who have not had experience for at least eighteen months of work below ground in a mine does not exceed fifty, he performs other duties in relation to the mine.

(7) Where a training officer is not required under this regulation to devote his full time to his duties as such the manager of the mine shall give notice to him of the days or parts of the days in each week on which he is required to perform such duties and a copy of the notice while in force shall be kept at the mine at which he is to perform those duties or at such other place as may be approved by an inspector.

22.—(1) It shall be the duty of every training officer for a mine, or where there is more than one training officer, the duty of each of them to the extent to which duties are assigned to him pursuant to regulation 21(4)—

(*a*) to superintend the training and supervision provided at the mine in pursuance of these regulations;

(*b*) to keep records of the training superintended by him of any person employed at the mine in pursuance of regulations 7, 10 and 11 of these regulations and to furnish reports to the manager of the mine on the progress of that person during the period of his training, being reports made at the intervals specified in the scheme pursuant to which that person is receiving training, or, where intervals are not so specified, reports made weekly;

(*c*) to keep records of the supervision provided under his superintendence for any person employed at the mine in pursuance of regulation 12 of these regulations and to furnish weekly reports to the manager of the mine on the progress of that person during the period of his supervision;

(*d*) to make recommendations to the manager of the mine in regard to any training for the future employment of any person employed thereat;

(*e*) to furnish quarterly reports to the manager of the mine on the progress of any person employed below ground thereat who has not had experience for at least eighteen months of work below ground in any mine;

(*f*) to supervise the welfare while at work at the mine of any person employed thereat who has been employed for less than six months at a mine.

(2) It shall be the duty of a training officer for a mine or a person whose appointment for the purpose has been notified to the inspector for the district, being in either case a person who has superintended the giving of the whole or part of the training provided for any male young person who has not attained the age of sixteen employed at the mine, to keep records of the whole of that training, showing separately the instruction received by that young person in pursuance of regulation 16 of these regulations.

(3) The records and reports described in the foregoing paragraphs of this regulation shall be kept for twelve months at the office at the mine at which the person to whom they relate is employed or at such other place as may be approved by an inspector.

(4) The manager of every mine shall ensure that every record and report which is so kept relating to a person who has ceased to be employed thereat or a copy thereof shall be sent forthwith to the manager of the mine (if any) at which that person is next thereafter employed upon being given notice of his employment at that mine by the manager thereof.

APPROVED APPRENTICESHIP SCHEMES

The following apprenticeship schemes are approved for the purposes of Regulations 14(2) and 19(*b*) of the Coal Mines (Training) Regulations 1967.

(*a*) The National Coal Board Engineering Craft Apprenticeship Scheme.

(*b*) The National Coal Board Student Apprenticeship Schemes in Mining, Electrical and Mechanical Engineering.

VENTILATION

THE COAL AND OTHER MINES

(VENTILATION) REGULATIONS 1956

S.I. 1956 No. 1764

(As varied by the Coal and Other Mines (Ventilation) (Variation) Regulations 1960, S.I. 1960 No. 1116 and the Coal and Other Mines (Ventilation (Variation) Regulations 1966, S.I. 1966 No. 1139)

Arrangement of Regulations

PART I

Application

1. These regulations shall apply to every mine of coal, stratified ironstone, shale or fireclay, and in these regulations, unless otherwise expressly provided, 'mine' means such a mine.

PART II

Provisions relating to firedamp content

Inflammable gas in intake airways

2. (1) Without prejudice to the generality of section fifty-five of the Act the manager of every mine shall take such steps as are necessary for securing that every airway therein which as regards any working face* is an intake airway and the air in which has not previously ventilated a working face shall normally be kept free from inflammable gas:

Provided that the requirements of this regulation shall not apply to any part of such an airway within three hundred feet of the first working place at that working face.

(2) For the purposes of this regulation an airway shall be deemed not to be normally kept free from inflammable gas if the average percentage by volume of inflammable gas found in six samples of air taken by an inspector in the general body of the air in that airway at intervals of not less than fourteen days exceeds one quarter.

---

*This expression, as used here and subsequently in these Regulations, has the meaning defined in Regulation 33 (1).

Determinations of firedamp content

3. (1) Where in any part of a mine in which the use of lamps or lights, other than permitted lights*, is unlawful electric power is used at or within one hundred and fifty feet of a working face, the manager shall make and secure the efficient carrying out of arrangements whereby determinations of the percentage of inflammable gas present in the general body of the air (in these regulations referred to as 'the firedamp content') are made in that part in accordance with the provisions of the four next following regulations, and of Regulation 7A.

(2) Where in any part of a mine of coal the use of lamps or lights, other than permitted lights, is unlawful and in any part of that mine which comprises a working face shots are fired in the ordinary course of working, the manager shall make and secure the efficient carrying out of arrangements whereby determinations of the firedamp content are made in accordance with the provisions of the four next following regulations in the part of the mine in which shots are so fired.

4. (1) Determinations of the firedamp content shall be made—

(*a*) by means of apparatus of a type approved for the purpose by the Minister, by a competent person appointed for that purpose by the manager of the mine; or

(*b*) by means of samples of air taken by a competent person so appointed and analysed within four days of the taking thereof.

(2) In reckoning a period of four days for the purposes of this regulation no account shall be taken of any Saturday, Sunday or day of general holiday.

5. (1) Where determinations of the firedamp content in any part of a mine which comprises a longwall face are required to be made by virtue of the use of electric power at or within one hundred and fifty feet of that face or the firing of shots in that part of the mine, those determinations shall be made at or as near as is practicable to the point in each airway serving that face thirty feet from the nearest working place at that face. If the air ventilating that longwall face has ventilated or will ventilate another longwall face determinations shall also be made at such a point in each airway serving each such other face.

(2) An inspector may serve on the manager of the mine a notice requiring determinations to be made also at one or more additional points at any such longwall face or in any airway serving such a longwall face being points specified in the notice.

6. (1) Where determinations of the firedamp content in any part of a mine which comprises a working face other than a longwall face are required to be made by virtue of the use of electric power at or within one hundred and fifty feet of that face or the firing of shots in that part of the mine, those determinations shall be made at suitable points fixed by the manager in respect of each air current in that part of the mine.

(2) An inspector may, if he is of opinion that any point so fixed is unsuitable, serve on the manager a notice requiring him to fix some other point in substitution therefor and may serve on the manager a notice requiring determinations to be

*This expression, as used here and subsequently in these Regulations, has the meaning defined in Section 182 (1) of the 1954 Act.

made at some other point specified in the notice in addition to those required by the preceding paragraph.

7. (1) Determinations of the firedamp content shall be made at every point required by or under the two last preceding regulations once in every week:

Provided that—

(*a*) if any determination at any such point shows a firedamp content exceeding 0·8 per cent by volume determinations shall be made at the corresponding point at intervals not exceeding twenty-four hours so long as the content is shown to exceed or to have exceeded that percentage and for the seven next following working days, unless an inspector by notice served on the manager otherwise consents;

(*b*) if every determination made during a period of thirty days at any such point showed a firedamp content not exceeding 0·6 per cent by volume it shall be sufficient to make determinations at the corresponding point at intervals not exceeding thirty days for so long as the firedamp content shown thereby does not exceed that percentage.

(2) Notwithstanding anything in the last preceding paragraph whenever any alteration is made in the arrangements for ventilating a mine which affects or may effect substantially any part of the mine in which determinations of the firedamp content have to be made, a determination of the firedamp content at each point in that part shall be made as soon as any substantial effect of the alteration would be apparent.

(3) Any determination of the firedamp content shall be made, if the relevant face is machine-cut, during the latter part of the cutting shift or, if the face is not machine-cut, during the latter part of the filling shift:

Provided that if it appears to the manager or an inspector, as the case may be, that the firedamp content is normally greatest at any point at any other stage of the operations, determinations at that point may be made at that stage if an inspector by notice served on the manager consents thereto and shall be made at that stage if an inspector by such notice so requires.

(4) The provisions of Part XV of the Act* with respect to references upon notices served by inspectors shall apply to a notice of requirement under the last preceding paragraph and either of the following shall be a relevant ground of objection to such a notice, namely—

(*a*) that the firedamp content at the point in question is not normally greatest at the stage referred to in the notice;

(*b*) that the greater firedamp content at that stage at that point is transitory.

(5) Where determinations of firedamp content are made once in every week or thirty days they shall as far as practicable be made on the last occasion during the week when the appropriate stage of the operations referred to in paragraph (3) occurs, not being an occasion during a shift beginning on a Saturday.

7A. On every occasion on which a determination of firedamp content is required to be made at or as near as is practicable to the point in an airway

*See Section 170 of the 1954 Act.

serving a longwall face thirty feet from the nearest working place at that face, being an airway which as regards that face is a return airway, a determination of firedamp content shall also be made as near as is practicable to the point in that airway thirty feet from the junction thereof with any other return airway.

8. (1) Particulars of every determination of firedamp content made in accordance with these regulations shall be recorded forthwith in a book* provided for that purpose by the owner of the mine.

(2) If any determination other than one made pursuant to regulation 7A shows a firedamp content at any point exceeding one per cent by volume the manager of the mine shall forthwith give notice thereof to the inspector for the district unless—

(*a*) the excess was caused by temporary derangement of the ventilation at the mine which has been remedied; or

(*b*) the inspector by notice served on the manager has otherwise directed.

Measurements of quantity of air

9. (1) The manager of every mine shall make and secure the efficient carrying out of arrangements whereby the quantity of air passing each of the points hereinafter mentioned is measured at intervals not exceeding thirty days.

(2) The points at which such measurements are to be taken are—

(*a*) in every intake airway starting at an entrance to a shaft or outlet, a point as near as is practicable to that entrance;

(*b*) in every split by which air leaves an air current except a split at a longwall face, a point as near as is practicable to the junction;

(*c*) in any part of the mine in which determinations of firedamp content are required to be made, the points at which those determinations are made, excluding any point at which determinations are made because it has been specified in a notice served on the manager by an inspector; and

(*d*) in any part of the mine containing a working face, being a part in which determinations of firedamp content are not required to be made under these regulations, a point in each road, which as regards a working face is an intake airway and the air in which has not previously ventilated a working face, as nearly as practicable four hundred and fifty feet from the nearest part of the said working face with respect to which that road is an intake airway, unless that point would be within three hundred feet of a point at which measurements are taken under sub-paragraph (*a*) or (*b*).

(3) A measurement of the quantity of air at a point specified in sub-paragraph (*c*) of the last preceding paragraph shall be taken on an occasion when a determination of firedamp content is made thereat.

(4) Notwithstanding anything in paragraph (1) of this regulation, whenever any alteration is made in the arrangements for ventilating a mine which affects

*M. & Q. Form No. 226.

or may affect substantially the quantity of air passing any point at which measurements thereof have to be taken, a measurement of the quantity at each such point shall be taken as soon as any substantial effect of the alteration would be apparent.

(5) Particulars of every measurement taken in accordance with this regulation shall be recorded forthwith in a book* provided for the purpose by the owner of the mine together with any other information incidental thereto for which provision is made in that book.

PART III

Firedamp detectors

10. (1) At every mine in any part of which the use of lamps or lights, other than permitted lights, is unlawful, there shall be provided appliances for detecting the presence of inflammable gas being appliances of a type approved by the Minister for use in mines generally or in mines of a class to which that mine belongs or in that mine (hereinafter called 'detectors') in such number as will enable the provisions of these regulations to be complied with.

(2) Those detectors shall be adjusted, maintained and tested in the manner (if any) specified in the relevant approval.

11. (1) The manager of every mine at which detectors are required to be provided shall—

(*a*) make arrangements to secure that detectors are in use at the places and in the numbers specified in, and otherwise in compliance with, the three next following regulations;

(*b*) appoint competent persons and make arrangements to secure that each detector required to be in use is in the personal charge of such a person.

(2) In any prosecution for a contravention of this regulation it shall be a defence to prove that the manager has made the necessary arrangements for the training of a sufficient number of persons and made reasonable efforts to induce appropriate persons to be trained and that the failure to comply fully was due to an insufficiency of trained persons willing to take charge of detectors at that mine.

(3) In the case of any person appointed under this regulation who may be in charge of a detector which is a flame safety-lamp, his competence to recognise actual gas caps as they appear on the lowered flame of the lamp shall be certified by such person and in such form as the Minister may direct.

12. (1) The places for and the number of detectors to be in use thereat, being places in a part of the mine in which the use of lamps or lights, other than permitted lights, is unlawful, are as follows—

(*a*) at each longwall face, one detector for each eight persons, and one detector for any person or persons not thus taken into account, in the total number of persons wholly or mainly employed at that face during the shift;

---

*M. & Q. Form No. 226.

(*b*) at each other working face (including a cross measure drift or heading in stone), one detector;

(*c*) at each place in an airway which as regards any working face is a return airway being a place at which one or more men are engaged in repair work, one detector;

(*d*) at each place at which apparatus comprising an electric motor is in operation at or within three hundred feet of a working face, one detector.

(2) Any detector required by sub-paragraph (*d*) of the last preceding paragraph shall be in addition to any detector required by any other sub-paragraph thereof.

13. (1) If electric power is being used at a working face and the average of the last six determinations of firedamp content made in pursuance of these regulations at the point on the return side of that face at which such determinations are required to be made exceeds 0·5 per cent by volume—

(*a*) any detector required to be in use at that face by virtue of sub-paragraph (*d*) of paragraph (1) of the last preceding regulation shall be an automatic detector;

(*b*) in the case of a longwall face, at which by virtue of sub-paragraph (*a*) of that paragraph not less than eight detectors are required to be in use, one out of each complete eight of those detectors shall be an automatic detector.

(2) Nothing in the last preceding paragraph shall require the provision of more than two automatic detectors at any single-unit conveyor face nor more than four automatic detectors at any double-unit conveyor face.

(3) If broken working is being carried on immediately adjoining the waste in any part of a mine in the course of bord and pillar or a similar system of working and—

(*a*) the average of the last six determinations of firedamp content made in pursuance of these regulations on the return side of that part of the mine exceeds 0·5 per cent by volume; or

(*b*) if such determinations are not required to be made, the average of a series of at least six determinations of firedamp content made by an inspector at intervals of not less than fourteen days exceeds 0·5 per cent by volume (being where more than one such series of determinations has been made the most recent series);

then, in a case in which not less than four detectors are required to be in use in those broken workings, one out of each complete four of those detectors, and, in any other case, one of those detectors, shall be an automatic detector.

14. The manager of every mine at which detectors are required to be in use shall give directions to the persons who are to have charge of detectors (other than detectors which operate automatically) as to the minimum number of tests for inflammable gas to be made by them.

15. (1) A person in charge of a detector which is a flame safety-lamp shall not, except with the written permission of the manager of the mine, use any other lamp as his working light.

(2) No person in charge of a detector which is a flame safety-lamp shall when testing for inflammable gas raise the lamp higher than is necessary to allow the presence of gas to be detected.

16. If any person in charge of a detector which is a flame safety-lamp detects the presence of inflammable gas therewith he shall not throw away that detector or attempt to extinguish it by blowing or jerking it but shall take it out of the gas steadily, holding it near the floor and sheltering it. If the gas fires in the detector and he cannot immediately take it out of the gas he shall smother the light.

17. Nothing done in pursuance of the preceding regulations relating to detectors shall affect any obligation imposed on any deputy to make any inspection or any obligation to test for inflammable gas in connection with shot firing.

PART IV

Ventilating machinery

18. (1) There shall be provided and maintained in connection with every ventilating fan driven by mechanical power (other than an auxiliary fan) a water gauge and either an automatic indicator registering the number of revolutions of the fan or an automatic indicator registering the ventilation pressure.

(2) The manager of every mine shall give directions as to the speed at which any machinery driving such a fan is to be run to the person in charge of that machinery.

19. (1) The person in charge of the machinery driving such a fan shall examine the machinery and observe the water gauge and automatic indicator at intervals not exceeding—

(*a*) in the case of a mine in any part of which the use of lamps or lights, other than permitted lights, is unlawful, a half hour or such longer time as an inspector may approve by notice served on the manager;

(*b*) in the case of any other mine, two hours.

(2) Where an automatic indicator registering the ventilation pressure is not in use the person in charge of the machinery driving such a fan shall at the end of each period of two hours enter in a book* provided for the purpose by the owner of the mine the number of revolutions of the fan and the pressure shown by the water gauge at the end of that period.

(3) The person in charge of the machinery driving such a fan shall forthwith report to the official of the mine under whose directions he works—

(*a*) any damage to or defect or derangement in or stoppage of that machinery; and

(*b*) any unusual variation in the pressure shown by the water gauge.

---

*M. & Q. Form No. 227.

PART V

Prevention of leakages of air

Air-locks

20. (1) In each shaft and outlet which is connected by a drift to a fan on the surface of the mine, which was so connected after the thirty-first day of July, nineteen hundred and forty-seven, and which is ordinarily used for winding or haulage there shall be provided and maintained an efficient air-lock.

(2) An inspector may serve on the manager of a mine a notice requiring the provision and maintenance of such an air-lock at any shaft or outlet specified in the notice being a shaft or outlet which is connected and used as aforesaid but which was not so connected after the said date. The provisions of Part XV of the Act* with respect to references upon notices served by inspectors shall apply to a notice served under this paragraph and any of the following shall be a relevant ground of objection to such a notice, namely—

(*a*) that there is insufficient space for an efficient air-lock;

(*b*) that by reason of the shortness of the period during which the mine is expected to be worked the requirement is unreasonable;

(*c*) having regard to the provision made to ensure the proper ventilation of all parts of the mine, the requirement is unnecessary.

(3) If the Minister is satisfied that the requirements of this regulation are inappropriate to the circumstances of any mine, he may by notice served on the manager exempt that mine from those requirements.

(4) The provisions of this regulation shall not apply to a mine at which not more than thirty persons are employed below ground.

21. (1) Any road not required for the working of a mine and connecting airways which as regards any working face are intake and return airways shall forthwith be so stopped off as to minimise leakage of air through it.

(2) In a mine of coal any such stopping between a main intake airway† and a main return airway† shall be—

(*a*) constructed of a tight packing at least fifteen feet thick of stone, dirt, sand or rubbish; or

(*b*) constructed of a tight packing at least nine feet thick of stone, dirt, sand or rubbish having the end of the packing nearest the intake airway faced with a wall not less than nine inches thick of masonry, brickwork or concrete the face of which is covered with a coating of mortar so as to prevent leakage of air.

In either case each space between the face of the stopping and the airway shall be kept clear.

(3) Nothing in paragraph (2) shall apply to any mine in South Staffordshire in which the unworked coal is liable to spontaneous combustion.

---

*See Section 170 of the 1954 Act.

†This expression, as used here and subsequently in these Regulations, has the meaning defined in Regulation 33 (1).

Ventilation doors and sheets

22. (1) In every road which is required for the working of a mine and which is a connection between—

(*a*) a main intake airway and a main return airway; or

(*b*) airways which as regards any working face are intake and return airways and in either of which the quantity of air passing any point is required to be measured under regulation nine;

there shall be provided and properly maintained at least two suitable doors to minimise the leakage of air, or, if in any case it is impracticable to provide such doors, other suitable means of minimising such leakage.

(2) In any other road the ventilation in which is to be restricted by means of any door or sheet for the purpose of preventing short-circuiting of an air current, there shall be provided and properly maintained at least two doors or, if that is impracticable, at least one door and one sheet or two sheets.

(3) Doors and sheets provided in pursuance of this regulation shall be so spaced that whenever one door or sheet is opened at least one other door or sheet provided for restricting the passing of air can be kept shut, or, if in any case it is impracticable so to space such doors and sheets, other measures to minimise the leakage of air through them shall be taken.

(4) Doors provided in pursuance of this regulation shall be self-closing. No person shall prop or fix such a door open except where and for so long as it is necessary to allow a vehicle to pass through it. Any such door when not in use shall be taken off its hinges and placed in a position in which it will not obstruct the air current.

(5) Any person who opens any such door shall secure that it is closed as soon as possible.

PART VI

Ventilating fans below ground

23. (1) No person other than the deputy in charge of a district affected or an official of the mine authorised by the manager or a person authorised by such a deputy or official shall start, stop, remove or alter any fan installed below ground at any mine.

(2) A deputy or official shall not start or authorise any person to start such a fan on any occasion unless the deputy or official is satisfied that it is safe for the fan to be so started.

24. (1) No auxiliary fan shall be installed at any place in a mine unless the manager is satisfied—

(*a*) that the quantity of air reaching it at all times will be sufficient to ensure that it does not re-circulate air; and

(*b*) that air circulated by it will not be contaminated by any substantial quantity of any noxious gas or dust;

and no such fan shall be worked at any time at which either of those conditions is not satisfied.

(2) No auxiliary fan shall be installed at a point within, or less than fifteen feet from the nearer side of the entrance to, the place to be ventilated by it; so however that in the case of two or more fans installed in series this requirement shall apply only to one of them.

(3) Any forcing auxiliary fan shall be installed on the intake side and any exhaust auxiliary fan on the return side of the place to be ventilated by it.

(4) There shall be installed and maintained with every auxiliary fan such an air duct for conducting air to or from the face of the place to be ventilated as ensures adequate delivery of air within fifteen feet of the face and minimises leakage.

(5) Every auxiliary fan, whether driven electrically or otherwise, shall be so connected with earth as to prevent the accumulation of an electro-static charge.

25. (1) In respect of every auxiliary fan at a mine the manager shall fix the minimum quantity of air to be delivered or exhausted per minute at the end of the air duct.

(2) The manager shall make and secure the efficient carrying out of arrangements whereby at least once in every week a competent person appointed for that purpose by him measures the quantity of air being so delivered or exhausted and determines whether any air is being re-circulated by that fan.

(3) Particulars of the quantity fixed under paragraph (1) and of every measurement and determination made under paragraph (2) shall be recorded forthwith by the manager or the competent person, as the case may be, in a book* provided for that purpose by the owner of the mine.

26. (1) Two or more auxiliary fans shall not be installed in any section of narrow or panel workings so as to draw air from the same air current unless there is kept at the mine an accurate plan showing the general system of ventilation in that section and the quantity of air in each air current therein.

(2) Upon the preparation of such a plan the manager of the mine shall send a copy thereof to the inspector for the district, and, if any change in the system of ventilation or any substantial variation in the quantity of air in any air current thus shown is made, the manager shall send an amended plan or otherwise give notice of the change or variation to that inspector as soon as the effect thereof can be ascertained.

27. Without prejudice to the generality of subsection (5) of section fifty-five of the Act, where a place is provided with an auxiliary fan, no workman shall enter or remain in that place while the fan is not operating unless the deputy in charge of the district or some other official appointed for that purpose by the manager has inspected the place and found it safe.

28. (1) No fan (not being an auxiliary fan) shall be installed at any place below ground in a mine, unless the manager is satisfied that it is necessary or expedient to install it at that place for the proper ventilation of the mine, having taken into account a survey of the ventilation of every part of the mine which would or might be substantially affected and a report upon the appropriate type,

*M. &. Q. Form No. 228.

size and location of the proposed fan, being a survey and report made by persons experienced in those matters appointed for the purpose by the owner of the mine or the manager.

(2) If any such fan is installed at any place below ground the manager shall forthwith give notice thereof to the inspector for the district, attaching thereto particulars of the survey and a copy of the report made in relation to that installation.

PART VII

General

Ventilating Sheets

29. In any mine in which naked lights are in use, every ventilating sheet shall be of fire-resisting material and shall be properly maintained.

30. Any person who moves any ventilating sheet shall secure that it is replaced as soon as possible.

31. Wherever sheets or ducts are used to secure the ventilation of any working place not being a working place in a shaft in the course of being sunk, it shall be the duty of the deputy or other official in charge of that part of the mine to ensure that they are so placed and maintained that an adequate amount of air reaches that place.

Exemptions

32. The Chief Inspector of Mines if he is satisfied that the application of any provision in Part II, V or VI of these regulations (other than a provision in relation to which an express power of exemption is contained in these regulations) is inappropriate in relation to any mine or part thereof, may by notice served on the manager of that mine exempt it or a part thereof from the application of that provision.

Interpretation

33. (1) In these regulations the following expressions have the meanings hereby respectively assigned to them, that is to say—

'the Act' means the Mines and Quarries Act 1954;

'auxiliary fan' means a fan used or intended to be used below ground wholly or mainly for ventilating a heading, drift or blind end;

'deputy' has the meaning assigned thereto in the Coal and Other Mines (Managers and Officials) Regulations 1956;*

'detector' has the meaning assigned thereto in regulation ten;

'electric power' does not include electricity used in a portable safety-lamp or detector, shot-firing apparatus, a scientific instrument, signalling apparatus or a telephone;

'firedamp content' has the meaning assigned thereto in regulation three;

*See page 188.

'main intake airway' means a length of intake airway which begins at a shaft or outlet or a length of airway the current of air in which is subsequently split and which as regards two or more working faces is an intake airway;

'main return airway' means a length of return airway which ends at a shaft or outlet or a length of airway the current of air in which has been split and which as regards two or more working faces is a return airway;

'mine' has the meaning assigned thereto in regulation one;

'working face' does not include a place in a road or roadhead at which ripping or work of repair is in progress.

(2) Where a determination of the firedamp content made for the purposes of any of these regulations is made by means of a sample of air it shall be deemed to be made at the time and place at which the sample is taken.

(3) Expressions to which meanings are assigned by the Act or by these regulations shall (unless the contrary intention appears) have the same meanings in any document issued under the provisions of these regulations.

(4) The Interpretation Act 1889 shall apply to the interpretation of these regulations as it applies to the interpretation of an Act of Parliament.

LIST OF PROVISIONS IN THE MINES AND QUARRIES ACT 1954 WHICH EXPRESSLY PROVIDE THAT A PERSON IS GUILTY OF AN OFFENCE (SECTION 152(1) OF THE MINES AND QUARRIES ACT 1954)*

Section	*Subject*
65 (1)	Damaging, destroying or losing a safety-lamp or allowing it to be damaged, destroyed or lost . . . . .
65 (2)	Tampering with a safety-lamp . . . . . .
66 (1) & (3)	Having a cigar or cigarette, a pipe or other contrivance for smoking, or a match or mechanical lighter in or when about to go into a safety-lamp mine or safety-lamp part of a mine
66 (6)	Refusal to allow searching . . . .
89	Contravention of certain rules or directions made or given by the owner or manager . . . .
90 (1)	Negligent or wilful acts or omissions likely to endanger the safety of the mine or the safety or health of persons thereat
90 (2)	Removal or alteration of, or tampering with, anything provided for securing the safety or health of persons employed . .
116 (3)	Failure of actual employer, who is not the owner, to report an accident to the responsible person . . . . .
145 (2)	Offences in relation to the powers and duties of Inspectors .
153	Inducing or procuring, or consenting to or conniving at, the commission of an offence under the Act . . . .
160	Liability of the parent for the employment of a young person in contravention of the Act . . . . . .
161 (1)	Forgery of certificates, or the making of false statements, etc.
162	Removal of, injury to, or defacement of a notice or of a document in the accommodation provided in pursuance of Section 135 . . . .

*See 'The Law Relating to Safety and Health in Mines and Quarries' Part 1.

REFERENCES UPON NOTICES SERVED BY INSPECTORS MATTERS TO WHICH PROVISIONS OF SECTION 170 OF THE 1954 ACT APPLY

MINES AND QUARRIES ACT 1954

	Subject	Page
	The Coal and Other Mines (Mechanics and Electricians) Regulations 1965	
Regns. 5, 6 & 7	Requirement that mechanic/electrician shall be in charge whenever a prime mover/electric motor is used for purpose not specified in the Regulations	192
10	Amendment to scheme for systematic examination and testing of apparatus	194
	The Coal Mines (Clearances in Transport Roads) Regulations, 1959	
Regn. 8	Widening of clearances in old roads	257
	The Coal and Other Mines (Ventilation) Regulations, 1956	
Regns. 7	Change of point at which determinations of fire-damp content are to be made	319
20	Provision and maintenance of an air-lock at a shaft or outlet connected by a drift to a surface fan before 31st July, 1947	324

PROVISIONS REGARDING EXEMPTIONS, APPROVALS, ETC., GIVEN UNDER EARLIER LEGISLATION

The Orders listed below provide that any certificate, exemption, consent, approval, authority, etc., granted under earlier legislation (shown in col. 3) and which was in force at the commencement of the Mines and Quarries Act 1954, i.e., 1st January, 1957, in so far as it could have been granted or made for the purposes of the Regulations (shown in col. 2) made under those Orders shall have effect as if it had been so granted or made.

Order	Regulations	Earlier legislation
Col. 1	Col. 2	Col. 3
The Coal and Other Mines (Managers and Officials) Order 1956	The Coal and Other Mines (Managers and Officials) Regulations 1956	Coal Mines Act, 1911, sections 14, 15, 17, 63, 64, 65 and 66 (as amended by the Coal Mines (Officials and Inspections) General Regulations 1951).
		General Regulations, dated 10th July, 1913, Regulations 30, 36 to 38, 40, 42 to 45, 104, 180, 182 and 184.
		Coal Mines (Officials and Inspections) General Regulations 1951 and 1952.
		Coal Mines (Miscellaneous) General Regulations 1953, Regulation 1.
The Coal and Other Mines (Mechanics and Electricians) Order 1956	The Coal and Other Mines (Mechanics and Electricians) Regulations 1956	General Regulations dated 10th July, 1913, Regulations 131(*g*) and 132(iii)
		Coal Mines (Mechanics and Electricians) General Regulations 1954.
The Coal and Other Mines (Surveyors and Plans) Order 1956	The Coal and Other Mines (Surveyors and Plans) Regulations 1956	Coal Mines Act 1911, Sections 20 and 21 as amended by the Coal Mines (Surveyors and Plans) General Regulations 1952.
		General Regulations dated 10th July, 1913, Regulation 31.
		Coal Mines (Surveyors and Plans) General Regulations 1952.
The Coal and Other Mines (General Duties and Conduct) Order 1956	The Coal and Other Mines (General Duties and Conduct) Regulations 1956	Coal Mines Act 1911, Section 74.
		General Regulations of 10th July, 1913, Regulations 3, 4, 5, 9, 11, 12, 17, 19, 27 and 68.
		Coal Mines (Mechanics and Electricians) General Regulations 1954, Regulation 10.
The Coal and Other Mines (Shafts, Outlets and Roads) Order 1956	The Coal and Other Mines (Shafts, Outlets and Roads) Regulations 1956	Coal Mines Act 1911, Section 40 (as amended by the Coal Mines (Winding and Haulage) General Regulations 1937 and 1948 and the Coal Mines (Miscellaneous) General Regulations 1953).

Order	Regulations	Earlier legislation
Col. 1	Col. 2	Col. 3
(cont.) The Coal and Other Mines (Shafts, Outlets and Roads) Order 1956	*(cont.)* The Coal and Other Mines (Shafts, Outlets add Roads) Regulations 1956	Coal Mines Act, 1911, Sections 43, 44 (as amended by the Coal Mines (Winding and Haulage) General Regulations 1948).
		Coal Mines Act 1911, Sections 46, 53 (2) and (3) and 66 (1).
		General Regulations dated 1st April, 1913.
		General Regulations dated 10th July, 1913, Regulations 3, 20 to 23, 25, 26, 39, 63 to 68, 79 to 81, 92 to 96, 98 to 101, 103, 172 to 174, 176, 177, 181, 183 and 186 to 190.
		General Regulations dated 30th July, 1920.
		Coal Mines General Regulations (Winding and Haulage) 1937.
The Coal and Other Mines (Support) Order 1956	The Coal and Other Mines (Support) Regulations 1956	Coal Mines Act 1911, Section 50 (as amended by the Coal Mines (Support of Roof and Sides) General Regulations 1947 and the Coal Mines (Miscellaneous) General Regulations 1953).
		Coal Mines (Support of Roof and Sides) General Regulations 1947.
The Coal and Other Mines (Ventilation) Order 1956	The Coal and Other Mines (Ventilation) Regulations 1956	Coal Mines Act 1911, Section 29 General Regulations dated 10th July, 1913, Regulations 15, 16, 69–73 and 91.
		Coal Mines General Regulations (Firedamp Detectors) 1939.
		Coal Mines (Ventilation) General Regulations 1947.
		Coal Mines (Officials and Inspections) General Regulations 1951, Regulation 8.
		Coal Mines (Explosives) Order 1951, Articles 34 and 54.
The Coal and Other Mines (Safety-Lamps and Lighting) Order 1956	The Coal and Other Mines (Safety-Lamps and Lighting) Regulations 1956	Coal Mines Act 1911, Section 34 (as amended by the Coal Mines General Regulations (Safety-Lamps) 1927).
		General Regulations dated 10th July, 1913, Regulations 13, 14, 37, 122 and 135.
		Coal Mines General Regulations (Firedamp Detectors) 1939, Regulation 7.
		Coal Mines (Lighting) General Regulations 1947.
		Coal Mines (Officials and Inspections) General Regulations, 1951 Regulation 17.

Order	Regulations	Earlier legislation
Col. 1	Col. 2	Col. 3
The Coal and Other Mines (Electricity) Order 1956	The Coal and Other Mines (Electricity) Regulations 1956	Coal Mines Act 1911, Section 60. General Regulations dated 10th July, 1913 (as amended by the Coal Mines (Electricity) (Earthing Systems) Regulations 1953, Regulations 118 to 132, 134 and 137). General Regulations dated 30th July, 1920, Regulation 28. Coal Mines General Regulations 1938, Regulation 8.
The Coal Mines (Explosives) Order 1956	The Coal Mines (Explosives) Regulations 1956	Coal Mines (Explosives) Order 1951.
The Coal and Other Mines (Fire and Rescue) Order 1956	The Coal and Other Mines (Fire and Rescue) Regulations 1956	Coal Mines Act 1911, Sections 69 and 70. General Regulations dated 10th July, 1913, Regulation 122(*c*). General Regulations dated 30th July, 1920, Regulation 9. Coal Mines General Regulations (Rescue) 1928 (as amended by the Coal Mines General Regulations (First Aid) 1930 and the Coal Mines (Rescue) Amending Regulations 1935). Coal Mines General Regulations 1938, Part 1.
The Coal Mines (Precautions against Inflammable Dust) Order 1956	The Coal Mines (Precautions against Inflammable Dust) Regulations 1956	Coal Mines Act 1911, Section 62. Coal Mines General Regulations (Precautions against Coal Dust) 1939.
The Coal and Other Mines (Precautions against Inrushes) Order 1956	The Coal and Other Mines (Precautions against Inrushes) Regulations 1956	Coal Mines Act 1911, Section 68. Coal Mines (Shallow Workings and Dangerous Deposits) General Regulations 1952.
The Coal and Other Mines (Locomotives) Order 1956	The Coal and Other Mines (Locomotives) Regulations 1956	Coal Mines (Locomotives) General Regulations 1949
The Coal and Other Mines (Steam Boilers) Order 1956	The Coal and Other Mines (Steam Boilers) Regulations 1956	Coal Mines Act 1911, Section 56. General Regulations dated 10th July, 1913, Regulations 74 to 76.
The Coal and Other Mines (Sidings) Order 1956	The Coal and Other Mines (Sidings) Regulations 1956	General Regulations dated 10th July, 1913, Regulations 23, 150, 151, 153 to 155, 157 to 169 and 171.

Order	Regulations	Earlier legislation
Col. 1	Col. 2	Col. 3
The Coal and Other Mines (First Aid) Order 1956	The Coal and Other Mines (First Aid) Regulations 1956	Coal Mines General Regulations (First Aid) 1930. Coal Mines (First Aid) Amending Regulations 1937.
The Coal Mines (Medical Examinations) Order 1956	The Coal Mines (Medical Examinations) Regulations 1956	Coal Mines (Medical Examinations) General Regulations 1952
The Coal and Other Mines (Sanitary Conveniences) Order 1956	The Coal and Other Mines (Sanitary Conveniences) Regulations 1956	General Regulations dated 10th July, 1913, Regulations 106 to 112.
The Coal and Other Mines (Horses) Order 1956	The Coal and Other Mines (Horses) Regulations 1956	Third Schedule to the Coal Mines Act 1911 (as amended by the Coal Mines General Regulations of 10th February, 1922 and the Coal Mines (Horses) General Regulations 1949).

LIST OF M. & Q. FORMS RELATING TO MINES OF COAL, STRATIFIED IRONSTONE, SHALE AND FIRECLAY

	M. & Q. Form No.
Notices	
Notification to District Inspector of appointment by mine owner (Section 15)	201
Notice of accident or dangerous occurrence (Sections 116 and 117)	206
Notice fixing periods of employment and intervals allowed for meals or rest for women and young persons (Section 128) .	208
Notice for giving (*a*) name of mine, name and address of owner, name of manager; (*b*) name and address of Inspector for the District; (*c*) situation of covered accommodation required by Section 135 (Section 136)	204
Notification of beginning and ending of certain mining operations (Section 139) or of change of ownership or name of a mine (Section 140)	212
Notice of result of proceedings (Section 165)	209
Notice of proposal to fix maximum exceeding 10 shots on any one shift for a deputy (Coal Mines (Explosives) Regulations 1961), (Regn. 45 (2))	242
Notice of intention to use electrical apparatus (Coal and Other Mines (Electricity) Regulations 1956), (Regn. 2 (1)) . .	263
Notice to instructor or supervising workman of person to be supervised and nature of work to be performed (Coal Mines (Training) Regulations 1967) (Regn. 12 (2)) . . .	225
Report Books and Registers	
The Mines and Quarries Act 1954	
Reports of withdrawal of persons employed in cases of danger (Section 79)	210
Reports of inspections on behalf of workmen (Section 123) .	216
Register of women and young persons employed (Section 131), Part I—Young persons employed above and below ground; Part II—Women	311
The Coal Mines Regulation Act 1908	
Register of times at which men are lowered into and raised from the mine (Section 2 (1) as amended by the Mines and Quarries Act 1954)	203
The Coal Mines (Precautions against Inflammable Dust) Regulations 1956	
Record of analyses of dust samples (Regn. 7 (4))	207
The Coal Mines (Explosives) Regulations 1961	
Record of cleaning, overhaul and test of electric shot firing apparatus (Regn. 26 (*e*))	240
Daily record of shots fired and miss-fires (Regns. 36 and 72) .	241
Record of maximum number of shots to be fired by shot firers (Regn. 46 (1))	243
The Coal Mines (Cardox and Hydrox) Regulations 1956	
Reports of examinations of shells (Regn. 6 (2))	229
Record of number of shells fired (Regn. 28)	230

	M. & Q. Form No.
The Stratified Ironstone, Shale and Fireclay Mines (Explosives) Regulations 1956	
Record of cleaning, overhaul and test of electric shot firing apparatus (Regn. 17 (*e*))	221
Daily record of shots fired, quantity of detonators and explosives used, and number of miss-fired shots (Regns. 27 and 41 (4))	222
The Coal and Other Mines (Fire and Rescue) Regulations, 1956	
Reports of fires or suspected fires (Regn. 11 (3))	261
The Coal and Other Mines (Horses) Regulations, 1956	
Horse-keepers daily report on horses employed (Regn. 10 (2))	265
The Coal and Other Mines (Locomotives) Regulations, 1956	
Record of inspections of locomotive roads (Regn.) 10 (2) (*b*)	269
Record of determinations of firedamp content in locomotive roads (Regn. 15)	270
Record of daily external examinations of locomotives (Regn. 23 (1))	271
Record of examinations and tests of locomotive brakes (Regn. 24)	273
Record of analyses of exhaust gases of diesel engines and air sampled at appointed places (Regn. 31 (4))	274
The Coal and Other Mines (Managers and Officials) Regulations 1956	
Deputy's pre-shift report (Regn. 24 (1))	231
Deputy's general report (Regn. 25)	232
Reports of inspections of places outside deputies' districts (Regn. 29 (*a*) and (*b*))	234
Reports of weekly inspections of airways and roads (Regn. 29 (*c*))	235
The Coal and Other Mines (Mechanics and Electricians) Regulations 1965	
Reports of defective mechanical apparatus (Regn. 14)	267
Reports of defective electrical apparatus (Regn. 14)	268
The Mines (Medical Examinations) Regulations 1964	
Medical examinations book (Regn. 8)	312
Copy of the certificate and other entries in the medical examinations book in respect of a medical examination (Regn. 5 (6))	313
The Coal and Other Mines (Safety-Lamps and Lighting) Regulations 1956	
Record of damage to safety-lamps or detectors (Regn. 2 (3))	214
Reports of tests of pneumatic electric lighting units (Regn. 19 (5))	215
The Coal and Other Mines (Shafts, Outlets and Roads) Regulations 1960	
Reports of examinations of shafts, staple-pits and unwalkable outlets through which persons are carried (Regn. 18)	275
Reports of examinations of winding ropes (Regn. 19 (3))	277
Reports of tests of automatic contrivance to prevent overwinding (Regn. 19 (4))	278

MINING QUALIFICATIONS BOARD

Mining Qualifications Board Rules

Certificate of Competency Rules

Surveyors' Certificates Rules

Mechanics' and Electricians' Certificates Rules

Deputies' Certificates Rules

Shot Firers' Certificates Rules

Certificate Fees Order

General provisions about the grant, cancellation and suspension of certificates, and provisions governing the constitution of the Mining Qualifications Board, are contained in Part XII of the Act.

If further details are required about any particular point inquiry should be made to the Secretary, The Mining Qualifications Board, Ministry of Technology, Thames House South, Millbank, London, S.W.1.

THE MINING EXAMINATIONS (CERTIFICATES OF COMPETENCY) RULES 1962*

PART I

1. (1) An applicant for any certificate of competency under the Act must comply with the provisions of this Part of these rules.

(2) An applicant for any certificate of competency valid only with respect to mines of stratified ironstone must comply with the provisions of Part II of these rules.

(3) An applicant for any certificate of competency other than a certificate valid only with respect of mines of stratified ironstone must comply with the provisions of Part III of these rules:

2. An applicant for a certificate of competency must produce to the Board with his application, the following documents:

(*a*) a birth certificate, or other evidence of his age satisfactory to the Board;

(*b*) two testimonials, on forms provided for the purpose by the Board, of his good character;

(*c*) a certificate that he is the holder of a qualification in first aid approved by the Minister of Power for the purpose of the Coal and Other Mines (First Aid) Regulations 1962 obtained within the last preceding three years;

(*d*) a certificate concerning his ability to test for gas, and his hearing, being a certificate which would be valid for the purposes of paragraph (2) of regulation twenty-six of the Coal and Other Mines (Managers and Officials) Regulations, 1956†, as amended by the Coal and Other Mines (Managers and Officials) (Variation) Regulations, 1961; and

(*e*) particulars of his actual and prospective practical experience in mining referred to in rule three.

3. (1) Subject to any reduction determined by the Board, an applicant for a certificate of competency must:

(*a*) satisfy the Board that he has had, prior to making his application, not less than four years practical experience in mining; and

(*b*) before or within nine months after the examination provided for in Part II, Part III or Part IV of these rules, or within such longer period as the Board may in a particular case allow, satisfy the Board that he has then had not less than five years such experience.‡

(2) The practical experience aforesaid must:

(*a*) be experience:

(i) under the National Coal Board's Mining Engineering Training Scheme; or

---

*As amended by the Mining Examinations (Certificate of Competency) (Amendment) Rules 1963 and 1964 (No. 2).

†See page 185.

‡For reduced periods see Note 1 at end of these rules.

(ii) below ground in mining which includes the performance, immediate supervision or responsible control, during periods amounting in all to not less than two years, subject to any reduction determined by the Board, of the getting of minerals (by hand or mechanical methods) or work at the face directly connected with such getting, setting of supports or repairing and stonework;

(*b*) be experience either wholly in one or more mines of coal, stratified ironstone, shale or fireclay in the United Kingdom, or partly in one or more such mines and partly in one or more mines of coal, stratified ironstone, shale or fireclay, outside the United Kingdom with respect to which the Board are satisfied that it or they provided equivalent experience;

(*c*) in relation to an applicant for a certificate of competency valid only with respect to mines of a specified class or description, include not less than three years' experience in one or more mines of that class or description.

(3) Any reduction of practical experience as aforesaid shall be such reduction in respect of any qualifications or experience (including performance of national service) acquired by the applicant as the Board may determine having regard to any directions given to them by the Minister.

PART II

4. An applicant for a second class certificate of competency valid only with respect to mines of stratified ironstone must qualify after attaining the age of twenty-one years at a written examination held by the Board on the subjects specified in the first part of the first schedule to these rules.

5. An applicant for a first class certificate of competency valid only with respect to mines of stratified ironstone must qualify after attaining the age of twenty-one years at a written examination held by the Board on the subjects specified in the second part of the first schedule to these rules.

PART III

6. An applicant for a second class certificate of competency under this Part of these rules must produce to the Board, with his application, evidence that he is:

(*a*) the holder of a higher national certificate in mining; or

(*b*) the holder of any degree or diploma specified in the second schedule to these rules;

and must qualify after attaining the age of twenty-one years at a written examination held by the Board on the subject of mining law.*

7. An applicant for a first class certificate of competency under this Part of these rules must produce to the Board, with his application, evidence that he is the holder of any degree or diploma specified in the second schedule to these

*For syllabus see Note at the end of these rules.

rules and must qualify after attaining the age of twenty-one years at a written examination held by the Board on the subject of mining law.*

8. The Board may if they are satisfied that an applicant under this Part of these rules holds a degree or diploma of a standard of knowledge and competency at least equal to one of the degrees or diplomas specified in the schedule to these rules, obtained by examination after an equivalent course of study, exempt that applicant from the provisions of rule six or of rule seven so far as they require evidence that he is the holder of a degree or diploma specified in that schedule.

8A. The Board may, if they are satisfied that an applicant under this Part of these rules has, after attendance for at least two years at a course intended to lead to a National Diploma in Mining awarded by the Institution of Mining Engineers and Department of Education and Science or by that Institution and the Scottish Education Department, attained in an examination in the subject of Mining Technology, Mining Surveying, Colliery Electrical Engineering and Colliery Mechanical Engineering a standard equal to a pass in the examination for the higher national certificate in mining, exempt that applicant from the provisions of rule 6 so far as they require evidence that he is the holder of a certificate, degree or diploma referred to in that rule.

PART IV

(relates to examinations which ceased after May, 1963)

PART V

11. The times and places at which examinations are to be held under these rules shall be published by the Board in such publications as the Board may from time to time think fit.

FIRST SCHEDULE

Rules 4 and 5

(*Mines of Stratified Ironstone*)

PART I

Second Class Certificates

Methods of working
Ventilation, Ignitions, Underground Fires and Inundations
Machinery
Surveying and Levelling
Mining Legislation relating to stratified ironstone mines

PART II

First Class Certificates

Winning and working
Theory and Practice of Ventilation
Ignitions, Underground Fires and Inundations
Machinery
Surveying, Levelling and Drawing
Mining Legislation relating to stratified ironstone mines

*For syllabus see Note 2 at end of these rules.

SECOND SCHEDULE

Rules 6, 7 and 8

Degrees and Diplomas

BENARES HINDU UNIVERSITY: Degree of B.Sc. in Mining Engineering
*BIRMINGHAM UNIVERSITY: Degree of B.Sc. in Mining
*DURHAM UNIVERSITY: Degree of B.Sc. in Applied Science (Mining Engineering); Honours Degree of B.Sc. in Applied Science (Mining Engineering); General Degree of B.Sc. in Applied Science (Mining Engineering); Diploma in Mining Engineering
*EDINBURGH UNIVERSITY: Degree of B.Sc. in Mining
*GLASGOW UNIVERSITY: Degree of B.Sc. in Mining Engineering; Certificate of Proficiency in Mining
†*HERIOT-WATT COLLEGE, EDINBURGH: Associateship in Mining
INDIAN SCHOOL OF MINES, DHANBAD: Associateship in Mining Engineering
LEEDS UNIVERSITY: Degree of B.Sc., in Mining;‡ Degree of M.Sc. (Mining) for students who have already graduated in Engineering; Diploma in Mining*
LONDON UNIVERSITY: Degree of B.Sc. (Eng.) in Mining
NOTTINGHAM UNIVERSITY: Degree of B.Sc. in Mining
ROYAL SCHOOL OF MINES, LONDON: Associateship in Mining
UNIVERSITY OF NEWCASTLE-UPON-TYNE: Degree of B.Sc. in Applied Science (Mining Engineering)
§*ROYAL COLLEGE OF SCIENCE AND TECHNOLOGY, GLASGOW: Associateship in Mining Engineering; Diploma in Mining Engineering
*SHEFFIELD UNIVERSITY: Degree of Bachelor of Engineering (Mining); Degree of Master of Engineering (Mining)
UNIVERSITY OF WALES: Degree of B.Sc. in Mining Engineering
UNIVERSITY COLLEGE OF SOUTH WALES AND MONMOUTHSHIRE: Diploma in Metalliferous Mining
*WIGAN AND DISTRICT MINING AND TECHNICAL COLLEGE: Diploma in Mining
INSTITUTION OF MINING ENGINEERS AND DEPARTMENT OF EDUCATION AND SCIENCE (jointly): National Diploma in Mining
INSTITUTION OF MINING ENGINEERS AND SCOTTISH EDUCATION DEPARTMENT (jointly): National Diploma in Mining
INSTITUTION OF MINING ENGINEERS: Pass in the Associate Membership Examinations.

Notes on the Certificate of Competency Rules

1. The practical experience required before a certificate can be granted is as follows: for candidates with university or college mining degrees, etc.; or holders of the National Diploma in Mining, three years (including eighteen months face work). Completion of the National Coal Board's Mining Engineering Training Scheme or Student Apprenticeship in Mining Engineering will be accepted as fulfilling the practical experience requirements.

2. The syllabus for the examinations in Mining Law is as follows: statutory requirements (including regulations and orders) relating to safety, health and conditions of employment in mines under the Mines and Quarries Act.

---

*No longer granted.
†Now known as Heriot-Watt University—B.Sc. in Mining.
‡No longer accepted.
§Now known as University of Strathclyde and awarding B.Sc. in Mining Engineering.

THE MINING EXAMINATIONS
(SURVEYORS) RULES 1962*

1. An applicant for a surveyor's certificate under the Act (in these rules referred to as 'an applicant') must produce to the Board with his application, the following documents:

(*a*) a birth certificate or other evidence of his age satisfactory to the Board;

(*b*) two testimonials on forms provided for the purpose by the Board of his good character; and

(*c*) particulars of his actual and prospective experience in surveying mines referred to in rule two.

2. (1) Subject to any reduction determined by the Board, an applicant must:

(*a*) satisfy the Board that he has had, prior to making his application, not less than three years' experience in surveying mines; and

(*b*) before or within nine months after taking the examinations provided for in rule three, or within such longer period as the Board may in a particular case allow, satisfy the Board that he has then had not less than four years such experience.

(2) The experience mentioned in sub-paragraph (*b*) of the foregoing paragraph of this rule must:

(*a*) include experience in surveying and levelling (including chain reading) below ground for periods amounting in all to not less than two thousand hours, subject to any reduction determined by the Board; and

(*b*) be experience:

(i) in mines in the United Kingdom; or

(ii) partly in such mines during periods amounting in all to not less than one year and partly in mines elsewhere with respect to which the Board are satisfied that they provided equivalent experience.

(3) Any reduction of experience as aforesaid shall be such reduction in respect of any qualification or experience (including performance of national service) acquired by the applicant as the Board may determine having regard to any directions given to them by the Minister.

3. An applicant must qualify at a practical examination held by the Board after attaining the age of twenty years before the first day of May immediately before the date of the examination on the subjects of:—

(i) surveying on the surface (including the use and adjustments of a theodolite) and levelling (including the adjustments of the level and flying and sectional levelling); and

(ii) surveying below ground (including the use of a theodolite and level) and the correlation of surface and underground surveys.

4. . . . an applicant must produce to the Board with his application evidence that he is the holder of a higher national certificate in mining surveying having

*As amended by the Mining Examinations (Surveyors) (Amendment) Rules 1967.

attained such standard in qualifying therefor as the Board may require or has passed the Intermediate Examination of the Royal Institution of Chartered Surveyors in the Mining Surveying Section thereof:

Provided that the Board may, if they are satisfied that an applicant holds a qualification of a standard of knowledge and competency at least equal to one of the qualifications mentioned in this rule, obtained by examination after an equivalent course of study, exempt that applicant from the requirements of this rule.

5. . . .

(Rule 5 relates to examinations which ceased after May, 1963)

6. The times and places at which examinations are to held under these rules shall be published by the Board in such publications as the Board may from time to time think fit.

MINING QUALIFICATIONS
(MECHANICS AND ELECTRICIANS) RULES 1955*

PART I

General

1. In these rules:

'engineering' and 'plant' mean:

(*a*) in relation to an applicant for a mechanical engineer's certificate or a mechanic's certificate Class I or Class II, mechanical engineering and mechanical plant respectively;

(*b*) in relation to an applicant for an electrical engineer's certificate or an electrician's certificate Class I or Class II, electrical engineering and electrical plant respectively;

'the regulations' means the Coal and Other Mines (Mechanics and Electricians) Regulations 1965.

2. Any reduction of practical experience for which provision is made in these rules shall be such reduction in respect of any qualification or experience acquired by the applicant as the Board may determine having regard to any directions given to them by the Minister.

2A. The provisions of rule six and rule ten that an applicant must satisfy the Board that he has had practical experience in engineering for not less than five years must be complied with—

(*a*) in the case of an applicant for a Mechanical Engineer's Certificate or Electrical Engineer's Certificate who qualifies at a written examination held by the Board pursuant to head (i) of sub-paragraph (*c*) of paragraph (2) of rule seven, or an applicant for a Mechanic's Certificate Class I or Electrician's Certificate Class I who qualifies at a written examination held by the Board pursuant to head (i) of sub-paragraph (*b*) of paragraph (2) or head (i) of sub-paragraph (*c*) of paragraph (3) of rule eleven by—

(i) producing with his application evidence satisfactory to the Board that he has had, prior to making his application, not less than four years such experience; and

(ii) before or within nine months after that examination or within such longer period as the Board may in a particular case allow, producing evidence satisfactory to the Board that he has then had not less than five years such experience;

(*b*) in any other case by producing with his application evidence satisfactory to the Board that he has had, prior to making his application, not less than five years such experience.

---

*As amended by the Mining Qualifications (Mechanics and Electricians) (Amendment) Rules 1958, 1959 and 1962.

3. The times and places at which examinations are to be held by the Board under these rules shall be published by the Board in such publications as the Board may from time to time think fit.

PART II

Mechanical Engineers' Certificates and Electrical Engineers' Certificates

4. An applicant for a mechanical engineer's certificate or electrical engineer's certificate under the Regulations other than such a certificate expressed to be valid only with respect to mines of stratified ironstone must comply with the provisions of this part of these rules.

5. An applicant under this part of these rules must produce to the Board with his application, the following documents:

(*a*) two testimonials, on forms provided for the purpose by the Board, of his good character;

(*b*) particulars of his practical experience in engineering.

6. Subject to any reduction determined by the Board*, an applicant under this part of these rules must satisfy the Board that he has had practical experience in engineering for not less than five years, being experience acquired—

(*a*) during periods amounting in all to not less than two years, under training of a kind approved by the Board in one or more engineering workshops, and

(*b*) during periods amounting in all to not less than two years, in the use, examination, testing and maintenance of plant or the supervision of such operations; and

including experience acquired—

(i) during periods amounting in all to not less than eighteen months, either wholly at one or more mines to which the Act applies, or partly at one or more such mines and partly at one or more mines outside the United Kingdom of coal, stratified ironstone, shale or fireclay which provided equivalent experience, and

(ii) during periods amounting in all to not less than two hundred working days, below ground in one or more such mines.

7. An applicant under this part of these rules must—

either (1) qualify at a written examination held by the Board on the subjects specified in the first or second part (as the case may require) and the seventh part of the first schedule to these rules;†

or (2) (*a*) be the holder of—

(i) a higher national certificate in engineering;

(ii) a degree in engineering granted by any university in the United Kingdom;

---

*For reduced periods see note at end of these rules.

†In practice M.Q.B. only examines in mining legislation.

(iii) an honours certificate in engineering granted by the Association of Mining Electrical and Mechanical Engineers;* or

(iv) any other qualification in engineering which, in the opinion of the Board, has required the attainment of a standard not inferior to the standard required to have been attained by a holder of any qualification specified in the three last preceding heads of this sub-paragraph;† and

(*b*) in any case in which the Board so require, satisfy them that in the course of attaining any qualification specified in sub-paragraph (*a*) of this paragraph or the qualifying standard at any examination approved by the Board he has undergone examination in writing on each of the subjects specified in the first or second part (as the case may require) of the said first schedule; and

(*c*) (i) qualify at a written examination held by the Board on the subject of mining legislation,* or

(ii) satisfy the Board that in the course of attaining any qualification specified in sub-paragraph (*a*) of this paragraph he has attained a standard in the subject of mining legislation not inferior to the standard required to be attained by an applicant who qualifies in that subject under the last preceding head of this sub-paragraph;

or (3) in the case of any applicant born before the first day of January, nineteen hundred and twenty-six who has had special practical experience in engineering approved by the Board, satisfy the Board, who may for this purpose require him to present himself for an interview, that his standard of knowledge of each of the subjects specified in the first or second part (as the case may require) and the seventh part of the said first schedule is not inferior to the qualifying standard required to be attained by an applicant at a written examination held by the Board on those subjects for the purpose of paragraph (1) of this rule.

PART IIA

Mechanical Engineers' Certificates and Electrical Engineers' Certificates expressed to be valid only with respect to mines of stratified ironstone

7A. An applicant for a mechanical engineer's certificate or electrical engineer's certificate under the Regulations, being such a certificate expressed to be valid only with respect to mines of stratified ironstone, must comply with the provisions of this part of these rules.

7B. An applicant under this part of these rules must produce to the Board with his application, the following documents—

(*a*) two testimonials, on forms provided for the purpose by the Board, of his good character;

(*b*) particulars of his practical experience in engineering.

*The certificate at 7(2)(*a*)(iii) now exempts from M.Q.B. mining legislation examination.

†This is intended to provide for qualifications such as suitable degrees in engineering of overseas universities.

7C. An applicant under this part of these rules must—

either (1) (*a*) subject to any reduction determined by the Board, satisfy the Board that he has had practical experience in engineering for not less than five years, being experience acquired—

(i) during periods amounting in all to not less than two years, under training of a kind approved by the Board in one or more engineering workshops, and

(ii) during periods amounting in all to not less than two years, in the use, examination, testing and maintenance of plant and the supervision of such operations; and

(*b*) be the holder of—

(i) a higher national certificate in engineering;

(ii) a degree in engineering granted by any university in the United Kingdom;

(iii) an honours certificate in engineering granted by the Association of Mining Electrical and Mechanical Engineers; or

(iv) any other qualification in engineering which, in the opinion of the Board, has required the attainment of a standard not inferior to the standard required to have been attained by a holder of any qualification specified in the three last preceding heads of this sub-paragraph;

or (2) in the case of any applicant born before the first day of January, nineteen hundred and thirty-two, and subject to any reduction determined by the Board, satisfy the Board that he has had practical experience in engineering for not less than five years, being experience acquired—

(*a*) during periods amounting in all to not less than two years, under training of a kind approved by the Board in one or more engineering workshops, and

(*b*) during periods amounting in all to not less than two years, including periods amounting in all to not less than one hundred working days at one or more mines or quarries of stratified ironstone, in the use, examination, testing and maintenance of plant and the supervision of such operations.

Part III

Mechanics' Certificates Class I and Electricians' Certificates Class I

8. An applicant for a mechanic's certificate Class I or electrician's certificate Class I under the Regulations must comply with the provisions of this part of these rules.

9. An applicant under this part of these rules must produce to the Board with his application, the following documents—

(*a*) two testimonials, on forms provided for the purpose by the Board, of his good character;

(*b*) particulars of his practical experience in engineering.

10. Subject to any reduction determined by the Board*, an applicant under this Part of these rules must satisfy the Board that he has had practical experience in engineering for not less than five years, being experience of the kinds specified in rule six.

11. An applicant under this part of these rules must—

either (1) qualify at a written examination held by the Board on the subjects specified in the third or fourth part (as the case may require) and the seventh part of the first schedule to these rules;†

or (2) (*a*) be the holder of—

(i) a certificate in engineering specified in the first or second part (as the case may require) of the second schedule to these rules; or

(ii) (in the case of an applicant for a mechanic's certificate Class I) either of the certificates specified in Division A, and either of the certificates specified in Division B, of the third part of that schedule; or

(iii) (in the case of an applicant for an electrician's certificate Class I) either of the certificates specified in Division C, and either of the certificates specified in Division D, of the fourth part of that schedule; and

(*b*) (i) qualify at a written examination held by the Board on the subject of mining legislation‡, or

(ii) satisfy the Board that in the course of attaining any one or more of the certificates specified in the second schedule to these rules he has attained a standard in the subject of mining legislation not inferior to the standard required to be attained by an applicant who qualifies in that subject under the last preceding head of this sub-paragraph;‡

or (3) (*a*) be the holder of any qualification in engineering which, in the opinion of the Board, has required the attainment of a standard not inferior to the standard required to have been attained by an applicant who complies with the provisions of sub-paragraph (*a*) of paragraph (2) of this rule; and

(*b*) in any case in which the Board so require, satisfy them that in the course of attaining any qualification specified in the last preceding sub-paragraph or the qualifying standard at any examination approved by the Board he has undergone examination

---

*For reduced periods see note at end of these Rules.
†In practice M.Q.B. no longer holds examinations for Class I certificate.
‡All the certificates in Parts I and II of the Second Schedule to these rules except City and Guilds certificates issued before 1960 now exempt from M.Q.B. mining legislation examination.

in writing on each of the subjects specified in the third or fourth part (as the case may require) of the first schedule to these rules; and

(*c*) (i) qualify at a written examination held by the Board on the subject of mining legislation; or

(ii) satisfy the Board that in the course of attaining any qualification specified in sub-paragraph (*a*) of this paragraph he has attained a standard in the subject of mining legislation not inferior to the standard required to be attained by an applicant who qualifies in that subject under the last preceding head of this sub-paragraph;

or (4) in the case of any applicant born before the first day of January, nineteen hundred and twenty-six who has had special practical experience in engineering approved by the Board, satisfy the Board, who may for this purpose require him to present himself for an interview, that his standard of knowledge of each of the subjects specified in the third or fourth part (as the case may require) and the seventh part of the said first schedule is not inferior to the qualifying standard required to be attained by an applicant at a written examination held by the Board on those subjects for the purpose of paragraph (1) of this rule.

PART IV

Mechanics' Certificates Class II and Electricians' Certificates Class II

12. An applicant for a mechanic's certificate Class II or electrician's certificate Class II under the Regulations, must comply with the provisions of this part of these rules.

13. An applicant under this part of these rules must produce to the Board with his application a document specifying particulars of his practical experience in engineering.

14. Subject to any reduction determined by the Board*, an applicant under this part of these rules must satisfy the Board that he has had practical experience in engineering for not less than five years, being experience acquired—

(*a*) during periods amounting in all to not less than two years, under training of a kind approved by the Board in one or more engineering workshops, and

(*b*) during periods amounting in all to not less than two years, in the use, examination, testing and maintenance of plant; and

including experience of the kinds specified in sub-paragraphs (i) and (ii) of rule six.

15. An applicant under this part of these rules must—

either (1) qualify at a written examination held by the Board on the subjects specified in the fifth or sixth part (as the case may require) and the seventh part of the first schedule to these rules;†

*For reduced periods see note at end of these rules.
†In practice M.Q.B. does not hold examinations for Class II certificates.

or (2) be the holder of—

(i) (in the case of an applicant for a mechanic's certificate Class II) any one of the certificates specified in the first part of the third schedule to these rules;

(ii) (in the case of an applicant for an electrician's certificate Class II) any one of the certificates specified in the second part of that schedule; or

(iii) any other qualification in engineering which, in the opinion of the Board, has required the attainment of a standard not inferior to the standard required to have been attained by a holder of any one of the certificates specified in the first or second part (as the case may require) of that schedule;

or (3) in the case of any applicant born before the first day of January, nineteen hundred and twenty-six who has had special practical experience in engineering approved by the Board, satisfy the Board, who may for this purpose require him to present himself for an interview, that his standard of knowledge of each of the subjects specified in the fifth or sixth part (as the case may require) and the seventh part of the said first schedule is not inferior to the qualifying standard required to be attained by an applicant at a written examination held by the Board on those subjects for the purpose of paragraph (1) of this rule.

PART IVA

Mechanics' Certificates and Electricians' Certificates expressed to be valid only with respect to mines of stratified ironstone

11A. An applicant for a mechanic's certificate or electrician's certificate under the Regulations, being such a certificate expressed to be valid only with respect to mines of stratified ironstone, must comply with the provisions of this part of these rules.

11B. An applicant under this part of these rules must produce to the Board with his application a document specifying particulars of his practical experience in engineering.

11C. An applicant under this part of these rules must—

either (1) (*a*) subject to any reduction determined by the Board, satisfy the Board that he has had practical experience in engineering for not less than five years, being experience acquired—

(i) during periods amounting in all to not less than two years, under training of a kind approved by the Board in one or more engineering workshops, and

(ii) during periods amounting in all to not less than two years, in the use, examination, testing and maintenance of plant; and (*b*) be the holder of—

(i) (in the case of an applicant for a mechanic's certificate) any one of the certificates specified in the first part of the fourth schedule to these rules;

(ii) (in the case of an applicant for an electrician's certificate) any one of the certificates specified in the second part of that schedule; or

(iii) any other qualification in engineering which, in the opinion of the Board, has required the attainment of a standard not inferior to the standard required to have been attained by a holder of any one of the certificates specified in the first or second part (as the case may require) of that schedule;

or **(2)** in the case of any applicant born before the first day of January, nineteen hundred and thirty-two, and subject to any reduction determined by the Board, satisfy the Board that he has had practical experience in engineering for not less than five years, being experience acquired—

(*a*) during periods amounting in all to not less than two years, under training of a kind approved by the Board in one or more engineering workshops, and

(*b*) during periods amounting in all to not less than two years, including periods amounting in all to not less than one hundred working days at one or more mines or quarries of stratified ironstone, in the use, examination, testing and maintenance of plant.

FIRST SCHEDULE

Rules 7, 11 and 15

PART I

Mechanical Engineer's Certificate

Applied Mechanics and Materials
Applied Heat and Hydraulics
Colliery Mechanical Engineering

PART II

Electrical Engineer's Certificate

Electrical Technology
Colliery Electrical Engineering

PART III

Mechanic's Certificate Class I

Mechanics and Applied Heat
Workshop Technology and Practice
Colliery Mechanical Engineering

PART IV

Electrician's Certificate Class I

Electrical Technology
Colliery Electrical Testing and Practice

PART V

Mechanic's Certificate Class II

Mechanical Technology
Mechanical Practice

PART VI

Electrician's Certificate Class II

Electrical Technology
Electrical Practice

PART VII

All Certificates

Mining Leglisation

SECOND SCHEDULE

Rule 11

Name of Institution by which Certificate Granted	*Description of Certificate*

PART I

Mechanic's Certificate Class I

Association of Mining Electrical and Mechanical Engineers	First Class Certificate (Mechanical)
City and Guilds of London Institute	Colliery Mechanic's Advanced Certificate

PART II

Electrician's Certificate Class I

Association of Mining Electrical and Mechanical Engineers	First Class Certificate (Electrical)
City and Guilds of London Institute	Colliery Electrician's Advanced Certificate

PART III

Mechanic's Certificate Class I

DIVISION A

Institution of Mechanical Engineers and Department of Education and Science (jointly)	Ordinary National Certificate in Mechanical Engineering
Institution of Mechanical Engineers and Scottish Education Department (jointly)	Ordinary National Certificate in Mechanical Engineering

DIVISION B

Institution of Mining Engineers and Department of Education and Science (jointly)	Ordinary National Certificate in Mining (granted in respect of Group Three subjects)
Institution of Mining Engineers and Scottish Education Department (jointly)	Ordinary National Certificate in Mining (granted in respect of Group Three subjects)

Name of Institution by which Certificate granted	*Description of Certificate*

PART IV

Electrician's Certificate Class I

DIVISION C

Institution of Electrical Engineers and Department of Education and Science (jointly)	Ordinary National Certificate in Electrical Engineering
Institution of Electrical Engineers and Scottish Education Department (jointly)	Ordinary National Certificate in Electrical Engineering

DIVISION D

Institution of Mining Engineers and Department of Education and Science (jointly)	Ordinary National Certificate in Mining (granted in respect of Group Four subjects)
Institution of Mining Engineers and Scottish Education Department (jointly)	Ordinary National Certificate in Mining (granted in respect of Group Four subjects)

THIRD SCHEDULE

Rule 15

PART I

Mechanic's Certificate Class II

Association of Mining Electrical and Mechanical Engineers	Second Class Certificate (Mechanical)
City and Guilds of London Institute	Colliery Mechanic's Certificate
East Midland Educational Union	General Certificate in Mining (Mechanical)
Institution of Mining Engineers and Department of Education and Science (jointly)	Ordinary National Certificate in Mining (granted in respect of Group Three subjects)
Institution of Mining Engineers and Scottish Education Department (jointly)	Ordinary National Certificate in Mining (granted in respect of Group Three subjects)
Northern Counties Technical Examinations Council	General Certificate in Mining (Mechanical)
Union of Educational Institutions	Coal Mining Certificate (Mechanical Section)
Union of Lancashire and Cheshire Institutes	Mining Industry General Certificate (Mechanical)
Yorkshire Council for Further Education	Colliery Mechanic's Certificate (Intermediate Grade)

PART II

Electrician's Certificate Class II

Association of Mining Electrical and Mechanical Engineers	Second Class Certificate (Electrical)
City and Guilds of London Institute	Colliery Electrician's Certificate
East Midland Educational Union	General Certificate in Mining (Electrical)

Name of Institution by which Certificate granted	*Description of Certificate*
Institution of Mining Engineers and Department of Education and Science (jointly)	Ordinary National Certificate in Mining (granted in respect of Group Four subjects)
Institution of Mining Engineers and Scottish Education Department (jointly)	Ordinary National Certificate in Mining (granted in respect of Group Four subjects)
Northern Counties Technical Examinations Council	General Certificate in Mining (Electrical)
Union of Educational Institutions	Coal Mining Certificate (Electrical Section)
Union of Lancashire and Cheshire Institutes	Mining Industry General Certificate (Electrical)
Yorkshire Council for Further Education	Colliery Electrician's Certificate (Intermediate Grade)

FOURTH SCHEDULE

Rule 11C

PART I

Mechanic's Certificate expressed to be valid only with respect of mines of stratified ironstone

Institution of Mechanical Engineers and Department of Education and Science (jointly)	Ordinary National Certificate in Mechanical Engineering
Institution of Mechanical Engineers and Scottish Education Department (jointly)	Ordinary National Certificate in Mechanical Engineering
Association of Mining Electrical and Mechanical Engineers	Second Class Certificate (Mechanical)
City of Guilds of London Institute	Colliery Mechanic's Certificate
Institution of Mining Engineers and Department of Education and Science (jointly)	Ordinary National Certificate in Mining (granted in respect of Group Three subjects)
Institution of Mining Engineers and Scottish Education Department (jointly)	Ordinary National Certificate in Mining (granted in respect of Group Three subjects)

PART II

Electrician's Certificate expressed to be valid only with respect to mines of stratified ironstone

Institution of Electrical Engineers and Ministry of Education (jointly)	Ordinary National Certificate in Electrical Engineering
Institution of Electrical Engineers and Scottish Education Department (jointly)	Ordinary National Certificate in Electrical Engineering
Association of Mining Electrical and Mechanical Engineers	Second Class Certificate (Electrical)
City and Guilds of London Institute	Colliery Electrician's Certificate
Institution of Mining Engineers and Department of Education and Science (jointly)	Ordinary National Certificate in Mining (granted in respect of Group Four subjects)

Name of Institution by which Certificate granted	*Description of Certificate*
Institution of Mining Engineers and Scottish Education Department (jointly)	Ordinary National Certificate in Mining (granted in respect of Group Four subjects)

SYLLABUSES

associated with the subjects in the First Schedule

Syllabus for Mechanical Engineer

Applied Mechanics and Materials

Force diagrams for frames structures. The link polygon.

Stress and strain due to tensile, compressive and shear forces.

Relationship between elastic constants. Combined stresses.

Eccentric loads. Resilience. Sudden and fluctuating loads.

Fatigue in metals. Torsion in shafts. Stresses in thin walled and thick walled cylinders under internal and external pressure.

Beams. Bending moments and shearing force diagrams. Stresses due to bending and moment of resistance. Section moduli.

Empirical formulae for struts.

Velocity and acceleration. Moment of inertia and radius of gyration. Centrifugal force. Brakes and dynamometers.

Transmission of power by shafts, belts, chain, gears and fluid couplings.

Clutches.

The mechanical properties of ferrous and non-ferrous materials. Safety factors. Heat treatment—annealing, normalising and tempering. Structure of alloys. Equilibrium diagrams. The iron-carbon diagram. Structure of carbon steels. Special steels and other alloys used in mining. Effects of work on structure and mechanical properties. Testing of materials. Common machines and instruments for investigation of mechanical properties. Forms of specimen, testing procedure and expression of results. B.S.I. specifications for materials.

Applied Heat and Hydraulics

Laws of thermodynamics. Characteristic equation of a gas.

Total heat and internal energy. Specific heats of gases.

Isothermal and adiabatic changes. Entropy. Temperature-entropy and total heat-entropy diagram for steam. The Carnot and the Rankine cycle. Callendar's steam tables.

Combustion. Calorific value of fuels. Air-fuel ratio.

Furnaces and draught. Flue gas analysis. Boilers, feedwater heaters, air heaters and superheaters. Boiler trials and heat balances.

The steam engine. Compounding and condensing. Effects of superheating.

Steam jacketing.

The steam turbine. Flow through nozzles. Impulse and reaction turbines.

Compounding. Velocity diagrams. Blade thrust. Stage efficiency.

Condensing plant. Performances and testing of steam plant and heat balances.

Principles and general application of gas turbines.

The internal combustion engine. Ideal working of cycles and their representation. Air-standard efficiencies, actual and ideal.

Volumetric efficiencies. Testing of I.C. engines and heat balances.

Theory of air compression. Conditions for maximum efficiency.

Stage compression. Flow of air in pipes: metering.

Hydraulics. Total energy in a fluid. Bernoulli's theorem and its applications. Flow through nozzles. Stream line and turbulent flow. Measurement of flow by orifices, notches, weirs and venturi meters.

Friction in pipes. Theory of reciprocating and rotary pumps.

Colliery Mechanical Engineering A

Shaft-sinking equipment, supports for water and compressed air pipes, cables, etc. Methods of guiding skips and cages.

The application and relative merits of parallel, clutched and bi-cylindroconical drum and Koepe winders with single and multiple ropes; winding diagrams. The advantages and disadvantages of skips and cages. Precautions which can be taken in the headframe, the sump and the engine to prevent over-winding or to minimise its effects. Types of brakes and the effect of the magnitude and direction of motion of unbalanced loads on rates of deceleration. The effect of the lay-out of the plant on the drum, sheave, rope, pulleys and headframe. Methods of loading and unloading cages and skips.

Types, construction, selection and installation of ropes. Cappings and attachments for winding and haulage ropes. Inspection, maintenance, re-capping and lubrication.

The application and relative merits of transport by wire ropes, locomotives, conveyors and trackless vehicles. Types of rope haulages and locomotives. Tracks, rolling stock, safety devices and manriding.

Types of coal cutting, loading and conveying machines, pneumatic picks, drilling machines, bits, rods and rigs. Pneumatic and mechanical stowing plant. Hydraulic props and chocks.

Application, lay-out and relative merits of reciprocating, turbine and other pumps. Their inspection and maintenance, including cleaning of pipes. Fire fighting systems and apparatus.

Colliery Mechanical Engineering B

The application, lay-out and relative merits of single and multi-stage reciprocating compressors and turbo-compressors both above and below ground. Inspection and maintenance and other precautions essential to both safety and proper operation.

Types and characteristics of mine fans. Methods of reversing the ventilation. Auxiliary and booster fans.

Steam power; types of boilers and accessories; stoking: ash disposal: feed water treatment. Lay-out and equipment of coal preparation plant, refuse disposal plant and sidings. Locomotives.

The application and relative merits of the usual types of A.C. and D.C. motors for driving mechanical plant above and below ground.

Systems necessary for the efficient maintenance of mechanical plant for various sizes and types of collieries. Detailed maintenance schedules for major items of plant.

Spare machines and spare parts.

Workshop stores and any other facilities for the repair of plant.

Necessary staff.

Siting, lay-out and organisation of workshops at the mine. The inter-relationship of the mine workshops to any central workshops for several mines and to services provided by manufacturers of plant and apparatus.

Ordering and inspection of materials, spares and plant.

Essential records.

Mining Legislation

The provisions of the Mines and Quarries Act and Regulations relating to the above subjects and to the duties of the mechanics of the mine.

Syllabus for Mechanic Class I

MECHANICS AND APPLIED HEAT

Measurement of force and its effects. Triangle and parallelogram of forces.

Resolution and composition of forces.

Moments and their applications. Centre of gravity.

Stress and strain. Young's modulus. Work power and energy.

Simple machines. Friction. Velocity ratio, mechanical advantage and mechanical efficiency. Transmission of power.

Laws of linear motion: velocity and acceleration. Force, mass and acceleration. Momentum and kinetic energy.

Angular velocity and acceleration and simple applications. Simple problems in hoisting and traction.

Strength of beams in relation to breadth, depth and span.

Behaviour of metals in tension, compression and shear. Simple treatment of torsion and bending. Testing of materials.

Factor of safety.

Hydraulics. Pressure on a submerged surface. Flow of water through pipes and orifices and over notches.

Applied heat. Heat and work. Mechanical equivalent of heat.

Relation between temperature, pressure and volume of a gas.

Properties of steam. Steam tables and their use. Dryness fraction.

Brief treatment of steam boilers, engines, turbines and condensing plant.

Principles of combustion. Calorific values.

Reciprocating steam engines. Mean effective pressure, indicated horse-power, brake horse-power and steam consumption.

Simple theory of air compression. Ventilating fans. Air flow in pipes and ducts.

Simple boiler and engine tests.

WORKSHOP TECHNOLOGY AND PRACTICE

Materials. The composition, physical properties and uses of plain carbon and alloy steels, brass, gun-metal, bronze, white metals and light alloys with special reference to their workability and applications.

Heat treatment. Simple consideration of the heat treatment of plain carbon steels. Normalising, annealing, tempering, and hardening. Effect of carbon content. Meaning of critical point and critical range. Colour method of judging temperature and its limitations. Use of a small tool furnace for single point tools.

Measurement and gauging. Elements of inter-changeability and limit gauging.

Limits and fits for plain and screwed work. B.S.I. standards. B.S.1916, part 1 and 2.

Tolerances: limits: clearance, interference and transition fits. Types of limit gauges and adjustable gauges.

Cutting tools. Cutting action of lathe tools, milling cutters, drills, taps and dies. Tool shapes and correct cutting angles, rake and clearance for different materials and purposes.

Machine tools. A general knowledge of the constructional features, accessories and use of lathes, saws, plain milling machines, drilling, shaping, slotting, planing and grinding machines. Conditions for accuracy. Marking out for accurate work. Coolants and lubricants.

Soldering, brazing and welding by electric and flame processes. Flame cutting. Precautions against fire.

Exercises in inspection, maintenance and repair of mining machinery.

Workshop drawings and blue prints. Exercises in reading.

B.S.308. First angle and third angle projection.

Safety measures and statutory regulations affecting the engineering workshop.

Colliery Mechanical Engineering

Shafts, methods of guiding skips and cages. Supports for water and compressed air pipes, cables, etc.

The inspection and maintenance of steam and electric winders. Precautions which can be taken in the headframe, the sump and the engine, to prevent overwinding or to minimise its effects. The testing of automatic contrivances and brakes. Plant for loading and unloading the cages and skips.

Types of ropes and their construction, selection and installation. Rope cappings and attachments for both winding and haulage. Inspection, maintenance, re-capping and lubrication.

Types of rope haulages, conveyors and locomotives. Arrangement of engine houses and garages and ancillary mechanical plant in haulage systems. Inspection and testing of manriding plant and of the brakes of haulages and locomotives.

General outline of types of face machinery and inspection and maintenance thereof.

General outline of inbye and main pumping plant and also of fire fighting systems and apparatus.

Generation and distribution of compressed air on the surface and underground. Precautions essential to safety.

Installation and maintenance of surface and underground fans.

Types of surface plant and the installation, inspection and maintenance thereof.

Mining Legislation

Provisions of the Mines and Quarries Act and Regulations for steam generating plant, shafts and winding apparatus, haulage apparatus, ventilating plant, all other machinery, gear and other appliances of the mine, and for surface lines and sidings, etc., and the duties of the mechanics of the mine.

Syllabus for Mechanic Class II

Mechanical Technology

Force and its effects. Tension, compression and shear. Units of force.

Stress and strain. Young's modulus. Composition and resolution of forces.

The parallelogram and triangle of forces.

Moments and their practical applications.

Friction and brakes. Lubricants and lubrication. Work and power.

The inclined plane. Machines. Velocity ratio, mechanical advantage and efficiency. Transmission of power by belts, ropes and gears.

Brief account of velocity, acceleration, momentum and inertia and their application in simple haulage and winding problems.

An elementary treatment of steam and its properties. Dryness fraction. Superheat. Total heat in steam. Outline of construction and principles of operation of boilers, feed pumps, feed heater, steam engines and condensers.

The meaning of indicated horsepower and brake horsepower.

Steam consumption. Steam pipes and valves. Provision for expansion and drainage. Lagging.

Outline of construction and principle of operation of I.C. engines used at collieries.

Generation, transmission and use of compressed air in mines.

Syphons and pumps. Measuring water and quantities and pressure.

Flow through pipes. Pipe friction.

Properties and use of cast iron, wrought iron and steel. Other alloys used in mining.

Chains and lifting gear. Haulage and winding ropes, their construction and examination.

Mechanical Practice and Regulations

Colliery workshops and their equipment. A general knowledge of the use of bench tools, lathes, drilling machines, grinders and millers. Consideration of speeds and feeds for machine tools. Marking out for hand and machine work. Use of gauges, blue prints and drawings.

A general outline of soldering, brazing, forging, electric and forge-welding, flame welding and cutting.

Heat treatment—normalising, annealing, hardening and tempering.

Operation, inspection and maintenance of:—(*a*) Steam plant, screening and cleaning plant and other machinery on the surface; (*b*) Winding plant, shaft equipment, cages, decking plant, creepers and tipplers; (*c*) Haulage engines, locomotives, conveyors, coal-cutters and other mining machinery, including the fencing thereof; (*d*) Reciprocating and rotary pumps, water pipes for pumping, fire fighting and dust suppression, air compressors and auxiliary ventilators.

Systems of underground haulage and the necessary equipment and safety devices.

Rope capping and rope splicing.

Bearings: types and properties, arrangements, alignment and lubrication.

Special dangers due to firedamp, coal dust and frictional heating underground.

The appropriate provisions of the Mines and Quarries Act and Regulations and the statutory duties of the mechanics of the mine should be included in the work of the syllabus.

Syllabus for Electrical Engineer

Electrical Technology A

Direct current; general circuit theory. Magnetic properties of materials. The magnetic circuit.

Alternating current circuit principles. Simple treatment of resonance and harmonics. Inductance, capacitance, reactance, impedance, power and power factor related to single and 3-phase circuits. Principles and economics of power factor correction.

Measurement of power and power factor in a balance 3-phase circuit; use of instrument transformers. Simple network calculations in D.C. and A.C. circuits. Calculations of distribution and short circuit current ratings for switchgear. Voltage drop and power loss in transmission: power calculations in D.C. and 3-phase circuits.

Simple treatment of unbalance in 3-phase circuits.

Principles of common methods of rectification with suitable circuits and control; applications.

Characteristics and efficiency of filament and discharge types of lamps. Factors governing choice of type. Lighting calculations.

Electrical Technology B

Construction, insulation and installation of high-voltage cables and overhead lines.

The D.C. generator and the alternator: construction and excitation; voltage regulation; parallel running and load adjustment; synchronising 3-phase machines.

The single phase transformer: principles and construction; cooling; installation; voltage regulation. The auto-transformer. The 3-phase transformer; connections and parallel operation.

Principles and construction of D.C. and A.C. motors used in colliery plant; starting and speed control; electric braking.

Motor generators, converters and rectifiers.

Characteristics, testing and efficiency of generators, transformers and motors.

Storage batteries: charging, maintenance and use.

Electrical welding equipment.

Colliery Electrical Engineering

Armoured cables, flexible cables, joints and repairs.

Switchgear for colliery use.

General lay-out of colliery electrical plant; public supplies, power stations, sub-stations and their equipment, fire protection methods. The colliery earthing system. Earth leakage protection. Selective protection of transmission lines, alternators and transformers; metering equipment.

Torque characteristics of typical colliery motor loads; suitable motors and starting methods. Special problems of coal face machinery; remote control; sequence starting and conveyor belt protection.

Electric winding systems; winding load cycle and load equalising; safety devices. Haulage and shaft signalling systems; telephones.

Electric locomotives, battery and trolley types.

Firedamp: occurrence, properties and ignition; gas testing by flame lamp and special apparatus. Principles of flameproofing and intrinsic safety.

Lay-out and equipment for the maintenance of portable electric lamps. Mains lighting, surface and underground.

Systematic inspection and testing involving insulation, earth continuity, intrinsically-safe apparatus, flameproof equipment and exploders.

Mining Legislation

The statutory provisions relating to:—

(*a*) the use of electricity in mines and the duties of the electricians of the mine;

(*b*) the installation, examination, testing and maintenance of electrical apparatus and cable at mines.

Syllabus for Electrician Class I

Electrical Technology

The heating, chemical and magnetic effects of an electric current with appropriate examples: fuses, bells, relays and tripcoils. Primary and secondary cells. Electrolysis.

Conductors and insulators. The electric circuit. Calculations on resistance, divided circuits, resistivity and voltage drop in D.C. circuits. Electrical units and measurement of resistance.

Electromagnetic induction. Principles of the induction coil, transformer, and generator.

Types and principles of operation of D.C. generators.

Force on a conductor carrying current in a magnetic field. D.C. motors, their operation and control.

Alternating currents. Single phase circuit. Frequency, r.m.s. value. Simple treatments of inductance, capacitance and impedance. Phase difference, vector representation. Power and power factor. The 3-phase system. 4-wire and 3-wire systems. Star and delta connections. The 3-phase induction motor: principles and action; cage and wound rotor types. Transformers: single and 3-phase.

Simple power and energy calculations applicable to D.C. and A.C. circuits.

Brief description of methods of converting alternating current to direct current.

Measurement of candle power and illumination.

Colliery Electrical Testing and Practice

Materials used in mining electrical plant. Construction of cables, including flexible cables; safe location and installation. Joints and cable couplers. Repair of cables. Insulation and continuity testing and simple fault location. Overload and earth leakage protection of circuits. Fuses and circuit breakers. Construction and use of ammeters, voltmeters and wattmeters on D.C. and A.C. circuits.

Connections, performances, control and maintenance of D.C. and A.C. generators and motors in common use; oil and airbreak control gear. Construction and use of circuit diagrams.

The 3-phase transformer: applications: housing.

Portable electric lamps. The storage battery and its maintenance. Equipment and procedure for charging. Mains lighting, surface and underground. Installation and testing of lighting circuits. Compressed air lamps.

Earthing of colliery electrical apparatus. The colliery earthing system. Earth leakage protection. Remote control systems.

Firedamp: occurrence, properties and ignition; gas testing by flame lamp and special apparatus. Principles of flameproofing and intrinsic safety.

Open sparking danger. Flameproof construction and maintenance. Intrinsically-safe apparatus.

Signalling systems for shafts and roadways. Simple telephone systems.

Installation and testing of signalling and telephone systems. Testing of exploders.

The Electrician's log book and reports.

Mining Legislation

The statutory provisions relating to:—

(*a*) the use of electricity and the duties of the electricians of the mine;

(*b*) the installation, examination, testing and maintenance of electrical apparatus and cable at mines.

Syllabus for Electrician Class II

Electrical Technology

Note. Emphasis should be laid throughout on the practical and experimental approach rather than on a mathematical treatment.

Heating, chemical and magnetic effects of an electric current.

Magnetic fields. Permanent and electro-magnets and their applications.

Principle of bells, relays, trips and telephones.

Simple electric circuits. Practical units—volt, ampere, watt, ampere-hour, kilowatt-hour. Horse-power. Ohm's law.

Conductors and insulators. Resistance and its measurement.

Voltage drop in cables.

Leclanche cells and dry batteries. Lead-acid and alkaline accumulators.

Elementary principles of the D.C. generator. Methods of excitation.

Voltage control.

The D.C. motor. Principle of operation. Motor types and their application.

Starters and speed control.

Comparison of A.C. and D.C. circuits. Outline of the operation of the alternator.

Explanation of common terms relating to A.C. circuits—inductance, capacitance, reactance, impedance, K.V.A., power and power factor. Elementary treatment of the 3-phase circuit. Star and delta connections.

Elementary principle of the induction motor. Squirrel cage and wound rotor motors and their control gear.

Principle of the transformer. Mining transformers.

Electrical instruments—ammeters, voltmeters, wattmeters and ohmmeters.

Shunts, multipliers and instrument transformers.

Note. In the treatment of the above subjects due regard should be paid to the application of the principles to the Mining Industry.

Electrical Practice and Regulations

Tools, materials and instruments used by the electrician.

Jointing and insulating. Simple circuit diagrams.

Installation and testing of signalling and telephone apparatus for haulage and winding.

Care and maintenance of miners' electric lamps, gas detectors, shot-firing batteries and pneumatic lighting units. Installation and testing of lighting circuits. Lighting transformers.

General outline of distribution from surface to coal face.

Types of cables and their construction; installation in shafts and roads.

Cable jointing. Connection of armoured cables to fixed apparatus. Flexible and semi-flexible cables and their connectors.

Continuity, conductivity and insulation tests. Simple methods of fault location.

Common faults in motors, switches and control gear. Simple repair work, mechanical and electrical.

Installation and operation of A.C. and D.C. motors and their control gear.

Methods of reversal and speed control.

Installation and maintenance of switchgear and transformers.

Circuit protection against over-current, under-voltage, earth leakage.

Interlocks and remote control and examples of sequence starting and conveyor belt protection.

Open sparking. Detection of firedamp with a flame safety lamp. Flameproof enclosure and intrinsic safety.

Routine tests and examinations. Importance of isolating and earthing before examination. The electrician's log book and reports.

Statutory provisions governing the use of electricity in mines.

Notes on the Mechanics and Electricians Rules

The practical experience required by the Mining Qualifications Board before a certificate can be granted is as follows:—

(*a*) Experience in engineering for not less than 5 years which must include at least 2 years under training of a kind approved by the Board in one or more engineering workshops and not less than 2 years in the use, examination testing and maintenance of plant. This experience must also include at least 18 months at a mine and at least 200 working days below ground in a mine: in certain cases these periods can be reduced to 9 months and 100 days. Up to one year's drawing office experience may be counted towards the total 5 years' requirement.

(*b*) In the case of an engineering graduate or the holder of a Higher National Diploma in engineering the 5 year period is reduced to 3 years and each of the 2 year periods to 18 months. Up to six months' drawing office experience may be counted towards the total 3 years' requirement.

(*c*) Completion of the National Coal Board's Engineering Training Scheme and certain National Coal Board Apprenticeships, in Mechanical and Electrical Engineering are accepted as fulfilling the practical experience requirements.

THE MINING EXAMINATIONS (DEPUTIES) RULES 1966*

Application for deputy's certificate

4. Each application to the Board for a deputy's certificate must be accompanied by—

(*a*) the applicant's birth certificate, or other evidence of his age satisfactory to the Board;

(*b*) particulars of his experience below ground in mines of coal, stratified ironstone, shale or fireclay in the United Kingdom (including the periods of his employment in each category of work), certified by or on behalf of the managers of the mines in which he was so employed;

(*c*) particulars of any experience below ground in a mine of any other class or description (including the periods of his employment and the categories of work); and

(*d*) evidence of qualifications held by him upon which he relies as enabling him to comply with any provisions of these rules.

ALL MINES CERTIFICATE

5.—(1) An applicant for an all mines certificate must be the holder of a shotfirer's certificate granted by the Minister of Technology on the recommendation of the Board or of a service certificate made under paragraph (6) of article 12 of the Coal Mines (Explosives) Order 1951 and must, subject to any reduction of practical experience determined by the Board pursuant to Rule 7, comply with one of the following paragraphs of this rule.

(2) An applicant for an all mines certificate who has obtained one of the certificates specified in Schedule 1 to these rules must—

(*a*) have had not less than four years practical experience below ground either wholly in one or more mines of coal, stratified ironstone, shale or fireclay in the United Kingdom, or partly in one or more such mines and partly in one or more mines of coal, stratified ironstone, shale or fireclay, outside the United Kingdom with respect to which the Board are satisfied that it or they provided equivalent experience of which not less than eighteen months was at the face of the workings;

(*b*) have attained the age of twenty-three years; and

(*c*) either have obtained one of the certificates specified in Schedule 2 to these rules or pass a practical test held by the Board† or a practical test held by the National Coal Board and approved by the Board for the qualification of deputies in which he satisfies the examiners that he can make reports adequate for a deputy, orally and in writing, on inspections.

(3) An applicant for an all mines certificate who has obtained one of the degrees, diplomas, associateships or certificates specified in Schedule 3 to these rules must—

(*a*) have completed the National Coal Board's Mining Engineering Training Scheme or an apprenticeship in Mining Engineering under the National

*As amended by Mining Examinations (Deputies) (Amendment) Rules 1967
†In practice M.Q.B. do not hold tests.

Coal Board's Student Apprenticeship Scheme or have had not less than three years practical experience as aforesaid, of which not less than eighteen months was at the face of the workings;

(*b*) have attained the age of twenty-three years; and

(*c*) either have obtained one of the certificates specified in Schedule 2 to these rules or pass a practical test held by the Board* or a practical test held by the National Coal Board and approved by the Board for the qualifications of deputies in which he satisfies the examiners that he can make reports adequate for a deputy, orally and in writing, on inspections.

(4) An applicant for an all mines certificate who does not hold any of the degrees, diplomas, associateships or certificates specified in Schedules 1 and 3 to these rules must—

(*a*) have had not less than five years practical experience as aforesaid, of which not less than two years was at the face of the workings;

(*b*) have attained the age of twenty-five years;

(*c*) have completed a course of technical instruction approved by the Board for the training of deputies; and

(*d*) either—

(i) have obtained the certificate specified in Part I of Schedule 2 to these rules; or

(ii) pass a written examination in the subjects of Mining Science, Mining Practice and Mining Machinery approved by the Board for the purpose of qualification of deputies, and held by one of the bodies specified in Schedule 4 to these rules, and within three years of passing such written examination, pass a practical test held by the Board* or a practical test held by the National Coal Board and approved by the Board for the qualification of deputies in which he satisfies the examiners that he can make reports adequate for a deputy, orally and in writing, on inspections:

provided that an applicant born before 1st January, 1934 need not comply with sub-paragraph (*d*) of this paragraph if he has either obtained the certificate specified in Part II of Schedule 2 to these rules or passes an oral test held by the Board* or held by the National Coal Board and approved by the Board for the qualification of deputies in which he satisfies the examiners that he has sufficient knowledge of the matters specified in Schedule 5 to these rules to enable him to perform the duties of a deputy and within three years of passing such oral tests passes a practical test held by the Board* or a practical test held by the National Coal Board and approved by the Board for the qualification of deputies in which he satisfies the examiners that he can make reports adequate for a deputy, orally and in writing, on inspections.

Restricted Certificate

6.—(1) An applicant for a restricted certificate must, subject to any reduction

*In practice M.Q.B. do not hold tests.

of practical experience determined by the Board pursuant to Rule 7, comply with one of the following paragraphs of this rule.

(2) An applicant for a restricted certificate who has obtained one of the certificates specified in Schedule 1 to these rules must—

(*a*) have had not less than four years practical experience as aforesaid, of which not less than eighteen months was at the face of the workings;

(*b*) have attained the age of twenty-three years; and

(*c*) either have obtained one of the certificates specified in Schedule 2 to these rules or pass a practical test held by the Board* or a practical test held by the National Coal Board and approved by the Board for the qualification of deputies in which he satisfies the examiners that he can make reports adequate for a deputy, orally and in writing, on inspections.

(3) An applicant for a restricted certificate who has obtained one of the degrees, diplomas, associateships or certificates specified in Schedule 3 to these rules must—

(*a*) have completed the National Coal Board's Mining Engineering Training Scheme or an apprenticeship in Mining Engineering under the National Coal Board's Student Apprenticeship Scheme or have had not less than three years practical experience below ground in a mine as aforesaid, of which not less than eighteen months was at the face of the workings;

(*b*) have attained the age of twenty-three years; and

(*c*) either have obtained one of the certificates specified in Schedule 2 to these rules or pass a practical test held by the Board* or a practical test held by the National Coal Board and approved by the Board for the qualification of deputies in which he satisfies the examiners that he can make reports adequate for a deputy, orally and in writing, on inspections.

(4) An applicant for a restricted certificate who does not hold any of the degrees, diplomas, associateships or certificates specified in Schedules 1 and 3 to these rules must—

(*a*) have had not less than five years practical experience as aforesaid, of which not less than two years was at the face of the workings;

(*b*) have attained the age of twenty-five years; and

(*c*) either—

(i) have obtained one of the certificates specified in Schedule 2 to these rules; or

(ii) pass an oral test held by the Board* or an oral test held by the National Coal Board and approved by the Board for the qualification of deputies in which he satisfies the examiners that he has sufficient knowledge of the matters set out in Schedule 5 to these rules to enable him to perform the duties of a deputy, and, except in the case of an applicant who is the holder of a shotfirer's certificate granted by the Minister of Technology on the recommendation of

*In practice M.Q.B. do not hold tests.

the Board or of a service certificate made under paragraph (6) of article 12 of the Coal Mines (Explosives) Order 1951, in which he also satisfies the examiners that he has sufficient knowledge of the duties of a shotfirer to enable him to perform the duties of a deputy, and pass a practical test held by the Board* or a practical test held by the National Coal Board and approved by the Board for the qualification of deputies in which he satisfies the examiners that he can make reports adequate for a deputy, orally and in writing, on inspections.

Reduction of practical experience for applicants with special qualifications

7.—(1) The Board may in respect of the special qualifications or experience of any applicant for a deputy's certificate (including the performance of national service) reduce in his case the experience required under such of the provisions of rules 5 and 6 as may apply to him;

Provided that the period of practical experience below ground shall not be reduced to less than three years nor the period of experience at the face of the workings be reduced to less than one year.

(2) An applicant, who desires the Board to reduce in his case the practical experience so required, must attach to his application for a deputy's certificate particulars of any special qualifications or experience on which he relies.

*In practice M.Q.B. do not hold tests.

SCHEDULE 1

(*Certificates enabling an applicant to make application under rules* 5 (2) *and* 6 (2))

Awarding Body	*Description of Certificate or Diploma*
City and Guilds of London Institute	Coal Mining Certificate Coal Mining Craft Certificate Coal Mining Advanced Certificate Coal Mining Technician's Certificate
East Midland Educational Union	General Certificate in Mining Craft Certificate in Mining
Institution of Mining Engineers and Department of Education and Science (jointly)	Ordinary National Certificate in Mining
Institution of Mining Engineers and Scottish Education Department (jointly)	Ordinary National Certificate in Mining
Northern Counties Technical Examinations Council	General Certificate in Mining Mining Craft Certificate
Union of Educational Institutions	Coal Mining Certificate Craft Certificate in Coal Mining (Production Group)
Union of Lancashire and Cheshire Institutes	Mining Industry General Certificate Mining Industry Craft Course, 3rd Year, Section A—Mining Certificate
Welsh Joint Education Committee	Mining Certificate
Yorkshire Council for Further Education	General Mining Certificate Coal Mining Certificate

SCHEDULE 2

PART I

(Certificate valid for the purposes of rule 5 (2) (*c*), 5 (3) (*c*) and 5 (4) (*d*) (i), and rule 6 (2) (*c*), 6 (3) (*c*) and 6 (4) (*c*))

Awarding Body	*Name of Certificate*
Union of Lancashire and Cheshire Institutes	Colliery Deputy's Proficiency Certificate

PART II

(Certificate valid for the purposes of rule 5 (2) (*c*), 5 (3) (*c*), proviso to rule 5 (4) and rule 6 (2) (*c*), 6 (3) (*c*) and 6 (4) (*c*))

Union of Lancashire and Cheshire Institutes	Colliery Deputy's Certificate

SCHEDULE 3

(*Degrees, diplomas, associateships and certificates enabling an applicant to make application under rules* 5 (3) *and* 6 (3))

Degrees

University	*Name of Degree*
Benares Hindu	B.Sc. in Mining Engineering
Birmingham	B.Sc. in Mining*
Durham	B.Sc. in Applied Science (Mining Engineering)*
Edinburgh	B.Sc. in Mining*
Glasgow	B.Sc. in Mining Engineering*
Heriot-Watt	B.Sc. in Mining
Leeds	B.Sc. in Mining
	M.Sc. (Mining)†
London	B.Sc. (Eng.) in Mining
Newcastle upon Tyne	B.Sc. in Applied Science (Mining Engineering)
Nottingham	B.Sc. in Mining
Sheffield	B.Eng. (Mining)*
	M.Eng. (Mining)*
Strathclyde	B.Sc. in Mining Engineering
Wales	B.Sc. in Mining Engineering

Diplomas, Associateships and Certificates

Awarding Body	*Name of Diploma, Associateship or Certificate*
Durham University	Diploma in Mining Engineering*
Glasgow University	Certificate of Proficiency in Mining*
Heriot-Watt College, Edinburgh	Associateship in Mining*
Indian School of Mines, Dhanbad	Associateship in Mining Engineering
Leeds University	Diploma in Mining*
Royal School of Mines, London	Associateship in Mining
Royal College of Science and Technology, Glasgow	Associateship in Mining Engineering*; Diploma in Mining Engineering
University College of South Wales and Monmouthshire	Diploma in Metalliferous Mining
Wigan and District Mining and Technical College	Diploma in Mining*
Institution of Mining Engineers and the Department of Education and Science (jointly)	Higher National Certificate in Mining; National Diploma in Mining
Institution of Mining Engineers and the Scottish Education Department (jointly)	Higher National Certificate in Mining; National Diploma in Mining

*No longer granted.

†No longer accepted.

SCHEDULE 4

(Examining bodies for the purposes of rule 5 (4) (*d*) (ii))

East Midland Educational Union.
Northern Counties Technical Examinations Council.
Scottish Association for National Certificates and Diplomas.
Union of Educational Institutions.
Union of Lancashire and Cheshire Institutes.
Welsh Joint Education Committee.
Yorkshire Council for Further Education.

SCHEDULE 5

(Subjects of oral examination under proviso to rule 5 (4) and under rule 6 (4) (*c*))

(i) methods of working and haulage;
(ii) nature of the atmosphere and mine gases; ventilation; dust control;
(iii) support of roof and sides; withdrawal of supports;
(iv) maintenance of direction of roadways;
(v) flame and electric safety lamps;
(vi) safety in use of machinery;
(vii) fires; fire-fighting and equipment; and
(viii) law applying to safety and health in mines.

MINING EXAMINATIONS
(SHOT FIRERS) RULES 1952

An applicant for a shot firer's certificate must either—

(*a*) be the holder of a certificate of qualification in shot firing approved by the Board for the purposes of these rules*; or

(*b*) satisfy the examiners at an oral and practical test held by the Board† under these rules that he has sufficient knowledge of the following matters to enable him to perform the statutory duties of a shot firer:—

(i) inflammable gas and gas testing (including tests with gas detection apparatus);

(ii) dust suppression and fumes in relation to shot firing;

(iii) use and handling of explosives and detonators;

(iv) drilling and placing of, and breaks in, shot holes;

(v) shots fired singly and in rounds; use of delay detonators; testing of circuits and treatment of miss-fires; determination of danger zones and safe shelter; examinations after shot firing;

(vi) the keeping of records; and

(vii) the law relating to shot firers.

---

*The following are the approved certificates:—

UNION OF LANCASHIRE AND CHESHIRE INSTITUTES: Certificate for Shot Firers.
WELSH JOINT EDUCATION COMMITTEE: Certificate for Shot Firers.
YORKSHIRE COUNCIL FOR FURTHER EDUCATION: Shot Firers' Certificates.
NATIONAL COAL BOARD: Shotfiring Test Certificate.

†In practice M.Q.B. do not hold oral and practical test.

THE COAL MINES

(CERTIFICATE FEES) ORDER 1961

S.I. 1961 No. 713

1. This order shall come into operation on the first day of May, nineteen hundred and sixty-one, and may be cited as the Coal Mines (Certificate Fees) Order 1961.

2. (1) Subject to the provisions of paragraph (2), the fee to be paid by any person who applies for the grant by the Minister of Power on the recommendation of the Mining Qualifications Board of any of the following certificates shall be the amount stated in relation thereto, namely—

	£.	s.	d.
(*a*) a first-class certificate of competency	5	10	0
(*b*) a second-class certificate of competency	2	15	0
(*c*) a surveyor's certificate	4	10	0
(*d*) a mechanical or electrical engineer's certificate ..	4	10	0
(*e*) a mechanic's or electrician's certificate class I ..	2	5	0
(*f*) a mechanic's or electrician's certificate class II ..		5	0
(*g*) a deputy's certificate	1	7	6
(*h*) a shot firer's certificate		17	6

(2) In any case where an applicant for a deputy's or shot firer's certificate does not intend to submit himself for any practical test or oral and practical test, as the case may be, held by the Mining Qualifications Board for applicants for such certificates the fee to be paid by such person shall be .. .. 5s. 0d.

3. The Coal Mines (Deputies' Certificates) (Fees) Order 1952, the Coal Mines (Certificates of Competency, Shot Firers' and Surveyors' Certificates) (Fees) Order 1954, and the Coal Mines (Mechanics' and Electricians' Certificates) (Fees) Order 1955, as having effect by virtue of subsection (1) of section one hundred and ninety-one of the Mines and Quarries Act 1954, are hereby revoked.

INDEX

---

* relate to mines of coal only.
† relate to mines of stratified ironstone, shale and fireclay only.

* apply to Mines of Coal only.
‡ See also Sections 4 and 6 of the 1954 Act.

Printed in England for Her Majesty's Stationery Office by A. Wheaton & Co., Exeter.
Dd. 500259 K.120 6/70